Adventures of the Symbolic

COLUMBIA STUDIES IN POLITICAL THOUGHT/POLITICAL HISTORY

Columbia Studies in Political Thought/Political History
Dick Howard, General Editor

Columbia Studies in Political Thought/Political History is a series dedicated to exploring the possibilities for democratic initiative and the revitalization of politics in the wake of the exhaustion of twentieth-century ideological "isms." By taking a historical approach to the politics of ideas about power, governance, and the just society, this series seeks to foster and illuminate new political spaces for human action and choice.

Pierre Rosanvallon, *Democracy Past and Future*, edited by Samuel Moyn (2006)

Claude Lefort, *Complications: Communism and the Dilemmas of Democracy,* translated by Julian Bourg (2007)

Benjamin R. Barber, *The Truth of Power: Intellectual Affairs in the Clinton White House* (2008)

Andrew Arato, *Constitution Making Under Occupation: The Politics of Imposed Revolution in Iraq* (2009)

Dick Howard, *The Primacy of the Political: A History of Political Thought from the Greeks to the French and American Revolution* (2010)

Robert Meister, *After Evil: Human Rights Discourse in the Twenty-first Century* (2011)

Paul W. Kahn, *Political Theology: Four New Chapters on the Concept of Sovereignty* (2011)

Stephen Eric Bronner, *Socialism Unbound: Principles, Practices, and Prospects* (2011)

David William Bates, *States of War: Enlightenment Origins of the Political* (2011)

Adventures of the Symbolic

POST-MARXISM AND RADICAL DEMOCRACY

Warren Breckman

COLUMBIA UNIVERSITY PRESS

NEW YORK

Columbia University Press
Publishers Since 1893
New York   Chichester, West Sussex
cup.columbia.edu
Copyright © 2013 Columbia University Press
Paperback edition, 2016
All rights reserved

Library of Congress Cataloging-in-Publication Data
Breckman, Warren, 1963-
  Adventures of the symbolic : post-Marxism and radical democracy / Warren
Breckman.
    pages cm. —(Columbia Studies in political thought/political history)
  Includes bibliographical references and index.
  ISBN 978-0-231-14394-3 (cloth: alk. paper)—ISBN 978-0-231-14395-0 (pbk. : alk.
paper)—ISBN 978-0-231-51289-3 (e-book)
  1. Political science—Philosophy.   2. Social sciences—Philosophy.   3. Philosophy,
Marxist.   4. Democracy.   5. Radicalism.   I. Title.
  JA71.B734 2013
  321.8—dc23
                                                          2012037769

Columbia University Press books are printed on permanent and durable acid-free paper.
Printed in the United States of America

COVER IMAGE: Dieter Roth, *Literaturwurst* (1969). Copyright © Dieter Roth Estate.
Courtesy of Hauser & Wirth. Copyright © The Museum of Modern Art/Licensed by
SCALA / Art Resource, NY.

COVER DESIGN: Milenda Nan Ok Lee

References to Web sites (URLs) were accurate at the time of writing. Neither the author
nor Columbia University Press is responsible for URLs that may have expired or changed
since the manuscript was prepared.

For Cordula

Contents

Foreword

Dick Howard

THE PARALLEL OF BRECKMAN'S TITLE and his critical analysis to Maurice Merleau-Ponty's *Adventures of the Dialectic*, which was published in 1955, is well taken. Merleau-Ponty was concerned with the fate of Marxism in the postwar climate. He sought to understand the reemergence of dialectical thought as an attempt to overcome the challenge to classical liberalism that Max Weber formulated as the opposition of an ethics of conviction and an ethics of responsibility. Dialectical Marxists, most prominently Georg Lukács, sought to go beyond the antinomies of liberalism by finding a synthesis incarnated by the proletariat; the working class was said to be both the subject of history and its product, a being that was both individual and yet total, one that incarnated the future in the present. The triumph of Leninism, then Stalinism, put an end to this revolutionary synthesis, and the Trotskyist opposition was not able to restore the historical hope. Merleau-Ponty concluded his account with a devastating critique of what he called Sartre's "ultra-bolshevism," which he considered a voluntarist attempt to "go beyond history . . . when Marx understood communism as the realization of history."

The parallel account in Breckman's *Adventures* is concerned with the fate of what he calls post-Marxism. Merleau-Ponty and Breckman differ, of course, in many ways; Breckman is a historian, not a philosopher; as he says at several points, rather than offer its own normative construction, his work "assesses" or "evaluates" a complex path, which he "narrates."

But if there is not an exact parallel there is, to use a term from the Romantics that Breckman stresses elsewhere, an analogy between the projects. Just as Merleau-Ponty began his story with an account of the constitution of his object of study, the dialectic, from the work of Max Weber, so Breckman begins his history with the constitution of its object, the *symbolic*. Breckman begins with the problem posed to the young (or "left") Hegelians by the insistence of the late Schelling and his Romantic followers that the real is not only, or truly, the rational; how, then, is one to understand the irreducible otherness of the world to thought? This is territory that Breckman had covered from one perspective in *Marx, the Young Hegelians, and the Origins of Radical Social Theory*; he retraces in this new work, compactly, the process by which the Hegelian opposition, and finally Marx, built their theory on a *desymbolization*, the reduction of the transcendent to the immanent and the secularization of social relations. But Marx had no monopoly on radical social theory; in his second chapter Breckman underlines the place of another line of leftist theory whose first formulation he finds in the "romantic socialism" of Pierre Leroux. This alternate orientation sets the stage for the climb back to a *resymbolization* of radical thought whose avatars were the fathers of what came to be known as "French theory": Lévi-Strauss, Althusser, and Lacan. Breckman interprets this process of resymbolization, which is often referred to as the "linguistic turn," as an attempt to "rescue radical thought from Marxism" and its dialectical misadventures. While this claim is questionable in the case of Althusser's structural Marxism, Breckman's interpretation of the structuralist movement is suggestive.

These first two chapters are only the beginning of Breckman's attempt to present "a more or less coherent narrative that has something like a beginning, a series of variations that rearticulate that first insight, and a conclusion that returns to that beginning in order to reaffirm its basic insights." He then turns in the second section to the central chapters of the book, which treat first Cornelius Castoriadis, then Claude Lefort. The former comrades, ex-Trotskyists become Marx critics, bring front and center the problem of democracy. Broadly interpreted, resymbolization replaces the base/superstructure account with a vision of the social world as "constructed"; it replaces the determinism of historical materialism by a recognition of indetermination and stresses democracy rather than a state-centered, planned political world. But this changed perspective poses a new question: what is the *foundation* of social relations? The search for the grounds of social relations and the source of social values points beyond the immanence of secular society toward the dimension of transcendence that had been the domain of theology before the avatars of modernity and Marxism challenged its credibility. The challenge of Schelling to Hegel's rationalism returns, now in the various forms of deconstruction, of which Breckman offers a coherent panorama that richly repays reading. But he goes on to point to the richness of the alternate paths proposed by Castoriadis and Lefort.

The fact that reason here recognizes its limits does not mean that it lapses into unreason; rather the idea of a society whose relations could be rationalized is replaced by the search for the grounds of what both Castoriadis and Lefort call "the political." Although they define it differently, as Breckman shows, their basic insight is that the political is a symbolic power that structures or institutes both society and social institutions. Their respective critiques of totalitarianism led them to challenge the Marxist reduction of the political to the social. For Castoriadis, the political depends on the interplay between what he calls the (social) "imaginaire" and the "radical imaginary," which creates the conditions for human and social autonomy. Autonomy, in its literal Greek sense of *autos* + *nomos,* means that the law is self-given; its only justification is the will of the participants, and this is just what is entailed by democracy. For Lefort, the modern concept of the rights of man—which should not be confused with classical liberal philosophy—becomes the foundation of a democratic politics that is radical because it can never overcome the difference between its symbolic foundation (the rights of man) and its socially bound reality. The result, says Breckman, is a "robust theory of the uncertainty and indeterminacy of the democratic condition," which leads Lefort to praise democracy "not [for] what it does, but [for] what it *causes to be done"* (ooof). Because the political transcends the society that it institutes, it can never be incarnated (by the proletariat, the party, or any social institution); it can only be represented because, in itself, it must always remain "an empty place." The same logic holds for democracy, the rule of the *demos*: because the people can never be incarnate in any institution, *all* institutions can claim to represent the people, and their competition (in the separation of powers) protects the rights and freedoms of democratic individuals.

The final section of *Adventures of the Symbolic* recalls Marx's famous aphorism in *The Eighteenth Brumaire of Louis Napoleon*: the first time is tragedy, the second time is farce. Once again, Breckman retraces the movement from the symbolic to a desymbolization that opens the door to political voluntarism. The first phase of the development is found in Ernesto Laclau and Chantal Mouffe's *Hegemony and Socialist Theory*, which reformulates proletarian dialectics into a theory that explicitly acknowledges the power of the symbolic as well as its debt to Lefort's theory of democracy. Laclau's subsequent explorations, and criticisms, of deconstructionist philosophy and of Lacanian psychoanalysis are shown to be directed by his and Mouffe's concern to understand how radical politics can find its place in a world whose institution is ultimately symbolic and in which no agent or actor comparable to the dialectical proletariat can—or should—be imagined. An early ally in this search was the young Slavoj Žižek, a dissident Slovene intellectual who had imbibed the heady culture of radical Paris. Breckman reconstructs their emerging disagreements, which became explicit in a jointly published volume (with Judith Butler), *Contingency, Hegemony, Universality*. Agreement on the first two terms was marred by disagreement concerning the third. For Žižek, "universality" is, because of its abstraction, complicit with capitalist domination. On the contrary, his idiosyncratic interpretation of Hegel's idea of a concrete universal led Žižek increasingly to believe in the (perhaps fleeting) reality of something like the "revolution" that Merleau-Ponty had denounced, with biting irony, in *The Adventures of the Dialectic* as a "sublime point" that would put a (totalitarian) end to history. For his part, Laclau insisted that while political universality cannot be actualized in reality, it must nonetheless always be sought as a constituent element in the quest to create a hegemonic politics of social change. In this way, Laclau can be said to reformulate Lefort's concept of the political as a symbolic structure that can never be incarnated because its foundation is an empty space.

The second chapter of part 3 completes what Breckman calls the "narrative arc" of his book, setting the context and following Žižek's tumultuous evolution from the primacy of the symbolic to an unintended repetition of the movement that culminated in the Marxist desymbolization in part 1. Breckman's ability to punch through Žižek's verbal fireworks and tenuous interpretations, for example of Hegel or Lacan, lends coherence to what often seems arbitrary rhetorical spins. He does denounce as "disturbing" some of Žižek's bluster and his "inconsistent and at times deeply disturbing pronouncements," but here as elsewhere the reader will come to appreciate the *historian* who makes the strands of the past cohere in a narrative. At the same time, the political thinker will recognize the way in which the guiding thread through this maze is suggested by the retrodevelopment from symbolic political socialism to reductionist Marxism that was dissected in part I. For example, Žižek attempts to combine reductionism and voluntarism into what he (and Alain Badiou) calls a "positive vision" that he identifies now with "communism," now with "Leninism," and then again with the terrorist actions taken by self-defined leftist groups in Peru or Vietnam. In so doing, says Breckman, Žižek is trying to "fill in the hole," to overcome the indeterminacy, and to secularize the transcendence of the political to the social. And that, after all, is just what the young Marx proposed to accomplish in his "On the Jewish Question" (1843), the missing link in his move away from Hegelianism and toward the discovery of the proletariat as the subject-object of history. From that point forward, Marx would interpret religious and ideological questions as the expression of social relations and soon would interpret political problems in terms of economic relations.

It is of course a broad step to lay responsibility on the flighty figure of Žižek, whose rhetoric could change tomorrow. But, if it changes, he would have a material explanation for the new position. The point is that his evolution testifies to the culmination, apparently real, of the adventures of the symbolic. With it comes the end of the hope of saving radicalism by resymbolizing Marxism. Breckman admits his frustration with this conclusion, for there remains much indeed to criticize about contemporary capitalism. But this is no reason to accept the surface plausibility of Žižek's (or Badiou's or others') return to Marxism-Leninism; perhaps, ironizes Breckman, citing Žižek, miracles do happen, but don't count on them, for the desymbolizing project is doomed to political failure. Breckman himself stands on the critical left; but his left is built on the democratic imperative. Yet democracy, he concludes sagely, is "not a solution; it is a problem, inseparably philosophical and political." Breckman has no solution; that's not his job. But his historical reconstruction of the modern history of political thought is innovative, refreshing, and a marvelous mirror through which we can see more clearly how we have come to be who we are and why we have the theorists that we have.

Acknowledgments

THIS BOOK TOOK A LONG TIME TO WRITE. Along the way, there have been many distractions, mostly good, some bad. What has remained unwavering throughout is my gratitude to the many people who have supported, encouraged, fed, entertained, and sparred with me. One of the many perks of finally finishing a project like this, beyond a huge sigh of relief and a moment of existential angst about what comes next, is the opportunity finally to offer thanks.

I should begin by acknowledging the institutions that allowed me to pursue this work. The University of Pennsylvania supported a year of leave, which allowed me a long sojourn in Paris, and the École des hautes études en sciences sociales welcomed me as a visiting scholar while I was there. Penn proved flexible in allowing me to take time away from teaching when further opportunities presented themselves. The Institute for Advanced Study in Princeton provided support and a tranquil environment in the otherwise turbulent year of 2001. A fellowship from the Alexander von Humboldt-Stiftung in 2004–2005 allowed me to spend a wonderful year in Germany affiliated with the research group on "Symbolische Kommunikation und gesellschaftliche Wertsysteme vom Mittelalter bis zur französischen Revolution" in Münster. Though personal circumstances led me to live in Berlin, I am grateful to the Münsteraner for their hospitality. The opportunity to serve as the academic director of the Berlin Consortium for German Studies in 2008–2009 brought me back to that city, and though it was a year full of official duties, it was a time of great strides toward completion of this book.

I have presented elements of this project at many conferences and invited lectures in America, Canada, Europe, Turkey, and Israel, and I am thankful for these invitations and the engaged audiences who responded to my work. Many people discussed my ideas with me, read and improved my drafts, and generally bore with me as I groped around for the proper paths. For all sorts of help, criticism and encouragement, thanks go to Andrew Arato, Andrew Baird, Jonathan Beecher, Michael Behrent, Benjamin Binstock, Julian Bourg, James Brophy, Roger Chartier, Andrew Chitty, Jean Cohen, David Ames Curtis, Laurence Dickey, Ben Dorfman, Johan von Essen, Bernard Flynn, Don Forgay, Peter Gordon, Anthony Grafton, Stephen Hastings-King, Andreas Hetzel, Dick Howard, Gerald Izenberg, Martin Jay, Andreas Kalyvas, Randy Kaufman, Dominick LaCapra, Ernesto Laclau, Anthony La Vopa, Claude Lefort, Suzanne Marchand, Paola Marrati, Clara Gibson Maxwell, Allan Megill, Douglas Moggach, Dirk Moses, Samuel Moyn, Carmen Müller, Theresa Murphy, Elliot Neaman, Andrew Norris, Heiko Pollmeier, Jean-Michel Rabaté, Anson Rabinbach, Ulrich Raulff, Michèle Richman, Wolfert von Rahden, Camille Robcis, Paul Rosenberg, David Ruderman, Hans Christoph Schmidt am Busch, Ulrich Johannes Schneider, Joan Scott, Bernd Seestaedt, Jerrold Seigel, Ralph Shain, Jonathan Sheehan, Ludwig Siep, Gareth Stedman Jones, Andrew Stein, Christian Strub, Tom Sugrue, Judith Surkis, Luke Thurston, Lars Trägårdh, Hent de Vries, Norbert Waszek, Richard Wolin, and Rachel Zuckert. I'm indebted to Lynn Hunt in a slightly perverse way. Her invitation to contribute a volume on European Romanticism to her series with Bedford/St. Martin's sidetracked me for at least a year, but it forced me to think more deeply about that pivotal phenomenon. More straightforwardly, as my colleague at Penn, Lynn first encouraged my idea to depart radically from the field of my first book on Karl Marx and the Young Hegelians and embark on a project on recent thought. Zoé Castoriadis opened her doors to me and attended patiently as I worked in the well-organized archive now housed in the home she had shared with her husband Cornelius. Claude Lefort was generous in meeting with me while I lived in Paris in 1998. My undergraduate and graduate students at Penn have risen to the challenges of seminars taught on various aspects of my project, and they've often given back at least as much as they've taken. I have also benefited from a number of diligent research assistants, particularly Eric Leventhal and Alex Zhang.

I am ever grateful to my parents and my family for all that they have given me in love and support. Above all, I owe the existence of this book to Cordula Grewe. In her, I have been graced with the best of companions. Ours is a romantic friendship in every sense, for she is not only my wife and closest friend, but also a great historian of Romantic art and aesthetics. She has been a limitless partner in my own explorations. This book reflects her influence in more ways than I could count. Our relationship began almost exactly when this book began and I hope it will continue decades after the ink is dry. But it gives me boundless pleasure to thank her, underway and in the middle, for bringing me this far.

I have published earlier versions of some of the material in this book. It appears here revised, extensively in most cases. I am grateful for permissions to use the material here: "The Symbolic Dimension and the Politics of Young Hegelianism" in Douglas Moggach, ed., *The New Hegelians: Politics and Philosophy in the Hegelian School*, copyright © 2006 Cambridge University Press, reprinted with permission; "Politics in a Symbolic Key: Pierre Leroux, Romantic Socialism and the 'Schelling Affair,'" *Modern Intellectual History* 2, no. 1 (2005): 61–86, copyright © 2005 Cambridge University Press, reprinted with permission; "Democracy Between Disenchantment and Political Theology: French Post-Marxism and the Return of Religion," *New German Critique* 94 (Winter 2005): 72–105, copyright © 2005 New German Critique, Inc., reprinted with permission; "The Post-Marx of the Letter" in Julian Bourg, ed., *After the Deluge: New Perspectives on Postwar French Intellectual and Cultural History*, copyright © 2004 Lexington Books, reprinted with permission; "The Return of the King: Hegelianism and Post-Marxism in Žižek and Nancy" in Warren Breckman, Peter E. Gordon, A. Dirk Moses, Samuel Moyn, and Elliot Neaman, eds., *The Modernist Imagination: Intellectual History and Critical Theory. Essays in Honor of Martin Jay*, copyright © 2009 Berghahn Books, reprinted with permission.

Adventures of the Symbolic

Introduction

Post-Marxism and the Symbolic Turn

IN THE DARK DAYS OF LATE 2008, as the world economy slid toward the abyss, commentators in Europe began to notice a curious side effect of this unfamiliar sense of epochal crisis. People were reading Karl Marx again. The collapse of the East Bloc in the late 1980s and early 1990s and the triumphant march of liberal capitalism across the globe had made it easy to relegate Marx to the dustbin of history. His diagnosis of capitalism's tendency toward crisis seemed fully belied not only by the disappearance of any serious alternative world order but also by steadily accumulating profits and the evident capacity of states and markets alike to learn from past mistakes how to manage risk. How quickly those beliefs reversed in the months after September 2008. The learning curve of markets and governments turned out to be more like a Möbius strip where strategies of risk management twined in a feedback loop with self-confirming models of perpetual growth. Steadily accumulating profits turned out to be largely illusory, resting on dubious financial instruments and credit conjured out of thin air. Before the fall some observers had described a strong tendency toward ever intensifying concentrations of wealth, but as long as profits rose the new "gilded age" seemed robust enough to spread the goods. With the collapse disparities of wealth suddenly became conspicuous, the spectacle of bankers and financiers cavorting like ancien régime aristocrats objectionable. It was enough to make one nostalgic for the good old days when capitalists at least *made* things, but the captains of industry surrendered their ships to the pirates of finance long ago. Even in America, where any mention of social class in public discourse in the 1980s and 1990s was met with crushing opprobrium, high profile opinion makers seemed just about ready to endorse Bertolt Brecht's claim that robbing a bank is nothing compared to founding one.[1]

Within this suddenly changed environment, it seemed that Marx had something relevant to say. In Germany, sales of *Das Kapital* rose to levels not seen in decades. Reinhard Marx, Roman Catholic archbishop of Munich, issued his own protest against capitalism in a book called *Das Kapital: Eine Streitschrift*.[2] Even if Reinhard Marx—no relation to Karl—is interested mainly in moderating, and not overthrowing, capitalism through a renewal of Catholic humanism, he shares some of Karl Marx's outrage at the effects of an unbridled market and his yearning for social justice. Although Reinhard Marx considered his book to be an argument against Marxism, it opens with a "letter" to his namesake. That opening, plus the intentional confusion created by the two Marxes and the two *Das Kapitals*, had the effect of putting Marx on the agenda as indispensable interlocutor. Marx's return to public visibility reached what may be its climax when *Time* magazine published a story on Marx in early February 2009. Though it was only the European edition of February 2 that placed Marx's image on the magazine cover, the article asked what Marx might have to say about the economic crisis. The answers were predictably trite, but the mere fact that Marx was presented not as the godless enemy of liberty but as a potential source of insight was itself striking. In light of this reversal of Marx's fortunes, one must agree with various commentators who have ventured that Marx may have been wrong about communism, but he may have been right about capitalism.

Yet that proposition itself suggests the real situation of Marxism: the possibility that Marx may speak again to an age that has discovered anew the fragility and inequity of capitalism coupled with the complete collapse of the political alternative that Marx had envisioned. Indeed, it may be that the mainstream media has been willing to invoke Marx precisely because he no longer represents something positive, some *other* possibility. Shorn of this dimension of radical otherness, Marx becomes a marker within a discourse of contradiction that capitalism has fully absorbed into its own self-referential cosmos. It is not just that the communist experiment in the twentieth century proved to be such a tragic failure that political projects aligned with Marxism have lost credibility, whatever the distance between Marx and the regimes that ruled in his name. The romance with revolution has evaporated, and along with it the fear of revolution—at least in Europe and North America, as both the left and right have come to acknowledge the complex and resilient structures of the existing social order. Insofar as governments in late 2008 began pouring billions of dollars into the economy, they did so partly in order to rescue capitalism from its own excesses and partly to alleviate the misery inflicted on millions of people. But they did not do so to avert revolutionary upheaval. Even the surprising return of popular protest in 2011 does not contradict this assertion. The rebellions that overturned regimes in parts of the Arab world objected to authoritarian governance, but not to the regime of private property and the capitalist structuring of the economy. Likewise, Occupy Wall Street, which spread from New York to other cities in America and Europe in the autumn of 2011, objected to what many Americans deemed an excessive and unbearable level of economic inequality and the corporate manipulation of democratic politics. But the Occupy movement rebelled against a certain kind of capitalism, not against capitalism *as such*. Undoubtedly, the paranoid use of police force to contain the occupiers and eventually expel them from their encampments would seem to lend new credibility to Marx's view of the bourgeois state as the guardian of private property, but a Marxist call for revolution could not be counted even as a minor key in the chorus of protests rising from the Occupy movement.

The intellectual underpinnings of Marxism have also crumbled. Gone is belief in a dialectic objectively operating in history and with it the primacy once assigned to class as both the bedrock of social analysis and the agent of historical change. That in turn has dealt a death blow to the old Marxist, and especially Marxist-Leninist, belief in the unity of theory and praxis, a belief that assigned a central role to revolutionary intellectuals. Even as affirmative an assessment as that of Göran Therborn, whose panoramic survey of contemporary leftist politics and intellectual activity certainly supports his claim that "left-wing intellectual creativity has not ceased," concedes that "its greatest moments may have passed." Speculating on the future, Therborn writes, "Twenty-first-century anti-capitalist resisters and critics are unlikely to forget the socialist and communist horizons of the past two hundred years. But whether they will see the dawn of a different future in the same colours is uncertain, perhaps even improbable. New cohorts of anticapitalist social scientists will certainly emerge, and many will read Marx, but it may be doubted whether many will find it meaningful to call themselves Marxists."[3]

So back to the general situation: the economic catastrophe of 2008 led more people to renewed recognition that capitalism is a problematic system. But if Marx may have been even partly right about capitalism, he was entirely wrong about communism. Which means that we are still left with the gaping hole where the Marxist political project used to stand. This book is concerned with several important attempts to address that gaping hole, that empty place.

People reflexively turn to symbols to organize their historical experience, and it is conventional to date the end of communism in November 1989, the fall of the Berlin Wall. Of course, more sophisticated political histories challenge the simplicity of that symbol of the "end" with analyses of a process that stretches back before 1989 and, in various ways, projects forward beyond 1989. Likewise with the history of Marxism's collapse as an intellectual system. I was in Berlin when the wall fell, having recently arrived there to begin research on a dissertation concerned with Marx and the Left Hegelians. A week or so after the great event, one of my friends asked me if my topic wasn't beating a dead horse. The question had occurred to me, but ultimately I never felt undone by history, unlike a hapless West German acquaintance who had submitted a massive *Habilitationsschrift* on East German property law to the law faculty of the Free University just days before the collapse of the regime. For one thing, I was already convinced that Marx was "for the ages," an unavoidable and indispensable part of history and, much as he would loathe such a description, a classic within the philosophical tradition. But, more importantly, it did not require the fall of the Berlin Wall to alert me to the weaknesses and deeply problematic status of Marxist thought. At the time, I would have been hard-pressed to reconstruct a satisfying genealogy of my own intellectual distance from Marxism, but I was more or less aware that I was an inheritor of a longer historical process whereby Marxism's hold on left-wing intellectuals had steadily weakened.

The collapse of Marxism as the dominant paradigm of progressive intellectuals was, perhaps, nowhere felt more profoundly than in France. After all, the collapse dramatically reversed the elevated status that Marxism had enjoyed among French intellectuals after World War II. That prominence was the outcome of a confluence of circumstances: the politicization of intellectuals during the Second World War; the prestige of the Soviet Union, which was seen as the country that had borne the brunt of Nazi furor, turned the war's tide at Stalingrad and shared the greatest credit for the Allied victory; the success of the postwar communist left in grafting itself to the memory of the Resistance; the widespread conviction that the Bolshevik Revolution was the legitimate heir to Jacobinism; the more or less contingent fact that a number of particularly gifted intellectuals like Jean-Paul Sartre and Simone de Beauvoir chose to champion Marxism. The power of Marxism lasted right up to 1968, and then it began to unravel. Corresponding to the intensity of the experience of Marxism's collapse was the vigor with which certain French intellectuals have sought new paradigms of radical thought beyond Marxism. These efforts extend also to non-French thinkers who have heavily drawn upon the resources of French thought. The mere fact that French intellectuals experienced the fall of Marxism in a particularly intense way would not be enough to justify my decision to concentrate so heavily on this French and French-inflected discourse. After all, the intellectual crisis of Marxism has international dimensions, which could embrace an enormous cast of characters ranging from Jürgen Habermas to Barry Hindess, Paul Hirst, and Judith Butler, to name just a few; moreover, a narrative of the crisis could encompass much of the twentieth century, as Stuart Sim implies when he chooses to title a chapter of his history of post-Marxism "Post-Marxism Before Post-Marxism: Luxemburg to the Frankfurt School."[4]

What makes the French case so powerful and influential is the fact that the collapse of Marxism coincided with a larger phenomenon of radical skepticism. This has gone under various rubrics, none of them entirely satisfying: French theory, poststructuralism, deconstruction, postmodernism. The general contours are too familiar to detain us here. The point is that from the heyday of structuralism in the 1960s and on through the works of Derrida, Lacan, Lyotard, Deleuze, Nancy, Lacoue-Labarthe, Kristeva, and numerous others, French thinkers waged a highly influential attack on the rational norms, transcendental grounds, and metanarratives that had provided the foundations for modern philosophical discourse. This unrelieved skepticism contributed significantly to the undermining of the philosophical grounds of Marxism. The epistemological realism that had dominated Marxist thought collapsed as radical constructivism dissolved the "real" referent of "class" and "society" into the fluid of language; belief in the meaningful structure of history, the modern metanarrative of emancipation, gave way to an acute awareness of historical contingency; totalizing styles of thought yielded to the fragmentary; unity yielded to heterogeneity, identity to difference, dialectical development to indeterminate ruptures; Hegel and Marx lost ground to Nietzsche and Heidegger; the very idea of emancipation seemed imperiled by the critique of the subject and the "humanism" that had allegedly dominated the West since the advent of the modern period.[5]

Did these shifts in the intellectual landscape precipitate the crisis of Marxism, or were they symptoms of that crisis? That question is, in the end, unanswerable in any strict sense, yet, whether as cause, symptom, or both, the larger intellectual context of the collapse of Marxism in France has also complicated the search for alternatives. This quest typically involved a return to political philosophy, rejection of the totalitarian legacy of really existing socialism, a self-critique of intellectuals' evident attraction to totalizing styles of thought per se, and a turn toward open models of democracy. Yet the same widespread skepticism about the foundational discourses of modern politics that shook Marxism to its core makes it impossible to return to a naive conception of democracy. As Marcel Gauchet described the situation in 1988, "The more we are led to acknowledge a universal validity to the principles of Western modernity, the less we are able to ground them in a history of progress of which they represent the fulfillment."[6] In the context of this convergence of Marxism's eclipse and the decline of foundational principles, what are the prospects for regenerating critical social and political philosophy beyond the Marxist framework? What are the possibilities of creating and sustaining a positive emancipatory project?

This book explores these questions through a series of historically and philosophically informed studies of several major thinkers who confront us with contrasting approaches to the challenges of political philosophy in the postfoundational and post-Marxist context. These figures include Cornelius Castoriadis, Claude Lefort, Marcel Gauchet, Ernesto Laclau, Chantal Mouffe, and Slavoj Žižek. Claude Lefort and Cornelius Castoriadis played crucial roles in the so-called return of political philosophy in

1980s France. Decades earlier, in 1948, the two founded the group and journal *Socialisme ou Barbarie*. A Greek leftist forced into exile in Paris after World War II, Castoriadis strove to rethink revolutionary politics as the "project of autonomy"; his exertions led to an increasingly deep critique of the Western philosophical tradition and an exploration of the "social imaginary" as the source of radical creativity in history. Claude Lefort broke with *Socialisme ou Barbarie* in the late 1950s and went on to write highly influential works on the nature of modern democracy and totalitarianism. Unlike Castoriadis, who avowed the revolutionary project right up to his death in December 1997, Lefort rejected the idea of a revolutionary transformation of society; his embrace of pluralism and, in the 1980s, the politics of human rights could seem to mark him as a liberal centrist. But, in fact, his mature theory involved a robust conception of democracy and, indeed, of the social basis of rights, which cannot be subordinated to liberalism. Accordingly, his theory could and did inspire radical democratic projects. But in an attenuated form, it could also nurture a more conservative project, as we will see in the trajectory of Lefort's student, Marcel Gauchet. Gauchet teaches philosophy at the École des hautes études en sciences sociales and is head of the journal *Le Débat*. He rose to significance through an impressive oeuvre investigating political power, subjectivity and psychoanalysis, and the relationship of modern democracy to religion. Ernesto Laclau, Chantal Mouffe, and Slavoj Žižek are not French, but their engagement with French thought is so deep that in many ways they represent the continuation of certain French trajectories. Laclau, an Argentine who has taught mainly at Essex, England, and his wife, Chantal Mouffe, a Belgian who has also made a career in England, are best known for their book *Hegemony and Socialist Strategy* (1985). Since then, Laclau has attempted to place the central concepts of that important book— hegemony, antagonism, and radical democracy—into an explicitly universalist frame. Laclau's conviction that the future of the left depends on rediscovering a dimension of universality beyond postmodern identity politics is shared by Žižek, though they have developed sharply conflicting visions of what that dimension might be. The prolific theorist from Slovenia has come to occupy a position of almost unrivaled international visibility through a cascade of works, with trademark leaps between philosophy and popular culture and an idiosyncratic synthesis of Hegel and Lacan. If

Žižek began as a supporter of Laclau and Mouffe, the final chapter will trace Žižek's rejection of the post-Marxist project and his return to an equally idiosyncratic and deeply problematic revolutionary language.

Three major caveats are in order right away. First, my aim is not to provide an exhaustive survey, neither of the terrain of recent French political thought nor of post-Marxism. Rather, I have selected these figures because they provide an important range of different though related responses to the challenge of generating a new political language that retains a commitment to the radical possibility of theory and its potential interaction with political movements at a time when the inadequacies of inherited modes of radical thought have become clear but no alternative has really emerged. Moreover, and here I reveal myself as a historian, this cast of characters allows me to narrate a story in an economical but, I hope, compelling way: a more or less coherent narrative that has something like a beginning, a series of variations that rearticulate that first insight, and a conclusion that returns to that beginning in order to reaffirm its basic insights. Second, as is already clear, the grouping is not exclusively French. The French context is crucial for reasons I have already indicated; yet, as I will argue, the collapse of Marxism in France during the 1970s and 1980s created an inhospitable atmosphere for the task of responding positively to the crisis. Certainly one can point to important and creative efforts within France to rethink radicalism, such as those of Alain Badiou, Étienne Balibar, and Jacques Rancière, but some of the most influential deployments of French intellectual resources developed beyond the Hexagon. Third, I am by necessity forced to use the term *post-Marxist* somewhat loosely. Among the central figures of this book, only Laclau and Mouffe, and, with some qualifications, Žižek, have applied this term to themselves. Castoriadis and Lefort are post-Marxists by dint of biography. Quite simply, they were Marxists and then they ceased to be. Nonetheless, as with Mouffe and Laclau, though less explicitly, both Lefort's and Castoriadis's intellectual development after their Marxist period continued to bear the stamp of their past. Gauchet was never a Marxist, but his thought orients itself toward problems opened by the collapse of Marxism. So, post-Marxism functions in this book variously as a "period" concept, a self-description, a biographical fact, and a designation of continuity—whether explicit or implicit—in the way in which questions are posed and even judged important.

The group at the heart of this book does not form a school or a move-ment. The differences that divide them are at least as important and inter-esting as the commonalities that unite them. But there are commonalities. Two recent books suggest possible ways of understanding these. Oliver Marchart groups Lefort and Laclau together with Alain Badiou and Jean-Luc Nancy under the rubric of *Post-Foundational Political Thought*.[7] Yannis Stavrakakis, building on an analogy to the Hegelian left, groups Castoria-dis, Laclau, and Žižek, along with Badiou, in his book *The Lacanian Left*.[8] Certainly, all the figures I will concentrate on are postfoundational; they all participated in and have been shaped by the larger intellectual context I have already sketched. Likewise, Jacques Lacan is an important point of reference for all the figures under discussion. Indeed, Lacanian thought undoubtedly provides one of the master keys to late twentieth-century thought in France and beyond, as we shall see in the chapters that follow. Yet the idea of grouping the figures of this book under the name *Lacanian left* is unsettling. Consider Stavrakakis's analogy to the Hegelian left of the 1840s. Figures like Ludwig Feuerbach, David Friedrich Strauss, and Bruno Bauer were fully converted to Hegel's teachings in their youth. Each of their trajectories involves a passage through youthful encounter, conver-sion, growing doubt, and apostasy; at the crucial stages along this path, even after explicitly breaking with Hegel, Hegelianism remained the crucial template for their thought. By contrast, Lacan's role in the history of post-Marxism is much more varied. Castoriadis and Lefort both read Lacan as mature thinkers. In Castoriadis's case a brief period of openness to Laca-nian ideas was followed by polemical rejection; it is true, as we will explore in detail, that Castoriadis's ideas formed partly through this critical engage-ment with Lacan, but a negative abreaction does not qualify Castoriadis for inclusion in any form of Lacanian left, however attenuated that member-ship may be construed. Lacanian ideas play a more positive role in both Lefort and Gauchet, but by no means is Lacanianism the determinative force. Laclau and Mouffe's *Hegemony and Socialist Strategy* draws on Lacan, but only as one among numerous theoretical resources. Laclau's subsequent work more explicitly engages Lacan, but even Stavrakakis acknowledges that Laclau's appropriation of Lacan is quite selective.[9] That would leave Slavoj Žižek. Žižek is probably the world's most prominent proponent of Lacanian ideas, and there is scarcely a page in Žižek's oeuvre that doesn't mention Lacan. Yet, even here, one of the best books on Žižek claims, perhaps perversely, that, for Žižek, Lacan is a machine for reading Hegel.[10]

Behind the shared reference to Lacan is a factor that operates more loosely and broadly, but is at the core of what unites this diverse group. That is, in one way or another, they each turned away from Marx's ontological assumptions—Marxism's belief that society is grounded upon the material foundation of economic life. In place of Marxism's ontological and epistemological *realism*, each of these thinkers turns toward the sphere of representation; contrary to Marx's belief that symbolic forms belong to the superstructure, they each adhere to the basic notion that the social world is constituted as a symbolic order. In this sense, they participate in one of the most fundamental tendencies of modern French thought; indeed, as Alain Caillé suggests, "the bulk of the liveliest French thought of the postwar period gravitates around this notion of symbolism."[11] This is a trajectory with a complicated genealogy, reaching from poststructuralist figures like Jacques Derrida, Julia Kristeva, and Jean Baudrillard back through structuralist thinkers like Roland Barthes, Louis Althusser, Jacques Lacan, and Claude Lévi-Strauss to interwar figures like Georges Bataille, Michel Leiris, the Collège de sociologie, and the surrealists to Marcel Mauss, Émile Durkheim, and Ferdinand Saussure.

The sea change that transformed almost every aspect of the social sciences and humanities in France after World War II usually goes under the name the *linguistic turn*. It is a commonplace that Claude Lévi-Strauss, the key figure steering postwar French thought toward a preoccupation with the symbolic, conceived structural anthropology on the linguistic model pioneered by Saussure, Jakobson, Greimas, and others. Building on Saussure's exclusion of the historical dimension of language in order to establish a synchronic science of language as a system, Lévi-Strauss defined the symbolic as a closed order of social representations that form a system, the function of which is to render the perception of the world coherent by superimposing on the continuum of reality a grid of taxonomic oppositions and syntagmatic associations.[12] Likewise, Lévi-Strauss drew heavily from Saussure's semiological principle, in which linguistic values emerge through differential relations among signs. Linguistics, as Marcel Hénaff writes, opened for Lévi-Strauss a new approach to the study of myth, indeed of all cultural systems: "what is important is not the figures or themes as such but the system of their differences, of their reciprocal relations."[13]

Accordingly, Lévi-Strauss and those directly influenced by him studied symbolism as a code, as an invariant structure, at the expense of acts of speech within living contexts.

Ever since Lévi-Strauss hammered out this new paradigm, critics have objected that the linguistic model employed by Lévi-Strauss and his followers is at best a loose and partly metaphorical borrowing from the tradition of structural linguistics and at worst a gross distortion of scientific linguistics.[14] In light of these objections to the dubious precision of the linguistic model in post-1945 thought, I would propose the term *symbolic turn* as a better description of the loose set of affiliated ideas and approaches that characterize a broad range of thinkers who have stressed the noncorrespondence of words and things, the nontransparency of language, and the power of signs to constitute the things they purportedly represent. The notion of a symbolic turn gains further credibility if we bear in mind the relationship of French structuralism and its heirs to wider currents of twentieth-century thought, such as both Freudian and Jungian psychoanalysis, phenomenology, nonstructuralist anthropology, and philosophical anthropology. Whether we are speaking of Freud, Jung, or Cassirer, they may have considered language to be the primary medium of symbolization, but not the only one.[15] Moreover, the broader twentieth-century fascination with the symbolic did not categorically reduce the symbolic to the model of semiological value embraced by Lévi-Strauss. The greatest advantage in emphasizing the *symbolic* in the sea change of twentieth-century thought is one that is central to this book: namely, that the attempt to reduce the symbolic to the structural linguistic model was doomed to fail not only because it provoked external opposition but also because every theory of the symbolic, including that of structuralism, mobilizes a polyvalent range of meanings that cannot be fully mastered. To speak of the symbolic turn thus brings us back from the deliberate reductionism that was a core strategy of almost all the variants of the twentieth-century linguistic turn.[16]

For thinkers oriented toward radical politics yet convinced of the inadequacy of existing models, the symbolic construction of the sociopolitical world offered an irresistible way out of the perceived reductionism of Marxism. However, it also posed a difficult challenge. For the influential model that took shape in the structuralism of Lévi-Strauss and Lacan privileged a transcendent symbolic order standing over and above contextualized speech, intentions, actions, and events. The symbolic order, always already there before our speech, leaves little room for classically modern (including Marxist) ideas about the autonomous human subject and the potentiality of human creativity. Moreover, structuralism's heavy emphasis upon the synchronic operations of a closed system makes it exceedingly difficult to conceptualize historical change as a dialectical process. To be sure, the structuralist model of the symbolic, rooted in linguistics, structural anthropology, and Lacanian psychoanalysis, provided Louis Althusser with the conceptual tools for his short-lived though influential attempt to rethink Marxism from *within*; the same is more or less true of Jean Baudrillard in the period when he wrote *For a Critique of the Political Economy of the Sign* (1972). Elements of this model even helped to shape the post-Marxist thought of Laclau, Mouffe, and Žižek. Nonetheless, the version of the symbolic turn inherited from the structuralist era was as much an obstacle as a vehicle for the various political projects to be discussed in this book. The structuralist understanding of the symbolic is incapable of conceiving forms of critical thought and action that could disrupt hegemonic ideological forms, as structuralism takes these to be constitutive of our subjectivity itself.

Post-Marxism involves a confrontation between the relatively rigid semiotic concept of the symbolic order and looser, less formulaic and less deterministic ideas of the symbolic. These more open concepts tap the complicated legacy of the symbolic turn, a history with roots deeper than the twentieth century. The polyvalence of the concept of the symbolic opens up the terrain of post-Marxism: on one hand, the view of the symbolic as a "gargantuan" matrix, a ubiquitous ideological grid.[17] On the other hand, the symbolic draws on roots in aesthetic and religious thought to indicate a special kind of representation, a representational form that oscillates between creating a certain kind of presence and remaining permanently flawed, shot through with that which it is not and cannot be. Viewed in this way, the symbolic opens the possibility for reorienting critical theory toward radical democracy, conceptualizing the power of symbols to body forth ideas, while at the same time viewing the social space as open and unmasterable. These conceptions of the symbolic overlap and frequently conflict in the course of radical thought in the aftermath of Marxism. The notion of the symbolic is too polyvalent, and the uses to which it has been put too diverse, to permit singular definitions or solutions or a singular line of development. Rather, from the basic problem, we encounter a series of variations on its theme; the original problematic is never wholly overcome, but by following the peregrinations of the concept we may gain a better understanding of that problematic, its history, and its possible implications for contemporary theory and practice.

In brief, I believe that the history of post-Marxism should be narrated as an adventure, as the adventure of the symbolic. In the early 1950s, when Maurice Merleau-Ponty set out to chart the course of Marxism in the twentieth century, he titled his important book *Adventures of the Dialectic*. In echoing Merleau-Ponty, I want to suggest the analogous need to mark out the course of post-Marxism. But I also want to highlight yet another ambiguity in the history being explored here. What is, in fact, the relationship between the *dialectic* and the *symbolic*? To judge from Lévi-Strauss's searing criticisms of Jean-Paul Sartre's version of Hegelian Marxism, the symbolic, conceived as an invariant code, is the opposite of the dialectic.[18] Then again, the notion of semiotic value is strictly relational, and that might suggest dialectics; but semiotic value seems to lack the dynamic transformative relationships characteristic of dialectical thought. Consider the fact that several writers, including Lacan, lay stress on one of the earliest meanings of the word symbol, *sumbolon*, which means bringing together. Lacan refers to the Greek word *tessera*, which denotes tokens such as two halves of a broken piece of pottery that allowed initiates of early mystery religions to recognize each other.[19] The structuralist symbolic is a form of social contract, as Lévi-Strauss made clear in his sense of affinity with Rousseau, Lacan in his claim that "symbol means pact."[20] The ancient meaning of symbol thus has the implication of a union, or more precisely of reunion, insofar as we take the notion of the *sumbolon* seriously.[21] This idea of (re)union thus returns us to the function of a code, of an established system of meaning, not to the idea of union as a dynamically transformative process. If we extend the definition of symbolic beyond structuralism, to consider the symbolic as a flawed form that is in permanent tension with that which it purports to represent, then we may also see it as a nondialectical form. Certainly, the young Jean Baudrillard saw in the symbolic a form of heterogeneity that resists dialectical resolution. We encounter Ernesto Laclau contrasting his concept of "antagonism," which he takes as a form of radical difference, to dialectics: "dialectical transitions are not only compatible with contradiction but have to rely on contradiction as the condition of their unity within a homogeneous space," he writes.[22] A similar resistance to the dialectical movement of contradiction and reconciliation is a powerful motif in Castoriadis, who turned sharply against the determinism that he believed was intrinsic to dialectical form.

So there are grounds for seeing the post-Marxist symbolic turn as a move against dialectical thought. Conversely, the question of the dialectic does not disappear. Žižek, for example, rejects the "postmodern doxa" concerning the "illusion of the Hegelian *Aufhebung* ('sublation': negation-conservation-elevation)."[23] In Žižek's unconventional reading, Hegel is a philosopher of contingency, and the dialectic rests on a radical negativity that undoes the imaginary drive to wholeness. Moreover, for Žižek, the symbolic itself is the proper place of the dialectic, not only because the symbolic involves an endless series of mediated interactions but also because it is always in relation to that which exceeds it. Lacan's position on the dialectic is itself divided. On the one side, he frequently attacks the Hegelian dialectic: "this dialectic," he writes in an exemplary passage, "is convergent and proceeds to the conjuncture defined as absolute knowledge. As it is defined, this conjuncture can only be the conjunction of the symbolic with a real from which nothing more can be expected."[24] On the other side, he continually construes his own work as dialectical, whether we speak of his interwar openness to the Hegelian dialectic of recognition, his 1950s and 1960s structuralist emphasis upon the workings of the symbolic, or his later stress on the agonistic relationship between the symbolic and the real. Even his view of the decentered subject involves a dialectic that disjunctively relates structure and subject.[25] Indeed, he pointedly contrasts this view to "the antidialectical mentality of a culture which, dominated as it is by objectifying ends, tends to reduce all subjective activity to the ego's being."[26] We could pursue the roots of this open, nontotalizing dialectic back and back, at least to the early German Romantics, where we find Friedrich Schlegel defending dialectic as an "*eternal* determination by a never-ending separation and combination." This is a dialectic, sustained by irony, that does not settle into sedimented truth: "The actual *dialectic* has always been in play around necessity and freedom, the highest good, etc. Here *irony* is one and all."[27]

The complex relationship between the dialectic and the symbolic is heightened when we remember that Merleau-Ponty himself turns to the symbolic as a way of rescuing the dialectic from the vulgar, mechanical Marxism that had come to dominate twentieth-century communism.

Repeatedly, *Adventures of the Dialectic* returns to Marx's description of the economic apparatus as "a relationship between persons mediated by things." "This order of 'things' which teaches 'relationships between persons,' sensitive to the heavy conditions which bind it to the order of nature, open to all that personal life can invent, is, in modern language, the sphere of symbolism, and Marx's thought was to find its outlet here. The Marxist orthodoxy, however, does not frankly consider the problem."[28] Speaking of this "interworld" of "history, symbolism, truth-to-be-made," in which all action is symbolic, Merleau-Ponty draws large conclusions for Marxists trying to break out of the rigid base-superstructure model and conceive a more flexible relationship between theory and practice: "If politics is not immediate and total responsibility [*contra* Sartre], if it consists in tracing a line in the obscurity of historical symbolism, then it too is a craft and has its technique. Politics and culture are reunited, not because they are completely congruent or because they both adhere to the event, but because the symbols of each order have echoes, correspondences, and effects of induction in the other."[29]

Adventures of the Dialectic traces this view of the symbolic back through Georg Lukács and Karl Korsch to the interpretive sociology of Max Weber. But, in other work written in the 1950s, Merleau-Ponty located his thinking about the symbolic in a French trajectory stemming from the two roots of Ferdinand Saussure and Marcel Mauss. Already, in a 1951 essay, he embraced Saussure's thesis that language's "expressive value is not the sum of the expressive values which allegedly belong individually to each element of the 'verbal chain.' "[30] This enthusiasm for Saussure dovetailed with his friendship with Claude Lévi-Strauss. In a 1960 essay Merleau-Ponty drew a direct link between Lévi-Strauss and Mauss, whose notion of the *total social fact* is "no longer a massive reality but an efficacious system of symbols or a network of symbolic values."[31] Titling this essay "From Mauss to Lévi-Strauss," Merleau-Ponty explicitly endorsed Lévi-Strauss's own effort to legitimate his program by leaning on Mauss's claim that anthropology should learn from linguistics.

Lévi-Strauss's *Introduction to the Work of Marcel Mauss* (1950) served as something of a manifesto for the new structuralist agenda, laying out its main premises in rapid succession. First, although people may use *symbols* consciously, the *symbolic* functions primarily unconsciously. Consistent with the thrust of structural linguistics, Lévi-Strauss avoided recourse to the conscious speaking subject, emphasizing instead the unconscious operation of structure. Lévi-Strauss's "unconscious" is not to be confused with Freud's, for it is without personal affect, content, or historicity. It is an empty site where the symbolic function takes place. This view of the unconscious undergirded Lacan's famous return to Freud, but Lacan's distance from conventional Freudianism can be measured by an exchange with the philosopher Jean Hyppolite. When Hyppolite attended Lacan's seminar in 1952–1953, he remarked, "The symbolic function is for you, if I understand you correctly, a transcendent function." Lacan's reply was that the transcendence he had in mind was that of an implacable ideal machine.[32] In certain ways, Lévi-Strauss's move built on Mauss. After all, in a 1924 lecture on psychology and sociology, Mauss had argued that the two disciplines came together in the idea of the symbolic, and he had granted that in symbolic communication "the layer of individual consciousness is very thin."[33] However, Lévi-Strauss's much more radical insistence on the emptiness of the unconscious can be seen in his critique of Mauss's attempt to explain *mana*, the intense power residing in the symbolic objects circulated within the economy of the gift. Lévi-Strauss condemned Mauss's idea of an "emotional-mystical" cement holding together the symbolic system as offering nothing more than the self-understanding of the participants, and instead he emphasized the relationships produced by the interactions of the system's elements.[34]

This rejection of any sort of depth model and insistence on explanation at the level of the symbolic itself was fully consistent with a second of Lévi-Strauss's major premises. Radicalizing Durkheim's insistence that society is sui generis, Lévi-Strauss insisted on a radical discontinuity between the symbolic order and other levels of reality: "Like language, the social *is* an autonomous reality (the same one, moreover); symbols are more real than what they symbolize, the signifier precedes and determines the signified." For Lévi-Strauss, "it is not a matter of translating an extrinsic given into symbols, but of reducing to their nature as a symbolic system things which never fall outside that system except to fall straight into incommunicability."[35] This raises a final point. Again in keeping with the paradigm of structural linguistics, the symbolic system is to be understood in strictly relational terms. Meanings are created through differential relations between the terms of the system. These relations are transferable, substitutable, comparable, and reducible. Thus Lévi-Strauss's repeated insistence that symbolic operations can ultimately be reduced to a small number; hence his frequently expressed interest in "combinatorial analysis" within modern mathematics and his desire to mathematize the field of ethnography.[36]

In the definitive study of Mauss's concept of the symbolic, Camille Tarot does not deny affinities between Mauss and Lévi-Strauss, but he does severely qualify them. Mauss developed his thinking about the sociological role of the symbolic in close collaboration with his uncle, Émile Durkheim, whose *Elementary Forms of the Religious Life* contains the claim that "social life, under all its aspects and all the moments of its history, is possible only thanks to a vast symbolism."[37] In his 1924 lecture on psychology and sociology, Mauss depicted his ideas modestly as a collaboration with his uncle: "It is a long time now since Durkheim and I began teaching that communion and communication between men are possible only by symbols, by common signs, permanent ones, external to individual mental states which are quite simply sequential, by signs of groups of states subsequently taken for realities."[38] True as that image of cooperation is, Mauss departed from Durkheim in important ways. Durkheim ultimately subordinated symbolic forms to a realist ontology, in which symbols are seen as representations of an anterior social reality. Hence, Tarot maintains that Durkheim treated symbols as allegories to be deciphered in order to expose their reference to reality.[39] Far from offering to "decode" symbols, Mauss emphasized their polyvalent meanings and multiple associations. Again, unlike Durkheim, Mauss did not locate the epistemological value of symbols in their capacity to "represent" society, but rather in their capacity to *create* the order, relation, and bonds of society. Mauss's final refusal to decipher symbols points to his most basic innovation, namely his shift from individual symbols to symbolic systems. In Mauss's classic essay *The Gift*, gestures and objects signify more than they are worth, or rather, are worth only what they signify.[40] Mauss is not interested in deciphering isolated elements of this exchange of symbolic goods, but in the dynamic exploration of relations that are generated and mediated by the symbolic system. As Camille Tarot writes, "The symbolic is this concatenation of symbols, their structure in a network. The symbolic is the death of the isolated symbol."[41]

Tarot presents Mauss as the pioneer within the French context of an understanding of society as a symbolic construction. But, while he acknowledges Mauss's influence on structuralism, he also insists on distance. Mauss's own understanding of language was rooted in Sanskrit studies and the nineteenth-century philological tradition in which he had been educated. Regarding Ferdinand Saussure's new synchronic approach to language, Tarot finds that Mauss was skeptical and reserved. He had doubts about Saussure's insistence upon an abstract linguistics removed from sociology.[42] And indeed, Saussure distinguished between "symbols" as motivated signs and arbitrary "signs." Only the arbitrary sign could be the basis for the science of semiology; the motivated sign is too ambiguous, too polyvalent, and too social to play anything but a minor role in semiology. "From the instant at which a symbol becomes a symbol," wrote Saussure, "which is to say, from the instant at which it becomes immersed in the social mass which at any given moment establishes its value, its identity can never be fixed."[43] The complex social life of the symbolic was precisely what attracted Mauss, and this is, for Tarot, the ultimate distinction between Mauss and structuralism.[44]

Tarot's insistence that Durkheim's approach to the symbolic was ultimately *allegorical* leads him to draw a contrast between Mauss and Durkheim. Mauss maintained that symbols are irreducibly complex. They are polysemic and always open to interpretation, as Saussure acknowledged in the act of pushing symbols to the margins of his linguistic science. Moreover, Mauss recognized that a singular and uniform concept of the symbolic could not be achieved: the concept could not be rendered transparent, but it nonetheless remained essential.[45] As Daniel Fabre has argued, it was important for the subsequent history of the concept of the symbolic that Mauss did not enclose it in a single definition, but stressed the interplay of arbitrary and motivated symbols, polysemy, the relational values of symbolic systems, and the capacity of symbols not only to possess plural meanings but also to produce chains of associations.[46] Surveying the innovations of Mauss's thought, Tarot suggests that Mauss's symbolic sociology ultimately developed a more "Romantic" version of Durkheimianism. That helps explain why Mauss could have a double posterity, influencing not only the hyperrationalist structuralist current but also the irrationalist currents of surrealism and members of the Collège de sociologie such as Georges Bataille.[47]

Judith Butler once insisted that the structuralist idea of the symbolic is the exact opposite of the German Romantic meaning of the symbolic, which she defined as "the fusion of sense and sound, characteristic of poetic language."[48] Recent German commentators have made similar distinctions. So, for example, Rudolf Schlögl speaks of the "old European semantic of the symbol, which even into the modern era emphasized not the referential character of the symbolic, but its power to make present [*Vergegenwärtigung*]."[49] Karl-Siegbert Rehberg distinguishes between the theory of the symbol as "presence-creating" (*Präsenzsymbolik*) and the theory of arbitrary signs. "Today the arbitrariness of signs and complexes of symbolization is nearer to us, more distant is their double existence as the presence of something else, along with their authoritative structure."[50] That is to say, there is something archaic about the latter. Such distinctions immediately get complicated, for we see Rehberg assert in the same text that the theory of "presence-creating" symbolism is indispensable to the analysis of modern institutions because of the ongoing need for power and order to make themselves visible through symbolic embodiment and presence.[51] Indeed, Rehberg suggests that one might speak of a progressive dissolution of the old modes of symbolism if it were not for the persistence of countercurrents and knots tying us to underlying continuities.[52] Schlögl, too, acknowledges that at present a unified theory of the symbolic is not available.[53] This probably means it never will be. Far from being crippling, this "fecund uncertainty," as Daniel Fabre calls it, may be intrinsic to the concept of the symbol.[54] So, for example, Vincent Descombes insists on the "irreducible duplicity" of the symbol, between the strictly conventional sign and the motivated symbol that evokes the unsayable, as Romantic philosophy insisted, but, even further, Descombes argues that the symbolic sits between two stools, between the *algebraic* and the *sacred*.[55] Likewise, Jean-Joseph Goux maintains the equivocal oscillation between "abstract operational symbolization" and "cryptophoric symbolization." "There is no true symbolism," he writes, "that is not cryptophoric: the symbol is a visible substitute that replaces something hidden, something that is not presentable."[56] We need to hold onto this sense of polyvalent, overlapping, and sometimes conflicting concepts of the symbolic if we are to follow the twists and turns of post-Marxism's adventure of the symbolic.

Jean-Joseph Goux argues that the ambiguities in the word symbol do not need to be reconciled, but "correspond to different logico-historical moments in the evolution of the symbol."[57] In Goux's presentation, the cryptophoric symbol yields to a rationalized, instrumentalized, and abstract symbolization appropriate to the capitalist world. In one way or another, the engagement with the history of the symbolic typically involves some form of exit narrative. As Sven Lütticken has written, "In the end, all genealogies of the symbol seem to end in practices of radical de-symbolization."[58] Indeed, one could see this as the basic premise of the Enlightenment: myth yields to science, a world of opaque meanings evolves into a world of rationally transparent relations, belief in the real power of symbols gives way to a recognition of their status as fictions, the power of symbols to *present* fades before the function of signs to *represent*, the forest of symbols is cleared to make way for a field of truth. This position governs Ernst Cassirer's philosophy of symbolic forms, insofar as symbols have a "liberating power," to borrow a term from Jürgen Habermas, not only because symbolic activity per se is the properly human mode of life that lifts humans out of the immediacy of nature but also because symbolic form itself tends increasingly toward more abstract conceptual expression.[59] Lévi-Strauss strongly subscribes to a process of desymbolization, despite his commitment to the symbolic as the basis of anthropology. This is the burden of his use of the term "floating signifier", to designate an undetermined signifier, such as *mana*, which operates as a supplement that seeks to remedy "the intellectual condition of man, in which the universe is never charged with sufficient meaning and in which the mind always has more meanings available than there are objects to which to relate them."[60] This condition may in essence be permanent, but it is not static. In his essay on Mauss, Lévi-Strauss suggested that the domain covered by the floating signifier is shrinking as the intellectual practices of humans develop: we "acknowledge that the work of equalising of the signifier to fit the signified has been pursued more methodically and rigorously from the time when modern science was born."[61] As Marcel Hénaff writes, "this presentation demonstrates an optimistic vision of science and assigns it a precise task regarding symbolic thought. One should be able to say that science takes over for such thought and, especially, relieves it of its duties. This would mean, at the limit (or, in any case, in principle), that symbolic thought could completely disappear in a universe where objective knowledge has responded to the totality of available signifiers."[62] Even deconstruction, that wayward offspring of structuralism, has been seen in this light, though here it is the hypergrowth of symbolic plurality that ironically seems to undo the power of the symbolic. It amplifies the consciousness of the unconnectedness of symbolism and hence its liberation from the various attempts to anchor it in an authoritative structure. Thus Umberto Eco calls deconstruction the "ultimate epiphany of the symbolic mode": radically secularized, semiotically adrift, and with no "outside."[63]

Grosso modo, another term for desymbolization is *secularization.*

It is no accident that Karl Marx insisted on the necessity of turning to religion when he strove to understand the function of symbols in society. He well recognized the power of symbols: what is money, after all, other than a symbol? Even gold, often thought of as more *real* than paper species, is already symbolic; and the commodity is a symbol of the value generated by labor. Value is a social relation that gets condensed into the commodity, making every product a "social hieroglypic."[64] To find an analogy to this process, Marx wrote, "we must have recourse to the mist-enveloped regions of the religious world." It is worth recalling this famous passage from *Das Kapital:* "In that world the productions of the human brain appear as independent beings endowed with life, and entering into relation both with one another and the human race. So it is in the world of commodities with the products of men's hands. This I call the Fetishism which attaches itself to the products of labour, so soon as they are produced as commodities, and which is therefore inseparable from the production of commodities."[65]

In thus seeking to decipher the social hieroglyph, Marx drew directly on the critical mode first formulated by the Left Hegelian critique of religion. He tied the enlightened drive toward desymbolization directly to the epochal task of secularizing the world. Communism was to be the last act in the secularization of humanity. In the light of Marx's critique of the commodity, it is not particularly surprising that the Hegelian left sharpened its blades for combat with Romanticism; nor, given our discussion thus far, should it come as a surprise that the Left Hegelians attacked Romantic concepts of symbolic form. Just as the Romantic ideal of the symbol was anchored in the desire to present the unpresentable, so too was the Left Hegelian rejection of the symbolic deeply implicated in their campaign against religion. Marx followed the Left Hegelians in associating human emancipation with the task of overcoming the otherness, heteronomy, and unmasterability implied by symbolic representation. Not all of the Left Hegelians' contemporaries on the left set themselves against the Romantics, however. Indeed, for the French "Romantic socialist" Pierre Leroux, the ambiguity and transcendentalism implied in the Romantic concept of the symbolic offered a way to conceive social life as a communion and preserve the openness of the social world for artistic and political creativity. The desymbolizing and secularizing line staked out by the Hegelian left and radicalized by Karl Marx won and came to exercise a dominant influence on the European left.

We will gain a deeper sense of the complexities, echoes, and subterranean continuities of post-Marxism's adventure of the symbolic if we recall the early European left's critical engagements with Romanticism. Accordingly, the book begins with two chapters on the Hegelian left and the Romantic socialist Pierre Leroux respectively. The point is not to argue for direct lines of influence. Rather, in keeping with my remarks on the insurmountable polyvalence of the symbolic itself, to mobilize the symbolic is to play with a range of meanings from the algebraic to the sacred. The collapse of Marxism prompted numerous thinkers to attempt to reconceptualize the emancipatory project with the resources of the symbolic turn. That collapse has in turn reopened the question of religion, which classical Marxism had pushed to the sidelines of its analysis of capitalist modernity. So we must add to the questions posed earlier in this introduction about the possibilities and prospects for regenerating critical social and political philosophy beyond the Marxist framework. With the collapse of Marxism, what is the status of the European left's longstanding commitment to secularism? What is the relationship between the post-Marxist symbolic turn and the Enlightenment project of desymbolization?

It seems wise to close this introduction with a note on how one might read this book. Every author hopes his book will be read from cover to cover, and I am no exception. Certainly, I conceived this book to be read from beginning to end. It builds a coherent set of themes and elements of a narrative, though its narrative is by no means linear. The thorough reader will be rewarded, I hope. But this book may be gainfully approached in two other ways. First, each chapter is a substantial treatment of its subject: each one stands to a considerable extent on its own and may be read as an individual study. Second, I have constructed the book as a series of contrapuntal exchanges. Accordingly, the six chapters comprise three separate paired discussions. The first two chapters explore two quite different ways in which the emerging western European left engaged Romanticism in the early nineteenth century. Chapters 3 and 4 treat Castoriadis and Lefort, the cofounders of *Socialisme ou Barbarie*, whose subsequent work shared numerous features but diverged in significant ways. Finally, chapters 5 and 6 are driven by the relationship between Laclau, Mouffe, and Žižek.

CHAPTER ONE

The Symbolic Dimension
and the Politics of Young Hegelianism

IS STRUCTURALISM A PRODIGAL CHILD of German Romanticism? If we follow hints from Pierre Bourdieu and François Dosse, the answer would seem to be yes. Thus, in his major work on the history of structuralism, Dosse follows Roland Barthes in suggesting that Saussurean linguistics heralds a democratic model insofar as the conventional nature of the sign establishes a homology between the linguistic contract and the social contract. "An entire lineage here refers to structuralism's enduring rootedness," writes Dosse. "Poetry, according to the Schlegel brothers, was supposed to be a Republican discourse, and there is indeed a debt to German Romanticism, which had argued for a notion of art as a structure freed of mimesis."[1] In a similar vein, Pierre Bourdieu writes: "proceeding, in accordance with [Friedrich] Schelling's wish, to a properly *tautegorical* (in opposition to *allegorical*) reading which refers the myth to nothing outside itself, structural analysis aims at laying bare the structure immanent in each symbolic production."[2] The attempt to link structuralism to Romanticism hits a snag the moment we recall a distinction made by Kant, whose role in the Romantic theory of the symbol was instrumental. For Kant, a symbol creates visibility—it appeals to sensual intuition. In thus defining the symbol, Kant broke with the conceptual vocabulary of eighteenth-century rationalism, which had defined the symbol as an abstract sign that serves discursive knowledge.[3] So, complained Kant, "The use of the word *symbolic* in contrast to the *intuitive* kind of representation has, of course, been accepted by recent logicians, but this is a distorted and incorrect use of the word: for the symbolic is merely a species of the intuitive."[4]

As Bengt Algot Sørenson, the great student of Romantic symbol theory, suggests, the idea of the symbol almost immediately forked off from Kant. Kant, after all, believed that the symbol makes concepts visible by analogy, not by participation in or identity with the conceptual object, which itself remains sensuously unpresentable; the sensual and the intellectual are permanently divided. Ultimately, the role of the Kantian symbol is to lead us toward clarity on our concepts, as when Kant famously declares that "the beautiful is the symbol of the morally good."[5] Goethe, inspired by Kant but not satisfied with the restriction of the symbol to an analogical function, insisted that the symbol touches the object itself.[6] Romanticism, as we shall see, did not decisively settle on one side or the other of the alternatives posed by Kant and Goethe, but oscillated between the notions that the symbol presents the unpresentable and that it participates in the object it presents. Complicated as the history of this idea immediately becomes, we can agree with Tzvetan Todorov that Kant and the Romantics who followed *resubstantialized* the idea of the symbol.[7]

One of Saussure's inaugural gestures, let us not forget, was to separate the symbol from the sign, and what is really meant when mid-twentieth-century structuralism speaks of the Symbolic is the system of signs. So in fact structuralism is not so much Romanticism's distant heir as its overcoming, achieved, ironically, by resurrecting the eighteenth-century association of the symbol with the conventional sign. When we turn to what is known—somewhat problematically—as postmodern or poststructural thought, the connection to Romanticism looks more promising. There is, for example, the revival of interest in the "sublime" pioneered by Jean-François Lyotard, whereby the attempt to "present the unpresentable" comes to define a general condition of communication in an epoch shadowed by the figure of a radical heterogeneity that disrupts all efforts at closure, totalization, and seamless narrativity.[8] Scholars are quick to point out the gulf separating the Romantic from the postmodern sublime. For example, Edward Larrissy describes postmodern sublimity as "ironic, self-conscious, lacking in metaphysical confidence," and Paul Hamilton asserts that "the Romantic trope of sublimity recasts failures of understanding as the successful symbolic expression of something greater than understanding; Postmodernism rereads this success as indicating only the indeterminacy of meaning."[9] Yet, the relationship of postmodernism to Romanticism seems to go beyond this latter-day act of demystification, for the experience of indeterminacy is not at all alien to Romantic thought. While Kant seemed confident that the symbolic could lead us toward an intellectual comprehension of that which cannot be presented, Romanticism did not produce a similar sense of certainty. The Romantic quest to "say the unsayable" ensured that truth is a goal we never reach; Andrew Bowie writes of the Romantic sensibility that "all we can assert is that our experience of truth is of an ongoing insufficiency which yet sustains the continuing demand for a better account."[10]

If we can agree with François Dosse that Romanticism broke with mimetic theories of art, this did not produce a Romantic theory of a self-enclosed and endlessly self-referential discursive system. Rather, the break from mimesis led to a new appreciation for the constitutive role of representation, for the power of language to reveal or disclose a world. Of course, this could and did produce an exalted sense of the imagination's autopoietic power and of an artistic freedom operating beyond existing rules. Yet it also produced a refined and sometimes dizzying sense of irony. Work by the young Friedrich Schlegel often reads like an uncanny primer for Jacques Derrida; Schlegel's ironic claim that "it is equally fatal for the mind to have a system, and to have none" anticipates Derrida's habit of placing words under erasure in order to warn readers that he is using concepts that he can neither fully accept nor do without.[11] Further, Derrida did not believe that one could ever neglect the associations that belong to the intuition that underlies the signified meaning: one cannot assume that the signifier communicates an intended meaning without carrying traces of other associations. "In other words," writes Kathleen Dow Magnus, "by Derrida's assessment, the transition from the symbolic to the sign-making imagination can never be complete."[12] The fact that Derrida makes this point about signs and symbols in an essay directed against Hegel suggests the need for a refinement of my description of structuralism.[13] Perhaps it is more accurate to say that structuralism is the *second* overcoming of Romanticism.[14] Generations earlier, Hegel had already, after his own fashion, campaigned against the Romantic symbol in favor of the sign.

The status of the symbolic was one of the important divisions between Hegel and his Romantic contemporaries. The symbolic expressed the Romantics' paradoxical quest for the unity of the perfectly individual with the fully universal, their contradictory combination of yearning for the fullest possible presence of meaning and their fascination for the inexpressible, unapproachable, and inscrutable. The symbol, to cite Friedrich Schelling, creates an "inner bond uniting art and religion," and, further, the symbol establishes the philosophy of art "as the necessary goal of the philosopher, who in art views the inner essence of his own discipline as if in a magic and symbolic mirror."[15] Hegel, by contrast, judged the symbol to be inadequate for philosophy. How, he asked in the *Aesthetic*, is the idea supposed to take form in the symbolic?[16] Even stronger is his insistence in the *Lectures on the History of Philosophy* that "whoever hides thoughts in symbols has no thoughts at all."[17] The linguistic sign was, in Hegel's view, the privileged medium of the science of the concept. It is a commonplace among theorists of symbolism that all symbols are signs, but not all signs are symbols.[18] Hegel's distinction between the symbol and the sign hinges on the sensuous or intuitive dimensions of symbolism. According to him, a symbol conveys its meaning through the presentation of some quality or qualities it has in common with that meaning. By contrast, the specific virtue of the sign is precisely its arbitrariness. Because its capacity to convey meaning depends only on convention and agreement, the sign can be purged of the naturalness and intuitiveness that linger in the symbol. It can shed the symbol's ambiguity and become the transparent medium of spirit's self-determination. The tension between the sign and the symbol opens the heart of the conflict between Hegel and the Romantics.

Hegel's impulse toward desymbolization came to exercise a powerful influence upon the Left Hegelian movement that emerged into public discussion with the publication of David Friedrich Strauss's *Das Leben Jesu* in 1835. Strauss's initial campaign against Christian belief rapidly grew more radical in the writings of figures like Ludwig Feuerbach, Bruno and Edgar Bauer, and Karl Marx. From the outset, this attack on religion was not without profound political meaning, particularly within the restorationist Prussian context, where the state staked its legitimacy on its Christian mission; in the hands of Feuerbach, Bauer, and Marx, the political dimension became more explicit and ever more insistent. Still, even if Marx declared the critique of religion finished in Germany in the year 1843, the arsenal developed by the Left Hegelians had an enduring effect on social and political criticism, not least that of Marx himself. Compelled by the attempt to free humanity from religion, radical Hegelians like Arnold Ruge, Theodor Echtermeyer, and Friedrich Theodor Vischer sharpened Hegel's opposition to the Romantic sensibility. Ruge and Echtermeyer's polemical manifesto *Der Protestantismus und die Romantik* (1839–1840) is emblematic of this. Claiming that philosophy must now form a party against the dead past in the name of the true present, Ruge and Echtermeyer declare the Romantics to be the "living dead."[19] Against the Romantic taste for the "indeterminate, the ungraspable, the twilight, and the flitting," they pitted the "self-conscious spirit, that seeks to firmly appropriate the divine."[20] Ruge and Echtermeyer were much blunter than Hegel in linking Romantic aesthetics to the reactionary politics of the post-Napoleonic era and connecting spirit's struggle to overcome the heteronomy of the divine with the struggle for political emancipation.[21]

The main tendency of Left Hegelianism was opposed to Romanticism and, by extension, Romantic ideas about symbolic form. Nonetheless, as this chapter will show, there were subtleties in the way this critical distance from Romanticism played out. To explore these, this chapter will discuss the divergent tracks taken by Bruno Bauer and Ludwig Feuerbach. Bauer's philosophy of self-consciousness radicalized Hegel's emphasis on the potential transparency of language and meaning, thereby tying the emancipatory project to a radical process of desymbolization. Feuerbach's position was more conflicted. Although he developed a radical hermeneutic that had a tremendous impact on the development of left-wing thought, Feuerbach's naturalism led him toward a stance in which the Hegelian schema of the subject's appropriation of meaning contended with a resistant natural kernel that called for the reintroduction of symbolic representation as the only mode of signification appropriate for this unsayable and unmasterable element. This was a position that conflicted with main tendencies in Left Hegelianism, and even in Feuerbach's thought itself, and it eventually drew criticism from Karl Marx. Yet, in pointing to the irreducibility of the symbolic dimension, Feuerbach anticipated possibilities for conceptualizing the link between philosophical meaning and emancipatory politics that resonate with radical theory in the period of Marxism's collapse.

The Symbol from Classicism to Romanticism

The symbol held something of an absolute status for the Romantics. Nicholas Halmi has emphasized that Romantic symbolist theory was less concerned with identifying and interpreting particular symbols than with "establishing an ideal of meaningfulness itself."[22] This is an intuitively persuasive claim. The notion of the symbol carried far too much weight in the Romantic mind to be merely a rhetorical figure. Indeed, it seemed to speak directly to an acute sense of need. It was, after all, a time of crisis, when revolutionary upheaval cast existing convictions into doubt. Everyone, wrote the young Friedrich Schlegel, was caught up in this process of fermentation, whether he liked it or not, yielding to it or struggling against it.[23] The experience of the age—its politics, its social transformations, its dominant modes of analytic rationality inherited from the Enlightenment—produced a widespread sense of division and dualism. It is symptomatic of such a time that Novalis should describe philosophy as "homesickness—the desire to be everywhere at home."[24] Such a sensibility placed tremendous strain on existing modes of aesthetic and linguistic representation, which had already become sources of anxiety for Enlightenment thinkers. In the tempestuous climate opened by the French Revolution, eighteenth-century semioticians' emphasis on natural signs that consist in mimetic representations, or causal relations, but lack metaphysical content seemed both complicitous in the political, artistic, and epistemological ancien régime and of questionable service in the emerging new order.[25] Under such circumstances, the symbolic seemed to promise a more adequate mode of representation, one that better addressed this desire to overcome dualism. This is certainly the function that Halmi focuses on when he describes the Romantic symbol in terms of its claim to unify being and meaning through the sign's participation in the ontological order of the thing it represents.[26]

Where Halmi dispassionately searches for the genealogical sources of this emphatic ideal of the identity of sign and thing, critics of Romanticism have focused on its fantasmatic or mystifying dimensions. So, for example, Walter Benjamin valued Baroque allegory precisely because its evident reliance on arbitrary conventions accentuated the gap between meaning and being; Romantic symbolism, he argued by contrast, rested on a dream of fusion and identity, whereby the gap between signifier and signified is to be transcended by what Benjamin called "the idea of the unlimited immanence of the moral world in the world of beauty."[27] Paul de Man considered all writing an attempt to come to grips with the insurmountably temporal nature of our condition, and he judged allegory especially suited to revealing this situation. Allegory, writes de Man, "designates primarily a distance in relation to its own origin, and, renouncing the nostalgia and the desire to coincide, it establishes its language in the void of this temporal difference." The symbol, by contrast, "postulates the possibility of an identity or identification": within this view, the central feature of Romanticism is "a conflict between a conception of the self seen in its authentically temporal predicament and a defensive strategy that tries to hide from this negative self-knowledge."[28] Indeed, modernity or, more precisely, postmodernity has sometimes been seen as intrinsically *allegorical* (which would be to say *antisymbolic*) because it has forever foreclosed on the fantasy of immediacy, presence, identity, and transcendence.[29]

Insofar as such twentieth-century approaches distinguish strongly between allegory and Romantic symbolism, they are not without some grounding in Romanticism itself. Hence the young Friedrich Schelling articulated a dialectical triad, with the symbol serving to reconcile two opposed terms: *Schematismus*, which, following Kant's terminology, signifies the particular through the general, and *Allegorie*, which signifies the general through the particular. The "synthesis of the two, in which the general does not signify the particular nor does the particular signify the general, but in which the two are absolutely one, is the *symbolic*."[30] As opposed to allegory, the symbol creates a relationship of identity, not simply of signification, between the general and the particular. The symbol *is* what it signifies; it presents, rather than represents. Thus Schelling offers as an example Mary Magdalen, who "does not only *signify* repentance, but is living repentance itself."[31]

Schelling's emphasis on presence and participation accentuated a change in German aesthetic discourse already observable in predecessors like Karl Phillip Moritz and Goethe. Moritz articulated a notion of the beautiful object as the *in sich vollendet*, that which is perfect in itself. "An authentic work of art," wrote Moritz, "a beautiful poem, is something finished and completed in itself, something that exists for itself, and whose value lies in itself, and in the ordered relationship of its parts."[32] The beautiful cannot be translated into another medium, and it is, as Tzvetan Todorov emphasizes, radically "intransitive": "The beautiful object does not require an end out-side itself, for it is so perfected in itself that the entire purpose of its existence is found in itself."[33] Goethe formalized this ideal of the beautiful in his concept of the symbol. "True symbolism," wrote Goethe in 1797, "is where the particular represents the more general, not as a dream or a shadow, but as a living momentary revelation of the Inscrutable."[34] Goethe identified this ideal through a contrast to allegory.[35]

Where the Baroque period has been called the climactic age of the al-legory, by the later eighteenth century, critics were attacking allegory for various reasons, some of them mutually contradictory. So, for Gottsched, allegory's reliance upon the sensuous embodiment of ideas means that al-legory appeals to the senses and thus is not sufficiently rational, whereas Lessing maintained that because allegory relies upon a system of conven-tional signs—the blindfold signifying impartiality, for example—which is understood cerebrally, it cannot generate an affective response to art.[36] A new basis for the critique of allegory emerged with Goethe and Moritz's *Autonomieästhetik*. Allegory, in this view, represents a mechanical and self-conscious way of connecting the particular and the general. In creating an allegory, the poet seeks a particularity to typify a generality, thus the par-ticular serves merely to exemplify the general. By contrast, Goethe argued, the very nature of poetry lies in its expression of the particular, without thinking of or referring to a universal. To grasp this particular in a truly lively way, however, is also to come into contact with the general, though without immediate awareness or, at most, with an awareness that emerges only in reflection. "The allegory," wrote Goethe, "changes the phenomenon into a concept, the concept into an image, in such a way that the concept is always limited and complete in the image and expressed in the image." The symbolic, by contrast, "changes the phenomenon into an idea, the idea into an image, such that the idea remains always infinitely active and un-approachable in the image, and will remain inexpressible even if expressed in all languages."[37]

This formulation points to a tension in the *Autonomieästhetik*: the work may have a certain kind of autonomy insofar as it can never be reduced to something outside itself. But can a work of art be complete in itself when it opens up a potentially infinite activity of interpretation? Goethe's defi-nition vacillates between an ideal of the symbol as a form of presence, or, better, presentification, and as a figure that initiates a disruptive, open, and above all *inexhaustible* dialectic. Hence, Goethe spoke of the double nature of the symbolic artwork, whereby it is what it pretends to be and nonetheless embodies a different, general principle.[38] At times this could prompt descriptions that evoke an insurmountable circularity in this play of difference and identity: the symbol is "the thing, without being the thing, but nonetheless the thing."[39] Ultimately, it may be said that Goethe tried to contain the disruptive dimensions by insisting that the aesthetic symbol is a demonstrable perfection achieved in the greatest artworks. An observation from R. H. Stephenson suggests the self-imposed restriction this required: "Aesthetic expressibility, subject like everything else to polarity, evokes its opposite: ineffability. Any aesthetic symbol, marking an ultimate limit of articulation, necessarily evokes what may lie beyond: the transcendental. Aesthetic consciousness cannot, in the nature of things, vouchsafe insight into what lies beyond the little patch of order presented to it. An aesthetic symbol embodies an experience of presence; the absence which hovers about it is a matter for *religious* symbolism."[40]

The Romantics were unwilling to follow Goethe's self-restraint. The aesthetic and the religious mixed much more freely in Romantic thinking about the symbol.[41] Here we see the other side of how the idea of the symbol intersected with the sense of political and cultural upheaval around 1800. That is, the belief that the symbolic could overcome the dualisms of the age contended with a sense that the symbolic was actually a key index of unsurpassable dualism. Whereas Goethe and Moritz believed the symbol to be an achievable part of a classical ideal of completed aesthetic form, the Romantics tended to see the symbol as a condition of harmony and reconciliation that eluded the present. The symbol marked a lost past and an ideal future. Even Schelling, who offered perhaps the most emphatic formulation of the symbol as the organic fusion of particular and universal, maintained that whereas the classical Greeks had been able to create symbols of the infinite, Christianity, with its division of the world from the divine, could present only allegories of the infinite. Moreover, the modern commitment to originality and change made the symbol impossible in our age, for the symbol presupposes the constancy of a shared system of thought.[42] The symbol thus formed a cable in a temporal span suspended between the poles of recollection and imaginative invention, and the Romantics typically saw this bridge expanding infinitely in both directions. Though they strove for the perfect symbol, they were always underway toward it. In Schelling's opinion, the modern age—which in the broad Romantic usage meant essentially the Christian epoch—"must be allegorical, even if against its will, because it cannot be symbolic."[43]

With good reason, Sørenson places Schelling *between* Goethe's classicist idea of the symbol and that of the Romantics.[44] Some of Schelling's contemporaries moved more decisively away from the classicist ideal of the *in sich vollendet*. In the case of Friedrich Schlegel, Goethe's terminological distinction between symbol and allegory was of little significance; although he emphatically believed that all art is symbolic, he sometimes used allegory and symbol interchangeably, and at various points throughout his long career he privileged one term or another despite the fact that his basic view of the symbolic remained constant.[45] For Schlegel, the Christian narrative of Fall and Redemption meant that the symbol awaited the end of days, and until then the mediation of God and world could only be achieved indirectly. Allegory thus becomes the appropriate form of representation: "All beauty is allegory. One can only express the highest allegorically, precisely because it is inexpressible."[46] By allegory, it must be emphasized, Schlegel did not mean to designate the rhetorical trope or didactic device described by Enlightenment poetics; rather, Schlegel's "allegory of the infinite" spoke to the ontological situation of human beings and the limits of their systems of meaning.[47] We find a similar claim for the disruption of symbolic meaning in Novalis, for whom "the world's meaning has been lost."[48] For him, the symbol functions as a hieroglyph, gesturing toward a totality no longer understood in Goethe's and Moritz's terms as the perfected work of art, but as the numinous interpenetration of divinity and the world. Novalis thus imagined that the symbolic relationships constituting art paved the royal road to the recovery of lost meaning. However, because the symbol's ultimate pretext is the numinous, neither Schlegel nor Novalis believed that the symbol could be exhaustively decoded or understood.[49] Not surprisingly, Goethe never accepted the Romantic emphasis on the allegorical nature of modernity, a claim that would have nullified core values of his own aesthetics; nor was he at all happy with the Romantic tendency to steer the concept of the symbolic away from the clear light of artistic revelation toward the mystical domain of "shadow and dream." For Goethe, the Romantic tendency to mix the aesthetic with the religious and the allegorical with the symbolic were key symptoms of the immoderation that he believed was a discernible danger in modernity.[50] Quite by contrast, it was precisely the dynamic exchange between religion and aesthetics, the allegorical and the symbolic, the present and the absent, ultimately the interchange between possibility and impossibility that confirmed the moral grandeur of the Romantics' striving spirit, what Friedrich Schlegel called the "unformed colossalness of the moderns."[51]

Walter Benjamin and Paul de Man both recognized this tendency toward allegorical polyvalence and fragmentariness within Romanticism, even as they criticized what they considered Romanticism's main tendency toward fantasies of fusion, identity, and totality. The nuances of Benjamin and de Man's critique of Romanticism have frequently disappeared in work inspired by them. The tension between symbol and allegory, which of course was a feature of the Romantic era itself, frequently hardens into an opposition. And, by extension, the notion that the postmodern age is allegorical rests inherently on a contrast to a modern age that was symbolic. It should be clear from the present discussion that it is a mistake to elevate one dimension of Romantic symbol theory above the polyvalence that lies at its core: the symbol is simultaneously a figure that concentrates *and* disperses meaning; it is a powerful figure, not just one sign among all others, but one that has the paradoxical power both to present or body forth *and* to accentuate the gap between the sign and the signified. It is, in Cordula Grewe's words, "both insufficient and overfull, insufficient in its inevitable failure to express the divine, overfull in its poetic surplus of meaning."[52] It is with good reason that Umberto Eco asks whether the Romantic symbol is an instance of "an immanence or of a transcendence" and then leaves the question unanswered.[53] The polyvalence is further accentuated when we consider that the same Romantics who distinguished between symbol and allegory often used the terms interchangeably and collapsed the two into a general idea that the modern age is itself allegorical. That is, modernity is a state of longing for an impossible unity. This understanding of modernity bridges the divide between the early Romanticism of the Jena group, which recent scholarship has embraced for its politically progressive and conceptually daring attitudes,and later Romanticism, whose Christian and politically conservative impulses continue to make it suspect. Further, this Romantic epochal concept establishes an affinity with the sensibility of much recent theory, even if generations of countervailing philosophical thought erected taboos that continue to hinder our recognition of that affinity.

Hegelian Spirit from Symbol to Sign

Hegel had little sympathy for the Romantic concern for the symbolic intuition of divinity. In his eyes, the Romantics' "nebulous representation [*Vorstellung*] of the Ideal" exemplified their flight from the world into the extremes of subjectivity.[54] Where the symbol and the allegory—whether as opposed terms or as synonyms—preoccupied Romantic theorists, Hegel was far more concerned with the distinction between symbol and sign. Indeed, Hegel presented allegory merely as a type of "conscious symbolism"; he thus turned allegory back from the kind of metaphysical and ontological meaning assigned it by Romantics like Friedrich Schlegel to the place it had held in eighteenth-century poetics, namely a rhetorical form ranked along with riddles, metaphors, images, and similes as modes of comparison. At one level, Hegel's lack of concern with the contrast between symbol and allegory may reflect the fact that these terms never became fixed in the contemporary debate. The Romantics themselves were not consistent in their usage, a lack of clarity that may be explained not only by the dependence of the concept of the symbolic on the intrinsically murky categories of the intuition but also by the fact that both symbols and allegories ultimately share a common identity as forms of sensuous imagery or as indirect representations of concepts. Yet, at another level, Hegel's relative indifference to the distinction between allegory and symbol underscores the greater significance he assigned to the distinction between sign and symbol.

As Kathleen Dow Magnus writes, "Hegel defines the act of symbolization as the imagination's use of sensuous appearances or images to represent by analogy conceptions '*of another kind*'; the symbol conveys a meaning through the presentation of some quality or qualities that it has in common with that meaning. The sign, by contrast, presents its meaning through an 'arbitrary connection' with it." The sign and the symbol each has a meaning that is different than its immediate sensible expression. However, where the symbol is both identical to and different from its meaning, the sign expresses its meaning through an indifference to its expression. The symbols *lion* and *fox,* for example, work because they "themselves possess the very qualities whose meaning they are supposed to express."[55] The sensuous form of symbolic expression introduces ambiguity in that the sensible expression does not fully coincide with its meaning. For example, "mountain" could symbolize sublimity or self-transcendence, but it could also mean obstacle or peril. As Hegel wrote, "the symbol, strictly so-called, is *inherently* enigmatic because the external existent by means of which a universal meaning is to be brought to our contemplation still remains different from the meaning that it has to represent, and it is therefore open to doubt in what sense the shape has to be taken."[56] The sign, by contrast, signifies only by convention. Its sensible expression has no value outside the agreement that establishes a link between expression and meaning; hence both the arbitrariness and the efficiency of *Fuchs, fox, renard.* Precisely by negating the significance of the relationship between meaning and the form of its presentation, the sign is able to mark identities and differences within a system of meaning. Purged of naturalness or intuition, the relationship between its expression and meaning clarified and explicit, the sign sheds the ambiguity of the symbol and exists only in its ability to signify. The sign is thus the privileged medium for philosophy, the science of the concept.

The nature of symbols establishes a connection between art and religion in Hegel's thought. As he writes, "In the case of art, we cannot consider, in the symbol, the arbitrariness between meaning and signification [which characterizes the sign], since art itself consists precisely in the connection, the affinity and the concrete interpretation of meaning and of form."[57] Likewise, as Magnus notes, religious consciousness tends toward symbolization. It assigns a *"general meaning or conception to immediacies"* that share something in common with that general meaning without being identical to it. It *"communicates its meaning ambiguously* because it does not clarify the basis or limitation of the identification it asserts." And finally, religious consciousness "in one way or another *sustains a divergence between its form and its meaning,* its activity of representation and the object it seeks to represent."[58] In drawing this connection between religion and art as symbolic forms, Hegel shared, in some ways, the impulse of his Romantic contemporaries to carry the idea of the symbol back and forth across the line separating religion and art. Yet Hegel took this to a quite different conclusion. Where the Romantic Schelling believed that art has the permanent task of teaching the philosopher to "recognize symboli-cally the way sensual things" emerge from the "true archetypes of forms," Hegelian philosophy was premised on the historical progression from symbols to signs.

Or, more precisely, where his contemporaries were interested in the ongoing viability of the symbol, Hegel created a tripartite history of the symbolic form that fit into his general account of the journey of spirit—humanity as a collective subject—from its immersion in nature to the free-dom of self-conscious self-determination. In his aesthetics Hegel main-tained that all art is, in a broad sense, symbolic insofar as it cannot express spirit as it is in itself but must rely on presentations in sensuous form.[59] Yet the only period in art history that Hegel called properly "symbolic" was the art of early civilizations like ancient Egypt.

In that early phase, spirit struggles to liberate itself from nature, but its limited success is reflected in an art that, in Hegel's view, imperfectly im-poses human meaning on the obdurate materiality of its main medium, stone. In this view the hieroglyph provides not a general template for art, as it did for a Romantic like Novalis, but an instance of a phase when consciousness remains indeterminate and unsure of its autonomy. Like-wise, the Sphinx serves Hegel as the "symbol of the symbolic itself," that is, the riddle-laden sign of spirit's unfree and half-conscious impulse to emerge from the animal domain.[60] In the subsequent classical period of ancient Greece, spirit is less bound by its interaction with the material. Classical sculpture transforms stone with less regard for its inherent prop-erties, and spirit seems to penetrate and illuminate the human forms that classical art took as its main subject matter. Indeed, so perfect is the unity of form and content that the artwork no longer signifies in the way a sym-bol does, but appears to be simply what it is. In a sense, Hegel thus treats the late-eighteenth-century classicist notion of the perfect work of art, the *in sich vollendet*, not as a timeless ideal but as a historical manifestation. Precisely this perfection proves to be the limit of classical art, because it hinders subjectivity from developing its own interior depths: "For spirit is the infinite subjectivity of the Idea, which as absolute inwardness cannot freely and truly shape itself outwardly if it remains poured into a bodily existence as the one appropriate to it."[61] It is precisely subjectivity liberated from the corporeality of its artistic presentation that characterizes the Ro-mantic period, which Hegel, in keeping with the Romantics he putatively opposed, equates with nothing less than the emergence of Christianity itself. Painting is Hegel's essential Romantic art. Where sculpture exists in natural space, painting creates its own unnatural space, an illusion of nature. Far from being a weakness, this creation of illusion exemplifies subjectivity's growing power of self-reflection and autonomy from the substantial world of nature. Under such circumstances, art once again becomes symbolic in the sense that there is yet again a discrepancy between the form and content of art. Yet symbolic art in Hegel's strictly technical and historical sense strove to find an adequate expression of a concept it held in an indeterminate way: as Hegel would remind his readers, the secrets *of* the Egyptians were also secrets *for* the Egyptians. By contrast, Romantic art expresses in a determinate fashion recognition that artistic form is exceeded by its spiritual content. Aware of a tension between itself and the sensuous, Hegel writes, spirit in its Romantic phase "dissolves that classical unification of inwardness and external manifestation and takes flight out of externality back into itself."[62] In the "free room for play" that spirit thus wins for itself, Romantic art reestablishes the typical tension of the symbolic, namely the gap between expression and meaning.[63]

There is much in this description that accords with Hegel's Romantic contemporaries: the general equation of the Romantic with the Christian period; the sense that the "modern" (that is, postclassical) period is allegorical, in the metaphysical sense intended by Friedrich Schlegel; even the contrast between sculpture and painting, which resonates with August Wilhelm Schlegel's contrast between the *plastic* spirit of classical art and poetry and the *picturesque* spirit of the moderns. However, Hegel departs sharply from the Romantics when he views this new symbolic phase as itself overcome by the progress of spirit. The end phase of Hegel's historical account of the aesthetic symbol coincides with his declaration that "art, considered in its highest vocation, is and remains for us a thing of the past," by which he never intended to suggest that art ceases to be produced but rather that it ceases to be an adequate medium for spirit's self-expression.[64] Human consciousness's reliance upon concrete sensual representations of itself weakens, even as spirit's ability to speak directly of itself grows. The Romantic form, writes Hegel, "passes over from the poetry of imagination [*Vorstellung*] to the prose of thought."[65] Or, more precisely, spirit never fully abandons sensual images, but it learns to distinguish with ever greater clarity between general ideas and attempts to give them visible form. Hence the history of the artistic symbol ends in *conscious* symbolism, a point where symbols can be known as symbols, that is, as humanly instituted conventions that function as components of human discourse.[66] The last symbolic stage of art is therefore the "conscious symbolic of the comparative form of art"; here, the artist has various possibilities at his disposal, such as metaphors, allegories, symbols, and parables, by which he may consciously compare and relate meaning and concrete appearance in the work of art. As Peter Szondi wrote, this is a "secularization of symbolic art," a rather flat matter of artistic choices about representational forms that no longer stands in the center of the historical process.[67] This attitude became even sharper among Hegel's liberal and left-wing followers. So, for example, the Young German Theodor Mundt and the Left Hegelian Friedrich Theodor Vischer believed that symbolic art continues to exist only as a relic.[68] Likewise, Arnold Ruge and Theodor Echtermeyer formulated a sarcastic "Catechism" for the Romantic living dead. Point number 4 reads: "the best will not become clear through words [*das Beste wird durch Worte nicht deutlich*]!"[69] Thus they pit the Romantic allegory directly against the ideal of discursive clarity.

A similar logic governs Hegel's treatment of symbolization in religion. Hegel assumes that "the object of religion, like that of philosophy, is the eternal truth, God and nothing but God and the explication of God."[70] Though philosophy and religion share an identical object, he nonetheless insisted on a distinction between the forms in which they express that content. Religion knows the Absolute naively because it does not recognize its absolute content thinkingly, but rather represents this content pictorially, symbolically. Consequently, religious consciousness knows the truth of religion in an unfree way, bound to the sensuousness of the image rather than liberated as a free self-determination of spirit. As he had done with art, Hegel inserted the history of religion into his account of the unified historical process of the evolution of consciousness, culminating in Christianity. A succession of "finite religions," such as Hinduism, Judaism, and Greek polytheism created a series of sensuous forms of the divine that allowed human subjectivity to establish identifications with the otherness of the divine, even if the forms of that identification did not yet permit the self-conscious recognition of the unity of the human and the divine. All historical religions prior to Christianity contain "some truth" as the different moments of the gradual yet determinate self-revelation and self-realization of spirit, but they remain fragmentary, representing a dualism in spirit between consciousness and self-consciousness. Only in Christianity, the "absolute religion," is God "*thought of* as self-consciousness" and hence it is only in Christianity that the self "beholds *itself* in the object."[71]

To be sure, in Christianity Hegel does see a continued role for the symbolic. However, because Christian symbols—most notably Christ himself as the incarnate God-Man—correspond to the structure of the Idea, symbols incline the Christian to reflect on the unity in difference of his own subjectivity and the divine as a moment of the self-relation of Spirit.[72] Absolute religion produces something equivalent to the condition of art in the period when art no longer is the privileged bearer of spirit's development, namely a *conscious* symbolism in which the nature and function of symbols becomes an object of self-conscious reflection. Religious consciousness thus moves toward philosophical consciousness, the symbol toward the sign. To be sure, Kathleen Dow Magnus is correct in arguing that Hegel reserved a place for the symbolic even in his conception of absolute spirit. Absolute spirit manifests itself in art, religion, and most fully in philosophy. Though philosophy's manner of knowing places it in the highest position within this triad, philosophy's own comprehensive grasp of identity in difference requires the persistence of art and religion in their relative autonomy, and this requires the persistence of the sensual and imagistic element that distinguishes art and religion from philosophy. In other words, the recalcitrant dimension of symbols gives us the opportunity to encounter a limit in our self-knowledge, to experience ourselves not knowing ourselves.

Ultimately, however, the obstacle of the symbolic acts as a catalyst propelling consciousness toward greater depths of self-comprehension and self-determination.[73] Magnus's detailed demonstration of the ongoing importance of the symbolic for Hegel remains tied to an understanding of human history as the dialectical movement of spirit toward absolute self-determination. The gulf between Hegel and the classicist and Romantic champions of the symbol remains unbridged. Where those champions insisted on both the untranslatability and intransivity of the symbol, Hegel's treatment is based on the claim that the symbol is both translatable and transitive. The highest aim of spirit is *thought*, and "in thought there is no longer any difference between ideas or pictures and their meaning; thought is its own meaning and in its existence it is what it is implicitly."[74] This conviction stamped Hegel's radical followers.

Left Hegelian Desymbolization

Writing in 1844, Bruno Bauer observed that the radical movement of Left Hegelianism had followed a pattern familiar in Germany, where revolutionary agitation and struggle played out as literary phenomena.[75] Bauer intended that to be a criticism of the *inverted* German world, much in the spirit of Marx's remark from the same year that "in politics, the Germans *thought* what other nations *did*."[76] However, if we take Bauer's claim seriously, then the notion that Young Hegelianism was a *literary* phenomenon ultimately rests on the fact that its radical politics began as a critique of religion. That meant, first and foremost, the criticism of religious texts. Insofar as Left Hegelianism may thus be understood as a practice of textual criticism, it is necessary to explore Bauer and Feuerbach's governing assumptions about referentiality and representation in the biblical text if we are to open the broader question of the status of the symbol in their thought. From there, finally, we will consider the political significance of their assumptions about the symbolic.

A first remark may be drawn from the preceding discussion of the Romantics and Hegel. For Left Hegelians like David Friedrich Strauss, Bruno Bauer, and Ludwig Feuerbach, the Romantic distinction between symbol and allegory seems to have had little significance. Rather, they tended to follow Hegel in treating allegory as a form of symbolic consciousness. Indeed, Left Hegelians used the terms *allegory* and *symbol* interchangeably and with less conceptual rigor than either the Romantics or Hegel. These terms functioned as roughly equivalent designations of the activity of symbolic representation; accordingly, in dealing with the Left Hegelians, it makes little sense to insist on the allegory-symbol distinction. While much of the specific conceptual weight of symbol and allegory was lost in the debates of the Left Hegelians, Hegel's distinction between the sign and the symbol was of far greater significance for them. Here it must quickly be said that the Left Hegelians did not explicitly, let alone rigorously thematize this distinction, nor did any of the Hegelian left significantly deepen Hegel's approach to this specific question. The distinction between sign and symbol was important more for the bedrock assumptions it entailed than for the conceptual clarity it might have brought to the discussion of religion and art.

What of the question of textual reference and representation in the biblical criticism of the Left Hegelians? Hegel's opposition between representation and concept authorized the dismantling of conventional schemes of biblical referentiality. Most dramatically, this meant the dissolution of the literal historical referent, reference to the biblical event, which by the later eighteenth century had become the hermeneutical model of biblical interpretation for orthodox defenders of the Bible and skeptical Enlightenment critics alike.[77] David Friedrich Strauss's 1835 *Das Leben Jesu* launched this critical trajectory by arguing that the Christian gospels were products of the *Volksgeist* of the ancient Hebrews, that is, mythical fulfillments of earlier messianic expectations. This was a hermeneutical position that absorbed both event and author into a collective mythological consciousness. It dealt a serious blow to supernaturalist theologians who read the Bible as a true and literal historical record of divine participation in human affairs; but it struck as well at rationalist Christian apologists who accepted the historical veracity of the biblical account, yet sought to explain away its more incredible episodes by recourse to natural causes. Further, Strauss's strategy undermined the long tradition of allegorical reading that discovered multiple levels of meaning in the Bible, for example Cassian's influential fourth-century account of the fourfold levels of meaning: the literal, the sacred historical or typological, the ethical, and the eschatological. Strauss nevertheless acknowledged that the allegorical mode of interpretation coincides with his own mythical approach "in relinquishing the historical reality of the sacred narratives in order to preserve to them absolute inherent truth."

Yet, Strauss quickly identified a crucial difference between the two approaches. The allegorical approach attributes the inspiration and truth of the narrative to "immediate divine agency," whereas the mythical method traces inspiration and truth back to the "spirit of a people or a community."[78] This distinction became blurred in the conclusion of *Das Leben Jesu*. There Strauss turned from the negative task of criticizing the historical claims of the New Testament to the positive task of discerning the true spiritual meaning of Scripture by reflecting upon the doctrinal significance of his critical life of Jesus. Indeed, Strauss offers what we might call an inverted allegorical reading as his mythical interpretation passes over into an exercise in Hegelian speculative reason. Arguing that God and man, the infinite and the finite, are complete only in each other, Strauss proceeds to deduce the *necessity* of the historical narrative of the God-Man from the conceptual truth of the union of human and divine natures. Deep meaning yields the surface narrative, an allegory in reverse. Reading Strauss today, it is difficult not to recall Heinrich Heine's exasperated observation that Kant's critical defense of belief in God reminded him of a student friend who smashed all the lamps in the city in order to lecture on the need for street lamps.

Under relentless attack from his many orthodox critics, Strauss retreated somewhat in subsequent editions of *Das Leben Jesu* from his initial assertion that every element of the biblical narrative is mythical. Even as Strauss backtracked, the Left Hegelian critique of religion rapidly moved beyond him. In 1837 Strauss described the Hegelian school as fragmented into a "right," "center," and "left," with himself occupying a lonely position as the sole figure on the left. By 1841 Strauss felt so insulted by the Hegelian left that he withdrew from the *Deutsche Jahrbücher*, the main organ of the movement.[79] Despite the souring of Strauss's relations with other Hegelian radicals, the rejection of historical referentiality that he articulated remained the bedrock of Left Hegelian biblical criticism. However, once the linguistic sign was detached from its conventional referent, the question of true reference became a matter of sharp debate, with Bruno Bauer and Ludwig Feuerbach defining the two most radical post-Straussian positions. In 1837 Strauss described Bauer as one of his main adversaries on the Hegelian right, because Bauer's articles in the *Jahrbücher für wissenschaftliche Kritik* between 1835 and 1837 amounted to the Prussian Hegelian establishment's official censure of *Das Leben Jesu*. By 1841 Bauer had entirely abandoned his defense of the accommodation between philosophy and theology. Bauer's evolution from a staunch defender of the accommodation between Hegelianism and orthodox Christianity to a militant Hegelian atheist may be traced through his unfolding critique of Strauss. The details of that engagement from Bauer's 1835 reviews of *Das Leben Jesu* through *Die Religion des Alten Testamentes* (1838), *Kritik der evangelischen Geschichte des Johannes* (1840), and *Kritik der evangelischen Geschichte der Synoptiker* (1841) cannot detain us here, except to repeat the frequently made observation that the continuous theme in these works is the role of human self-consciousness in its relationship to the infinite. However, where Bauer's early position centered on the "process of the subjective spirit which relates to God," that is, the understanding of God by the subjective spirit,[80] by 1841 he had arrived at the conclusion that religion is "nothing more than an inward relationship of self-consciousness to itself."[81] This was the most radical and influential stage of Bauer's development, which found its fullest expression in his *Kritik der evangelischen Geschichte der Synoptiker*. We will confine ourselves to this period and focus mainly on the extremely interesting preface to that work, which lays out Bauer's objection to Strauss and his alternative reading strategy.

In Bauer's view, Strauss's idea of a collective mythical consciousness is as alienating as the orthodox idea of revelation, for in both cases a transcendent explanation of the Scriptures conceals their true origin in human self-consciousness. In contrast, Bauer argued that the Synoptic Gospels were, in both form and content, the inventions of individual authors responding freely and pragmatically to the needs of their age. Bauer's insistence that individual authors created both the form *and* the content of Scripture was a dramatic departure from Strauss, as well as from those critical biblical scholars like Christian Gottlob Wilke, who had been willing to concede that humans had invented the Bible's literary forms but not the divinely revealed content. It enabled Bauer to claim that the Scriptures are "artistic" compositions through and through, and that both form and content were freely given by self-consciousness in accordance with the principles of authorship, even if self-consciousness did not yet recognize its own creativity at that stage in history.[82] The author's creation of both form and content, Bauer wrote, meant that there was no access to a "given and naked reality" outside the text.[83] Reference becomes a circular movement within the text itself, which now contains the signifier and the signified wholly within it. This would seem to link Bauer both backward to Karl Phillip Moritz's *Autonomieästhetik* and forward to Jacques Derrida's claim that there is nothing outside the text. Yet both associations need careful qualification. The relationship between Moritz and Bauer has yet to be explored in any depth, even though the last essay published in his lifetime was devoted to Moritz and Ernst Barnikol reports that Moritz was Bauer's favorite author.[84] This connection warrants investigation, but at present it suffices to assert that Bauer, like Hegel, would not have accepted Moritz's insistence on the radical intransitivity and untranslatability of the work of art. As for Derrida, Bauer would have had no patience for Derrida's radical skepticism about the capacity of language to serve as a transparent sign for thought. Indeed, far from either the self-contained wholeness of the work of art implied by Moritz or the displacement of referentiality along a chain of signifiers implied by Derrida, Bauer believed that the referent of the biblical text is in fact self-consciousness itself as it moves through history toward final recognition of itself as the "only power of the world and history."[85]

As religious self-consciousness, writes Bauer, the spirit is entirely gripped by the content of its own productions,

> cannot live without it, and without its continuous description and production, for it possesses in this activity the experience of its own determination. But as religious consciousness it perceives itself at the same time in complete differentiation from its own essential content, and as soon as it has developed it, and in the same moment that it develops and describes it, this essential content becomes for it a reality that exists for itself, above and outside religious consciousness, as the absolute and its history.[86]

The contrast here between manifest and essential content might look like a return to the allegorical mode, but it is not. For, as Bauer claims toward the end of the preface to the *Kritik der evangelischen Geschichte der Synoptiker*, the process of critique collapses the distinction between the content and the self-consciousness. There is no positivity in the text, no remainder. Or, to use Derrida's terminology, the materiality of the sign is effaced, because there is no slippage of meaning, no historical association or symbolic ambiguity that cannot be penetrated and mastered. Even with the alienated self-consciousness that composed the biblical text, self-consciousness recognizes something "homogeneous" with itself.[87] There is then no process of negotiation between signs and meaning, only the self-relation of a self-consciousness whose essential content is not its products, but its own productivity. Such transparency is the antithesis of the allegorical sensibility, which, if we follow Walter Benjamin, experiences the text, and indeed the world, as fragmentary and enigmatic, an aggregation of signs that adumbrate a truth that resides elsewhere. Allegory is literally "other-discourse," meaning that truth is, at most, "bodied forth in the dance of represented ideas."[88] By contrast, Bauer's critical assault on the gospels as well as on Strauss's mythical reading was motivated by his belief that "personality, reality and everything positive can in fact be gobbled up and consumed by the Hegelian idea."[89] Against critics who charged that he was animated only by the spirit of destruction, Bauer insisted in 1842 that "we fight for the honor and freedom of the positive, when we recognize and prove that it springs from the noblest thing there is, the historical self-consciousness."[90]

Feuerbach's *Das Wesen des Christentums* appeared in the same year as Bauer's *Kritik der evangelischen Geschichte der Synoptiker.* The two works share an emphasis on the development of human self-consciousness in relationship to religion; yet as both Feuerbach and Bauer recognized, they differed over the meaning of religion. Where Bauer regarded humanity's subjection to religious illusions as totally debasing, Feuerbach viewed religious feeling as alienated human species-being. Whereas Bauer sought to dissolve religious illusion, Feuerbach sought to return the projections of religion to their proper source in humanity, to restore the predicates of religious consciousness to their proper subject, man, and thereby to transform religious devotion into humanist devotion. Not surprisingly, Bauer denounced Feuerbach as a mystic and argued that the notion of species-being replicates the structure of theism insofar as it subordinates free self-consciousness to a substance that precedes and defines it.[91] As Bauer wrote in "Die Gattung und die Masse," "The essence which [man] does not make . . . is rather the expression of his weakness. The truly human in him would thereby be a barrier which is unattainable for him. His perfections, which confront him as hypostases or as dogmas, could at most be only the object of a cult or a faith."[92]

Feuerbach, for his part, maintained in the preface to the second edition of *Das Wesen des Christentums* (1843) that "Bauer takes for the object of his criticism the evangelical history, i.e., biblical Christianity, or rather biblical theology."[93] There are two implicit criticisms embedded in this seemingly neutral comment. First, Feuerbach always drew a sharp line between theology and the essence of faith; whereas faith expresses emotional and psychological needs that in themselves are authentic, even if misplaced, theology is an abstract discourse that distorts the content of faith and distances religion from its emotional core. So, from Feuerbach's perspective, Bauer's focus on the intellectual discourse of biblical theology obstructed his access to the essence of religion. Second, Bauer's exclusive focus on the theological text replicated what Feuerbach had come to regard as Hegel's greatest fault, namely, his identification of thought and being or, as Feuerbach insisted in his 1839 critique of Hegel, his confusion of the form or rhetoric of philosophy with the thing itself.[94] In contrast to Bauer, Feuerbach insisted that his own object "is Christianity, is Religion, as it is the *immediate object*, the *immediate nature*, of man." Religion as an object of reflection and intellection only comes afterward. Hence Feuerbach divided *Wesen des Christentums* into a first section dealing with "The True or Anthropological Essence of Religion" and a second section treating "The False or Theological Essence of Religion."

To put this another way, in Feuerbach's view Bauer operated *as if* there were nothing outside the text, or at least no truth that is not textual, which in Bauer's view is the privileged site of self-consciousness's creative self-realization. In contrast, Feuerbach insisted that his position does not "regard the *pen* as the only fit organ for the revelation of truth, but the eye and the ear, the hand and the foot; it does not identify the *idea* of the fact with the fact itself, so as to reduce the real existence to an existence on paper, but it separates the two, and precisely by this separation attains to the *fact itself*."[95] The line drawn between representation and the object itself, between thought and being, had been a feature of Feuerbach's thought ever since he jotted down some doubts about Hegel's logic in 1828. By the time he wrote his critique of Hegel in 1839, it had become a central motif of his thought. Manfred Frank has argued that Feuerbach formulated this critique under the influence of the later thought of Schelling, whose so-called positive philosophy had exercised such a complex and multivalent influence on the intellectual history of the 1830s.[96] We will discuss Schelling at greater length in the next chapter, and here it suffices to note that at the basis of positive philosophy was the claim that, instead of acknowledging their nonidentity, dialectical philosophy wrongly collapses being and consciousness into an identity. Rather than see the *Unaufhebbarkeit* or unassimilability of being as a restriction on human freedom, however, Schelling argued that precisely the gap between being and thought generates an unending open movement that resists closure in self-consciousness.

The Left Hegelian opposition to Schelling was generally unrelenting. Once again, we can point to Ruge and Echtermeyer's *Der Protestantismus und die Romantik*. There they complained that Schelling treats the thought process as too positive, too natural. In the absence of unity between thought and being within the "process of the Absolute," this unity occurs only in the form of an "intuition [*Anschauung*] of the Absolute, in which thinking is still not thinking, but remains immediate, in the form of *thinking phantasy* or *brilliancy of thinking* [*Genialität des Denkens*]." Failing to recognize the "self-movement of the Absolute, the true mediation of the finite and the concrete Spirit," Schelling consigns the human spirit to "subjective arbitrariness," in which an "alien objectivity" can only be mediated through "analogies and symbols." Schelling, so they argued, envisions no way for thought to "digest raw existence," because he lacks the "fluid dialectic of the free spirit." At the tail end of this particular metaphorical passage, Ruge and Echtermeyer diagnose Schelling to be sick from indigestion, though they leave unclear whether the result is constipation or diarrhea.[97]

Between 1835 and 1840 Feuerbach, too, directed a number of sharply critical essays against Schelling and his followers, yet there were sufficient overlaps with Schelling's positive philosophy that Schelling himself detected an underlying affinity.[98] Manfred Frank has even suggested that the vehemence of Feuerbach's critique of Schelling was motivated by a desire to distract attention from his reliance upon the anti-Hegelian philosopher. There are good reasons to remain skeptical of Frank's assertion of a direct reliance upon Schelling, though those cannot occupy us here.[99] However we judge that relationship, there can be little doubt that Feuerbach's recognition of the nonidentity of thought and being was a crucial impetus toward his attempt to construct a philosophy based on naturalism and sensuousness. He extended the principle of nonidentity into his attempt to rethink the human subject as an embodied subject. This effort formed the center of gravity in his 1843 *Grundsätze der Philosophie der Zukunft*, where he wrote, "Whereas the old philosophy started by saying, 'I am an abstract and merely a thinking being to whose essence the body does not belong,' the new philosophy, on the other hand, begins by saying, 'I am a real, sensuous being and, indeed, the body in its totality is my ego, my essence itself.'"[100] In the 1841 *Wesen des Christentums* the idea of embodied subjectivity was already present in Feuerbach's emphasis on the relationship of religious projections to humanity's sensuous needs, from carnal love to creaturely appetite. Yet here three qualifications are called for. First, what Van Harvey calls the "existentialist-naturalist" strand of Feuerbach's religious critique coexists uncomfortably with a "three-fold Hegelian schema of self-knowledge: objectification–alienation–reappropriation."[101] Second, embodiment has ambiguous consequences for Feuerbach's theory of knowledge. For although sensuousness disrupts the closed circuit of a mediation between thought and being that occurs one-sidedly in the dimension of thought, sensuousness opens the pathway toward more immediate, intuitive, and putatively more complete forms of knowledge. Hence, for Feuerbach, the "whole man," the man of "reason, love, and will" becomes the subject of a putatively deeper, fuller knowledge than the thin conceptual knowledge accessible to the abstract self-consciousness of Hegel or Bauer. If Bauer's biblical criticism drove the referent of language from history into the text, Feuerbach's religious criticism is not immune to the dream of bypassing the text in order to reach an anthropological core where language and activity are fused in the immediacy of human life. Indeed, he presented his humanist naturalism as a vital corrective to "the present age, which prefers the sign to the thing signified, the copy to the original."[102] Third, recognition of sensuous species-being was meant to bring the attributes of a transcendent divinity down into the immanent existence of humanity. However, Feuerbach was unable to balance this drive toward immanence against the return of the transcendent in the form of species-being itself. This was the burden of Bruno Bauer's charge that Feuerbach's concept of species acts as a surrogate god. In Derrida's language, we might say that the species furnishes a new transcendental signified. An observation made by Marcel Gauchet about a general tendency of the modern secularization process seems appropriate to this ambiguous aspect of Feuerbach: "It is as if the principle of collective order could only be returned to humans, to the visible, by setting up the invisible at the heart of the human order. It is as if we had to be dispossessed by collective-being's terrestrial transcendence if we were to be delivered from heaven's will. This is a remarkable example of realist fiction or effective symbolism."[103]

Feuerbach's Naturalist Symbol

Realist fiction or effective symbolism: the two are, arguably, not the same. Karl Barth, who viewed Feuerbach from a sharply critical if respectful distance, maintained that modernity suffers from the illusion of realism. In Barth's view realism, in both its literary and philosophical forms, expresses the highest point of confidence in the ability to represent. "Modernity," writes a student of Barth, "might be understood as an epoch in which the stability of Being and representation, the essential unity of Being and representation, went unquestioned—an epoch of forgetting."[104] Barth consecrated his theology to warning against this forgetting; that is, to recollecting the paradox that humans "need to posit theologically an otherness which cannot be posited within systems of human representation without undermining them."[105] Certainly, despite Feuerbach's insistence on the nonidentity of thought and being, he may be judged guilty of a certain blindness about his own procedure. He spoke of a kind of immediate sensuous knowledge beyond and behind philosophical language without problematizing the fact that he was representing this knowledge through philosophical language. Here again there is ambiguity, however. For there is good reason to argue that Feuerbach's thought rests on a gap between the necessity of textually representing the anthropological secret of religion and the claim that that truth lies beyond representation in a lifeworld constituted by the triangulated interactions of community, the embodied subject, and nature.

Rather than exemplifying Barth's realist illusion, Feuerbach represents a return to symbolic or allegorical styles of thought within Young Hegelianism. There is, first of all, his recognition that every system of thought or belief is a "presentation." That is, it is a means or vehicle for ideas that it can at best approximate. Not only the content of the system, but the form as well constitutes the presentation. It is striking that Feuerbach draws metaphorically on a different system of representation in order to accentuate the presentational dimension of philosophy that the Hegelian tradition specifically denied: "the systematizer is an artist—the history of philosophical system is the picture gallery of reason. Hegel is the most accomplished philosophical artist, and his presentations, at least in part, are unsurpassed models of scientific art sense and, due to their rigor, *veritable means for the education and discipline of the spirit.*"[106] Hedged with qualifications, we may evoke Richard Rorty's contrast between, on the one hand, the image of philosophy as "a chain of arguments and building a single coherent edifice on demonstrable foundations" and, on the other, philosophy as "edifying discourses," offering exemplary states of reflection, promising to take "us out of our solid selves by the power of strangeness, to aid us in becoming new beings."[107] Despite the fact that Feuerbach was, to say the least, significantly more committed to foundations than Richard Rorty, the notion of presentation entwines philosophy's task to make abstract arguments with its capacity to produce allegorical emblems of the examined life.

Feuerbach returns to the symbolic in another way. In the preface to *Das Wesen des Christentums*, Feuerbach performs an interesting move. There, he explicitly repudiates the allegorical mode: "we should not, as is the case in theology and speculative philosophy, make real beings and things into arbitrary signs, vehicles, symbols, or predicates of a distinct, transcendent, absolute, i.e., abstract being." Instead, Feuerbach urges us to take things for the "significance which they have in themselves, which is identical with their qualities, with those conditions which make them what they are. . . . I, in fact, put in place of the barren baptismal water, the beneficent effect of real water. How 'watery', how trivial!"[108] This is just the kind of thing that Karl Barth judged "extraordinarily, almost nauseatingly, trivial."[109] However, Feuerbach proceeds to reintroduce the symbol: "But while I thus view water as a real thing, I at the same time intend it as a vehicle, an image, an example, a symbol, of the 'unholy' spirit of my work, just as the water of Baptism—the object of my analysis—is at once literal and symbolical water."[110]

Feuerbach thus passed from the religious symbolic to the real to a reinvocation of the symbolic as an irreducible dimension of naturalism. In the Romantics, to be sure, there was an impulse toward the naturalization of the symbol. One sees this, for example, in Novalis, for whom all things relate to everything else in such a way that nature and art are both symbolic. Yet, if nature is symbolic, for Novalis this could only be because nature is suffused with divinity. For Feuerbach, symbolism functions in an immanent, humanist context. So, for example, noting that humans are both part of and distinct from nature, he writes, "The symbols of this our difference are bread and wine. Bread and wine are, as to their materials, products of Nature; as to their form, products of man." Bread and wine, core symbols of Christianity, become the symbols of the transformative powers of human labor:

Bread and wine are supernatural products,—in the only valid and true sense, the sense which is not in contradiction with reason and Nature. If in water we adore the pure force of Nature, in bread and wine we adore the supernatural power of mind, of consciousness, of man. Hence this sacrament is only for man matured into consciousness; while baptism is imparted to infants. But we at the same time celebrate here the true relation of mind to Nature: Nature gives the material, mind gives the form. . . . Bread and wine typify to us the truth that Man is the true God and Saviour of man.[111]

Bruno Bauer, by contrast, argued that the movement of self-consciousness absorbs the symbol. We see this, for example, in *Die evangelische Landeskirche Preussens und die Wissenschaft.* In 1817 Friedrich Wilhelm III had merged the Lutheran and Calvinist confessions into the Prussian "evangelical-Christian church." As Christopher Clark writes, the project of uniting the two churches reflected an "obsessive concern with uniformity that is recognizably post-Napoleonic: the simplification and homogenization of vestments at the altar as on the field of battle, liturgical conformity in place of the plurality of local practices that had been the norm in the previous century, even modular *Normkirchen* (standardized churches), designed to be assembled from pre-fabricated parts and available in different sizes to suit villages and towns."[112] Opposition to this effort grew after 1830 among groups who resisted this imposition of conformity. To a Hegelian like Bruno Bauer, who in 1840 had not yet lost his faith in the basic rationality of the Prussian state, such obdurate insistence on particularities must eventually disappear in the development of free self-consciousness:

> There is a oneness of the two churches which so strongly and thoroughly unites them that nothing can divide them. It is not symbols as such that form this oneness; if symbols are operative, then they separate, if the churches come together, then the symbols cease to have a binding effect. Wherein then does this unity lie? It lies in inwardness, into which the symbols have collapsed, in self-consciousness, into which the objective dogmatic consciousness has turned, in subjectivity.[113]

Even more clearly, in his 1842 book *Hegel's Lehre von der Religion und Kunst,* Bauer finds support in Hegel himself, quoting him at length: "The symbolical ceases immediately when the free subjectivity, and no longer merely general abstract conceptions [*Vorstellungen*] constitutes the contents of the representation [*Darstellung*]. Then the subject is the significant one for itself and the self-explaining [*das Bedeutende für sich selbst und das sich selbst Erklärende*]."[114] Hegel's end of art thesis has rarely been presented so succinctly. Bauer does more than faithfully present Hegel's aesthetics, however. For in fact he reverses the priority that Hegel had assigned to religion over art. For Bauer, the freely created sensuous representations of the individual artist supersede the sensuous representations of the alienated religious consciousness. Yet if Bauer's *Hegels Lehre von der Religion und Kunst* argues for the *Auflösung* of religion in art, the real point of the book is that the end of art marks the definitive end of religion. As Douglas Moggach has argued, Bauer's reversal of Hegel's elevation of religion over art was already present in Bauer's 1829 prize essay on Kant's doctrine of the beautiful.[115] Bauer's enduring emphasis on art would seem to suggest a place for symbolism in his thought. The 1829 essay opens with an epigraph: "Symbol: 'The seriousness in art is its joyfulness.'"[116] This invocation of joy seems to hover between Schiller's play impulse and Nietzsche's gay science, but in fact what is meant is that art is the "demonstrated and represented idea."[117] Art displays the unity of concept and object, thought and being, and thereby awakens "spiritual powers to their unhindered use," as he wrote in an 1842 essay on Beethoven.[118] Hence, when the very young Bauer claimed that "art is a symbol of philosophy," he immediately added that "no one, not even the artist, because he remains in immediacy, can penetrate [*durchschauen*] art more deeply than the philosopher, and knowledge of art can be given only through philosophy."[119]

Feuerbach did not spell out the differences between himself and Bauer at the level of aesthetics. However, consideration of the Young Hegelian Hermann Hettner underscores the contrast I have drawn. Hettner's 1845 article "Gegen die spekulative Aesthetik" employs Feuerbachean principles to criticize Hegel's aesthetics. While Hettner defended the cognitive vocation of art, he insisted that art communicates truth differently than does conceptual reflection. As Ingrid Pepperle writes, for Hettner, the "aesthetic disclosure of truth [*Wahrheitsfindung*] is 'aglow with the pulsing blood of concrete form,' and it is not simply overtaken by formal thought, but is an 'essential and necessary enlargement of systematic [*wissenschaftlichen*] thinking.' The pleasure of art can never be replaced by abstract thought. It is pleasure of the whole human being, 'which is both sensuous and spiritual.'"[120] Feuerbach was less explicit than Hettner about the aesthetic implications of his naturalism; still, as we have seen, he reappropriated the Romantic emphasis on the opacity of the symbol, but defined that opacity not by reference to the divine but to human subjectivity's embodied presence in the world. Bauer's position from 1829 onward rested on the assumption that the symbol is translatable without remainder. In this conviction, Bauer was more typical of the Young Hegelians than was Feuerbach, as Peter Uwe Hohendahl's characterization of Left Hegelian literary criticism would suggest: "In the final analysis it is the task of philosophical-critical argumentation to annihilate art as such and, by conceptualizing art in its historical development, to carry its living remains into philosophical-conceptual discourse; hence, the minimal interest in hermeneutical problems."[121]

Ambiguity and Radical Democracy

In *Theology and Social Theory* the so-called postsecular philosopher John Milbank makes an observation about Spinoza's biblical criticism that is relevant to the present discussion. Milbank notes that Spinoza's effort to create scientific criteria for biblical criticism was meant to free the reader; yet, writes Milbank, "although each free individual confronts the Biblical text without traditional mediation, this confrontation paradoxically *irons out* all idiosyncrasy, because the Bible, like nature, is [presumed to be] a self-interpreting totality, a world articulated by its own widest and most unambiguous meanings, as is nature by the most general motions."[122] What must be banished from such readings, he insists, is allegory, the uncontrollable proliferation of Christocentric meaning. Milbank sees this " 'capturing of the Biblical text' " as a constitutive dimension of modern politics, a commitment to "the illusion of spatial immediacy and to the exorcism of the metaphorically ambiguous."[123] This leads Milbank to vilify modern secularism and lament the decline of a theistic world. Moreover, it compels him to defend the metaphorical richness of the biblical text against the tradition of secular reading that one might say opens with Spinoza and stretches through the Enlightenment, the Left Hegelians, and into our own time. I have no interest in following Milbank down this path. Indeed, one of the questions that lurks behind our investigation of the post-Marxist adventure of the symbolic is whether a secular politics can recapture a vital sense of complexity and ambiguity without lapsing into the explicit or covert theological view that Milbank believes exercises a monopoly over these qualities. More precisely, I am concerned with the survival of complexity and ambiguity within the modern emancipatory project, not just as obstacles that will be overcome but also as irreducible—and even enabling—conditions for the attempt to create meaning.

The Left Hegelians' critique of religion presents something of a privileged moment for examining the hinge that connects the struggle for autonomy with the problem of meaning. It is not just that they confronted a deeply rooted system of religious heteronomy with the most radical claims for human self-sufficiency that had yet been uttered; rather, it is the fact that they confronted an age-old system of meaning with a philosophical guarantee of their own historical victory. That guarantee granted both the future and the past to an omnivorous self-consciousness that recognizes itself behind every mask and sees every window as a mirror. Bruno Bauer took this much further than Ludwig Feuerbach. Although Feuerbach also placed religion into the framework of a history of self-consciousness's self-actualization, he reserved a place of tension between textual representation and the world, subject and object, clarity and obscurity, the visible and the invisible. Having said this, it is equally important to qualify it. This was, after all, just one impulse in his work, and it was generally subordinated to his desire for immediacy and the essential presence of the species. Yet, in preserving a referential gap that leaves open the ambiguity of the symbol, Feuerbach embraced precisely the dimension of *positivity* that Bauer's philosophy of self-consciousness sought to "gobble up" and that Ruge and Echtermeyer diagnosed as the source of Schelling's indigestion. If the Young Hegelians continue to have relevance for philosophical debate, I wager that it rests largely in the lessons to be drawn from the confrontation between the unprecedented assertion of self-consciousness and the positive remainder. The remainder, was, of course, the theme of Schelling's later "positive philosophy," and it helps to explain the interest Schelling has held for a number of postmodern thinkers, from Heidegger through Jean-Luc Nancy, Gianni Vattimo, and, as we will see in chapter 6, Slavoj Žižek. Insofar as Feuerbach's thought represents the incursion of this positivity into the heart of a philosophical discourse oriented toward the full self-possession of human spirit, it belongs to this contemporary debate, as does the clash among Left Hegelians over this issue.

The next chapter concerns a different variation of the encounter between Hegelianism and the remnants of Romantic symbol theory, the scandal created among Left Hegelians when Pierre Leroux, one of the leading figures of the French left in the 1830s and 1840s, chose to embrace Schelling. Leroux's decision opens up a quite different perspective on the political valences of the symbolic. Let me conclude the present chapter by linking once again the Left Hegelian critique of Romantic symbol theory to the broad themes of this book. Ambiguity and positivity are of interest to more than the aesthetic theorist who recognizes the need to preserve hermeneutical complexity in approaching the expressive art object. The question is also of paramount concern to democratic political theory. To return to Marcel Gauchet's observation about the impulse to resurrect the transcendental within the disenchanted heart of the immanent, he raises an important point about the investments we make in transcendent collective bodies: this impulse, Gauchet writes, has given rise "to a new category of sacred beings, abstract individuals, collective apparitions, that we belong to and which crush us, immanent deities which, though never seen, continue to receive our devotion: the invisible State and the everlasting Nation. The personification and subjectivation of transcendent entities is the key to modern political development whose most original contribution, namely the system of impersonal institutions, is incomprehensible if we do not take into account the formation of these entities, as effective as they are fictitious."[124] For over two hundred years, the revolution unleashed by the struggle to replace personal power by impersonal institutions has intertwined and overlapped with the invention of quasi-transcendental entities like State, Nation, and, of course, Class. The historical and conceptual intersections of the democratic project with these new "immanent deities" compel us to recognize the unavoidable symbolic dimension of politics. Radical democracy demands preservation of nonidentity between the symbolic and the real, renunciation of full possession, acknowledgment of the power of symbols, and recognition that the impossibility of fixed and univocal meaning opens the symbolic domain to the possibility of a constant activation of the quest for autonomy.

CHAPTER TWO

The Fate of the Symbolic from Romantic
Socialism to a Marxism *in extremis*

IN 1843 KARL MARX MOVED to Paris to begin his life as a political exile.
His plan was to establish with his fellow Left Hegelian exile Arnold Ruge
a new journal that would unite the best of German radical thought with
the political savvy of the French left. Shortly after his arrival in Paris,
Marx wrote to Ludwig Feuerbach soliciting a contribution for the first issue of the *Deutsche-Französische Jahrbücher*. Unlike many editors seeking
to win an article from a prominent author, Marx did not leave the choice
of subject open. Rather, he urged Feuerbach to do a "great service to our
enterprise" by contributing a "characterization of [F. W. J.] Schelling to the
very first issue."[1] Marx's motive stemmed from his disappointing encounters with the Parisian socialists. Not only were they far too religious, but
some of them were enthusiastic for Schelling. "How cunningly Herr von
Schelling enticed the French," wrote Marx, "first of all the weak, eclectic
Cousin, then even the gifted Leroux. For Pierre Leroux and his like still
regard Schelling as the man who replaced transcendental idealism by rational realism, abstract thought with flesh and blood, specialized philosophy
by world philosophy!" As it turned out, Feuerbach declined to write the
article, the *Deutsche-Französische Jahrbücher* did not survive beyond its first
issue, and Marx's hoped-for alliance with French socialists never developed
momentum. Although he interacted with the French leftists, read their
works, and likely drew ideas from them, he ultimately found many of them
too religious for his taste.

The various currents of leftist thought in early nineteenth-century France did not fare well in the hands of Marx and Engels. Granted, *The Communist Manifesto* praised "Critical-Utopian Socialism and Communism" for providing "the most valuable materials for the enlightenment of the working class."[2] Yet the *Manifesto*'s overall assessment of the political effects of these currents was unequivocally negative; and this was a judgment given canonical form decades later in Engels's *Socialism: Utopian and Scientific*. As for Pierre Leroux, Marx nominated him for membership in the Central Council of the International Working Men's Association and hoped to include "*all* working-class Socialists"—"Proudhonists, Pierre-Lerouxists and even the more advanced sections of the English Trades Unions"—in the First International. Nonetheless, Marx's serious engagement with Leroux was very limited. Undoubtedly, Leroux's decision in 1841 to publish a French translation of Schelling's 1841 inaugural lecture at the University of Berlin along with his own lengthy essay defending Schelling against the Hegelians produced ripples through the ranks of the Hegelian left. After all, Schelling had long before abandoned his youthful Romanticism and was known in Germany as an orthodox theist, political conservative, and staunch opponent of dialectical thought. German leftists viewed his call to the chair in philosophy at the University of Berlin once occupied by Hegel as nothing less than the defeat of progressive politics and thought in Prussia. Karl Rosenkranz hastily published his *Sendschreiben an Pierre Leroux*, intended to neutralize any support Leroux might give to Schelling. Arnold Ruge took Leroux for a stroll in the Tuileries Garden to set him straight. And Marx called upon Schelling's German critics, like Feuerbach, to correct French leftists' misunderstanding of Schelling.[3] Once the dust settled on this affair, Marx seems not to have concerned himself again with Pierre Leroux.[4]

In 1843, the "gifted" Pierre Leroux was in mid-career and undoubtedly one of the most prominent of French socialists, having built his reputation through his work as an editor and his writings on politics, literature, aesthetics, philosophy, and religion. Of working-class background and trained as a typographer, he was the quintessential self-made intellectual, known as the most philosophical of proletarians and the most proletarian of philosophers. He had first gained prominence as a founder and editor of *Le Globe*, which became the main journal of the young French liberals after its creation in 1824.[5] In 1831 Leroux broke with liberalism, announced his conversion to Saint-Simonianism, and bequeathed the editorship of *Le Globe* to the Saint-Simonian Michel Chevalier. It was a short-lived alliance, however. Within a year, Leroux broke with the Saint-Simonians and henceforth pursued an independent career as a writer and publisher. He was a founder and coeditor of *L'Encyclopédie nouvelle* (1836–1843), to which he contributed numerous articles, and the founder and editor of the *Revue indépendante* (1841–1848). From the printing company that he founded in accordance with his ideas about cooperative labor in 1844 in Boussac, he also published work by George Sand, who revered Leroux as her oracle. After the outbreak of the Revolution of 1848, he was elected to the constituent assembly and then to the legislative assembly. Following Louis-Napoleon Bonaparte's coup in 1851, Leroux went into exile in Jersey. When Napoleon III issued a general amnesty of the 1848 revolutionaries in 1869, Leroux returned to Paris, where he died in April 1871.

Like numerous early left-wing theorists and activists, Leroux was eventually eclipsed by Marxism. Why devote discussion to him in a book about the Marxist and post-Marxist engagement with the problem of the symbolic? Very simply, at the moment when the nascent German left was stridently campaigning against Romanticism, Pierre Leroux's socialism was candidly Romantic. At the time when German leftists excluded symbolic modes from their vision of emancipation, Leroux's political project rested on a symbolic sensibility. Whereas the Germans construed the symbolic as anathema to the liberation of human beings from all forms of heteronomy, Leroux attempted to construct a democratic politics structured on the relationship of transcendence and immanence and the "opening" that results from the nonidentity of the symbolic and the real. In brief, Leroux offers a fascinating counterexample to the philosophical current that would eventually come to dominate the history of later nineteenth- and twentieth-century socialist thought. The style of Leroux's thinking was destined to fall out of fashion in the wake of the Revolution of 1848. However, even as Marxism came to dominate the intellectual and political field of the left, the problems that Leroux confronted continued to have resonance in the subsequent history of the European left. Marx, as we shall see, was attentive to the symbolic dimension of social phenomena, but his basic impulse was to seek its cause in an allegedly anterior material reality. Among many twentieth-century Marxist philosophers, Marx's devaluation of the symbolic and—what many viewed as practically synonymous—the cultural and ideological dimension was the source of misgiving, and it spurred various attempts to augment or correct Marxism's social ontology by turning to the symbolic. The final sections of the chapter will explore three such efforts within the French context. The chapter thus traces the fate of the symbolic from pre-Marxist Romantic socialism through Marx and twentieth-century philosophical Marxism up to the threshold of French Marxism's collapse.

Leroux and the Aesthetic Symbol

In 1833 Leroux neatly summed up his project, in which politics, religion, philosophy, and aesthetics all intersected, when he declared: "We believe in individuality, personality, liberty; but we also believe in society."[6] This statement neatly evokes Leroux's own history: on the one hand, his affiliation with the *Doctrinaire* liberals while he served as the editor of *Le Globe*, on the other hand, his short-lived acceptance of the organic socialism of Saint-Simonianism. Leroux's declaration of belief thus tied him to two positions that he had already abandoned in their unalloyed form; but this gesture toward his own past served to emphasize that his convictions would find fulfillment only in a future synthesis. For, at present, these two principles were like "two loaded pistols aimed at each other."[7] Having witnessed the failure of the Saint-Simonians to create a synthesis based on an association that subordinated all individuals to the hieratic authority of Père Enfantin, Leroux sought a model of association that reconciled individualism and socialism. Leroux's search was not merely for harmony between individual and society, but for an association that related the two poles while preserving them in their difference. Undoubtedly, the desire for mediation between individualism and socialism was not uncommon during the years from the July Revolution to 1848. One could even say this desire was one of the unifying elements of French Romantic socialism, the "generous, conciliatory, humanitarian" leftism that enjoyed considerable prominence in the years before the divisive conflicts of 1848.[8] Yet, in the context of the French left under the July monarchy, Leroux was remarkable not only for the clarity of his resistance to socialism's powerful current of anti-individualism but even more so for the complexity and richness of his attempt to theorize a social association based on the interplay of identity and difference. This was an attempt that led Leroux into an engagement with virtually all the intellectual resources of the age and launched him into flights of grandiose speculation, as his contemporaries noted with varying degrees of appreciation.[9]

Leroux's undertaking was at once social, political, and religious. But, it was also aesthetic. Indeed, the aesthetic dimension provides a key point of entry into Leroux's political thought. In a series of extraordinary articles from the late 1820s and 1830s on the history of European literature from Goethe's *Werther* to Byron, Lamartine, and Hugo, Leroux identified what he called the *style symbolique* as the hallmark of the Romantic "revolution." While Leroux's writings on literature have been quite thoroughly explored, the relationship between Leroux's aesthetic ideas and his political philosophy has seldom been probed. This is unfortunate, for the aesthetic and the political stand in close relationship in Leroux's thought. Indeed, the aesthetic category of the symbol played a vital role in Leroux's effort to rethink socialism as a reconciliation of individualism and society. It must be stressed that this role did not take the form of a direct and explicit transfer of aesthetic categories into the political realm. Rather, Leroux's political thought is itself articulated within the *style symbolique*.

In the mid-1820s Romanticism was a subject of heavy controversy in France. The "immortals" of the Académie Française expressed the conservative opinion of the cultural and political elites when they denounced Romanticism in 1824. In the pages of *Le Globe*, the debate was heated. The opinion of the liberal contributors to the journal split between Étienne Delécluze, who defended classicism in a series of articles from 1825, and Stendhal, who championed the new style in the same year. It was only in ensuing years that Romanticism became closely identified with political liberalism, although as with most aspects of the liberalism of the *Globe* group, "Romantic" liberalism remained a "hazy" matter, oscillating between an individualism that derived its paradigm from the creative artist and a collectivism that regarded the artist as the voice of the zeitgeist or even of God.[10] Leroux was not uncritical of Romanticism, but he sided with its "liberal" defenders in the late 1820s. Indeed, Leroux's initial attachment to French Romanticism's liberal ideal of free, expressive, and creative individuality remained a tenacious kernel of his thinking even after he renounced his ties to liberalism. So, for example, even during his short-lived alliance with Saint-Simonianism, his conception of the relationship between the artist and the aims of progressive politics was much looser and less doctrinaire than that of Émile Barrault, the main aesthetician of the Saint-Simonians.[11]

Leroux's differences with the Saint-Simonians over the artist's social role were consistent with his understanding of Romanticism, which he articulated in articles spanning his liberal phase in the 1820s and the period after his break with the Saint-Simonians. For Leroux, the heart of the Romantic "revolution" lay in the *style symbolique*.[12] There is some tension here between Leroux's depiction of the symbol as the defining feature of Romanticism and his description of the symbol as the "very principle of art."[13] Indeed, he viewed the symbol as a dimension of a general epistemological phenomenon, insofar as all human knowledge depends on comparison, metaphor, and processes of substitution. "What does the poet do, in effect, what does every artist do, and what do all humans in general do, if they do not continually substitute pure conceptions with the sensible or in other words seize relations and substitute them with identical relations taken from another order of ideas?" The artistic symbol thus belongs to the larger human reliance upon comparison and analogy whereby abstract ideas acquire substance and intelligibility. The symbol is unique insofar as it is "a figure that permits the continual substitution of abstract terms with images, proper expression with a vague and indeterminate expression."[14] In this sense, Romanticism might be characterized merely by its more frequent use of symbols. Yet Leroux identified a deeper novelty. The general tendency of human knowledge, he argued, is to develop an abstract idea itself; images may serve as valuable illustrations, but the articulation of the abstract idea remains primary. The *style symbolique,* by contrast, develops uniquely the second idea, that is to say, the image; the symbol thus becomes the vehicle of thought rather than merely its ornament. One would search in vain for this style in French classicism, Leroux asserted, whereas one could infinitely multiply the examples in contemporary literature. "To talk by symbols, to allegorize, *voilà*, that seems to us to be the great innovation in style during the last fifty years."[15]

In a discussion of Madame de Staël's approach to symbolism, Paul Bénichou emphasizes the tension in Romantic thinking between the poet as an inventor of symbolic language and the poet as a hierophant of the symbolic correspondences of the world itself. Madame de Staël ultimately sided with the artist as inventor, because to give the symbol an ontological ground would separate poetic intuition from scientific rationalism and elevate poetry over science. In Leroux's case, by contrast, it seems important to remain, as Bénichou puts it, "in the ambiguity that is characteristic to this intellectual theme, and to make of the symbol both a human invention and a characteristic of being itself."[16] For he did not treat symbolism as a mere dimension of rhetoric. Rather, he argued that the symbol gives poetry its expressive power by establishing new relationships between word and world. The symbol connects the human subject to the world because the artist cannot create *ex nihilo*, but must strive to embody his interior life in what already exists.[17] As Leroux wrote in 1831, by opening new channels between the subjective life and the world, the poet "glides at will through the entire world of the spirit." There the poet encounters manifold phenomena vibrating in tune with certain laws and communicating these vibrations to other regions. The privilege of art is to detect and express these relations, hidden in the unity of life itself. The expression of these relations is the symbol. "*Voilà*, that's why art is the expression of life, the sensation of life, and life itself."[18] Through art the entire world becomes symbolic. The invisible finds representation in the visible.

Much of the French debate about Romanticism centered on the alleged foreignness of the Romantic sensibility to a supposedly indigenous French classicism. Given the charged nature of this question of national style, it is not surprising that Leroux equivocated on the origins of the *style symbolique*. In 1829 he countered Étienne Delécluze's charge that symbolism is a foreign import by insisting that the *style symbolique* is not a "puerile imitation" but emerged in France as a response to "the need of poetry, renovation of moral and religious ideas, and the study of nature and its mysterious harmonies."[19] However, immediately following this insistence upon a native origin in the spiritual needs of the French, Leroux acknowledged that the turn to foreign literatures was crucial. And in the 1839 introduction to his translation of Goethe's *Werther*, Leroux noted that the initial French response to Goethe was uncomprehending because "in that epoch, the poetry of style, the poetry that lives from figures and symbols, was little known among us."[20] As for the sources of his own thinking, he likewise equivocated. On one hand, he claimed in *Réfutation de l' éclectisme* that "we have come to philosophy by the pathway of France and not by the pathway of Germany."[21] On the other hand, his thoughts on the symbol do seem indebted to Germans like Goethe, Friedrich and August

Wilhelm Schlegel, Novalis, and Schelling, the writers who formulated the Romantic theory of the symbol.

Paul Bénichou has argued that the poetic doctrine of the symbol had become sufficiently rooted in France that it formed "nearly a common-place in 1830." The earliest conduits for German Romantic aesthetics were Frédéric Ancillon's *Mélanges de littérature et de philosophie* and then, shortly after, Mme. de Staël's enormously influential *De l'Allemagne*. Mme. de Staël seized the essence of the German symbolic conception, particularly the intuition of mysterious parallels between the world and the intellect, the notion that every portion of the universe appears to be a mirror in which the whole of creation is represented, and the idea that the infinite can be depicted "only symbolically, in pictures and signs," to use August Wilhelm Schlegel's terms. Largely through Madame de Staël, the symbolic idea influenced Cousin and Jouffroy, the royalist Romantics around the *Muse Française*, and even the *Globistes*, who were devotees of Staël despite their ambivalence toward the German philosophy she celebrated. As for Leroux, there is no evidence that he had first-hand knowledge of the great German Romantic theorists beyond his brief discussion of Jean-Paul Richter and his many references to Goethe, particularly his *Werther*, which was, in any case, a product of the *Sturm und Drang*, not Romanticism. While Leroux's thinking about symbolism seems to have drawn heavily on the "alliance of the human spirit and of poetic symbolism" that was, as Bénichou puts it, "in the air," one particular German source may have exercised an influence on him, namely Friedrich Creuzer's *Symbolik und Mythologie der alten Völker*, published in four volumes between 1810 and 1812.[22]

Joseph Guigniaut's 1825 French translation of the *Symbolik* provoked controversy, with conservative Catholics echoing German Catholics' praise for Creuzer's vision of an ancient hieratic monotheism and liberal opinion ranging from Cousin's qualified appreciation to Jouffroy's outright contempt.[23] As for the *Globe* group, a pair of articles by Paul Dubois seems representative. Dubois expanded on Creuzer's symbolic conception of the world, which he traced to Schelling and a whole "school," presumably the German Romantics.[24] He praised Creuzer's erudition, but ultimately he shared the concerns of Creuzer's liberal critics in Germany about the irrationalist tendency of the symbolist doctrine as well as the illiberal implications of Creuzer's esoteric, hermetic interpretation of religion. In sum, the general tenor of Dubois's discussion reflected the prejudices of the

Globistes, who regarded Schelling and contemporary German philosophy with a mix of respect for the spiritual and philosophical culture flourishing beyond the Rhine and suspicion of the Germans' tendency toward mysticism and pedantry.

The exception within the *Globe* circle was Pierre Leroux. Leroux was by no means an adept of mystical orientalism or of the theological camp that found ammunition in Creuzer's thesis. Like Dubois, he must have known of the political controversies that had enveloped Creuzer's *Symbolik* in Germany, and the depiction of a mystery religion guarded by a priestly caste could hardly have appealed to him. Nonetheless, Leroux seems to have taken a number of things from Creuzer, including support for his own emerging conviction that the various religions through the ages are transient and progressive revelations of an eternal truth, as well as for his belief that that eternal truth depends on an aesthetic order, since it finds formulation only in "expressive figures" and "images charged with sense."[25] Creuzer's emphasis on the simultaneity of symbolic comprehension may have influenced Leroux's discussion of the symbol's ability to compress meaning and to communicate at an immediate intuitive level.[26] Further, Creuzer emphasized that a symbol is distinguished by an incongruity between essence and form, an "overabundance of content in comparison with its expression."[27] Finally, it is possible that it was through Creuzer that Leroux had his first encounter with Schelling's thought.

When Heinrich Heine set out to explain recent German intellectual history to a French readership in the early 1830s, he complained that the French had learned little about Germany since Madame de Staël. And, indeed, the processes of transmission whereby German ideas reached a man like Leroux are quite vague. Nonetheless, the extent to which he mirrored the German discourse is quite remarkable. This extends to his repetition of a basic tension within German symbol theory. On the one hand, the symbol seemed to have the power to fuse content and form. On the other hand, the failure of the symbol fully to communicate was intrinsic to its capacity to communicate. The symbol's possibility as an expressive and communicative form rested in turn on a further tension, between the *impossibility* of full presence of meaning and the overabundance of meaning in relation to the form of expression. Pierre Leroux fully partook of these paradoxical impulses. Hence he approached the core of Schelling's idea of symbolic identity of form and content when he spoke of Victor Hugo's poem "Mazeppa."

Mazeppa, the sixteenth-century Ukrainian who was sent into the wilderness bound naked to a horse as punishment for adultery, only to become the chief of the Cossacks who rescued him, becomes a "perfect symbol" of the artist carried by speeding genius itself. In Mazeppa, waxed Leroux, "the fusion of the moral idea and the physical image takes place; the assimilation is perfect. The genius, his interior torments, the blasphemies that pursue him at first, the adorations that succeed to the blasphemies, all these pure conceptions of the intelligence have become visible. We have a symbol and not a comparison."[28] Yet if Leroux thus echoed the German Romantics in identifying the symbol with fusion and presence of meaning, he also repeated their emphasis on the inexhaustibility of symbolic meaning. To recall a passage cited earlier, the symbol replaces "abstract terms with images, proper expression with a vague and indeterminate expression." If the advent of the *style symbolique* marks the disappearance of "abstraction" from the "poetry of the people," it also heralds the birth of "mystery."[29] This tension in the understanding of symbolism, whereby the symbol embodies a meaning but remains indeterminate precisely because the meaning itself is unmasterable, lies at the heart of Leroux's thinking about poetic style, and it deeply inflects his political thought.

The *Style Symbolique* and the Question of Society

How do these aesthetic ideas relate to Leroux's political project? In 1833 Leroux proclaimed his faith in both the individual and society. For him, both *individualisme* and *socialisme* as they were understood in his time had negative connotations. On one side was the *socialisme absolu* of the Saint-Simonians, which Leroux attacked because it submerged the individual fully under the weight of collective life. On the other side was an *individualité absolue* stemming from the eighteenth century that took the atomized, solitary individual for the only reality, thereby ignoring the bonds that tie us to society and, through the mediation of society, to humanity and to God. In opposition to both, Leroux wrote in 1845, "we are socialist if one intends by socialism the doctrine that does not sacrifice any of the terms of the formula, *Liberté, Fraternité, Egalité, Unité*, but reconciles all of them."[30]

Leroux insisted on the right of individual liberty, but his conception of the individual, in contrast to liberalism, rested on the assumption that the human being is formed by social relationships. There is no self-sufficient individual, only a person "tied to an incessant communication with his fellow creatures and with the universe. What he calls his life does not belong entirely to him and is not in him exclusively; it is in him and outside of him."[31] Unlike Marx, who would trace these relations to the processes of production and division of labor, whereby society reproduces itself, Leroux revealed his affiliation with other Romantic socialists by contrasting the antagonistic form of present-day commercial society to the possibility of a society bound together by love and emotional solidarity. Yet Leroux also differed from many of his socialist contemporaries in his vision of the form that this new social bond should take. In the case of the Saint-Simonians, the *nouveau christianisme*'s bond of love was supposed to move history from antagonism to association, from a critical age to an organic age, and direct all human energies toward common social goals. Even more radically, Abbé Alphonse-Louis Constant preached a gospel of the "unity before which all egoism and personality disappear."[32] Étienne Cabet offered, in his 1840 utopian work *Voyage en Icarie,* a similar vision of radical egalitarianism and communal property that won many followers among artisans but drew the criticism of more libertarian figures like Victor Considerant and Leroux because of the unrelenting conformism of Icarian communism.[33] While Leroux shared the French left's critique of the fragmented, egoistical society that had emerged in the eighteenth century, he sharply distanced himself from visions of synthesis that achieved social unity at the expense of the person's individual liberty.

It is with this objection to the fantasy of social fusion in mind that Leroux's definition of society as a "milieu" is very striking. "It is the new milieu, the true milieu, the only milieu where that new being, who has left behind the animal condition and calls itself man, develops its existence."[34] Society as milieu defines a space in which we live, but it is a temporality as well, insofar as it gathers together a past and a future as the meaning-giving horizons of the present. Hence, his definition of *milieu* as "tradition": "Society is a milieu that we organize from generation to generation to live there."[35] The intersecting notions of society as a human milieu that is not reducible to other levels of being and of society as a tradition in which we live and communicate with each other and with the world combine to form a conception of society as a symbolic space.[36] In a political context where the terms *individual* and *society* had become reified objects, between which the politically engaged felt obliged to choose, it was a bold and creative innovation to displace the social onto a self-consciously symbolic register. In Leroux's view, society is not something we relate to, but something that enables relation. Hence, he repeatedly stressed, "society is not a being in the same sense that we are beings."[37] Even more strongly, in "De l'individualisme et du socialisme," Leroux wrote: "do not make of society a great animal of which we will be the molecules, the parts, the members, of which some will be the head, others the stomach, others the feet, the hands, the fingernails or the hair."[38]

Leroux thus rejected the metaphor of the body politic, a metaphor with a long history in Western political thought, but one that had become much more literal in Leroux's time, insofar as the Saint-Simonians conceived the science of social organization on the model of a physiology of organized bodies.[39] Yet, having discarded the metaphor, Leroux returned in the same text to qualify himself: "Yes, society is a body, but it is a mystical body [*corps mystique*], and we are not members of it, but rather, we live in it."[40] The redefinition of the body politic as a *corpus mysticum* immediately complicates the question of the social bond. For it suggests that the bond is not one of "identity" between the individual and society, but of *relation* and *correspondence* because the *corpus mysticum* is by definition an invisible body. The *corpus mysticum* thus depends on symbolic mediation if it is to be brought into the visible world. The complicated theological and political history of the idea of the *corpus mysticum* in Christian culture cannot detain us here.[41] The point to emphasize in Leroux's recourse to this age-old Christian trope is that by redefining society as *corpus mysticum* he underscored his distance from the tendency of his contemporaries on the left to collapse the gap between the social and their representation of it, between the social totality and its alleged incarnation in any one party, figure, or historical agent. Leroux's reference to the *corpus mysticum* accentuates his intention to establish his political project on the tension between, on the one hand, the capacity of symbolic representation to make the intangible thing present and, on the other hand, the excess and inexhaustibility of the intangible in relation to all symbolic presentations.

In an 1841 letter to George Sand, Leroux remarked that he would prefer to replace the increasingly popular word *communisme* with the word *communionisme*, which better expresses "a social doctrine founded on fraternity."[42] The evocation of the sacral ritual whereby the mystical body of

Christ is made present could not have been unintentional for a thinker who had elsewhere identified society as a *corpus mysticum*. Leroux himself never detailed the ritualistic dimensions of his vision of socialism as communion.[43] However, as the elected deputy from Boussac in the National Assembly in 1848, he proposed a constitutional scheme that followed closely the symbolic logic implied by the idea of the *corpus mysticum*. In his proposal, the state was to be composed according to an idea of representation that rests firmly on Leroux's penchant for triadic structures, a habit of mind that has been described as Leroux's belief in "number symbolism as a clue to reality."[44] From Leroux's belief that God possesses the divine qualities of *force, amour,* and *intelligence,* he argued that man possesses the corresponding qualities of *sensation, sentiment,* and *knowledge.* From these qualities, he deduced three groups in society, the industrialists, artists, and savants, and, from there, a state comprised of three bodies, the executive, legislative, and judicial or scientific. Each of these bodies would be formed of three hundred elected citizens, making nine hundred representatives in total. The three bodies would be distinct yet without essential separation, forming together a "body that is one and at the same time triple."[45]

There is in this fantasy of the national state as a sort of Trinitarian mystery much that expresses the Romantic quest for fusion and full presence. True to Leroux's Romanticism, however, this dream of the presentation of the invisible body of society in the visible bodies of the state is complexly related to his awareness of the impossibility of surmounting the gap between the symbol and the thing itself. Society is not a thing that one can seize or know in its full measure; it is, rather, a mystical body, an enveloping milieu that no one or no thing can exhaustively incarnate. The same is true of "humanity," another lynchpin of Leroux's thought. For Leroux, the relationship of the individual to humanity is not one of identity, but of latency or virtuality. As Leroux wrote in 1840, "Humanity is virtually in each man, but there are only particular men who have a true existence within eternal Being." And, he added: "Humanity is a generic or universal being; but universals, as the Schoolmen said, do not have a veritable existence."[46] Nonetheless, at the same time as he denied a certain kind of reality to universal entities such as humanity, he also criticized the eighteenth-century axiom that only individuals exist and that all collective or universal beings are only abstractions. "Those philosophers were in grave error. They did not comprehend anything that was not tangible for the senses; they did not comprehend the invisible."[47] We are back to the language of the symbol, where the intangible exists, but in an unspecifiable mode whose power manifests itself only through symbolic mediation.

Leroux's repeated recourse to the mediating role of the symbolic points to a complex sense of interplay between the universal and the individual, in which neither is seen to prevail but both are held in a state of relation and correspondence. It is useful to recall Schelling's definition of the symbol as a figure in which the "finite is at the same time the infinite," but without the finite simply collapsing its distance from the infinite. This basic orientation guided Leroux's aesthetic judgments, for example his preference for Victor Hugo, who maintained the "sentiment of finite beings, even when he has the most profound sentiment of the infinite," over Alphonse de Lamartine, whose poems contemplate only "that vast ocean of Being where everything is engulfed."[48] And it deeply inflected his approach to political problems. For Leroux's concerns about the threats of both "absolute individualism" and "absolute socialism" led him to reject any politics that either exaggerated *or* flattened the distinction between the individual and society, the part and the whole; the symbolic style of mind seemed to offer him a way to think both relation *and* difference simultaneously.

Another way to summarize what this discussion reveals is to say that for Leroux the biggest problem of politics is the tendency to seek an incarnation of political meaning. On the one side, liberalism would incarnate the political in the sovereign individual; on the other side, socialism would incarnate the political in the collective or, as Saint-Simonianism had already demonstrated, in some sort of political avant-garde that claims to embody the essential interests of the class, society, or even the historical process itself. Incarnation was not an obscure or esoteric matter in the time when Leroux wrote; indeed, it had gained a pressing importance in the wake of the French Revolution. After all, the revolutionaries had executed the king, thereby destroying the embodiment of law and power as well as the political logic of incarnation that had governed the ancien régime. In the unsettled decades after the revolution, as Claude Lefort has observed, a wide range of thinkers "all looked to the religious for the means to reconstitute a pole of unity which could ward off the threat of the break up of the social that arose out of the defeat of the *Ancien Régime*."[49] This turn to religion often expressed itself as the temptation to return to the logic of political incarnation, whether in the form of a restored monarch, the nation, or a social class. Lefort mentions Pierre Leroux as an example of the powerful attraction of religion for early nineteenth-century thinkers; but within that context Leroux was actually something of an exception for his resistance against incarnation.

Not surprisingly, for a Romantic thinker who drew no rigid distinctions between art, society, and religion, this resistance extended to his interpretation of Christianity. Leroux defined his own religiosity as post-Christian, fully convinced as he was that both Catholicism and Protestantism had reached a state of exhaustion. Like many radicals of his age, Leroux found inspiration in the prophecy of Joachim of Fiore, who reimagined the Christian trinity as a historical progression from the age of the Father, to the age of the Son, to the age of the Holy Ghost.[50] Saint-Simon's *nouveau christianisme*, Moses Hess's *heilige Geschichte* of humanity, and August Cieszkowski's *Historiosophie* all equated the third age with a social solidarity cemented by pantheistic belief in the ubiquitous presence of divinity in the world. Leroux, by contrast, opposed pantheism and insisted on a transcendent deity. Where Hess and Cieszkowski envisioned the trinity as the immanent process of historical development itself, we have already seen in Leroux's 1848 proposal for a constitution that his conception of the Trinity rested on a symbolic conjugation of unity and difference. Rather than tie the Holy Ghost to a prophecy of the coming identity of man and God, he emphasized that the Trinity symbolically communicates a true "ontological conception," namely that there are *several* "persons" in being.[51] As with *homme* and *société* or *homme* and *humanité*, the relationship between man and God could thus never be one of identity, but only of *relation* and *correspondence*, a mirror play between the divine being and created beings.

If Leroux thus rejected the inclination to cast socialist arguments as prophesies of the coming identity of God and man, he simultaneously took his distance from the other tendency of contemporary socialism to draw sustenance from an emphatically christocentric reading of Christianity.[52] Where figures like Félicité de Lamennais and Étienne Cabet depicted socialism as the true imitation of Christ, Leroux's theology was based on the idea of a progressive revelation of an eternal truth; hence, Jesus's incarnation could only be a *relative* truth. As Leroux claimed in 1840, "Jesus . . . is God only because all men are from God or because God is immanent in every man."[53] At a first glance, this would seem to align Leroux with the German Young Hegelians. Indeed, it was such statements that led the radical Hegelians to believe Leroux was really one of them and to feel betrayed when he wrote appreciatively of the theologically inflected thought of the elderly F. W. J. Schelling, who had become the bête noire of the Left Hegelians. Yet it was not at all Leroux's intention to deify human being. As he wrote in an imagined address to Giordano Bruno: "You, like Spinoza, like Schelling and Hegel, who have followed from you, are right to say that in a man you see being, substance, God. But you, and Spinoza, and Schelling, and Hegel, you are wrong to say because of that that [man] is God. He is God in as much as he comes from God, proceeds from God."[54] Two years later, Leroux criticized as "a vague pantheism" the notion that God is incarnated in man; he also insisted more rigorously than he had previously that Jesus cannot be identified with God. Jesus "sensed God in him, without doubt, but he never said as a result: I am God. The name of the *son of God* that his disciples gave to him does not annul that meaning. Jesus always established an incommensurable distance between himself and God."[55] Once again, Leroux leads us to the borderline between the visible and the invisible where the symbol is the only adequate means of representation. In religion, as in politics, neither the finite nor the infinite, neither the individual nor the collective become absolutely fixed poles; but neither do they become sufficiently fluid as to flow into one. Both humanity and divinity exist virtually in the human person; both humanity and divinity are universal beings that remain radically alterior to every other form of being.

Leroux's hostility toward the logic of incarnation extended to a critique of Hegel, whom he regarded as the philosopher of incarnation par excellence. He summarized Hegel's philosophy of religion in the following terms: "All religion consists in the incarnation of God in man," with Christianity as the "absolute form" of incarnation.[56] Like the Hegelian left, Leroux recognized that, for Hegel, it was as a symbolic representation of the identity of humanity and divinity that Christ had philosophical meaning. For the Young Hegelians, this Hegelian formula collapsed when they reimagined Spirit as a collective human essence existing solely in nature and history. Likewise, when the Young Hegelians rejected Hegel's apparent claim that philosophy had come to its fulfillment in his philosophy, they dismissed the idea that any philosophy could incarnate the absolute. So, for example, in 1838 Ludwig Feuerbach depicted Hegel as a

would-be philosophical Christ, but asserted that "it is speculative super-
stition to believe in an actual incarnation of philosophy in a particular
historical appearance."[57] Accordingly, Feuerbach and a host of other progressive Hegelians insisted that the Hegelian dialectic must either describe an open-ended historical process or lapse into a reactionary absur-
dity. This latter theme emerged in Leroux when he blamed the Hegelian
doctrine of incarnation for corrupting the Saint-Simonians and leading
them into the grave error of worshipping Henri Saint-Simon as something like a demigod and Père Enfantin as *the* "Revealer."[58] Like the Young
Hegelians, Leroux condemned this fixation on incarnation as an obstacle
to the infinite progress of nature and humanity.

Whereas the Young Hegelians sought to reconstitute the absolute as
a purely immanent product of human self-consciousness, Leroux, a believer in a transcendent deity, opened the development of human self-
consciousness to what Marcel Gauchet calls "the dynamic of transcendence," namely a paradoxical process whereby human freedom grows
precisely through the distancing of the human from the divine source.[59] It
seems that Leroux's wager was that a transcendent God is a key to opening
the social space as a milieu for free human social interaction, a milieu that
sustains people, enables their interactions, but does not engulf them. Operating as a principle of alterity, the horizon of transcendence breaks the
hold of deterministic rationalism and opens human beings to their individual and collective possibilities for free action.[60]

Perhaps the best illustration of this is Leroux's discussion of revelation.
Revelation, he insisted, is permanent and progressive, but it does not lead to
the convergence of God and man. The distance between human and divine
is permanent, "incommensurable," even if there is a possibility of relation
and communication. God may be in the revealer, but so too is finite human
nature. Revelation is divinely inspired, but it is spoken by human mouths
and through the intermediary of society. The language of revelation may
become authoritative, and it may even create human institutions, but it will
always be symbolic, remaining in the tension between the visible and the
invisible, the sayable and the unsayable. And, in its inexhaustibility, it should
be open to a collective hermeneutical process that aims simultaneously at
disclosing the divine truth and constituting the human order. Leroux tried
to drive home this point in a book-length refutation of Joseph de Maistre's
authoritarian interpretation of Church history, where Leroux argued that the

Catholic Church had democratic origins in the efforts of early Christian councils to interpret and institutionalize Christ's revelation.[61] Leroux could agree with the Young Hegelians' effort to overcome the idolatry of the conventional Christian understanding of incarnation; he could even endorse their desire to disclose the human agency in biblical revelation. But he could not sanction the Young Hegelians' reduction of the Word to an immanent order of reality, to a single present dimension of meaning. Hence, he complained, "All the divine and eternal truths that Christianity contains in its symbols elude the disciples of Hegel."[62]

Marx and the Symbolic

In a sharply critical 1844 article titled "La poésie symbolique et socialiste," the literary critic Paulin Limayrac insisted on an elective affinity between symbolism and socialism, which according to him together comprised a "true kingdom of the vague."[63] This vagueness, for Limayrac, found its epitome in a doctrine that conflates human sociability with man's communion with God and nature. Limayrac's critique was directed at the poet Victor de Laprade, but his attack on the alliance of symbolism and socialism might as readily have been aimed at Leroux. Measuring the faddish efflorescence of symbolist poetry against the deep roots of the French classicist tradition, Limayrac forecast a short life for the symbolic style. In light of the long history of French symbolism, stretching from Baudelaire through Verlaine and Mallarmé and into the twentieth century, he was clearly wrong. As to his insistence on an affinity between socialism and symbolism, that had at best a momentary legitimacy in the period of Romantic socialism. If, as we have seen, the *style symbolique* formed a core component of Leroux's search for a third way at the very moment when the characteristic modern tension between liberalism and socialism was being born, the direction pointed by the radical German Hegelians was much more indicative of the course that European leftism would take in the later nineteenth and twentieth centuries.

The German left viewed the Romantics' symbolic conception of the world with hostility. This was a tradition of suspicion starting with Hegel's own critique of symbolism as too ambiguous and polyvalent for philosophical discourse, running through Heine's critique of major symbolists of the *Frühromantik* like Novalis and the Schlegel brothers, to Ruge and Echtermeyer's *Der Protestantismus und die Romantik*. For the main current of the German left, the way toward emancipation lay in overcoming religion, and for that project the symbolic conception seemed too loaded with theological baggage to be of any use. The Hegelian "hermeneutics of desymbolization," to use the phrase of Frank Paul Bowman, may even have played a crucial role in moving French intellectuals away from Romanticism. If we follow Bowman's account, then already Victor Cousin's 1827 Sorbonne lectures applied Hegelian categories to unpack and dissolve the symbolic form of Christianity; by the late 1830s the French controversy over David Friedrich Strauss's *Life of Jesus* intensified this French turn toward a desymbolizing intellectual style. In fact, spurred by the original instance of Strauss, who, as Bowman puts it, "desymbolized the most important symbol of Christianity, Jesus himself," the problem of symbol and desymbolization came to occupy a central place in mid-nineteenth-century French discussions about theology, law, and literature.[64]

As examples like Strauss and Feuerbach and indeed Hegel himself show, the Hegelian interpretive style typically recognized value in the symbol, but then proceeded to expose the truth that was veiled in the symbolic expression. This strategy characterizes Karl Marx as well.

In his adolescence, Marx seems to have been deeply attracted to the Romantic sensibility. The teenage Marx did not write philosophical prose on Romantic themes, but he did compose poems. In the poem "Creation," Marx depicts a cosmos animated by creative spirit, while in a companion poem titled "Poetry" he presents the human creation of symbols as a repetition of this demiurgic power.[65] Beyond the reasonable supposition that a voracious young reader like Marx would have been familiar with the works of major German writers of the recent past, there is some circumstantial evidence to suggest that he had some knowledge of the theoretical stances of the Romantics. At the University of Bonn, Marx attended August Wilhelm Schlegel's lectures in the winter semester of 1835–36, and a preparatory note for Marx's dissertation on ancient atomism refers approvingly to Friedrich Schlegel's concept of irony.[66]

By the late 1830s, however, Marx had turned away from Romanticism, largely as a result of the powerful anti-Romantic currents of Hegelianism. Convinced of the reactionary and irretrievably Christian nature of Romanticism, Marx was, by the early 1840s, ready to accept Bruno Bauer's invitation to write an article that would serve as a companion to Bauer's own polemic against Romanticism, *Hegels Lehre von der Religion und Kunst von dem Standpunkt des Glaubens ausbeurteilt* (*Hegel's Teachings on Religion and Art Judged from the Standpoint of Faith*). Marx reported that his essay against Romanticism was growing toward book length, but, unfortunately, the manuscript was never finished and became lost.[67] Even in the absence of this text, it seems clear that Marx was already launched into the themes that would dominate his discussions of aesthetics throughout his mature period. Like Heine, Ruge, and Bauer, his tastes leaned decisively toward classical Greek and Roman literature; later he and Engels would embrace literary realism. Further, influenced by Feuerbach, he sought to reveal the sensuous materialist base of art.[68] This early impulse gained historical concreteness in step with the further development of his thought, and over the years he would return on various occasions to the question of the relationship between art and the dominant social mode of production. While Marx tended to subordinate art to the economic structure, he did not rest with a straightforward deterministic model.[69] Nor did he fully abandon the notion that the artwork has its own internal logic, beyond simply reflecting the social world.[70] Nor, finally, did he ever fully abandon his early hope that communism would overcome the division of labor whereby certain activities took the form of creative, artistic practice, while most labor was stripped of creative, expressive dimensions. Still, if he thus hoped to reunite labor with its alienated creative side, this was clearly animated by a desire to demystify creativity and not to mystify labor.

As Alvin Gouldner has pointed out, this move to bring creativity down to earth had broad implications for Marx's vision of society: "While installing labor and productivity as the uniquely human form of creativity, in contrast to the Romantics' accent on the *symbolic* aspects of creativity, Marx, correspondingly, diminishes the significance of symbolic activity in its everyday, prosaic forms as language, speech, symbolic interaction, and culture. Humanity is thus largely viewed as *self-produced* and defined by labor, rather than its symbolic talents and linguistic heritage. The human 'essence' is now work, not language, not the symbolic, not culture."[71] Gouldner is just one of a host of modern commentators to note that Marx downplays the symbolic dimensions of social life. The examples could be multiplied at length. In *Adventures of the Dialectic*, Merleau-Ponty complained about the "ABC's of Marxist philosophy, namely, the definition of truth as 'the harmony of representation with the objects which are outside it.' " This species of epistemological realism, warned Merleau-Ponty, converts Marxism into a "massive positivity."[72] Jürgen Habermas criticizes Marx for reducing "communicative action" to "instrumental action."[73] Pierre Boudieu charges Marx with overemphasizing the material-economic structure, and in his own work Bourdieu shifts to symbolic struggles within culture. Jean-Joseph Goux complains that Marx rejects the "hieroglyphic valence" that Goux believes inhabits every true symbolism.[74] In terms that resonate with the Lacanian language we will encounter in the following chapters, Bernard Flynn notes that for Marx the disjunction between the real and the symbolic is socially produced and can be socially overcome; in denigrating the symbolic order, Flynn writes, Marx aims at the "total appropriation of society by itself," a "project of rendering society totally transparent to itself."[75] Indeed, considered in its hard form, historical materialism is an extreme instance of desymbolization, which dissolves the apparent autonomy of the merely symbolic by exposing its genesis and meaning in the material substratum of labor and value.

If Marx's thought aims at desymbolization, it is nonetheless also true that Marx was keenly aware of the power of the symbolic. One sees this in his analyses of earlier social forms. So, for example, Marx maintained that mythology did not simply veil the real conditions of ancient Greek social life, but in some sense was the ground of that social life: "Greek art," wrote Marx in 1857, "presupposes the existence of Greek mythology, in other words, nature and even the social forms have already been worked up in an unconsciously artistic manner by the popular imagination."[76] In *Capital* Marx argued in similar vein that while it is true that in our own time, "in which material interests preponderate," the economic structure of society is the "real basis on which the juridical and political superstructure is raised," it is not true for "the middle ages, in which Catholicism, nor for Athens and Rome, where politics, reigned supreme." Still, if this remark accords a prominent role to symbolic, cultural, and superstructural dimensions, Marx nonetheless immediately underscored the primacy of the economic base: "This much, however, is clear, that the middle ages could not live on Catholicism, nor the ancient world on politics. On the contrary, it is the mode in which they gained a livelihood that explains why here politics, and there Catholicism, played the chief part."[77] The capitalist epoch itself is, in a strict sense, an agent of desymbolization, stripping tradition of its halo and bringing people face to face with the true circumstances of their lives, as Marx famously declared in the *Communist Manifesto*. And as capitalism extends its technological power, the psychological need for a certain kind of symbolic compensation for human impotence weakens: "All mythology subdues, dominates and fashions the forces of nature in the imagination and through the imagination; it therefore disappears when real domination over these forces is established."[78]

The demystifying power of capitalist modernity stands in a dialectical relation to the evident power of capitalism to generate new mysteries, new symbolic forms out of the stuff of material life itself. The analysis of the symbolic structures of money, the commodity, value, and class comprise a core dimension of Marx's mature work. Indeed, Claude Lévi-Strauss, who always acknowledged Marx's influence, suggested that Marx opened a door toward the analysis of "the symbolic systems which underlie both language and man's relationship with the universe."[79] This potentiality is reinforced if one considers a famous distinction Marx makes in *Capital*: "A spider conducts operations that resemble those of a weaver, and a bee puts to shame many an architect in the construction of her cells. But what distinguishes the worst architect from the best of bees is this, that the architect erects his structure in imagination before he erects it in reality."[80] This remark suggests that Marx recognized constructive and constitutive powers in imagination and cultural representations, even if he placed these idealist elements into an intimate dialectical relationship with practical activity and concrete need.[81] Rastko Mocnik has even argued that Marx attempted to conceptualize *"the symbolic efficacy of the economic sphere itself."*[82] From this perspective, the crucial moment in Marx's account of capitalism's symbolic efficacy is the development of the general value form, when the value of all products comes under the one general equivalent of all values, money. Mocnik sees in Marx's consideration of "intersubjectivity" an attempt to describe a symbolic efficacy, as if it were incumbent on Marx to demonstrate that the structural constraint of the "value-form symbolism" "effectuates the specific type of intersubjectivity dubbed in the sequel 'commodity fetishism.'"[83] In other words, the autonomous logic of this symbolic register constitutes a certain kind of human agent.[84]

It is worth recalling that Marx explicitly describes the commodity as a symbolic form. Regarded from the perspective of exchange, commodities are symbols of the value generated by labor. Insofar as labor is a social relation, this relation gets condensed into the commodity, making every product a "social hieroglyphic."[85] To recall a well-known passage already cited in the introduction, Marx insists that to find an analogy to the process whereby the commodity becomes a hieroglyph, "we must have recourse to the mist-enveloped regions of the religious world." In that world, he continues, "the productions of the human brain appear as independent beings endowed with life, and entering into relation both with one another and the human race. So it is in the world of commodities with the products of men's hands. This I call the Fetishism which attaches itself to products of labour, so soon as they are produced as commodities, and which is therefore inseparable from the production of commodities."[86]

Let us consider more closely a specific commodity, money: Marx's later works are loaded with references to money as a symbol of value. In one of the most detailed recent discussions of Marx's theory of money, Anitra Nelson argues that although Marx describes money as a symbol, ultimately a nominalistic or symbol theory of money is much less important to Marx than is a commodity theory of money.[87] Yet this is true only if one employs a limited notion of symbol, whereby money would be considered a conventional sign that is valueless in itself. This limited symbolic view certainly belongs to the intellectual history of money. In her history of money in early modern British thought and life, Deborah Valenze speaks of the recurrent notion that money is an ideal instrument of cognition because of its abstract, symbolic character. Thomas Hobbes described money as the "sufficient measure of value of all things else," and recognized the ability of money to represent "all commodities moveable and immoveable."[88] Roughly a century later, David Hume described money as the product of a conventional agreement in which a symbol would function as a guarantor of exchange.[89] In the 1810s, writes Nelson, "Hegel discussed money as a 'symbol' of value, as the 'abstract' expression of 'another universal,' value";[90] Moses Hess wrote that "money is for the practical world what God is for the theoretical world. . . . It constitutes the alienation of the idea of social value. . . . In other words, money is simply the inorganic symbol of our present social production that has broken free from our rational control and therefore dominates us."[91] Marx's earliest writings on money draw heavily on this theory of money as a symbol of value; and even in *Capital* he concludes that, just as all commodities symbolize value or social relations, so too is money a symbol.[92]

Marx's more mature work supplements this with a view of money as itself a commodity. As he reasoned, because the value of a commodity cannot be directly expressed, a "third commodity" is necessary to express the value relation between any two commodities being exchanged.[93] Nelson and various other analysts distinguish sharply between this commodity theory of money and the symbol theory. However, it seems more accurate to say that Marx's theory of money as a commodity reinterprets money through the matrix of the theory of the symbol forged by German idealism and Romanticism.

After all, the notion of money as an abstract sign, a conventional marker, would be an instance of what Immanuel Kant considered a *misuse* of the word *symbol*. As we recall from chapter 1, Kant complained that logicians had come to use the word *symbolic* in contrast to intuitive presentation, whereas symbolic presentation is "only a kind of intuitive presentation."[94] Marx echoed Kant's idea that a symbol makes the invisible visible when he wrote, "Exchange value as such, of course, can exist only symbolically, although this symbol, in order to be usable as a thing—not only as imaginary form—possesses an objective existence; is not only an ideal notion, but actually represented in an objective way."[95] In chapter 1 we saw further that the Romantics who followed after Kant insisted on a *synecdochical* relation between the object of intuition and the concept, a manner of participation between sign and thing.[96] Marx's theory of money operates within the horizon of this conception of the symbol. Money can become a symbol of value because it too has value. "Hence," wrote Marx in the *Grundrisse*,

> in order to realize the commodity at a stroke as exchange value and to give it the general effect of exchange value, its exchange for a particular commodity is not sufficient. It must be exchanged for a third thing which is not itself a particular commodity but the symbol of the commodity as commodity, of the commodity's exchange value itself; *which therefore represents, say, labour time as such*, say, a piece of paper or leather which represents a certain portion of labour time. (Such a symbol presupposes general recognition; it can only be a social symbol; in fact, it only expresses a social relationship.)

"This symbol," he added, "this material sign of exchange value, is a product of exchange itself, not the execution of a preconceived idea. (IN FACT, the commodity which serves as the mediator of exchange is only transformed into money, into a symbol, gradually . . .)."[97] That is, it emerges not as the result of a convention, but rather in the process of exchange over time. Instead of merely being an abstract sign, money is a concrete particular that comes to serve as a universal symbol, as the general equivalent within the total value form: "As a result of the transformation of the commodity into general exchange value, exchange value becomes a particular commodity. But this is possible only if one particular commodity acquires over all others the privilege of representing, of symbolizing their exchange value, i.e. of becoming *money*."[98] Like the Romantics, Marx was concerned to demonstrate that this symbol was not the product of an arbitrary convention, but was rather a motivated sign; hence, his investigation into the qualities of various precious metals. Even if a certain kind of object, such as slips of paper that are in themselves devoid of value, may be arbitrarily assigned an exchange value, this comes only when the transformation of a specific commodity into a symbol of exchange is already very far advanced. At that point, a "symbol of the mediating commodity can in turn replace the commodity itself. It now becomes the conscious token of exchange value."[99] Paper money is thus a symbol of the symbol.[100] In saying this, one could suggest that Marx moves from one register of the symbolic to another: first, the Romantic synecdoche between the particular and the universal allows him to explain the emergence of the general equivalent and, second, the notion of a conventional sign allows him to explain paper currency.

Marx's analysis of the commodity form is a compelling example of his dominant attitude toward symbolic forms, namely that they are mystifying knots of meaning that hold people captive. By tracing the symbol back to its origin in social relations, Marx's aim was not only to release us from its thrall but also to aid people in their struggle to transform social relations from the source of alienation into the condition of human flourishing. This was the strategy already enunciated in Marx's famous remarks on religion in his 1844 "Contribution to the Critique of Hegel's *Philosophy of Right*: Introduction," which make clear his profound debt to the Left Hegelians even as he pushes beyond their desymbolizing agenda by insisting that the critique of religion must lead to the critique of law, politics, and society. Marx's debt to the Left Hegelian strategy of recognizing a human truth veiled in the religious symbol would still be evident years later in his analysis of commodity fetishism. Yet, alongside this predominant desymbolizing impulse, our brief foray into Marx's analysis of symbolic forms reminds us that his efforts at demystification are coupled with a sophisticated awareness of the complexity of these forms. In Marx we frequently sense that his attempt to create a descriptive language adequate to reality contests with his awareness that he is confronting a reality that continually exceeds the capacity of language to represent it.[101] There is thus sufficient ambiguity in Marx to help account for the divergent paths that Marxism took in the twentieth century.

Marxism *in extremis*: Merleau-Ponty, Althusser, Baudrillard

These divergent paths are neatly illustrated if we return to Merleau-Ponty. On the one hand, as we have seen, Merleau-Ponty railed against the vulgar form of epistemological realism that had come to dominate orthodox Marxism, the belief that truth is " 'the harmony of representation with the objects which are outside it.' "[102] On the other hand, in countering this orthodoxy by turning to the role of symbolism, Merleau-Ponty believed that this potentiality already resides in Marx himself. At his best, so he argued, Marx exemplifies the richest possibilities of dialectical thought, which in his words is a "paradoxical mode of thought, the discovery of an entangling relationship between the dialectician and his object, the surprise of a spirit which finds itself outdistanced by things and anticipated in them."[103] Admittedly, Merleau-Ponty sees a decline in Marx's own dialectical nuance as he moved toward the scientific socialism of his later years. In this regard, he does not consider Marx fully innocent of the tendency toward naive realism and positivism that he laments in twentieth-century Marxism. Still, if dominant Marxist currents have forfeited their claim to philosophical legitimacy, he readily defends the countercurrent that he detects even in the early Marx. Merleau-Ponty's Marxism is strongly influenced by a hermeneutical sensibility that he finds in Max Weber, but he qualifies Weber's own negative view of historical materialism as a form of reductionism. Indeed, he insists that the "best" Marxists in Weber's own time—above all Georg Lukács—actually resembled Weber, insofar as they too strove to develop a "theory of historical comprehension, of *Vielseitigkeit*, and of creative choice."[104] Merleau-Ponty is, of course, here touching on the rich and complex history of Western Marxism, a

designation he did not invent but did much to popularize. Alvin Gouldner's *Two Marxisms* labels the same current "Critical," as opposed to "Scientific Marxism"; Gouldner writes that if in Marx "the economic and instrumental side of human and social activity comes to overshadow the
symbolic and cultural," then this "is what the subsequent crystallization
of Critical Marxism, in some part, attempts to repair."[105] And indeed, that
heterogeneous grouping of thinkers—including Lukács, Korsch, Gramsci,
Bloch, Benjamin, Adorno, Horkheimer, Marcuse, and Sartre—spanning
several countries and several generations, strove to supplement classical
Marxism with richer theories of culture, ideology, and psychology.[106]
Above all, in one way or another, these critical Marxist philosophers sought
to avoid reductionism of the sort that would treat the cultural and political
superstructure as a reflection of the economic base and reduce consciousness to an epiphenomenon of social being.

When *Adventures of the Dialectic* appeared in 1955, Merleau-Ponty had
already traveled a great distance from his postwar investment in the communist cause. In 1947's *Humanism and Terror*, he readily defended some
of the worst offenses of Stalinism in the name of long-term progressive
historical change. In ensuing years the Soviet Union's obsession with its
own security at the expense of support for the western European working
class and the North Korean invasion of South Korea and the ensuing
proxy war soured his faith that "really existing socialism" was an agent of
emancipatory change, while the French Communist Party's relentless hostility to his work made it impossible to remain a fellow traveler.[107] *Adventures of the Dialectic* excoriates the vulgar Marxism that had come to dominate postwar French communism, but Merleau-Ponty is also not uncritical
of the various currents of Western Marxism. Insisting on the opacity of the
historical process, he challenges any theoretical position that pretends to
master history and reveal its total meaning. This critique touched not only
Lukács's view of the proletariat as the subject and object of history but also
Sartre's revolutionary voluntarism, which Merleau-Ponty denounced as
"Ultra-Bolshevism," as well as Merleau-Ponty's own confident proclama-
tions about the direction of history in *Humanism and Terror*. *Adventures
of the Dialectic* ultimately remains receptive to an open, nondogmatic
Marxism, but in retrospect it appears as a way station on the road to a much
more attenuated relationship to Marxism. Undoubtedly, his own unfolding process of reflection helps to explain this development; but in addition

Merleau-Ponty was, like so many leftists, deeply shaken by the Soviet Union's invasion of Hungary in 1956 and Kruschev's revelations of Stalin's crimes. By the time he published *Signs* in 1960, he could assert that "with the events of recent years Marxism has definitely entered a new phase of its history, in which it can inspire and orient analyses and retain a real heuristic value, but is certainly no longer true *in the sense it was believed to be true.*"[108]

Adventures of the Dialectic attempts to offset economistic determinism by appealing to an image of the complex symbolic fabric of the social world: "This order of 'things' which teaches 'relations between persons,' sensitive to all the heavy conditions which bind it to the order of nature, open to all that personal life can invent, is, in modern language, the milieu of symbolism, and Marx's thought was to find its outlet there."[109] In the face of the "obscurity of historical symbolism," both social theory and political praxis must become interpretive enterprises. The idea of the symbolic that circulates in *Adventures of the Dialectic* is decidedly expressivist, in the sense that Merleau-Ponty maintains that symbols give body and meaning to social relations and the experiences of personal life. This theory of the symbol supported his attachment to Weber's interpretive sociology. Strikingly, however, at the same time as he tried to build a bridge between Marx and Weber based on the expressivity of symbolic mediations, he was in fact becoming increasingly interested in the possibilities suggested by structural linguistics. Already in a 1951 essay, he embraced Ferdinand Saussure's thesis that language's "expressive value is not the sum of the expressive values which allegedly belong individually to each element of the 'verbal chain.'"[110] This view of a linguistic whole whose expressive power stems strictly from the relations of its parts suggested to Merleau-Ponty a broader social model, as he wrote in 1953: "Just as language is a system of signs which have meaning only in relation to one another, and each of which has its own usage throughout the whole language, so each institution is a symbolic system that the subject takes over and incorporates as a style of functioning, as a global configuration, without having any need to conceive it at all."[111] Merleau-Ponty's flirtation with the emerging structuralist paradigm culminated in his 1960 essay on Marcel Mauss and Claude Lévi-Strauss. There, he endorsed Lévi-Strauss's pathbreaking essay *Introduction to the Work of Marcel Mauss* (1950), which had argued that Marcel Mauss's call for anthropology to learn from linguistics was answered by Lévi-Strauss's structural anthropology. Closely echoing Lévi-Strauss's language, Merleau-Ponty wrote that Mauss's "total social fact," which is "no longer a massive reality but an efficacious system of symbols or a network of symbolic values, is going to be inserted into the depths of the individual."[112]

This observation in fact reveals what really interested Merleau-Ponty in structuralism, namely its potential as an ally in his long-running critique of the modern philosophy of the subject. It is not incidental that his friendship with Claude Lévi-Strauss strengthened after Merleau-Ponty broke with Jean-Paul Sartre.[113] Whereas Sartre emerges in Merleau-Ponty's work as the culmination of modern subjectivism—whether we speak of his criticism of Sartre's concept of freedom in the closing pages of *Phenomenology of Perception* or his attack on Sartre's "ultra-Bolshevism" in *Adventures of the Dialectic*—Lévi-Strauss seemed to offer a radically new departure. Hence, toward the end of his essay on Mauss and Lévi-Strauss, Merleau-Ponty steered the discussion back to the fundamental question of the human subject: "For the philosopher, the presence of structure outside us in natural and social systems and within us as symbolic function points to a way beyond the subject-object correlation which has dominated philosophy from Descartes to Hegel."[114]

Merleau-Ponty's enthusiasm for Saussure and Lévi-Strauss seems to have played an important role in helping structuralism rise to dominance in French intellectual life in the 1960s. Yet Merleau-Ponty was not a structuralist. For one thing, he consistently insisted that the tasks of the philosopher were not identical to those of a linguist or social scientist.[115] For another, he tried to integrate the insights of structuralism into his own philosophical agenda. Hence his abiding concern for a phenomenology of lived experience meant that for him the notion that meaning resides in a symbolic domain outside individual consciousness does not preclude the possibility that the individual receives and alters meaning in singular ways. Along the same track, Merleau-Ponty warned that an excessive emphasis on structure threatened to obscure the role of agency. Far from embracing structuralism's antihumanist potential, he insisted that the philosopher's task is to disclose the "dimension of coexistence—not as a fait accompli and an object of contemplation, but as the milieu and perpetual event of the universal *praxis*." Then, in a formulation that seeks to describe a nonreductive reciprocity between agency and structure, individual and collective, he asserts that "philosophy is irreplaceable because it reveals to us both the movement by which lives become truths, and the circularity of that singular being who in a certain sense already *is* everything he *happens to think*."[116] In short, structuralism gave Merleau-Ponty a further tool for decentering human subjectivity, for conceptualizing it as eccentrically situated within society and nature. But he likely underestimated the extremism of the structuralist break with subjectivity, seeing it as a critique rather than an erasure of the subject.[117] Even in praising Lévi-Strauss's reading of Mauss, he optimistically believed that recognition of the impersonal power of the symbolic order neither eliminated the individual nor forced a choice between the individual and the collective. In this sense, he remained true to the vision of *Vielseitigkeit*, to the many-sided view of history that he had praised in *Adventures of the Dialectic*. At the same time, his tempered approach to structuralism also fit with his evolving politics, which had taken him from the communism of the immediate postwar era, to a defense of undogmatic Marxism, to a pluralistic left-leaning liberalism at the time of his death in 1961. His untimely death meant that he never witnessed the more extreme antisubjectivist claims that characterized the structuralism of the 1960s or the displacement of his own brand of phenomenology by structuralist analysis.[118]

The same confluence of events that had contributed to Merleau-Ponty's increasingly distant relationship to Marxism had similar effects for many left-wing intellectuals. For many leftists in France, and, indeed, western Europe and North America, the Soviet invasion of Hungary in 1956 brought an end to their attachment to the respective communist parties and initiated the birth of the New Left, that fragmented international cadre of leftists who distanced themselves categorically from the Soviet Union and embraced less dogmatic and less statist forms of socialism. In France, *Socialisme ou Barbarie*, founded in 1948 by Cornelius Castoriadis and Claude Lefort, witnessed a marked rise in membership after the Hungarian invasion, although the group's historian, Philippe Gottraux, gives equal weight to the radicalizing effects of the Algerian War.[119] Other anti-Stalinist groups like the Situationist International and the *Arguments* circle emerged as direct responses to the Soviet aggression. However prescient these groups might look from our present vantage point, it was, ironically, Louis Althusser and structural Marxism that benefited most from the disenchantment of leftist intellectuals with the Parti communiste français. François Furet suggested in an important article of 1967 that the triumph of structuralism in the 1960s stemmed directly from "the dislocation of Marxist dogmatism."[120] It is a curious fact that structuralism served as an exit strategy for many disillusioned leftists who turned to anthropology and the eternal verities of peoples without history, or to psychoanalysis and the timeless unconscious, yet, at the same time, in Althusser, structuralism served as a way of rescuing Marxism. On this point the historian François Dosse writes that structural Marxism "was one response to the need to abandon an official, dogma-bound, post-Stalinist Marxism with an onerous past. . . . [Althusser] offered the exciting challenge to a militant generation that had cut its teeth in anticolonial combats of resuscitating a scientific Marxism freed of the scoria of regimes that had ruled in the name of Marxism."[121] Or, from Furet's closer and more jaundiced view, "the structuralist 'deideologizing' of Marxism undoubtedly offers a way of living through the end of the ideologies inside the Communist world."[122]

Althusser's structuralism possesses numerous qualities that exceed the linguistic model dominating Lévi-Strauss's thought. Nowhere is this more evident than in his effort to steer Marxism away from an expressive idea of the social totality. According to Althusser, the critical Marxism of the twentieth century had been enthralled by a Hegelian conception of totality in which the whole is unified by a core principle that is both the essence and the cause of all the parts. Against this conception of expressive totality, Althusser argued that society is a "*structured whole* containing what can be called levels or instances which are distinct and 'relatively autonomous,' and co-exist within this complex structural unity, articulated within one another according to specific determinations, fixed in the last instance by the level or instance of the economy."[123] Consistent with this understanding, Althusser proposed that the parts of the whole are not *determined* by an underlying essence, or within a hierarchy of cause and effect, as in the classic Marxist model of base and superstructure. Rather, the "levels" or "instances" are overdetermined through "structural causality." As he wrote, "structure is not an essence *outside* the economic phenomena which comes and alters their aspect, forms, and relations and which is effective on them as an absent cause. . . . Effects are not outside the structure, are not a preexisting object, element, or space in which the structure arrives to *imprint its mark*. The structure, which is merely a specific combination of its elements, is nothing outside its effects."[124] Except for Althusser's heavy emphasis on the synchronic operation of elements upon one another, this conception of structure arguably has more to do with Spinoza's idea of *natura naturans* than with Saussurean linguistics.

Nonetheless, Althusser drew upon the argot of structuralism when he tried to develop a new theory of ideology. In essays like "Freud and Lacan" (1964) he develops a theory of ideology leaning heavily on Lacanian psychoanalysis. Yet where Lacan continually balances tensions between the three registers of the real, symbolic, and imaginary, Althusser subordinates everything to the symbolic. The "real," that unmasterable domain beyond the symbolic, is fully absent from the account. The symbolic is, by Althusser's definition, nothing less than the "law of culture"; the imaginary, which for Lacan precedes the symbolic in the infant stage of individual human development and persists throughout adult life, disappears into the "*Law of the Symbolic.*" So, writes Althusser, "Even the moment of the imaginary, which, for clarity's sake, I have just presented as *preceding* the symbolic, as distinct from it—hence as the first moment in which the child *lives* its immediate intercourse with a human being (its mother) without recognizing it practically as the symbolic intercourse it is . . . —*is marked and structured in its dialectic by the dialectic of the Symbolic Order itself*, i.e., by the dialectic of human Order, of the human norm . . . in the form of the Order of the signifier itself, i.e., in the form of an Order *formally* identical with the order of language."[125] The formulations in this and other essays empty the individual human subject of any dimension of self-constitution or agency; the subject is a product of structural causality. In the 1969 essay "Ideology and Ideological State Apparatuses," Althusser borrowed from Lacan to define ideology as the "imaginary relationship of individuals to their real conditions of existence."[126] This would seem to allow no room for the role of the symbolic, but in fact, Althusser's formulation subordinates the imaginary entirely to the symbolic.[127] That is, in Althusser's account of ideology, the imaginary is structured by the "big Other," that point or place where the authority of the symbolic order is assumed to lie, that ultimate "quilting point" that stabilizes the entire system of signification. Further, insofar as Althusser believes that the human being is formed in and by language, he argues the human individual is always tied to a signifier that represents him for the other, thus loading him with a symbolic mandate and assigning him a position in the network of symbolic relations. Hence Althusser's notion of "interpellation," or hailing, as a constitutive moment of subjectivity, as when a policeman shouts "hey you!" and "I" turn in response.

Merleau-Ponty, as we saw, had straddled two conceptions of the symbolic in his critical engagement with Marxism, on one side, the expressive theory that underlies interpretive models such as Max Weber's and, on the other, the structuralist theory of symbolic order, wherein meaning emerges from synchronic operations within a relational field of signs. The tension between these two understandings of the symbolic would likely have become fully evident to Merleau-Ponty had he lived long enough to read Althusser's work in the 1960s. For, in presenting an "utterly consistent symbolic,"[128] a symbolic order with no outside and no disruption, Althusser pushed to an extreme the structuralist tendency to view the symbolic as an algebraic order. Excluded from Althusser's symbolic order is recognition of the polysemy that prevents a stable, unified theory of the symbolic: the "fecund uncertainty" of symbols,[129] the symbol's "irreducible duplicity" between the algebraic and the sacred,[130] the equivocal oscillation between "abstract operational symbolization" and "cryptophoric symbolization."[131] Yet, in the death throes of French intellectual Marxism, this dimension of symbolic polysemy did make a spectacular, if short-lived return in the work of Jean Baudrillard in the years immediately after 1968. It is impossible to close this chapter without mentioning this final twist in the entwined stories of Marxism's weakening hold and the vagaries of the symbolic.

We recall, from the introduction, Camille Tarot's suggestion that Marcel Mauss developed a "Romantic" version of Durkheimianism. Tarot is unable to account fully for Mauss's divergence from the sociology of Émile Durkheim, but he speculates that the German idealist and Romantic theory of the symbol may have influenced Mauss through his training as a philologist. For Tarot, Mauss's more supple, polysemic approach to meaning explains why his symbolic sociology had a double posterity, on the one hand, the hyperrationality of the structuralists and, on the other hand, the irrationalism of Georges Bataille and the Collège de Sociologie, with their fascination for excess, transgression, and what commentators have called the impure or transgressive sacred.[132] If Louis Althusser's attempt to wrest Marxism out of the hands of Hegelian humanists and put it on solid scientific ground exemplifies the one current, then Jean Baudrillard's work in the early 1970s represents the resurgence of the "Romantic" possibilities of the symbolic within a Marxism *in extremis*.

Baudrillard's two major works of his early career, *For a Critique of the Political Economy of the Sign* (1972) and *The Mirror of Production* (1973), mark a rapid turn away from Marx. The essays collected in *For a Critique of the Political Economy of the Sign* offer an amalgam of structuralist interest in the functioning of codes, Marx's discussion of money as the general equivalent of all value, and Guy Debord's description of an advanced stage of capitalism where capital has "accumulated to the point where it becomes image."[133] In Debord's account the reign of the commodity form has flattened all qualitative distinctions in a society of infinite exchangeability, and fetishism has grown so extensive that the lived reality of social relations has receded into an autonomous pseudoworld of representations, a system of signs that has coagulated into a mesmerizing and deceptive spectacle. Baudrillard accepts many elements of this depiction, as well as Debord's recognition that consumption has become a form of domination; but he views the commodity as just one instance of modern society's tendency to suppress qualitative differences beneath a logic of infinite sameness and abstract exchangability. Here, as Steven Best writes, Baudrillard "understood contemporary society not in terms of spectacle, but 'sign-exchange-value,' rooting the development of the commodity in the structural logic of the sign."[134]

Even as Baudrillard leans on structuralism in drawing this parallel between the logic of the commodity and the logic of the sign, he departs from structuralist nomenclature. Where the structuralist equates the symbolic order with the system of signs, Baudrillard pits the sign against the symbolic:

> The rationality of the sign is rooted in its exclusion and annihilation of all symbolic ambivalence on behalf of a fixed and equational structure. The sign is a discriminant: it structures itself through exclusion. Once crystallized on this exclusive structure, the sign aligns its fixed field, resigns the differential, and assigns [Signifier] and [Signified] each its sphere of systemic control. Thus, the sign proffers itself as full value: positive, rational, exchangeable value. All virtualities of meaning are shorn in the cut of structure.[135]

Baudrillard pointedly rejects the "classic semio-linguistic" definition of the term *symbol* as an "analogical variant of the sign."[136] Instead, the symbolic emerges as the radical other of the sign and, thus, a vital source of potential disruption: "Only ambivalence (as a *rupture* of value, of another side or beyond of sign value, and as the *emergence of the symbolic*) sustains a challenge to the legibility, the false transparency of the sign; only ambivalence questions the evidence of the use value of the sign (rational decoding) and of its exchange value (the discourse of communication)."[137] At one level, this disruptive force seems to reside as an ever present dialectical contradiction within the order of the sign itself. Hence, Baudrillard writes, "It is the symbolic that continues to haunt the sign, for in its total exclusion it never ceases to dismantle the formal correlation of [Signifier] and [Signified]."[138] Yet, at another level, the symbolic seems to belong to a historical destiny, as if the struggle of the sign to deny and repress openness will eventually generate its dialectical opposite. Accordingly, the main essay of the volume ends with a call for a revolutionary bonfire to consume both capitalism and semiotics:

> As the functional and terrorist organization of the control of meaning under the sign of the positivity of value, signification is in some ways kin to the notion of reification. It is the locus of an elemental objectification that reverberates through the amplified systems of signs up to the level of the social and political terrorism of the bracketing (*encadrement*) of meaning. All the repressive and reductive strategies of power systems are already present in the internal logic of the sign, as well as those of exchange value and political economy. Only total revolution, theoretical and practical, can restore the symbolic in the demise of the sign and of value. Even signs must burn.[139]

In *For a Critique of the Political Economy of the Sign*, Baudrillard believes that his analysis remains within a Marxist framework. By contrast, *The Mirror of Production* strikes a much more ambivalent stance: Baudrillard still leans heavily on Marxist categories, but at times he aggressively criticizes Marx. One aspect of this shift can be seen in his greater readiness to distinguish himself from Guy Debord and the situationists. They emerge as more or less conventional Marxists who ultimately operate within an orthodox social model, insofar as they speak of "the 'infrastructural' logic of the commodity" and believe that the "exploitation of labor power is still determinant."[140] In Baudrillard's more extreme challenge to that model, the autonomization of the sign, its detachment from reference to the real, and its capacity to oppress have become more or less absolute. "It is," he writes, "a matter of the passage of all values to exchange-sign value, under the hegemony of the code. That is, of a structure of control and of power much more subtle and more totalitarian than that of exploitation. *For the sign is much more than a connotation of the commodity*, than a semiological supplement to exchange value. It is an operational structure that lends itself to a structural manipulation compared with which the quantitative mystery of surplus value appears inoffensive" (121–122). Thus we see in *The Mirror of Production* the unmooring of the sign system, of signifiers from signifieds. Any meaningful notion of reality melts into air. This move would only gain in momentum in Baudrillard's subsequent work on simulacra and would eventually ensure his status as the most extreme and notorious representative of postmodernism.

Baudrillard's relentlessly bleak insistence that modern society stands fully under the dominion of the "super-ideology of the sign" (122) has invited comparisons with the Frankfurt school's idea of a "totally reified" society, but it must also remind us of Althusser's depiction of a fully consistent symbolic order. Yet, unlike Althusser, Baudrillard vacillates between this depiction of an entirely closed hegemonic order and a radically utopian leap beyond it. And once again, the notion of the symbolic plays the key role. But the register has shifted. In *For a Critique of the Political Economy of the Sign*, the issue of the symbol remains tied to questions of language—sign and symbol are dialectically entwined as two unsurpassable dimensions of communication. In *The Mirror of Production*, Baudrillard has shifted emphasis from semiotics to anthropology. His guiding lights are now Marcel Mauss and Georges Bataille, and his interest in the symbolic now centers on the contrast between primitive "gift" economies and modern capitalism. In the primitive economy, exchange is symbolic. It is expressive, it discharges energy and meaning, and it opens relations of reciprocity. In the modern economy the exchange of commodities ties us ever more tightly to the process of abstraction and the ever greater accumulation of capital.

Here, we encounter the second dimension of Baudrillard's sharpening critical distance from Marx. For he insists that Marx never managed to transcend the presuppositions of the era. That is, he failed to develop a critique of the two orders that Baudrillard believes act in total unison to dominate modern society: the "order of production and political economy" and the "form representation (the status of the sign, of the language that directs all Western thought)." The form *production* and the form *representation*, Baudrillard continues, "are the two great unanalyzed forms of the imaginary of political economy that imposed their limits on [Marx]" (20). Regarding production, Baudrillard takes Marx to task for failing to recognize the historical specificity of modern capitalism. Marx uncritically projected capitalism's productionist ideology onto all earlier epochs and thereby overlooked the radically different nature of symbolic exchange and its potentially disruptive effects within a commodity culture. Regarding representation, Baudrillard specifically attacks historical materialism for its realist epistemology, in short, its failure to recognize itself in the order of representation. Hence, he exposes the "'self-verification' of a model that is achieved through the adequacy of the rational (itself) and the real." Historical materialism is "an arbitrary model that verifies itself, like any self-respecting model, by its own circularity" (117). Such a perspective cannot think the symbolic: "If there was one thing Marx did not think about, it was discharge, waste, sacrifice, prodigality, play, and symbolism" (42). Within the productivist cosmos embraced by Marx, discharge of energy gets immediately translated into value, thus excluding "all symbolic *putting into play* as in the gift or the discharge" (44). "Labor," continues Baudrillard, "is defined . . . as what disinvests the body and social exchange of all ambivalent and symbolic qualities, reducing them to a rational, positive, unilateral investment. The productive Eros represses all the alternative qualities of meaning and exchange in symbolic discharge" (46).

The Mirror of Production posits an understanding of history in which the epoch of symbolic economy has been superseded by an epoch of political economy that fully represses the symbolic. Yet Baudrillard intimates that this repression cannot be fully successful. Even in the midst of the "triumphant abstraction" of the capitalist system, he writes, "the demand arises that nothing can be given without being returned, nothing is ever won without something being lost, nothing is ever produced without something being destroyed, nothing is ever spoken without being answered. In short, what haunts the system is the symbolic demand" (147). And so, at the end of a book about "coding, super-coding, universalization of the code," Baudrillard indulges a vision of radical alterity, a resurgence of the symbolic, as the utopian alternative to rational mastery and the dominance of the abstract code. Yet he insists that this must take the form of "revolt," not of "revolution," because the latter is far too entangled in a dialectical story of reality on its way toward completion. Hence, he seeks inspiration not in the Marxist yearning for proletarian revolution, but in "the cursed poet, non-official art, and utopian writings in general." Such figures of revolt, he writes, "are the equivalent, at the level of discourse, of the savage social movements that were born in a symbolic situation of rupture (symbolic—which means non-universalized, non-dialectical, non-rationalized in the mirror of an imaginary objective history). This is why poetry (not Art) was fundamentally connected only with the utopian socialist movements, with 'revolutionary romanticism,' and never with Marxism as such" (164).

Uncannily, at the extreme edge of Marxism's hold on the imagination of French leftist intellectuals, we find a summons to the Romantic socialists of the early nineteenth century. It is as if, in Marxism's implosion, history runs backward or, to be truer to Baudrillard's simulacral sensibility, as if history is a film playing in rewind. Passing back through Bataille and Mauss, Baudrillard tries to mobilize the Romantic recognition of the unmasterability of symbolic form as a weapon of revolt against the closed, rational order of late capitalism. This vision is, of course, mediated by Baudrillard's twentieth-century provenance and, more immediately, by the fresh memory of the heady days of May 1968, when stalwarts dreaming of communist revolution uncomfortably shared the Parisian streets with revelers in a carnivalesque revolt. And, among the various contemporaries who surface in *The Mirror of Production*—Kristeva, Lévi-Strauss, Deleuze, Althusser, Derrida, Marcuse—is one whose presence has scarcely been remarked in the sizable literature on Baudrillard. I am speaking of Cornelius Castoriadis, whose pseudonym Cardan appears at various pivotal moments in Baudrillard's book. It is from Castoriadis—not Lacan—that Baudrillard takes his notion of the "imaginary" of political economy, from Castoriadis that he draws his criticism of Marx's unwarranted projection of capitalist categories onto the universal history of earlier epochs. Indeed, it is through Castoriadis that Baudrillard arrives at the "radical hypothesis that not only have the categories of historical materialism no meaning outside of our society, but that *perhaps in a fundamental way they no longer have any meaning for us*" (108).

The striking disconnect between the evident impact of Castoriadis upon Baudrillard and Castoriadis's nearly total absence from scholarship on Baudrillard is emblematic of the fate of this Greek philosopher, who made his way to Paris in 1945 and there fashioned a singular political and intellectual career. If Castoriadis's influence on Baudrillard is palpable, nonetheless their thought and sensibility are in fact profoundly different. Baudrillard swings between sharply contrasting polar opposites: a despairing image of a totally ordered, dominated world and fantasies of breakthrough into an unimaginable plenitude. This oscillation is the first portent of what Martin Jay has diagnosed as the manic-depressive temperament of postmodernism, which mixes celebration of excess with apocalyptic visions of obliteration and dispersal.[141] Castoriadis never succumbed to this malady. Instead, when he abandoned Marxism as his guiding thread, he sought to detect the tension between openness and closure as present and active within the lived experience of social and political action. He rejected the binary opposition between an absolute oppression and an absolute freedom. Rather, he emphasized the extent of autonomy already won by historical actors in modernity, while also remaining unequivocal in his critique of the forms of domination at work in contemporary society. And, above all, he tried to conceptualize creativity in its full potency, not as an extraordinary visitation in moments of effervescent transgression, but as the truly distinctive feature of human society. The stridency of Baudrillard's insistence on the simulacral and his dualistic vision of freedom and oppression suggest that, even if only negatively, he remained captured by the moment of Marxism's implosion. He is a post-Marxist in the biographical sense only. Castoriadis, by contrast, leads us onto terrain where we recognize landmarks of a specific intellectual style and political vision that we may, with ample awareness of the perils of generalization, identify as post-Marxism.

CHAPTER THREE

From the Symbolic Turn to the Social Imaginary

Castoriadis's Project of Autonomy

STRUCTURALISM WAS WELL ON ITS WAY toward fully displacing Sartrean existentialism as the regnant intellectual style in France by the early 1960s. François Furet, as we saw in the previous chapter, explained this success as a "dislocation of Marxist dogmatism."[1] The Soviet invasion of Hungary, Khrushchev's revelations about Stalinism, the PCF's waffling on the Algerian war, the apparent waning of working-class activism, particularly the absence of resistance to Charles de Gaulle's power grab in 1958—these and other disappointments weakened the old attraction of Marxism-Leninism. Even as some disillusioned leftists turned to Lévi-Strauss and others turned to Lacanian psychoanalysis, still others embraced Louis Althusser's attempt to reinvent Marxism as a structuralist science. Remembering those years from the perspective of a committed political radical, Cornelius Castoriadis wrote, "Those who lived through those times can testify that being a militant at the beginning of the sixties in contact with certain student and university circles in Paris entailed taking a stand against structuralism in general and Althusser in particular."[2]

Castoriadis's recollection is fascinating because it comes from a political militant who in the mid-1940s had already denounced the communist world as a betrayal of Marxism and, by the early 1960s, had moved from a self-critique of Marxism to outright rejection of Marxism in the name of preserving revolutionary politics. Yet Castoriadis emphatically rejected both the retreat from Marxism into structuralism and the attempt to recast Marxism in structuralist terms. Instead, Castoriadis embarked on a sustained effort to reconceive radical politics as the project of autonomy. In its full articulation Castoriadis's position emphasized contingency in history, creativity at both individual and collective levels, and the emergence of novel forms of social life. At its core is the idea of the "imaginary," the workings of which Castoriadis tried to decipher at the levels of both the individual psyche and the "social-historical world." Imagination, in his view, animates a ceaseless process of self-transforming human activity. Though human existence is always self-creation, this process of self-production is typically occluded, covered over, assigned to an extrasocial source, as in religion, or to a deterministic process, as in modern philosophies of history such as Hegelianism and Marxism. Hence, the project of autonomy, as Castoriadis came to formulate it, demands that human beings recognize themselves as the source of their own creation and adopt a freeing and interrogative attitude toward their individual lives and their shared institutions.

By the late 1950s Castoriadis concluded that Marxism was an obstacle, not a resource in this effort to renew radical politics and human praxis. Indeed, he came to believe that Marxism itself is but the avatar of deeper tendencies in Western thought and culture toward determinism, scientism, and the covering over of the chaos and abyss that inhabits all of being. From this vantage point, structuralism could appear to be an heir to Marxism or, even more fundamentally, the latest manifestation of the West's deep-rooted penchant for deterministic, rationalist systems, a nullification of values Castoriadis cherished: human agency and creativity, contingency, the possibility of *true* historical time, marked not by repetition but by *alterity*, which he defined as the punctuating emergence of the "new." A 1977 statement can stand in for innumerable similar denunciations of structuralism: "The 'Law' and the 'symbolic' (just like the idea of structure in ethnology and sociology) erase the instituting society and reduce the instituted society to a collection of dead rules, indeed Rules of Death, in the face of which the subject (in order to be 'structured') must be immersed in passivity."[3] The terms here clearly reveal that for Castoriadis structuralism meant first and foremost Claude Lévi-Strauss and Jacques Lacan, the master structuralists who asserted claims over the two central domains of Castoriadis's concern, the social world and the psyche.

Moreover, as the passage suggests, Castoriadis saw that to champion the "imaginary" inevitably meant taking a stand on the "symbolic," for by the early 1960s these had become virtual antitheses in structuralist theory.

Castoriadis's magnum opus, *The Imaginary Institution of Society* (1975), opens with a sustained critique of Marxism, announcing in unequivocal terms his abandonment of Marx. In fact, however, that critique was essentially a summation of criticisms he had already formulated by the late 1950s. When it came to the articulation of his "positive" position in *The Imaginary Institution of Society*, the arguments and hypotheses that would earn him considerable fame and dominate the rest of his life's work, he did not develop these in direct confrontation with Marxism. Not Marxism but structuralism emerges in the pages of *The Imaginary Institution of Society* as the crucial foil for Castoriadis's own developing theory of the imaginary. Always a combative, polemical thinker, Castoriadis wasted no time in moving from opposition to Marxism to opposition to structuralism, which by the early 1960s had overtaken Marxism as the cutting edge of French intellectual life.

Vehement as Castoriadis's comments could be, his relationship to structuralism was in fact not merely a matter of drawing a rigid battle line. Indeed, his work entwined constructively with the broad shift in thinking represented most prominently by Lévi-Strauss and Lacan. He too rejected the idea that we have unmediated access to reality; he too rejected the idea of a sovereign conscious subject for whom language is a transparent medium of expression. He too believed that society is a symbolic construction made up of significations, and he spoke of "structures" shaping the material forms and mentalities of instituted society. That he shared many of the premises of structuralism makes it all the more intriguing, both theoretically and historically, that he worked his way toward such different conclusions. The nature of Castoriadis's engagement with structuralism did not emerge all at once, however. Rather, it evolved, and, as it did, the bull's-eye of his critical target shifted from Lévi-Strauss to Lacan. This fact is central to a historical account of the most crucial years of Castoriadis's philosophical development, stretching from roughly 1960 to the publication of *The Imaginary Institution of Society* in 1975. In truth, very little work has been done to comprehend Castoriadis's trajectory historically, beyond, that is, drawing a basic distinction between an "early" and a "late" period, between his overtly political Marxist, militant phase in the group

Socialisme ou Barbarie and the more philosophical post-Marxist phase beginning around 1960. Other than noting this shift, the majority of discussions have been more or less content to offer exegetical reconstructions and synoptic overviews of his thinking.[4]

One of the main culprits in perpetuating this rather undifferentiated view is *The Imaginary Institution of Society* itself. This large book immediately became the touchstone for anyone engaging Castoriadis's wide-ranging and challenging thought. Yet, behind the semblance of unity, the book actually comprises two documents, the first composed ten years earlier than the second. The first half, "Marxism and Revolutionary Theory," was written in the early 1960s and originally published in serial form from mid-1964 to mid-1965 in Castoriadis's journal *Socialisme ou Barbarie*.[5] A comparison between the content of this early text and the version printed in *The Imaginary Institution of Society* essentially confirms Castoriadis's claim that nothing was changed except for correction of typos and the insertion of some additional footnotes, duly marked so as to distinguish them from the original notes. The only real change—not acknowledged by Castoriadis— is the addition of chapter titles and subtitled sections to "Marxism and Revolutionary Theory," but that change is not trivial. It lends the text considerable programmatic clarity and strengthens its links to the later sections composed in the early 1970s. The last installment of the serialized text in *Socialisme ou Barbarie* in the summer of 1965 ends with the promise that the conclusion will follow in the next number; as it turned out, there was no number forthcoming, because the journal and the group reached an impasse that made it impossible to carry on any semblance of collective work. The unfulfilled promise of a conclusion drops out of the 1975 version of "Marxism and Revolutionary Theory," and instead Castoriadis moves straight to the second part of *The Imaginary Institution of Society*. The exigencies of the circumstances of Castoriadis's composition of "Marxism and Revolutionary Theory" are thereby effaced, the fact that it was written on the fly within a militant milieu being torn apart by internal strife at the center of which was Castoriadis's break with Marxism. Furthermore, the addition of the titles and subtitles and the erasure of the nonconclusion makes the relationship between the earlier and later halves of *The Imaginary Institution of Society* look more like the logical unfolding of an argument than two attempts to address the same cluster of issues separated by ten years of further theoretical refinement.

I use the word *refinement* deliberately, because I do not want to overstate the differences between the two parts of *The Imaginary Institution of Society*. Indeed, it is remarkable how assured Castoriadis's formulations in the early 1960s are and how well they flow into the arguments of the second part of the book. Still, there are differences, and they are not insignificant measures of shifts in Castoriadis's ideas, concerns, and engagements with his contemporaries and his philosophical sources. Castoriadis himself was entirely forthcoming about the unusual provenance of the book in his preface to *The Imaginary Institution of Society*, where he defended the inclusion of the essentially unaltered 1964 text as an effort to show the unedited process of theory making, much like an offer to reveal for once how sausages are made. He was equally candid that his thinking had evolved in the years between 1964 and 1975:

> The ideas which had already been brought out and formulated in the part of "Marxism and Revolutionary Theory" published in 1964–5— those of history as creation *ex nihilo*, of instituting society and instituted society, of the social imaginary, of the institution of society as its own work, of the social-historical as a mode of being unrecognized by inherited thought—had in the meantime been transformed for me from arrival points to starting points.[6]

Whereas none of Castoriadis's many commentators have really unpacked this observation, I will take it as my guide in exploring the development of Castoriadis's thought during the crucial period from 1960 to 1975. In that process of refinement and alteration, Castoriadis's long critical engagement with structuralism was an important vehicle. And at the center of that engagement was the question of the relationship between the imaginary and the symbolic, which he perceived as a nodal point in his efforts to rethink the radical project.

Arrival Points

The journey that found a temporary arrival point in "Marxism and Revolutionary Theory" began, in some respects, at least as early as Castoriadis's arrival in Paris in 1945. Born in 1922 in Istanbul of Greek parents, and raised in Greece, Castoriadis had joined the Greek Communist Youth in the late 1930s. During the German occupation of Greece, he was a left-wing student in Athens, where discontent with the Communists led him to participate in Trotskyist cells. The dangers of clandestine political activity under Nazi occupation were only slightly lessened when the Germans were driven out in October 1944, because in the ensuing chaos Communists embarked on a murderous campaign against the Trotskyists.[7] When Castoriadis was offered a bursary from the École française d'Athènes, he knew it was time to leave Greece. Setting sail on the *Mataroa*, a New Zealand military transport ship carrying a number of other young Greek intellectuals and artists, he reached Paris in late 1945. His intention was to complete a philosophy thesis with René Poirier demonstrating the intrinsic limits of rationalistic philosophical systems, a theme that looks portentous from the vantage point of his later work.[8] Instead, he became absorbed in the turbulent politics of the French left in the years immediately after the liberation. Already in 1946, Castoriadis and Claude Lefort, the brilliant young student of Maurice Merleau-Ponty, became the leading figures of a critical wing of French Trotskyism known as the Chaulieu-Montal tendency after their cover names, Pierre Chaulieu (Castoriadis) and Claude Montal (Lefort). By late 1948, the Chaulieu-Montal tendency announced its inability to continue with Trotskyism and declared the creation of the group and journal *Socialisme ou Barbarie*, borrowing its name from a phrase in Rosa Luxemburg's *Junius Pamphlet*. In the manifesto that opened the first issue of the journal and in the years to follow, Castoriadis and his comrades developed an ultra-left-libertarian position that was unique in the French political context. They rejected Trotsky's belief that Stalinism was a temporary aberration in the transition to classless society and attacked the Soviet Union for betraying Marx by developing a highly organized and particularly oppressive form of the "bureaucratic capitalism" that, in a more fragmented version, had come to dominate the West. Rejecting any firm distinctions between these two forms of "capitalism," they defined the core conflict in capitalism no longer as the struggle between owners of wealth and laborers without property, but as the conflict between "directors" and "executants" in the production process.[9] Years before the Soviet invasion of Hungary in 1956 produced wider disillusionment with communism, both Castoriadis and Lefort launched withering attacks against fellow-traveling French intellectuals like Jean-Paul Sartre.

Tremendously skeptical of the Marxist-Leninist idea of the vanguard role of the revolutionary party, Socialisme ou Barbarie attempted to subordinate their own theoretical work to the inventive power of workers' agency. Already by the early 1950s, in the face of the authoritarianism of the French Communist Party and the alliance of the Fourth Republic state with the large-scale corporations that were steering France's postwar economic modernization, Castoriadis redefined socialism as the struggle of people to gain control over their activities, what he called "autogestion" or "self-management."

Even as late as 1960, Castoriadis aligned his thinking with Marx, declaring that "every revolutionary worthy of the name will always remain a Marxist."[10] Yet the declaration concealed a process of questioning that had already taken him beyond anything resembling an orthodox Marxist framework. One sees this emerging clearly in the essays ranging from "On the Content of Socialism, I" (1955) to "Modern Capitalism and Revolution" (1960–61). Indeed, "On the Content of Socialism, II" (1957) notes that *Socialisme ou Barbarie* had already challenged core socialist ideas, including many held by Lenin and even by Marx; yet, he pointedly remarked, "we ourselves have failed to develop the content of our own ideas to the full," inhibited by "factors that have dominated the evolution of Marxism itself for a century, namely, the enormous dead weight of the ideology of exploiting society, the paralyzing legacy of traditional concepts, and the difficulty of freeing oneself from inherited modes of thought."[11] A number of major themes emerge in these essays, which anticipate the concerns of Castoriadis's "Marxism and Revolutionary Theory": first, the vision of history that takes shape here is no longer one of laws and deterministic processes, but rather of human self-creation; second, the question of "institution," a key element of Castoriadis's concept of historical creativity that denotes the process whereby a society draws on a well of significations to institute itself as a specific mode and type of human coexistence; third, a new concept of theory that abandons the pursuit of a closed order of truth in favor of "a living theoretical process, from whose womb emerge moments of truth destined to be outstripped."[12]

Castoriadis's rapid move from heterodox Marxism to an outright declaration that "Marxism quite simply no longer exists historically as a living theory" produced intolerable strains within Socialisme ou Barbarie.[13] Perhaps in an effort to defuse dissent, he insisted that the "Tendency" he now spearheaded "is the organic outcome of the line of development of the review. Indeed, it merely regroups and systematizes ideas already formulated in the review a long time ago."[14] At a certain level this was true, given the collective nature of the group's deliberations;[15] but it would be more accurate to say that it mainly systematized ideas that *Castoriadis* had already formulated; there had in fact always been debate on many points, even if there had been consensus on some basic principles. Castoriadis's decisive break with Marxism shattered that consensus, for it entailed a shift from quantity to quality that many members could not countenance. Jean-François Lyotard, who had been a member since 1954, led a scission in the name of upholding the commitment to Marxism. In a parting polemic aimed at Castoriadis, Lyotard denounced the new tendency as a form of "existentialism" because of its apparent subjectivism and voluntarism, and he predicted that Castoriadis would soon abandon revolutionary political activity altogether and fall into philosophy.[16] The charge of existentialism was entirely wrong, though Lyotard was not the last to make it; ironically enough, the fall into philosophy characterized Lyotard's own subsequent development, but it was certainly true of Castoriadis as well.

Indeed, even if articles of the later 1950s anticipated some of the themes of "Marxism and Revolutionary Theory," what could not have been foreseen was the philosophical tenor of the 1964–65 text. Philippe Gottraux rightly claims that "Marxism and Revolutionary Theory" was not only a rupture with Marxism but also a definitive rupture with the earlier form of Castoriadis's own writing. Undoubtedly, he remained oriented toward political questions, but, for the first time, he stepped out of the narrow milieu of the ultra-left and engaged in intellectual debate within the larger "intellectual field," to use Gottraux's Bourdieu-inspired terms.[17] Suddenly, Castoriadis's discourse burst the confines of an immanent critique based on the experience of working-class movements and capitalist societies and mushroomed into a philosophical reflection in which no question seemed off-limits. Prior to "Marxism and Revolutionary Theory," Castoriadis later observed, his writing contains "no mention of any philosopher whatsoever."[18] Now his text is full of references to Hegel, Husserl, Kant, Fichte, and Merleau-Ponty, social theorists like Ruth Benedict, Margaret Mead, and Lévi-Strauss, and the psychoanalysts Freud and Lacan. It turned out that Castoriadis had never stopped reading philosophy and social theory. Just to consider the 1940s, his copious reading list from his student days in

Athens include Ernst Cassirer's *Philosophie der symbolischen Formen* and works by Max Scheler;[19] he came to Paris intending to do a dissertation in philosophy; in the mid-1940s, he translated much of Hegel's *Wissenschaft der Logik* and considered translating Hegel's *Enzyklopädie*[20]; he and Lefort exchanged erudite remarks about Husserl;[21] and he never ceased to cultivate his deep interest in ancient Greek philosophy. By his own admission, the day job he held for years as an economist for the Organisation for Economic Co-operation and Development afforded him plenty of time to read and write for *Socialisme ou Barbarie.*

The Imaginary in Context

"Marxism and Revolutionary Theory" opens with a recapitulation and extension of the critique of Marx's economic theory and productivist orientation that Castoriadis had already developed. The opening sections are most striking for the significant deepening of Castoriadis's argument linking the deterioration of left-wing politics in the twentieth century to the emptying out of the meaning of praxis already implicit in the deterministic logic underpinning Marx's thought. This in turn led him to a much more comprehensive engagement with the question of historical determinism. Against Marx's rationalist philosophy of history, which Castoriadis described as an "inverted Hegelianism," he argued that no causal model could exhaustively account for history. "The non-causal," he wrote,

> appears as behaviour that is not merely "unpredictable" but *creative* (on the level of individuals, groups, classes or entire societies). It appears not as a simple deviation in relation to an existing type but as the *positing* of a new type of behaviour, as the *institution* of a new social rule, as the *invention* of a new object or a new form—in short, as an emergence or a production which cannot be deduced on the basis of a previous situation, as a conclusion that goes beyond the premises or as the positing of new premises. . . . History cannot be thought in accordance with the determinist schema (nor, moreover, in accordance with a simple "dialectical" schema) because it is the domain of *creation.*[22]

Castoriadis linked historical creation to the process of "signification," whereby "men give their individual and collective life a signification that is not preassigned, a signification that they have to make while they are at grips with real conditions, which neither exclude nor guarantee the accomplishment of their projects."[23]

The most novel dimension of "Marxism and Revolutionary Theory" is Castoriadis's effort to tie these ideas of creativity and institution to a new theory of the imaginary. There is a certain logic to Castoriadis's arrival at this concept, for having described history as a domain of creation, he next searched for its source. In his earlier writings, this source was simply *practice*, which he believed is never fully dictated by existing rules and procedures and produces in the aggregate an indeterminate openness to novelty. In shifting so emphatically to a philosophical register in "Marxism and Revolutionary Theory," Castoriadis seemed to respond to the need for an even more fundamental, perhaps even foundational source of creativity. A central feature of his theory of the imaginary is that it functions at two intersecting, yet distinct levels, that of society and that of the individual subject. In a sense reminiscent of Durkheim, Castoriadis designated the social-historical a sui generis domain that is "neither the unending addition of intersubjective networks" nor "their simple 'product.'"[24] The social-historical is, rather, "a dimension of the collective and the anonymous," which "is what is everyone and what is no one, what is never absent and almost never present as such, a non-being that is more real than any being, that in which we are immersed yet which we can never apprehend in 'person.'"[25] Castoriadis later compressed these various attributes into a succinct definition of the social imaginary: "Imaginary: an unmotivated creation, that exists only in and through the positing of images. Social: inconceivable as the work or the product of an individual or a host of individuals (the individual *is* a social institution), underivable from the psyche in itself as such."[26] If social significations are not traceable to the individual, neither is the individual imagination exhaustively traceable to the social-historical. This domain of individual imagination he called "radical imagination," signifying the power to make images arise in consciousness. We shall see shortly that Castoriadis's first formulation of the concept of radical imagination owed a great deal to phenomenology, whereas his subsequent formulations drew more heavily on psychoanalysis to describe radical imagination as a continual flux of representations, affects, and intentions that are virtually coextensive with the individual psyche per se. As he wrote in the later half of *The Imaginary Institution of Society*, the psychical and the social-historical are two domains of the radical imaginary, not reducible to each other but articulated together, not a mediated unity, but a "non-empty intersection between the private world and the public world."[27] "A full recognition of the radical imagination is possible," he claimed in 1978, "only if it goes hand in hand with the discovery of the other dimension of the radical imaginary, the social-historical imaginary, instituting society as source of ontological creation deploying itself as history."[28]

Castoriadis's theory of the imaginary is original, but it must be said that the term was in the air. There were, first of all, the surrealists, with their idea of the power of poetry to remake the world; André Breton fascinated the young Castoriadis, and two young surrealist poets, Benjamin Peret and Jean-Jacques Lebel, had considerable involvement with Socialisme ou Barbarie.[29] Jean-Paul Sartre had done a great deal to put the imaginary on the French philosophical agenda with his 1940 book *L'imaginaire*, which in turn was strongly indebted to Edmund Husserl. Gaston Bachelard also drew heavily on phenomenology in his works on imagination as well as on both Freudian and Jungian psychoanalysis. Bachelard's student Gilbert Durand further developed the implications of Bachelard's theory of archetypes of imagination in his 1963 book *Les structures anthropologiques de l'imaginaire: introduction à l'archétypologie générale*. Castoriadis studied Bachelard when he first came to Paris but rapidly grew dissatisfied with him.[30] While the grounds of this dissatisfaction in the 1940s are not entirely clear, it is not difficult to see differences from the perspective of Castoriadis's developed theory of the imaginary. Bachelard, and even more Durand aimed to classify the symbolic manifestations of the human imagination as these clustered around certain fundamental structures deriving from both human physiology and the human encounter with the world. While neither Bachelard nor Durand followed Carl Jung into the theory of a collective unconscious, their explorations of the symbolic forms of the imagination bore a timeless, archetypal quality.[31] By contrast, Castoriadis's concern was with the origin of images and symbols in a dynamic and endlessly creative imagination.[32]

His approach bears a somewhat closer relationship to Sartre's phenomenological path, but here Castoriadis is not the most reliable guide on the most crucial difference between himself and Sartre. In *The Imaginary* Sartre followed Husserl in contrasting perception to imagining. Whereas in perception consciousness observes an object that surpasses it, consciousness, in imagination, gives itself an object all at once. The object of perception exceeds consciousness, whereas "the object of an image is never anything more than the consciousness one has of it." Perception opens toward an infinitely rich world; imagination suffers an "essential poverty."[33] This removal of the image from the perceptual plenum points to a further attribute of the Sartrean imagination, namely that acts of creation are in fact *negations* of the existent, acts of positing a "thesis of irreality."[34] This view ultimately opens directly onto basic themes of Sartrean existentialism, for even though the imaginary suffers an "essential poverty" compared to the fullness of perception, the imagination is nonetheless the basis of our existential freedom because it is the source of man's transcendence of the real; though the imaginary may be the source of enslavement to our own fantasies, it is also the source of the spontaneous freedom of consciousness.

Castoriadis insisted on a firm distinction between this "purely negative" view of the imagination and his own creative view.[35] His imaginary is an "originary faculty to pose or give oneself, under the mode of representation, a thing and a relation that are not (things that are not or never have been given in perception)."[36] In a 1996 interview, Peter Dews and Peter Osborne rightly pressed him on this distinction, asking, "Isn't the philosophical structure of that process actually the same, with one side rather than the other being emphasized?"[37] Indeed, Castoriadis himself recognized that negation belongs essentially to the act of imagination, and he was as ready as Sartre to regard the capacity to negate as a crucial dimension of freedom.[38] Conversely, Sartre saw positing and negating as two sides of the same coin: "So to posit the world as world and to 'nihilate' it are one and the same thing."[39] Contrary to Castoriadis's depiction, imagining is in fact a good example of Sartre's *dialectical*, as opposed to purely *phenomenological*, style of analysis, wherein opposites are brought into play rather than bracketed as they would be in Husserl.[40]

The more significant difference to Sartre comes in Castoriadis's immediate response to Dews and Osborne's question, when he says, "there is no given without imagination."[41] That is, Castoriadis maintained that the imagination institutes "reality." Hence, for example, in "Marxism and Revolutionary Theory," he rebutted the orthodox Marxian determinism of the economic base by claiming, "The 'real social relations' concerned here are always *instituted*."[42] In the latter half of *The Imaginary Institution of Society*, he took this further when he claimed, "society as a whole and every society in particular constitutes the 'real' and its own 'real.'"[43] Sartre, by contrast, upheld a division between the real and the imaginary that rests on his initial division between perception and imagination. Here Sartre revealed the extent of his link to Husserl, for Husserl maintained that there is an "unbridgeable and essential difference" between "perception, on the one hand, and on the other, presentation in the form of an image."[44] As Richard Kearney writes, Husserl privileged "the perceptual mode of intentionality . . . because of [its] direct access to the flesh-and-blood *presentness* of things."[45] Castoriadis clearly took something from both Husserl and Sartre insofar as he embraced the notion of intentional consciousness, depicting the presentation of an image as an *act*, not an *object* of consciousness. Nonetheless, the form of realism evident in Sartre and Husserl's distinction between perception and imagination was one that Castoriadis could not accept.

In formulating his theory of the imagination, Castoriadis reached even further into the past, behind phenomenology back to Kant and Fichte. Kant, after all, had developed a theory of the transcendental imagination to account for the schemata whereby categories are applied to given objects. Yet, as Castoriadis argued in a later essay, Kant's transcendental imagination always produces the "Stable and the Same. There is nothing more deprived of imagination than the transcendental imagination of Kant." Indeed, Kant's epistemological framework would collapse if the transcendental imagination were at all capable of creating.[46] Not surprisingly, Castoriadis declared his greater affinity for Fichte, at least the Fichte of the first *Wissenschaftslehre* (1794/95), where the "productive imagination" (*produktive Einbildungskraft*) not only supplies schemata, as it did in Kant's first critique, but also produces the intuited objects themselves.[47] Fichte's radicalization of Kant's theory of the imagination is clearly described in the one pertinent source that Castoriadis cites in "Marxism and Revolutionary Theory," Richard Kroner's classic *Von Kant bis Hegel*.[48] Though Castoriadis never wrote extensively on Fichte, he clearly had an ongoing engagement with his thought. His unfulfilled plans for a magnum opus titled *L'élément imaginaire* called for studies of the *Sturm und Drang*, Fichte, the young Hegel and Schelling, and the Jena Romantics;

his unpublished working notes during the 1960s and 1970s contain many references to Fichte.

The influence of Fichte may, if anything, have grown in the years after "Marxism and Revolutionary Theory," as Castoriadis developed in greater detail his understanding of the psyche as "above all, a ceaseless surging of representations and the unique mode in which this representational flux exists."[49] This continual, unmasterable, and spontaneous flux of representations, desires, and affects is *creative*, in the truest sense of the word, because it begins with the emergence of representation itself. It is impossible not to hear in this "capacity to produce an 'initial' representation" an echo of Fichte's basic move when he addressed the impasses of K. L. Reinhold's attempt to create a philosophical science of "representations" based on the foundational "fact" (*Tatsache*) of self-consciousness. As Jerrold Seigel describes the problem, Fichte recognized there is a "basic incoherence in the notion that there is a self that can first come to know itself through conscious reflection: in order to recognize itself in the mirror it holds up, it must first know who it is."[50] In order to explain how the self can recognize a certain object as *itself*, there must already be a prereflective form of self-knowledge. This led Fichte to argue that the first principle is not a "fact" (*Tatsache*), but an "act" (*Tathandlung*) whereby the "I" posits itself. Fichte thereby shifted the conception of self-knowledge from one of relation to one of production. The imagination plays a crucial role here, for imagination must produce an "image" (*Bild*) of the self's own productive and self-determining activity if consciousness is to recognize itself as the source of this activity.[51] As we will see, a similar theoretical structure underlies Castoriadis's rejection of Jacques Lacan's theory of specularity.

Castoriadis repeatedly emphasized a crucial divide between himself and all earlier theorists of the imagination. Namely, where they remained at the level of the subjective imagination, his theory moved between the two poles of the individual subject and the social-historical world.[52] These poles, we have seen, are irreducible, and in this sense Castoriadis was a dualist. However, insofar as the subjective and the social meet in a "nonempty intersection," this junction is itself an "institution." Institution was the key concept allowing Castoriadis to link the two dimensions of his theory of the imaginary. Moreover, it played a vital role in his conception of autonomy. A constitutive tension runs through his view of the social-historical between the "instituted imaginary" and the "instituting imaginary":

"on the one hand, given structures, "materialized" institutions and works, whether these be material or not; and, on the other hand, *that which* structures, institutes, materializes. In short, it is the union *and* the tension of instituted and of instituting society, of history made and of history in the making."[53] Every human society is self-instituted, but generally institution happens behind people's backs, a product of the anonymous activity of the collective. Societies have typically repressed their instituting activity, assigning their instituted forms to extrasocial sources.[54] The paradox of self-institution is, therefore, that generally it has instituted society as heteronomy. Autonomous society demands a deepening recognition of the self-instituting activity of society, an open-ended interrogation of the instituted forms of society, and a willingness to change those forms when they cease to serve our needs.

In Castoriadis's capacious concept of "institution," the double meaning of the word is constantly in play, referring to both social forms and the act of creating them, but, beyond obvious social institutions as in church, hospital, university, or government, institution implies a certain kind of human being, a certain kind of world, and a certain kind of interaction between world and man. Institution is, to use a phrase of Maurice Merleau-Ponty, a *mise en forme du monde*, an articulation of the world. It is very difficult to resist turning to Merleau-Ponty in trying to get some hold on Castoriadis's theory. Curiously, Castoriadis later denied that Merleau-Ponty had anything to do with his attempt to understand the phenomenon of institution.[55] There can be no doubt about Castoriadis's general familiarity with Merleau-Ponty, however. The cofounder of Socialisme ou Barbarie was, after all, Claude Lefort, one of Merleau-Ponty's most brilliant students. Castoriadis himself wrote two lengthy and detailed essays on Merleau-Ponty in the course of his lifetime.[56] Merleau-Ponty's influence seems evident in many aspects of "Marxism and Revolutionary Theory," for example, in Castoriadis's discussion of embodiment as a counter to the "point-like ego" of the Cartesian tradition, and nowhere so clearly as in the theory of institution itself. Merleau-Ponty devoted his Collège de France lectures in 1954–55 to the problem of institution.[57] Institution served Merleau-Ponty as a way to shift his critique of subject-centered philosophy from the account of individual being-in-the-world found in *The Phenomenology of Perception* to an account of the social-historical mode of human being. He replaced the notion of the "constituting subject" with an "insti-

tuted and instituting" subject, a subject that is no longer the source of
meaning and coherence, but rather finds itself in a framework or space of
meaning that transcends it, even if the subject may help to produce the
institution and certainly reactivates it through actions and speech.[58] To
illustrate institution, Merleau-Ponty quoted Goethe, who said that genius
is posthumous productivity: just as genius creates a new frame that will
provoke and guide future work, so too the institution "sets on course an
activity, a succession, initiation into a present which is productive after
it."[59] Reinforcing the significance of this for the question of the human
subject, Merleau-Ponty emphasized that there is no "break" (*coupure*) between private and public institution, and he refused to assign a causal direction when speaking of the private and the public.[60]

The overlaps with Castoriadis are patent, and it is hard to believe Castoriadis's claim that Merleau-Ponty had nothing to do with his turn to the
topic of institution. Moreover, it is strange to see Castoriadis insist in his
interview with Dews and Osborne that, "there is no idea of creation or
creativity in Merleau-Ponty, as far as I can see."[61] After all, in the lectures
of 1954–55 Merleau-Ponty spoke of revolution as a "reinstitution" and even
"reversal" of the previous institution.[62] Still more fundamentally, even in
The Phenomenology of Perception Merleau-Ponty ascribed a creative dimension to perception itself, and Castoriadis himself noted that for Merleau-Ponty perception is "instituted," even if he also believed that Merleau-Ponty's process of self-liberation from the primacy of perception had
been cut short by his premature death.[63] It may be that Castoriadis's claim
was an instance of faulty memory—in the same interview he noted candidly how difficult it is to sort out one's own intellectual autobiography. It
may also be that Merleau-Ponty's endorsement of Saussurean linguistics
and his move in the 1950s toward Lévi-Strauss as an ally in his challenge
to the philosophy of the subject may have contributed to Castoriadis's assessment. Finally, although Merleau-Ponty clearly reserved space for deliberate human action, he was sufficiently Heideggerean that in the equation
between human activity and human receptivity, between the act of institution and institution as a new unveiling of being, the latter usually dominated. Castoriadis's values thus stood in some tension with Merleau-Ponty,
and, as we shall see in chapter 4, this would become a deep source of division between him and his erstwhile Socialisme ou Barbarie comrade
Claude Lefort, who closely followed Merleau-Ponty's attempt to embed the

conscious subject in a background that it neither creates nor explicitly thematizes.

Castoriadis *Contra* Lévi-Strauss

Merleau-Ponty was in fact never Castoriadis's critical target; indeed, he always retained a respectful and appreciative tone toward the great French phenomenologist. Instead, his formidable polemical energies moved quickly from Marxism to structuralism; to defend the idea of a radical project based on the pursuit of autonomy and the power of the imaginary in the early 1960s necessarily implied a fight against structuralism. The nodal point of Castoriadis's struggle against structuralism was the status of the symbolic, which was the heart of the structuralist theory of society. Undoubtedly, matters are complicated by Castoriadis's acceptance of certain aspects of the symbolic turn most prominently represented by Claude Lévi-Strauss.[64] Yet shared terrain immediately became divided again. The structuralists were interested in the process whereby cultural systems could be dissolved and reassembled into various codes or constituent elements according to the regular operations of structural laws. Lévi-Strauss's founding gesture repeated, or perhaps exaggerated, Ferdinand Saussure's exclusion of the temporal, and his work erased all question of origin by suggesting the fiction that the symbolic order must have appeared all at once.[65] Castoriadis, by contrast, searched for an understanding of symbolic activity compatible with his vision of social-historical creativity and the struggle for autonomy. Political stakes are never distant from his interrogation. Thus the final page of "Marxism and Revolutionary Theory" reverses Marx's "thesis eleven" to insist that we interpret the world in order to change it.[66] Accordingly, his interrogation aimed at the origins of the symbolic and the processes whereby new meaning emerges. To put it in Castoriadis's own terms, the question of the symbolic is inseparable from the question of institution.

A section titled "The Institution and the Symbolic" begins by emphasizing, "Everything that is presented to us in the social-historical world is inextricably tied to the symbolic." Although things, acts, and institutions are not reducible to the symbolic, Castoriadis pointedly emphasized that none of these things would be possible outside of a symbolic network.[67]

Castoriadis's crucial departure from structuralism lies in his insistence that "something else" is involved in symbolism. "The determinations of the symbolic," he wrote, "do not exhaust its substance. An essential, and, for our purposes, decisive component remains: the imaginary component of every symbol and of every symbolism."[68] Where Lévi-Strauss defines the "symbolic function" as a combination of diacritical elements within a structure, Castoriadis identifies the "symbolic function" with the "imaginative function," because the basic capacity of symbolism is identical to that of the imagination. That is, both presuppose a capacity to see and to think in a thing something that it is not.

> The deep and obscure relations between the symbolic and the imaginary appear as soon as one reflects on the following fact: the imaginary has to use the symbolic not only to "express" itself (this is self-evident), but to "exist," to pass from the virtual to anything more than this. The most elaborate delirium like the most secret and vaguest phantasy are composed of "images," but these "images" are there to represent something else and so have a symbolic function. But, conversely, symbolism too presupposes an imaginary capacity. For it presupposes the capacity to see in a thing what it is not, to see it other than it is.[69]

Castoriadis's emphasis on the imaginary element committed him to a theory of the symbol as an expression of meaning. Castoriadis saw that Lévi-Strauss was, by contrast, increasingly tempted to reduce institutions to symbolic networks in which "meaning is always the result of the combination of elements which are not in themselves meaningful."[70]

He warned against this tendency to do away with the question of content, to eliminate the reference to the signified.

> Institutions [cannot] be understood simply as symbolic networks. Institutions do form a symbolic network, but this network, by definition, refers to something other than symbolism. Every purely symbolical interpretation of institutions immediately opens the following questions: Why *this* system of symbols and not another? What are the *meanings* conveyed by the symbols, the system of signifieds to which the system of signifiers refers?[71]

This emphasis on the symbol's expressive power did not force Castoriadis to regress behind the insights of the "linguistic turn." He flatly rejected the idea of "expression" in the sense of a preexisting constituted meaning coming into form in language or other symbolic media. There is no "pure thought," but, just as equally, there is no "pure sign"; thinking and speaking are inseparable, and the "philosophy of a sovereign constituting consciousness" is just as mythic as "a structuralist or semiotic ideology, which takes account only of collections of arbitrary characteristics from which a combinatory would extract some will-o'-the-wisp meaning."[72] As Hans Joas has said, even as Castoriadis aimed to overcome the philosophy of consciousness, he also retained the seriousness of the struggle to express meaning—the process of "articulation"—as crucial to the task of securing "the possibility of novelty and creation against the view of a linguistically closed universe."[73]

Castoriadis's theory opens toward a hermeneutic impulse absent in Lévi-Strauss. Hence, wrote Castoriadis, "Understanding, and even grasping, the symbolism of a society is grasping the significations that it carries. These significations appear only as they are carried by signifying structures; but this does not mean that they can be reduced to these, that they result from them in a univocal manner, or, finally, that they are determined by them."[74] This position brings Castoriadis's theoretical statements back into communication with his political commitment to the transformation of society. For even though people communicate and cooperate in a symbolic milieu, this symbolism is itself *created*.

> History exists only in and through "language" (all sorts of languages), but history gives itself this language, constitutes it and transforms it. To be unaware of this aspect of the question is to continue to consider the multiplicity of symbolic systems (and hence institutional systems) and their succession as blunt facts about which there is nothing to say (and nothing to be done), to eliminate the prime historical question concerning the genesis of meaning, the production of new systems of signifieds and signifiers.[75]

"Marxism and Revolutionary Theory" attempts to conceptualize the symbolic constitution of society without lapsing into the polarity that defines much of later twentieth-century thought: the image of a fully present,

conscious subject, on the one side, and the image of the subject as an
empty intersection traversed by the traffic of signs, on the other. To bring
the imaginary and the symbolic into close communication, without collapsing the one into the other, is to acknowledge the power and indispensability of symbolic forms while preserving an element of individual and
social life that intertwines with symbolic networks but is not identical
with them. To insist on this principle of difference, which is not merely
the diacritical difference emerging from structure, is to insist on the open
and flexible relationship between our signifying systems and ourselves as
meaning-creating subjects, to insist equally on the role of symbols in determining domains of social life and the capacity for freedom and impro-
visation. At the same time, Castoriadis avoided two possible relapses.
First, he was attentive to the process whereby meaning gains clarity and
form in the process of articulation. There is no presymbolic meaning, but
there are representations, affects, and intentions that are not reducible to
the symbolic either in their form or origin. Second, while he thus avoided
positing a fully present subject, he also avoided a simple idea of referentiality. Symbols *refer*, but in contrast to Durkheim or the Anglo-American
functionalists, they do not refer to "social reality," the "natural world" or
functional needs. Rather, they refer to imaginary significations, meanings
that themselves are not reducible to "reality," but are, rather, active in the
institution of *social* reality.

This way of thinking about symbols circles back to an important distinction between *expressive* and *semiotic* theories of symbolism or, to use
Bourdieu's terms, between symbolic systems as "structuring structures"
and symbolic systems as "structured structures."[76] We can take up this
distinction in yet another formulation, that of Karl-Siegbert Rehberg from
his long introduction to the volume *Institutionalität und Symbolisierung*.
Rehberg distinguishes between *Präsenzsymbolik* (symbolic of presence) and
the *Zeichentheoretische Tradition* (semiotic tradition). In the first tradition
the symbol is not merely a sign; rather, it makes the absent thing present,
incarnates it. Typically, this is the idea of the symbol as the disclosure or
revelation of a different, higher order; it is linked most closely with the German Romantics and their enchanted vision of the world. By contrast, the
semiotic tradition belongs to the disenchanted, rational world. "Today,"
writes Rehberg, "the arbitrariness of signs and symbolizing complexes is
near to us; distant is the symbol's magical double existence as presence of

something other, as well as its authoritative structure. Compared to the older system—based on Ur-texts and religious conviction—of referral to the invisible, the doctrine of signs proves itself more modern."[77]

Castoriadis's approach shows the inadequacy of Rehberg's division. His distinction between symbols and imaginary significations underscores that symbols stand in close relationship to social meanings that are themselves not symbols but, rather, the stuff of symbolization. This is, admittedly, a difficult position. If one is to avoid a regress that is symbolic all the way down, one must accept that the imaginary presents a dimension of obscurity that may be significant, even constitutive, but is like the dark navel of a dream described by Freud as the limit of dream interpretation. Castoriadis himself recognized the difficulty of trying to grasp imaginary significations as such, when their accessibility is so entwined with symbols, and their own "mode of being" is a "mode of non-being."[78] Yet if one is to develop anything like a hermeneutic of social symbols and, even more importantly, a theory based on the emergence of novel meaning, it seems necessary to embrace a theory in which symbols refer to something other than more symbols in a symbolic matrix. However, because Castoriadis wished to break from the givenness of "reality," the primacy of perception, and the hold of functionalist rationality, the system of referral must open toward things that are not *there*. Hence, Castoriadis's theory of the symbolic returns to the dimension of *presence* dismissed as unmodern by Rehberg and, beyond him, figures like Walter Benjamin, Paul de Man, and Judith Butler.

One already detects this move in "Marxism and Revolutionary Theory," but it becomes fully explicit in the later half of *The Imaginary Institution of Society*. There one of the most frequent terms is the verb *presentify*, along with its noun form *presentification*. Toward the close of the book, *incarnation* also enters the discussion. Alluding to Durkheim's terminology, Castoriadis wrote: "It was found necessary to affirm that social facts are not things. In truth, what is to be said is that social things are not "things"; they are social things and *these particular* things only inasmuch as they "incarnate" or, better, figure and presentify, social significations."[79] The symbolic network thus has a vital relationship to the invisible, making it present and incarnate. Castoriadis noted pointedly that Marx revealed an awareness of this in his analysis of commodity fetishism, but whereas Marx thought this "hieroglyphic" character belonged strictly to the capitalist mode and would evaporate with the advent of socialism, Castoriadis saw it as a general feature of the social-historical world.[80] Yet in contrast to Romantic theory, Castoriadis's hieroglyphic refers not to what Novalis called a "numinous" realm, but to a magma of significations that forms "an indefinite skein of interminable *referrals to something other* than (than what would appear to be stated directly)."[81] Moreover, "presence" no longer implies a quasi-theological *manifestation* of the absent. Rather, Castoriadis mobilizes the language of phenomenology for a description of the act whereby consciousness spontaneously makes an image or mental object present. For this phenomenological terminology, one could go back at least as far as Kasimir Twardowski's *On the Content and Object of Presentations* (1894) and Husserl's *Philosophy of Arithmetic* (1891) with its distinctions between "intuitive" and "symbolic" presentations and its claim that the latter depends on the former.

Within the phenomenological tradition, "présentation" is the standard French translation of *Vorstellung*, not "représentation," as in the standard French title of Schopenhauer's *Die Welt als Wille und Vorstellung*.[82] Castoriadis showed himself fully aware of the subtleties, even if in the following passage he reintroduces some confusion by using the term *représentation* instead of *présentation* in the final sentence:

> The representative flux is, makes itself, as self-alteration, the incessant emergence of the other in and through the positing (*Vor-stellung*) of images or figures, an imaging which unfolds, brings into being and constantly actualizes what appears retrospectively, to reflective analysis, as the pre-existing conditions of its possibility. . . . Obviously, some representations are: for example, perceptive representations, called perceptions, the putting-into-images of . . . (something about which nothing can be said except in and through another representation). Here, it will be forever impossible absolutely to separate what comes from *that which is put* into images and *what puts* into images, the radical imagination, the representative flux. In the same way, representation (*Vorstellung*) is not re-presentation (*Vertretung*); it is not there for something else or in place of something else, to re-present it a second time.[83]

Castoriadis clearly realized that such formulations risked falling into "fictions of a thought without language, a transcendental language or language as condition external to thinking."[84] Here, again, it is important to repeat that even if Castoriadis denied the *identity* of meaning and forms of representation, he did not believe we have access to meaning outside our modes of presentation (*Vorstellung*) and re-presentation (*Vertretung*). This mutual inherence finds its clearest articulation in the following:

> Reciprocally, social imaginary significations exist in and through "things"—objects and individuals—which presentify and figure them, directly or indirectly, immediately or mediately. They can exist only through their "incarnation," their "inscription," their presentation and figuration in and through a network of individuals and objects, which they "inform"—these are at once concrete entities and instances or copies of types, of *eide*—individuals and objects which exist in general and are as they are only through these significations.[85]

Far from being unmodern, as Rehberg suggests, the notion of a *Präsenz-symbolik,* scrubbed clean of the mystical tones of Romanticism, reveals itself to be deeply attached to the modern tradition of phenomenology. Moreover, phenomenologists like Eugen Fink and Sartre and the militant philosopher Castoriadis suggest that the concepts of making present, bodying forth, and incarnating are difficult to avoid and perhaps even necessary when the goal is a theory of imagination that takes seriously the possibility of the new.

Starting Points

"Marxism and Revolutionary Theory" represented a dramatic shift in tone and conceptualization measured against Castoriadis's earlier *Socialisme ou Barbarie* writings. Yet, as he reported, striking as his innovations were, they rapidly evolved from "arrival points" to "starting points." If we compare the 1964–65 sections of *The Imaginary Institution of Society* to the sections first published in 1975, at least two major developments become apparent.

First, Castoriadis significantly deepened the ontological dimension of his thinking. "Marxism and Revolutionary Theory" rests on a critique of determinist models, but determinism's opposite, indeterminacy, is asserted rather than analyzed; even more important, little attention is paid to what kind of world *permits* societies to *institute* themselves locally as specific forms of human association and articulations. Without an answer to that question, Castoriadis would either lapse into subjective idealism or rest upon an untenable dichotomy in which the human freedom to create what the individual or collective imagination presents is blissfully unhindered by a world governed by its own laws. In short, he realized that he needed a more supple conception of the relations between the order of human significations and practices and the order of the world. A serious engagement with the philosophy and history of science during the later 1960s, as well as work on language, human activity, and technology, led Castoriadis to claim that the world is not uniformly determined. Indeed, he speculated that the world is in "fragments," and he suggested a "hitherto unsuspected stratification of [being] . . . an organization of layers that in part adhere together, in terms of an endless succession in depth of layers of being that are always organized, but never completely, always articulated together, but never fully."[86] Being is locally organizable or determinable, but, overall, being is chaos, abyss, and groundlessness.

He based this argument in part on the fact that science evidently has a *history* in the "strong sense": on the one hand, there has been a succession of physical theories that are not simply diachronically cumulative but are instead marked by ruptures and discontinuities and, on the other hand, as in the classic case of the transition from Newtonianism to twentieth-century physics, successive theories have proven capable of being both "false" in respect to the criteria of later theories and "true" in respect to their ongoing ability to account for significant classes of phenomena. Along with evidence from twentieth-century disciplines like physics and mathematics, which suggested a breakdown in conventional determinist models, he also drew support from examinations of human practices and technologies. Within this new vision of a fragmented and stratified world, Castoriadis hypothesized that science, all human doing, and, for that matter, all living things are possible because they exist in "parasitizing, or in ontological symbiosis with, a stratum of total being that is locally ensemblistic-identity," the latter being Castoriadis's neologism for determinate categories based on identity and difference and functional-instrumental goals.[87] The world thus *lends* itself to our descriptions, categories, and actions, and human creation "makes arbitrary use simultaneously of the rational make-up of the world *and* of its indeterminate interstices."[88] This ontological account furnished Castoriadis with an original way to argue for the freedom of human meaning and action vis-à-vis the "real" without giving up on the *realist* moment that vexes purely constructivist accounts.

Incidentally, this effort to avoid subjective idealism points to yet another way in which Castoriadis's project drew inspiration from Fichte, whose own "realist" moment has attracted increasing attention of late.[89] This refers to Fichte's description of the ego's encounters with a world whose capacity to resist human intentions can never be fully overcome; the recalcitrance of the world is the source of the *Anstoß*, the "check" and/ or "stimulus" that the thing-in-itself presents to the ego's activity. Castoriadis suggests something similar when he wrote in the latter half of *The Imaginary Institution of Society* that the world is neither devoured nor created by human significations. The world—the real—lends itself to signification, but it is also "an inexhaustible supply of otherness, and . . . an irreducible challenge to every established signification."[90] The Fichtean element becomes entirely clear in a remarkable text from 1986, "The State of the Subject Today." There Castoriadis began not with the conscious ego but with the organism in an effort to delineate the dynamics of closure and openness at work in the constitution of the individual entity. Speaking of the *X* that is the outside of the "for-itself" of the organism, Castoriadis wrote: "all we can say about it is that it creates a shock (*Anstoss*, to take up Fichte's term) which sets in motion the formative (imaging/imagining, presenting, and relating) capacities of the living being."[91] The Fichtean *Anstoß* must be understood as a companion to Castoriadis's use of a Freudian term, *Anlehnung*, to signify the way in which both the psyche and society "lean on" or "borrow" from a reality—whether in the form of nature or the organic basis of the psyche—that transcends both. Were there no such relationship, we would never meet anything but our own representations, an omnipotence of thought reserved for the psychotic.

The second major development after 1965, and the one that is of greatest relevance to the present discussion, is a marked turn toward psychoanalysis. Freudian influences are, of course, obvious in "Marxism and Revolutionary Theory." Clearly, Castoriadis was reading seriously in Freudian literature by the early 1960s, and he had entered analysis with Dr. Irène Perrier-

Roublef in 1960.[92] But the theory of the imaginary he elaborated in "Marxism and Revolutionary Theory" owes at least as much, if not more, to phenomenology and German idealism as it does to psychoanalysis. Indeed, although in 1964–65 Castoriadis already insisted on the nonidentity of the social imaginary and the radical imagination of the individual psyche, his ideas about the psyche were in fact relatively undeveloped. There is hardly any discussion of the dynamics of the psyche and how they might support his claims for the centrality of imagination; moreover, Castoriadis offers little on what actually happens in what he later called the "non-empty intersection" between the social-historical and the psychical. In search of a more adequate theory, Castoriadis turned to a much more serious study of psychoanalysis. And that meant, inevitably, a reckoning with Jacques Lacan. For, in 1960s France, Lacan's concepts of the symbolic and the imaginary provided the dominant framework for posing the question of the relationship between private fantasy and representations, on the one side, and social meanings, on the other. With Castoriadis's psychoanalytic turn, his campaign against structuralism shifted decisively from Lévi-Strauss to Lacan. Where his critique of Lévi-Strauss aimed to overcome the exclusion of the imaginary from the symbolic, his critique of Lacan attempted to preserve the imaginary as a dynamic productive force against Lacan's reduction of the imaginary to a structure of capture, fixation, and compensatory fantasy.

Considering the fact that he became an intransigent opponent of Lacan by the later 1960s, it is striking that Castoriadis referred to Lacan approvingly in the pages of "Marxism and Revolutionary Theory." In a section exploring the individual dimension of autonomy, Castoriadis tied his discussion to Freud's famous maxim: "Where Id was, Ego shall come to be." This passage essentially embraces Freud's idea that autonomy entails the establishment of conscious rule over the unconscious; in other words, autonomy is the struggle for "self-legislation" or "self-regulation" against heteronomous regulation by another, in this case, the unconscious itself. Here Castoriadis cited Lacan approvingly: "The unconscious is the discourse of the Other," which Castoriadis immediately linked to the infiltration of social significations into the unconscious. "The essential characteristic of the discourse of the Other," he continued, "is its relation to the *imaginary.*" A footnote added in 1975 acknowledged that in 1964–65 he had not yet adequately distinguished his own concept of the imaginary from Lacan's. For his argument here is that the subject is ruled by an imaginary that assumes the function of defining for the subject both reality and desire. The subject thus "takes himself or herself to be something he or she is not (or is not necessarily)," a misrecognition that consequently distorts the self, others, and the world.[93] This formulation, with its implication of an authentic self to be discovered beyond ideology and the dictates of the unconscious, is one that Castoriadis himself would greatly nuance as his idea of autonomy evolved. Moreover, although he aligned this remark with Lacan, it was in fact already at odds with Lacan. For Castoriadis's commitment to the "project of autonomy" pitted misrecognition against the ongoing struggle for autonomy, whereas for Lacan, to overcome misrecognition yielded a sharper insight into "the radical heteronomy that Freud's discovery shows gaping within man."[94] This marked a profound difference between Castoriadis and Lacan that rapidly came into focus as Castoriadis delved more deeply into psychoanalysis.

Castoriadis entered the world of French psychoanalysis in a particularly fraught phase of its rancorous history. Ever the enfant terrible, Jacques Lacan was expelled from the Société psychanalytique de Paris in 1936, and during the 1950s the International Psychoanalytic Association made various attempts to expel him because of his unorthodox training practices. That conflict came to a head in 1963 when the French Psychoanalytic Society, formed in 1953 by analysts driven out of the Société psychanalytique de Paris, removed Lacan from its list of approved training analysts. In reward, the international association recognized the French Psychoanalytic Society as the only authorized psychoanalytic organization in France. Lacan responded in June 1964 by creating the École Freudienne de Paris. Lacan transferred his weekly seminars from Sainte-Anne Hospital to the École Normale Supérieure, and there the medical people in his audience dwindled even as the ranks of philosophers, anthropologists, linguists, and literary critics swelled. The École Freudienne was itself to be a psychoanalytic society with a difference: no analytic hierarchy, no closed circle of analysts, but rather "a meeting place for the freest possible contact between psychoanalysts and members of other disciplines."[95] Lacan's excommunication and his dramatic entry into the broader intellectual milieus of Paris ensured him what Elisabeth Roudinesco calls a "paradoxical position, at once marginal and essential, to French academic life."[96]

Castoriadis was intimately related to these events. In 1964 he became a member of the École Freudienne, and his archive contains invitations to attend Lacan's seminar as well as notes on lectures by Lacan, André Green, Serge Leclaire, and Piera Aulagnier. Aulagnier, who married Castoriadis in 1968, was analyzed by Lacan between 1955 and 1961.[97] She had been a strong advocate of Lacan during the International Psychoanalytic Association's campaign against him, searching for a strategy of reconciliation and, when that failed, supporting the new Lacanian school. However, she and a number of colleagues soon became restive over what they perceived to be a growing authoritarianism within Lacan's circle. When Lacan introduced the so-called "pass" in 1967, wherein analysts in training had to submit to an elaborate interrogation before a panel presided over by Lacan himself, Aulagnier and her allies fell into open opposition. In 1969 Aulagnier and several other disaffected Lacanians formed the Organisation psychanalytique de langue Française, otherwise known as the Quatrième Groupe. In reaction against Lacan's authoritarian dictates, the group claimed a minimal ground of shared convictions, but above all it championed a pluralistic approach to theory and practice as well as an open institutional structure. Though Castoriadis was never a central figure in the group, his influence is manifest in its history. For example, a 1977 program urged its members to read his essay "Psychoanalysis, project and elucidation" on the subject of institution.[98] In turn, the circle of apostates from the École Freudienne clearly helped to shape Castoriadis's animus toward Lacan and the refinement of his theory of the imagination. His first extended discussion of psychoanalysis, the 1968 essay "Epilogomena to a Theory of the Soul Which Has Been Presented as a Science," was published just before the conflict produced an open schism in the École Freudienne. And for years there was a fruitful exchange of ideas between Castoriadis and Aulagnier; even after their marriage ended in a rancorous divorce, Castoriadis readily acknowledged his debt to her.[99]

In numerous works beginning with "Epilegomena to a Theory of the Soul," Castoriadis articulated the crucial difference between his and Lacan's conceptions of the imaginary, and the difference bore directly on questions of the human subject, creativity, agency, and self-transformation. Although Castoriadis and Lacan both endorsed the "decentering" of the ego implied by Freud's "discovery" of the unconscious, and in this sense both opposed American ego psychology, they did so in radically different ways. Lacan formed his core ideas on the ego in the 1930s by combining the work of the older French psychoanalyst Henri Wallon on the role of mirroring in the formation of the infant's sense of identity with Alexandre Kojève's Hegelian ideas about the role of a dialectical struggle for recognition in the development of subjectivity.[100] In his famous account of the mirror stage, Lacan depicted the ego as an imaginary construct produced through specular relations. The human infant overcomes its "motor incapacity and nursling dependence" by identifying itself with the image of corporeal wholeness presented by the "mirror," both the literal reflection and the constitutive gaze of others. The fixation of the psyche upon the image of bodily wholeness "situates the agency known as the ego, prior to its social determination, in a fictional direction."[101] The reflected image of its own body gives the infant its first object of desire, but in the form of an alienating desire for the other, desire for what is missing, for the lack which structures the unconscious. The mirror stage thus sets into motion a libidinal dynamism that operates within the field of tension between fantasies of mastery and/or identification with the object of desire and the impossibility of such union or control. "In the order of the imaginary," Lacan wrote, "alienation is constitutive. Alienation is the imaginary as such."[102] The "deflection of the specular *I* into the social *I*," that is, the transition into the Symbolic Order, demands that the hold of the imaginary be relaxed; but, as Richard Boothby notes, "Even under the influence of the most far-reaching effects of maturation and sublimation, the psychic organization remains at least partially oriented by the structure of the ego and can therefore never fully escape the orbit of the imaginary."[103]

According to Lacan, the emergence of desire and, indeed, of the ego rests on an "exteriority"—the image of the self as other—which he insisted is "certainly more constitutive than constituted."[104] Behind the imaginary construction of the ego through the other, Lacan detected an emptiness, an "ontological lack," the constantly shifting eye of a swirl of desires, which imaginary fantasies of wholeness and plenitude attempt to cover over or "suture." In Castoriadis's view, Lacan thus emptied out the interior of the psyche itself. "That which I call the imaginary," wrote Castoriadis in the 1975 preface to *The Imaginary Institution of Society*,

has nothing to do with the representations currently circulating under this heading. In particular, it has nothing to do with that which is presented as "imaginary" by certain currents in psychoanalysis: namely, the "specular" which is obviously only an image *of* and a reflected image. . . . The imaginary does not come from the image in the mirror or from the gaze of the other. Instead, the "mirror" itself and its possibility, and the other as mirror, are the works of the imaginary, which is creation *ex nihilo*.[105]

As Castoriadis underscored in 1986, "We are speaking here, of course, of the radical imagination: not the capacity to have 'images' (or be seen) in a 'mirror' but the capacity to posit that which is not, to see in something that which is not there."[106] In thus opposing Lacan's theory of specularity, Castoriadis pursued a strategy uncannily similar to Fichte's attempt to get beyond K. L. Reinhold's belief that the self first comes to know itself through conscious reflection. Recalling our earlier discussion of Fichte's reasoning, if the self is to be recognized in the mirror it holds up, it must first know who it is.[107] In similar manner to Fichte's shift from viewing self-consciousness as a fact (*Tatsache*) to viewing it as an act (*Tathandlung*), Castoriadis hypothesized that "psychical life can exist only if the psyche is this original capacity to make representations arise, and, 'at the start,' a 'first' representation which must, in a certain manner, contain within itself the possibility of organizing all representations."[108]

Although Castoriadis's commitment to a *realist* moment leads him to emphasize that the psyche, like society, leans on the "real," he insisted that the originary capacity to give psychical representation to the drives—as well as the perceptual flux of representations, affects, and desires—cannot be traced exhaustively to the "real." Castoriadis elaborated this claim for the rupture between the psyche and the real by introducing the idea of the "psychical monad." In a description resembling Freud's account of "primary narcissism," the monad in its primal phase is enclosed in a self-referring circuit, dominated by the pleasure principle, not distinguishing between represented desire and satisfaction.[109] The monadic core begins to break up under the pressure of bodily needs and the presence of another human being (in the typical case the mother). This socialization of the psyche involves "essentially imposing separation on it. For the psychical monad, this amounts to a violent break, forced by its 'relation' to others, more precisely, by the invasion of others as others, by means of which a 'reality' is constituted for the subject."[110] Even after the infant has become a "social individual" for whom social meanings have replaced purely private ones, the initial monadic pole continues to exert a powerful "tendency towards unification" over the psyche's representations.[111] The psyche, Castoriadis wrote, is its own lost unity, and unconscious fantasy interminably reconstitutes this initial world "if not in its now inaccessible untouched unity, at least in its characteristics of closure, mastery, simultaneity and the absolute congruence between intention, representation, and affect."[112] In the more socialized, conscious layers of the psyche, the unifying drive of the psychical monad operates as a power of synthesis creating the "relative unity of experience."[113]

The theory of the monadic core served various functions for Castoriadis, but one of the most vital was surely that it gave him a better way to theorize the relationship between the imaginary and rationality. In his 1964–65 formulation, he sometimes seemed close to drawing a division between reason and the imaginary. Yet toward the close of "Marxism and Revolutionary Theory," he made a highly suggestive claim regarding the beliefs of "ancient or archaic society": "This imaginary does not merely hold the function of the rational, it is already a form of the latter and contains it in an initial and infinitely fertile indistinction; in it, one can start to distinguish the elements presupposed by our own rationality."[114] He seemed to have in mind something like the primitive classification that Durkheim and Mauss had described as a propaedeutic to our own activity of rational ordering. Through the theory of the psychical monad, Castoriadis could shed the lingering implications of an evolutionary development and instead theorize a dialectical relationship between rationality and the imaginary in the individual subject. Thus the same processes that could yield the madness of the psychotic could also yield the creations of reason:

> One does not put reason where it should be, and, what is even more serious one cannot reach a reasonable attitude with respect to reason. . . . If one refuses to see in it something other than, of course, but *also*, an avatar of the madness of unification. Whether it is the philosopher or the scientist, the final and dominant intention—to find across difference and otherness, manifestations of the *same* . . . is based on the same schema of final, that is to say, primal unity.[115]

Castoriadis's theory of the radical imagination inverts the Lacanian imaginary, transferring the imaginary from the constituting operation of the exterior image to the productive dynamism of the psyche itself. Confronting the ontological lack that Lacan detected behind the imaginary construction of the ego, Castoriadis asked, "How can we speak of an object that is lacking if the psyche has not first posited this object as desirable? How can an object be desirable if it has not been invested (cathected), and how can it be invested if it has never been 'present' in any way?"[116] Castoriadis sought to replace *lack* as an ontological structure with the surplus, the plenitude, of the radical imagination, which posits lack, including the monadic self as a missing object of desire. Castoriadis's theory attempted to answer questions begged by Lacan's specular theory of the imaginary: How does the psyche register the image as itself? How does the image become effective in psychical life?

Castoriadis maintained that the premise of an originary capacity that links drives to psychical representations is inherently necessary in the Freudian problematic, but Freud's failure to make it explicit reflects a deeper reluctance to thematize the imagination as such. Although Castoriadis credited Freud for articulating the dynamics of the unconscious and posing the crucial question of how the initial psyche makes the transition from total self-absorption to socialized "normalcy," he criticized Freud for pressing his discovery into the positivist mold of the late nineteenth century and he vigorously attacked later ego psychology for its attempt to domesticate the "scandal of the Unconscious." This led Castoriadis to praise Lacan for shaking the psychoanalytic establishment's ossified "positivist" self-understanding. Significantly, however, Castoriadis argued that Lacan reached an impasse precisely because he continued to adhere to a traditional scientific understanding of psychoanalysis. Hence, Castoriadis wrote that the Lacanians could not cope with the tension between the irreducibly singular individual, who is psychoanalysis's object, and the general concepts and categories that analysis must necessarily deploy. Defeated by this tension, Lacanians conceive psychoanalysis only as a "projection, phantasm, delirium"—in other words, a defensive formation of the imaginary—insofar as it takes seriously the individual or as a "science" that establishes its rigor by exposing the individual as a product of the play of elements within a structure.[117]

If Castoriadis's theory of the imaginary inverts Lacan's, the same is true of his account of the socialization of the psyche and the torsions produced by that process. For Lacan, socialization is the (always incomplete) transition from the imaginary to the symbolic; for Castoriadis, it is the (always incomplete) entry of the individual psyche into a shared domain of social imaginary significations. Writing of Lacan's conception of the subject, Malcolm Bowie observes, "the subject is no *thing* at all and can be grasped only as a set of tensions, or mutations, or dialectical upheavals within a continuous, intentional, future-directed process."[118] In opposition to this perpetual coming-into-being, the ego is the sum of imaginary resistances and misrecognitions that attempt to stabilize and unify identity. This conception of the tension between the subject and the ego points to a contrast fundamental to Lacan, which Bowie puts succinctly: "Where the [Symbolic] is characterized by difference, disjunction, and displacement, the [Imaginary] is a seeking for identity or resemblance. . . . Wherever a false identification is to be found—within the subject, or between one subject and another, or between subject and thing—there the Imaginary holds sway."[119] Where Lacan proposed a discontinuity between the imaginary and the symbolic, Castoriadis deepened the view, already articulated in his 1964–65 critique of Lévi-Strauss, that the imaginary and the symbolic are entwined, though not identical, as are the psychical imagination and the social-historical imagination.

This image of an irreducible gap between the psychical and the social-historical led Habermas to complain that Castoriadis's theory of the psychical monad establishes a "metaphysical opposition" between psyche and society, which thereby fails to "provide us with a figure for the mediation between the individual and society."[120] Castoriadis countered this charge aggressively: "One should ask oneself, rather, what metaphysics is hidden behind the idea that every affirmation of irreducibility is 'metaphysical.' The answer is obvious: a unitary and reductionist metaphysics."[121] In fact, however, Castoriadis offered a more nuanced articulation of the relationship between psyche and society than he himself sometimes suggested. "There is no 'human individual,'" he wrote. "There is a psyche that is socialized, and in this socialization, in the final result, there is almost nothing individual in the true sense of the term."[122] Consistent with the vision of the social-historical world as a sui generis domain he had formulated in the late 1950s, he insisted that socialization involves the psyche's access to and accession to a "mode of being which the psyche could never give rise to starting from itself."[123] This is a "violent" process directed at the "internally wish-generated stream of representations and affects."[124] This language of violent imposition has misled some commentators, notably Peter Dews, to see between the social order of imaginary significations and the flux of representations that form the core of the individual psyche a permanent conflict that seems at odds with Castoriadis's political optimism.[125]

It is important to see that this imposition is also an introjection. For the psychical monad encounters not only obstacles and prohibitions to its own fantasy but also new "organizational schemata" that are enlisted in the psyche's activity. This is the double message suggested by Castoriadis's version of "sublimation"; he defined it as the "process by means of which the psyche is forced to replace its 'own' or 'private' objects of cathexis (including its own 'image' for itself), with objects that exist and are valid in and through their social institution, and out of these create for itself 'causes,' 'means,' or 'supports' of pleasure." This process implies the "psyche itself as imagination, namely as the possibility of positing this for that," even as it also implies "the social-historical as the social imaginary, namely as the positing, in and through the institution, of forms and significations which the psyche as such is absolutely incapable of bringing into existence."[126] Psychical processes are codetermined by the social, yet the psyche's entry into and participation in the social, in "language" and "*doing* as social activity," does not erase the monadic core of the psyche, but satisfies or does not satisfy psychical needs, as the case may be. In place of Habermas's desired "mediation" and in place of a "metaphysical opposition" between psyche and society, we find once again Castoriadis's image of a nonempty intersection.

The opposition between Habermas and Castoriadis returns us to Lacan; as numerous scholars have noted, for all their differences, both Lacan and Habermas converge in their "linguistification" of the unconscious.[127] Lacan's famous claim that the "Unconscious is structured like a language" links it to the constituting order of the symbolic. Of course, this claim is notoriously enigmatic. It could mean that the unconscious has a structure *like* language, in which case the unconscious would itself be a closed order operating according to laws of combination of differential elements. Or it might mean that the symbolic allows the articulation of the unconscious through a kind of translation. As Lacan wrote, "Like the unnatural figures of the boat on the roof, or the man with a comma for a head, which are expressly mentioned by Freud, dream images are to be taken only on the basis of their value as signifiers, that is, only insofar as they allow us to spell out the 'proverb' presented by the oneiric rebus."[128] Or, it could mean, as Boothby suggests, that the symbolic volatilizes the imaginary, confronting the fixations of the ego with the displacements and discontinuities of language. Against this penetration of the unconscious by the symbolic, Castoriadis insisted on what could be described as a more orthodox Freudian division between thing representations and word representations, between primary and secondary processes. In the unconscious, he argued, "there is no representation of words as *words* that would convey some sort of rationality; there is not, and cannot be, any symbolism, anything symbolic."[129]

In insisting so categorically upon a nonlinguistic and hence nonsocial psychical core, Castoriadis adopted quite an extreme position vis-à-vis a problem that became particularly pressing to many on the French left after the disappointment of May 1968, namely, how society penetrates and reproduces a socially normative individual.[130] Sherry Turkle writes that whereas many on the left prior to 1968 had still denigrated structuralism as overly deterministic, May 1968 lent credence to structuralism's claim that man is inhabited by the signifier rather than freely creating it: "What had seemed reactionary in structuralism now seemed merely realistic."[131] Lacan's influence found its way into the women's movement (Antionette Fouque, Luce Irigaray, Michèle Montrelay), French antipsychiatry (Félix Guattari, Gilles Deleuze), French Maoism (Jacques-Alain Miller, Judith Miller, Lacan's daughter), as well as textual theory (Philippe Sollers, Julia Kristeva).[132] Yet, if Lacan's depiction of a symbolic network enveloping the individual thus reshaped the sensibility of many left-leaning French intellectuals after 1968, the abiding leftist investment in progressive change produced a certain kind of schizophrenia: Precisely the omnipresence of the symbolic order prompted ideas of total escape, a leap into another way of being and speaking. Given what the failure of 1968 seemed to show, that the powers of the symbolic order could recuperate and reabsorb even the most radical of emancipatory impulses, the idea of revolutionary change had to migrate to a neverland bounded by its own pristine impossibility. This hardened into an impasse what Peter Starr defines as Lacan's "tragicomic" politics, which occupied a "vacillatory" space "where the prospect of a partial release from self-division intersects with the full awareness of all that opposes human redemption."[133] Lacan was drawn to the left

out of respect for the truth of revolutionary desire, yet he criticized emancipatory ideology for its pursuit of an impossible happiness; and he extended
his criticism of the demand for the unity of the "One" (truth, meaning,
system, ego) to political revolution. In this pursuit of an imaginary wholeness, he saw only the inevitable repetition, the specular doubling, of
power's own monological impulse to unify. He saw in every transgression
in the direction of *jouissance* an enforcement of the Law that opposes, yet
defines, transgression.[134]

Castoriadis's writings against the avant-garde styles of thought in the
1970s recognized clearly what Peter Starr later described. For example, in
a 1977 piece titled "The Diversionists," Castoriadis argued that structuralism arose as an evacuation of "living history" and political activism. It
could hardly be more opposed to the forces that erupted in 1968, he insisted. The waves of French theory that commanded the stage in the 1970s
completely sidestepped what Castoriadis regarded as the main challenge
posed by the events of 1968, namely how this explosion of political activism might go beyond its initial stage without losing its creativity, how this
"fantastic deployment of autonomous activity" might be able to "institute
lasting collective organizations that express it without drying it up or con-
fiscating it."[135] Castoriadis formulated this position even more forcefully
in a 1986 critique of Alain Renaut and Luc Ferry's book *La Pensée 68*. "It is
strange," he wrote,

> to hear people label today "68 thought" a set of authors who saw
> their fashionableness increase after the *failure* of May '68 and of the
> other movements of the time and who did not play any role even in
> the vaguest sense of a "sociological" preparation of the movement,
> both because their ideas were totally unknown to the participants
> and because these ideas were diametrically opposed to the partici-
> pants' implicit and explicit aspirations.

He went on,

> The effacement of the subject, the death of man, and the other asi-
> nine conceptions contained in what I have called the French Ideol-
> ogy had already been in circulation for some years. Their inescap-
> able corollary, the death of politics, could be made explicit without

much effort. . . . It is clearly incompatible with the very activities in which the participants in the movements of the sixties, including May '68, were engaged.[136]

Far from spurring revolt, he argued, the French ideology provided legitimation for "withdrawal, renunciation, noncommitment, or . . . a punctilious and measured commitment."[137]

Castoriadis also saw clearly the impasse structure that Peter Starr describes as one of the key features of 1970s French thought. Indeed, it is stunning that Castoriadis recognized this within weeks of May 1968 in his contribution to *La Brèche*, the volume he co-authored with Claude Lefort and Edgar Morin.[138] As he conceded, the upheavals of May speak to the dimension of *failure* in modern radical movements, the "enormous difficulty involved in extending critique of the existing order in practical and positive ways, the impossibility of assuming the goal of an autonomy that is at once individual and social by establishing collective self-governance." This failure has haunted modern revolutions; but Castoriadis cautioned that the failure has rarely been total. Like the Paris Commune, he predicted that May '68 is likely to leave deep marks on French mentalities and patterns of political behavior. And then, in an observation that anticipates the structure in 1970s thought described by Peter Starr, Castoriadis detected a tendency to overlook this historical remainder because the modern political imaginary is wedded to antinomic models of power and politics that fantasize either a leap into an unheralded kingdom of freedom or a fall back into the oppressive structures of the past.[139]

Castoriadis's corrective to this pathology of the revolutionary imagination points also to the most nuanced aspect of his campaign against the legacy of Lévi-Strauss and Lacan. Here, for all the fiery polemics of his attacks on Lacan, Althusser, Lévi-Strauss, Barthes, Foucault, and post-1968 currents like the philosophers of desire and the new philosophers, Castoriadis actually argued for a kind of middle ground, which equally rejected the sovereign ego of classical modern philosophy, the "lightning bolt" freedom of Sartrean humanism, and the "death of man" discourse. We encounter an exemplary instance of this middle ground stance in Castoriadis's writings on psychoanalysis, where he rejected the identification of psychoanalysis with science, therapeutic "technique," or even "philosophy" and redefined it as a *practico-poietic* activity aimed at transformation of the individual through a process of self-examination and learning. It is an activity of elucidation undertaken by both analyst and analysand. It aims not at knowledge, but at *autonomy*, at the "establishment of a certain relation of the individual to himself, the opening up to reason of the imaginary, or the transformation of the relations between unconscious intention and conscious intention."[140] This relationship can never be transparent, both because of the inexhaustible opacity of the unconscious and because other social-historical conditions for individual life exist beyond the domain of the psyche. However, between Lacanian practice and his own recognition of the impossibility, not to mention undesirability, of a victory of "ego" over "id," Castoriadis saw an insurmountable gulf.

Aimed at autonomy, psychoanalysis should take the "subject" not as its point of departure but as its end goal, as its *project*. Of course, we have seen that Castoriadis recognized that socialization intrudes on the psychical monad to produce an individual "that *functions* adequately for itself most of the time . . . and, above all, functions adequately from the point of view of society."[141] Yet he chided his contemporaries because "an enormous part of the rhetoric of the sixties and seventies concerning the subject as a simple effect of language and its 'unbeing' was in fact questioning only this social individual."[142] In contrast, Castoriadis insisted on the capacity for reflective self-representation and deliberate activity that allows the "subject or human subjectivity properly speaking" to put social boundaries and even itself into question. This type of subjectivity is an *ongoing project*, neither a static reality, nor an unattainable ideal, nor a fiction, nor a guaranteed telos. Situating the question of subjectivity and autonomy in this way makes it imperative that history be thought in its openness to the emergence of radically novel innovations. In this regard, Lacan, in common with all structuralists, excluded the essential dimension: temporality. In a vital passage, Castoriadis wrote of the meaning of temporality in the history of the psyche and in the practico-poietic activity of psychoanalysis:

It is because the history of the individual is also a history of self-creation that everything cannot be rediscovered in the present; it is because the individual is always borne forward from what he is that he can only rediscover himself by turning back from where he is now. The treatment's efficacy proceeds not from rediscovering the

past in the present but from being able to see the present from the
point of view of the past at a moment when this present, still to come,
was entirely contingent, and when what was going to fix it was still
in statu nascendi. . . . The practical essence of the psychoanalytic
treatment lies in the individual's rediscovery of himself as partial
origin of his history, his undergoing gratuitously the experience of
making himself, which at the time was not recognized for what it
was, and becoming once again the origin of possibilities, as having
had a history which was history and not fatality.[143]

Castoriadis's recovery of the temporal dimension, of *history* in the
strong sense as radical alterity—"ontological creation deploying itself as
history"—united his engagement with psychoanalysis with the redefinition of radical politics he had first offered in his writings of the early
1960s. The "project of autonomy" animated Castoriadis's efforts to rethink the social-historical world as the domain of human creation, to free
it from deterministic or functionalist logics, yet to understand its relationship to a "real" world that permits this creation. For Castoriadis, it is the
abyss of imagination that constitutes the democratic opening by bringing
forward "new figures of the thinkable." It is the radical imaginary that
opens the possibility of a struggle for a new "relation of society to its institutions, for the instauration of a state of affairs in which man as a social
being is able and willing to regard the institutions that rule his life as his
own collective creations, and hence is able and willing to transform them
each time he has the need or the desire."[144] In this vision of radical democracy one readily discerns traces of a classic theme of German political idealism, the association of freedom with the emergence of a self-conscious
recognition that it is human will that creates the institutions of society.
Yet if Castoriadis drew from that tradition, he recast the struggle for a
self-conscious relationship between citizens and their institutions in terms
that rejected the ideals of social transparency, determinism, and every sort
of absolute. Politics, like the individual psyche, is part of a world that is
obscure and unmasterable, yet capable of elucidation. Consistent with his
rejection of foundationalist logics, Castoriadis maintained that the value
of autonomy cannot be "grounded" or "proven"; at most autonomy can be
"reasonably argued for and argued about" once it has emerged historically
in the social imaginary.[145]

If the radical imagination is the "sperm of reason" and of personal and political autonomy, it is, as we saw, also potentially a "monster of madness." Castoriadis's hopes for emancipatory struggles were in fact tempered by recognition of impediments and obstacles. Democracy is "the tragic regime," he wrote, because it is that form of social life that explicitly renounces extrasocial support from gods or transcendent ideas and accepts its own responsibility and historical risk. Regressions and repetitions, for example, in the form of racist hatred, cannot be definitively avoided, though they may be exposed and resisted through an unceasing deployment of "collective activity," what Castoriadis called "explicit and lucid self-institution." To this end, in place of the rationalist language of much modern political philosophy, he revived ancient Greek terms that emphasize the discursive, activist, and agonistic dimensions of civic life: *phronesis* (prudential, practical wisdom) and *paideia* (education into citizenship). Alongside the negative potentialities intrinsic to a social-political order that has no limitation other than its own self-limitation, Castoriadis's notion of the "dual institution" of modernity also sobered his vision of autonomous society. "Autonomy," an imaginary signification of the modern period, has roots in the Western tradition every bit as deep as those of the ontological presuppositions that have fed the pursuit of rationalistic domination and technical efficiency. These imaginary significations, *autonomy* and *instrumentalist mastery*, constitute a conflict at the core of modernity, and Castoriadis saw no necessary or fixed outcome to this struggle.

In fact, however, he offered a bleak assessment of the present. To be sure, throughout his life, Castoriadis acknowledged and supported the struggles of women, students, workers, homosexuals, racial and ethnic minorities, and colonized peoples. But he believed that, at least in the wealthy countries of the West, relative affluence, consumerism, television, and leisure, as well as the decline of working-class politics in the postindustrial context, have produced a dominant tendency toward a passive, privatized citizenry and complacent immersion in the technical imaginary. Nonetheless, although Castoriadis clearly saw the obstacles to radical politics, he always stressed that the project of autonomy is "already in the process of being realized," even if it is never guaranteed.[146] Acknowledging the effectiveness of the "partial realization" of autonomy—like his recognition of the partial realization of a subjectivity beyond the social individual—was his answer not only to the collapse of the revolutionary dream of

Marxism but also to the paralyzing choice between the impossibility of emancipation and its full actualization that had led many of his contemporaries, including Lacan, into an impasse.

The group Socialisme ou Barbarie disbanded once and for all in 1967. That marked the end of Castoriadis's direct involvement in a militant group. He had, in any case, already made a decisive move from the marginalized intellectual and political milieu of the extreme left to a much broader and explicit engagement with the intellectual currents of the period when he began to publish "Marxism and Revolutionary Theory" in serialized form in *Socialisme ou Barbarie*. This trajectory reached its apogee with the later sections of *The Imaginary Institution of Society*, composed in the early 1970s, which articulated all the themes that would preoccupy Castoriadis for the rest of his career. The shift in style and content in the years since roughly 1960 was mirrored by a shift in the loci of Castoriadis's activities: he became a practicing psychoanalyst in the early 1970s and he was elected a directeur d'études at the École des hautes études en sciences sociales in 1980. A Greek expatriate who bypassed French education on his way to the radical peripheries of French politics, Castoriadis arrived at the upper reaches of French academe along a highly unconventional path. He always remained something of an outsider within the cliquish intellectual life of Paris, which he was sometimes able to regard with ethnographic curiosity, that is, when he was not attacking it with fury. His outsider status may help to explain his resistance to successive waves of intellectual fads, from communist fellow-traveling, Sartrean existentialism, and structuralism to poststructuralism, Foucauldianism, the new philosophers, and so on. Yet that explanation would ascribe too much causal power to sociological position, whereas what really seemed to sustain him was a clear-sighted fidelity to his own political commitments. With remarkable consistency, from the earliest days of Socialisme ou Barbarie onward, Castoriadis championed the idea that, in myriad ways, people may act creatively to alter the conditions of their lives. This idea not only weathered the changes in Castoriadis's writing and spheres of action, but it gained in power as Castoriadis articulated a deepening critique of Western ideas about being, society, history, and selfhood.

Castoriadis liked to insist upon the reality of *creatio ex nihilo* in the hope that this most extreme image of creation would sweep away " the subterfuges and sophisms concerning the question of the *new*: either there is creation or else the history of being (therefore also of humanity) is interminable repetition (or eternal return)."[147] Yet he was invariably quick to add that creation is *ex nihilo*, but not *in nihilo* or *cum nihilo*. That is, even if new forms cannot be deduced from existing elements, they do not emerge in a vacuum nor are they "made" from nothing. The history of Castoriadis's own thought certainly supports this image of creativity. As we have seen, his break from Marxism and attempt to rethink radical autonomy unfolded through a deep and evolving engagement with the resources of modern philosophy, from German idealism to phenomenology, and the psychoanalytic tradition. A crucial dimension of this process was his polemically charged relation to competing currents, from opposition to Stalinism and Trotskyism in the name of true socialism, to opposition to Marxism in the name of revolution, to opposition to structuralism in the name of human agency.

Castoriadis's argument with structuralism, so central to the years of his most fruitful theoretical development, in turn evolved from a critique of Lévi-Strauss's exclusion of the imaginary from the symbolic to a critique of Lacan's attempt to reduce the imaginary to a structure of capture and fixation. In the process, Castoriadis went from a superficial but essentially positive to a deep but explicitly hostile view of Lacan. Seen from a different angle, however, it is striking that Castoriadis always treated Lacan exclusively as one of the high priests of structuralism. Once he arrived at this negative judgment, he never acknowledged tensions, ambiguities, or developments in Lacan's position. It must be said that a lack of nuance or generosity toward his opponents was typical of Castoriadis, for whom the political stakes of theoretical debate were always immediate and paramount.[148] Undoubtedly, his work represents a vital and original contribution to the thought of the late twentieth century across a spectrum of fields and questions, but his approach to the work of other thinkers was almost invariably polemical. So, for example, his erstwhile comrade Claude Lefort once noted that Castoriadis's "desire to desanctify Marx, to shatter the myth attached to his name, while certainly legitimate, leads him to over-emphasize his rupture with Marx."[149] For similar reasons, Castoriadis may have overemphasized his rupture with the structuralism of Lévi-Strauss and Lacan, although, as this chapter has shown, far from discrediting his innovations, links to the styles of thought against which he rebelled lend his work additional power and interest.

The distance separating Castoriadis from Lacan was substantial, but not absolute; and this becomes even clearer if we recall Castoriadis's use of Fichte's idea of *Anstoß*, the check or stimulus that human significations experience when they encounter the inexhaustible otherness of the thing-in-itself. Castoriadis meant this to shatter structuralism's closed order of language and law. Yet we must not forget, as Slavoj Žižek repeatedly reminds us, that Lacan himself turned away from the structuralism of the 1950s, when the symbolic order functioned as a "proto-transcendental structural a priori," which "in advance predetermines the subject's acts, so that we even do not speak, but 'are spoken' by the Other."[150] The later Lacan turned increasingly to the real, that kernel or remainder of the unconscious that can never be dissolved or integrated into the symbolic order. It is as the philosopher of the real, of the disruption of the symbolic order, and hence, of the *flawed* symbolic, that Lacan has most palpably influenced the discourse of post-Marxism. Slavoj Žižek stakes his entire oeuvre upon the contrast between the early and the later Lacan, but even Claude Lefort and Marcel Gauchet, while certainly not disciples of Lacan, nonetheless drew upon him. If Castoriadis revealed the limits of Lacan's structuralist paradigm for a theory of radical politics, other thinkers perceived in the Lacanian theory of the real a more promising pathway for political thought.

CHAPTER FOUR

Democracy Between Disenchantment and Political Theology

French Post-Marxism and the Return of Religion

IS A SYMBOL CREATED OR FOUND? Does it reveal the freedom of human creation or does it disclose the form of the world? This was a perennial question for the Romantics. While some denied the instituted character of symbols in order to assert their correspondence with reality, others defended the autopoietic power of the human creator. In his theory of the radical imagination and his insistence on society's instituting creativity, Castoriadis was an emphatic heir of the latter camp. Yet, we should recall from chapter 2 that Paul Bénichou urges us to recognize within Romanticism "the ambiguity that is characteristic to this intellectual theme, and to make of the symbol both a human invention and a characteristic of being itself."[1] Claude Lefort, theorist of the "symbolic dimension" of the political, remained within this ambiguity. Indeed, many of the issues that came to divide Castoriadis and Lefort in the years after their intensive collaboration as cofounders of Socialisme ou Barbarie could be encapsulated in the contrast evoked by Bénichou. Where Castoriadis held that democracy emerged out of the exercise of human autonomy and further insisted that autonomy has the potential to become more and more lucid about its self-creating activity, Lefort came to believe that, even as democracy opened new circuits for the articulation and realization of autonomy, democratic power, indeed the political domain as such, remains unmasterable. Democracy, in Lefort's mature view, is enigmatically poised between human action and a disclosure or unveiling of being. Hence, political philosophy, if it is to remain true to the indeterminacy and unmasterability of democracy, must preserve metaphorically the insight of religion, "that human society can only open on to itself by being held in an opening it did not create."[2] Lefort thinks autonomy as inseparable from its Other (the "outside" [dehors]); the immanence of the social is always shadowed by the transcendent enigma of its institution, and political discourse is always inflected by the language of theology even as it gropes for a secular speech adequate to the mystery of democracy.

To Castoriadis, this was all foreign, indeed anathema. Castoriadis bluntly equated religion with heteronomy, with the concealment of the human act of signification whereby social life is given form. To attribute the origin of the social institution to a transcendent extrasocial source is to stabilize the enigma of human self-creation, assign it an origin, foundation, and cause outside society itself. Autonomy, he insisted, requires the final overcoming of religious exteriority and "the permanent opening of the abyssal question: 'What can be the *measure* of society if no extra-social *standard* exists, what can and what should be the law if no external norm can serve for it as a term of comparison, what can be life over the Abyss once it is understood that it is absurd to assign to the Abyss a precise figure, be it that of an Idea, a Value, or a Meaning determined once and for all?"[3] Translated into political terms, Castoriadis's vision of interminable questioning assumes an unbridgeable gap between religion as closure and democracy as openness to contingency and human self-creation.[4]

Bound by personal history and shared milieus, Lefort shared many of Castoriadis's political and theoretical concerns: with historical indeterminacy, the symbolic construction of social reality, the equation of democracy with a permanent interrogation of the terms of our collective lives, the expansion of autonomy, and so forth. He even shared Castoriadis's lack of personal religious belief. However, Lefort's turn to the language of theology, the ultimate figure of heteronomy, in order to describe the situation of democracy indicates a significantly different trajectory as he moved beyond the Marxist commitments of his radical youth. Entanglements of theology and politics in Lefort's thinking are nowhere explored with greater subtlety than in his 1981 essay "The Permanence of the Theologico-Political?" This seminal text will provide the following discussion with its point of departure and return as we trace the development of Lefort's thought.

If it is illuminating to keep Lefort in dialogue with Castoriadis, then it will be equally instructive to set Lefort into relationship with Marcel Gauchet, his most brilliant student. Four years after Lefort's essay, Gauchet cemented his reputation as a major thinker with the publication of *The Disenchantment of the World*, a magisterial book that offers an extraordinarily sweeping account of the emergence of modern democracy out of the collapse of the religious world. Gauchet's course in the years leading up to *The Disenchantment of the World* strongly reflects the influence not only of Lefort but also of Castoriadis. However, the particular style of Gauchet's engagement with the question of political autonomy's relation to religious heteronomy signaled political commitments that depart from those of *both* founders of Socialisme ou Barbarie. An exploration of the theologico-political problem in Lefort and Gauchet thus allows us to mark way stations in the collapse of revolutionary politics in France and the accompanying reorientation of progressive French intellectuals.

Two Turns and a Twist

French intellectual life in the late 1970s and 1980s was marked by so many announcements of "turns" and "returns" that one sometimes feels caught in a Paris traffic circle. Two stand out, not only for their lasting significance in the recent history of French thought but also for the manner in which they became twisted together. In 1976, a special issue of *Esprit* announced the "return of the political." Of course, politics had never gone away, least of all in the politically charged atmosphere of Parisian intellectual life in the decades since 1945. What *Esprit* had in mind were indications of a revival of politics as an object of serious historical and philosophical reflection. Numerous thinkers who had earlier viewed politics from a Marxist perspective, that is, as an epiphenomenon of the social base, now looked to the "political" as a field of "power and law, state and nation, equality and justice, identity and difference, citizenship and civility."[5] In this revival Castoriadis and Lefort played major roles. As the cofounders of Socialisme ou Barbarie, the two staked out a unique ground in French political culture; but unique positions are often marginal ones, as was certainly the case with Lefort and Castoriadis. This changed in the mid-1970s, when an altered context created a new and receptive audience.[6]

For one thing, the events of 1968 loosened the hold of the French Communist Party, producing a fragmented left, including the short-lived Maoist Gauche Prolétarienne and the so-called Deuxième Gauche, which subscribed to the self-management politics that Socialisme ou Barbarie had articulated. For another, the Common Programme, the 1972 electoral alliance between the French Communist Party and the Socialist Party, drove many noncommunist intellectuals further away from the major left-wing parties. Further, the French publication of Alexander Solzenitsyn's *Gulag Archipelago* generated an "electro-shock" that jolted leftist intellectuals and produced what one historian has dubbed the antitotalitarian moment.[7] The "Gulag Effect" yielded, among other things, the media savvy New Philosophers, who combined a hair-shirt-and-ashes rejection of their former leftism with bald claims that all forms of power corrupt equally. Though the New Philosophers tried to claim affiliation with Lefort and Castoriadis, both men stridently refused the compliment. Undoubtedly, however, the wave of antitotalitarian rhetoric renewed interest in three decades' worth of serious philosophical and political writing by Lefort and Castoriadis. Their example proved instrumental in helping to bring political reflection—as opposed to political posturing—back into the orbit of serious philosophical discussion.

The ideological conjuncture that thrust political philosophy and, more specifically, sustained reflection upon the experience of modern democracy and its doppelgänger, totalitarianism, into the center of French discussion may be traced in the sociology and institutional history of Parisian intellectual life. Between 1971 and 1980 Lefort and Castoriadis participated in founding two new political journals, *Textures* and *Libre*, along with others, such as the anthropologist Pierre Clastres and Lefort's students Marcel Gauchet and Miguel Abensour. Gauchet, who had studied with Lefort at the University of Caen in the 1960s, authored the article "L'expérience totalitaire et la pensée de la politique," which dominated the 1976 special issue of *Esprit* on the return of politics. Further, in 1980, Gauchet collaborated with Pierre Nora in launching the journal *Le Débat*, which quickly became the most influential Parisian periodical during the 1980s. François Furet's historical writings on the French Revolution broke with the Marxist school and explored the Revolution as modernity's first experiment with democracy, and under Furet's presidency the École des hautes études became the epicenter of this revival of political philosophy.

Under Furet's patronage, Lefort and Castoriadis were elected directeurs d'études at the École, Lefort in 1976, Castoriadis in 1980. Pierre Rosanvallon writes that their elections gave an *élan décisif* to political studies at the École.[8] A monthly seminar on politics, history of political thought, and political philosophy began at the École in 1977. As Rosanvallon remembers, "What made this group special is that it linked together two different generations. There was the generation of François Furet, Claude Lefort, Cornelius Castoriadis, Krzysztof Pomian, but there were also, from the very beginning, Marcel Gauchet, Bernard Manin, Pierre Manent, and myself."[9] In 1985 this same group founded the Institut Raymond Aron, a noteworthy tribute to the liberal political thinker who had long been overshadowed by his left-wing contemporary Jean-Paul Sartre. This institutional initiative was followed in the 1990s by the creation of numerous journals committed to political philosophy and the history of political thought.[10]

François Furet was the not-so-gray eminence behind most of these developments, including Lefort and Castoriadis's elections to the EHESS.[11] However, it would be a mistake simply to associate them with Furet's efforts to remake the École in his image. Indeed, both diverged from Furet's politics. Where Furet argued, in his highly influential work *Interpreting the French Revolution* (1978), that the Revolution's search for "pure democracy" formed nothing less than the matrix of totalitarianism, Castoriadis championed direct democracy right up to his death in 1997. Although Lefort was closer politically to Furet, he nonetheless criticized Furet's neo-Tocquevillean association of the Revolution with totalitarianism and emphasized instead its role in inaugurating the indeterminate, open social experience of democracy.[12] Where Furet's politics centered on the need for stable representative institutions, Lefort gave his support to the pluralistic activism of the new social movements that emerged after 1968. By contrast, Gauchet, who was a generation younger than Furet, Lefort, and Castoriadis, has commented that between himself and Furet there existed "that mysterious thing that is a deeply spontaneous accord."[13] With good reason, he was perceived as Furet's protégé. In fact, Furet's opponents blocked Gauchet's election to the École until Furet strategically withdrew his support for Gauchet in 1990.

With some historical distance, it is perhaps not surprising that the return of political philosophy and, more specifically, of democratic commitments coincided with a notable return of religion in French thought. So long as Marxism's social and economic model prevailed, the political domain could always be exposed as epiphenomenal in the last instance, while political philosophy could be dismissed as idealist. If, as Jacques Derrida once reminded us, Marx believed that "'Christianity has no history whatsoever,' no history of its own," then it must be added that, for Marx, politics has no history of its own, and for exactly the same reason.[14] Once the Marxist claim for the determinate role of the economic base collapsed, the field was cleared to see the creative and constructive role of cultural representations in forming the social world. Within such a constructionist perspective, both politics and religion could reemerge as irreducible systems of meaning that generate and not only reflect social-historical life. Yet that also brought these two symbolic systems into competition and threw up a series of questions. If we consider democracy as the domain of human self-determination and religion as the domain of human dependency, can democracy escape from its long entanglement in religion and quasi religions and establish its own autonomy as the self-instituting activity of human communities? Or must democracy draw on the otherness of religion to discover the meaning of democracy?

Karl Marx certainly thought the answers to these questions were clear. The young Marx fully embraced the Young Hegelians' critique of religion, which he believed demolished religion at the level of religion's own self-understanding. But he was convinced that his radical analysis led further down, down to religion's cause in something other than itself, down to the root that nurtured religious illusions. And he went still farther in his campaign against religion by applying the Young Hegelians' model directly to the political realm. Hence he declared the liberal state, the "atheistic state, the democratic state," to be the pure essence of the Christian state.[15] Turning to the most advanced model available, the American republic, Marx claimed that the state stands over society as heaven does earth; the sovereignty of the citizen rests on a Christian logic of incarnation that separates the individual from human species-being; the abstract universality of rights displaces the concrete universality of man's participation in collective social life. Marx regarded communism as the last great act in the history of secularization, returning the transcendent political state to its immanent place in society and removing the final obstacle to man's recovery of his alienated humanity.[16] The leap of faith was to be surpassed by the leap into the kingdom of freedom.

It is an irony of history that Marx's radical secularizing impulse has been almost fully eclipsed by the commonplace that communism itself was a religion, albeit an *ersatz*, secular collectivist faith. One would reasonably expect that as the authority of Marxism collapsed and leftist intellectuals turned to support one form or another of liberal democracy, there would be a double liberation from theology: not only from traditionalist ideas of the bond between religion and social order, but from (alleged) secular religions like Marxism. The story in France was not quite so simple. Take, for example, François Furet's final book, *The Passing of an Illusion: The Idea of Communism in the Twentieth Century*. The title immediately situates the analysis of communism in the framework of religion, for it refers unmistakably to Freud's main essay on religion, *The Future of an Illusion*, an allusion that is even blunter in the French title, where Furet's *passé d'une illusion* exactly mirrors Freud's *avenir*. Furet concludes that the collapse of the socialist dream undid a covert theological code by which the twentieth century had sought historical certainty. As he writes, "At the end of the twentieth century, deprived of God, we have seen the foundations of deified history crumbling." The apparent triumph of liberal democracy does not bring comfort, however: "history has become a tunnel that we enter in darkness, not knowing where our actions will lead, uncertain of our destiny." A democracy stripped bare of illusions proves itself to be an object of anxiety, because Furet judges this disenchanted condition "too austere and contrary to the spirit of modern societies to last." Democracy needs utopia, "a world beyond the bourgeoisie and Capital, a world in which a genuine human community can flourish."[17] Furet's book thus ends ambiguously. He hopes that democracy's inventiveness is not at an end, but he worries that it remains susceptible to dreams of historical redemption. If the exit from communist illusion has proven terminable, democracy's own exit from religion seems interminable.

Already in the late 1970s, the strident denunciation of totalitarianism was a central feature of Furet's critique of the French Revolution and the "revolutionary catechism" that he believed linked the French and Bolshevik Revolutions in the political imaginary of the French left. However, the ambivalence was also already there. Furet's insistence that the French Revolution was modernity's first experiment with political democracy was accompanied by a diagnosis of the slippage of the discourse of popular sovereignty into coercive civil religion and the Terror.[18] This mix of assertion and apprehension was in fact common to many French intellectuals in the late seventies, the "antitotalitarian moment" when the ideological hold of Marxism definitively broke and many leading leftist intellectuals turned toward a democratic politics of a decidedly more pluralistic, quotidian, and nonutopian sort. The apprehensiveness, if we may call it that, came from the paradoxical circumstances of this rediscovery of democracy. Consider a comment by Gauchet in 1988: "The more we are led to acknowledge a universal validity to the principles of Western modernity, the less we are able to ground them in a history of progress of which they represent the fulfillment."[19] Even more pointedly, Olivier Mongin, the editor of *Esprit*, recalls that it was "a bizarre period, when intellectuals increasingly distanced themselves from their self-image as proprietors of history and discovered democracy at the same moment when democracy was the object of increasing doubt."[20] Mongin's observation refers to the fact that French intellectuals' turn toward democracy coincided with a period of intensifying critique directed at the very foundational discourses and metanarratives—whether transcendental ethics, natural law, or the immanent rationality of the historical process—that had traditionally provided grounds for liberal democratic and revolutionary socialist politics alike.

Gianni Vattimo has identified the dissolution of philosophical metanarratives as the general precondition for the return of religion in recent philosophical discourse, because this situation has exposed the uncertainty and contingency of the process whereby the modern philosophical project was constructed on binary oppositions between the "rational" and the "irrational," "faith" and "knowledge," "secular" and "religious."[21] Vattimo's observation helps to explain the striking fact that accompanying the widespread democratic reorientation of French intellectuals was a resurgence of the theologico-political problem in French thought in the 1980s. In 1988 Marcel Gauchet and Pierre Nora identified the "rehabilitation of the religious problematic" as a spectacular phenomenon within a culture where almost all the dominant intellectuals, whether under the sway of Robespierre, Marx, or Nietzsche, had long dismissed religion as a dead letter.[22] Indeed, a French historian of the German secularization debate describes this as the third great reappearance of the theologico-political problem in the twentieth century, preceded by Carl Schmitt's illiberal political theology in the Weimar period and then by progressive German political theology and Latin American liberation theology in the

1960s and 1970s.[23] In contrast to those earlier moments, the French resurgence did not aim to reassert a theological language as a political strategy. Gauchet and Nora signaled the specific nature of this resurgence: "the return of religion as a central object of social theory and a legitimate object of laic reflection."[24] For lay thinkers, the goal was to assess the place of religion in the genealogy of political modernity. Yet this was more than an analytical question. The theologico-political question spoke directly to the paradoxical situation in which French intellectuals turned to democracy at the same moment that they perceived democracy's loss of substance and foundation. A century and a half after Marx detected a political theology at the core of liberal democracy and called for the final radical secularization of politics, post-Marxist intellectuals turned to political democracy as the only possible vehicle for emancipatory politics; but they did so in circumstances that returned with less confidence to the question of democracy's relationship to the ultimate figure of otherness.

The Thought of the "Political"

In a 1975 interview Claude Lefort taxed his former comrade Cornelius Castoriadis for perpetuating Marxism's dream of total revolution, a myth of a "society able to master its own development and to communicate with all its parts, a society able in a way *to see itself*."[25] This charge was not really fair, given Castoriadis's repeated insistence that neither society nor the individual psyche can ever be fully controlled by autonomous human action. However, the comment reveals a tremendous amount about Lefort's relationship to Castoriadis, as well as his commitment to a style of philosophizing that cleaves to the opacity, indeterminacy, and ambiguity of the social-historical world.

Lefort met Castoriadis soon after the Greek arrived in Paris. By then Lefort had been involved in Trotskyist circles in Paris since 1942. As Lefort relates in the 1975 interview, while still in his teens he had sought a "Marxism faithful to Marx, a radical critique of bourgeois society in all of its forms and linked to revolutionary action, a Marxism that manifested the alliance of theory and politics: an anti-authoritarian Marxism."[26] When his lycée instructor, Maurice Merleau-Ponty, the philosopher who would indelibly stamp almost every aspect of Lefort's subsequent thought, heard him speak of his loathing of the French Communist Party's heavy-handed manner, he immediately pointed his student toward Trotsky. Lefort's ensuing enthusiasm for Trotsky proved short-lived. Joining forces with Castoriadis in 1946, he moved rapidly from an effort to reform Trotskyism from within to the founding of Socialisme ou Barbarie in the first month of 1949. Though Castoriadis and Lefort agreed that Trotskyism was not the proper way forward, the two had differences right from the start. Above all, Lefort was less interested in forming a militant organization than in fostering a forum for discussion and information. He was, he later admitted sardonically, a "petty bourgeois intellectual, a stranger to revolutionary action."[27] That did not mean he opposed revolutionary action, just the ambition of intellectuals and vanguard politicians to dictate the terms of working-class politics or deduce the proletarian standpoint from a globalizing theory of history. Hewing closely to Merleau-Ponty's critique of any claim of absolute knowledge, he shied away from manifestos and programmatic pronouncements. Instead, he tried to develop a phenomenological account of the proletarian experience, one that would derive its categories concretely from the working class itself.[28] In retrospect, he would judge that effort flawed by a lingering adherence to deductive criteria, but, whatever its weaknesses, it signaled a quite specific political outlook that brought him into conflict with Castoriadis.

Both Castoriadis and Lefort shared a critique of bureaucracy; indeed, their shared perception of the Soviet Union as a calcified bureaucracy established to extract surplus value from the Russian working class was the key source of their misgivings about Trotskyism. Moreover, both Castoriadis and Lefort recognized the need to radically rethink the nature of militant organization if Socialisme ou Barbarie were to avoid repeating in miniature the mistakes of Lenin, Stalin, and Trotsky. Nonetheless, Lefort detected in his comrade a persistent tendency to see the group as a new vanguard. The impulse to formulate a revolutionary direction and a socialist program seemed to flatly contradict the group's insistence on the autonomy of the working class and its political struggles.[29] Lefort first formulated this worry in an article published in *Socialisme ou Barbarie* in the summer of 1952 in which he underscored his faith in the political creativity of the proletariat.[30] Responding sharply, Castoriadis denounced Lefort as a "spontaneist," and, immediately afterward, Lefort and his supporters announced they would leave the group.[31] Despite the affront, even as they parted, Lefort indicated his willingness to continue to collaborate; and indeed, he drifted back into involvement with Socialisme ou Barbarie. In 1958, however, the group opened a discussion aimed at clarifying its ideological and political direction. When a majority indicated a wish for a more structured organization, Lefort once again expressed his worries about repeating the slide toward bureaucracy. Castoriadis responded with an acidly polemical attack expressing the majority position. A second schism was unavoidable, and this time Lefort's departure was permanent.[32]

Lefort's 1958 break with Socialisme ou Barbarie coincided with his final adieu to Marxism. As he recounted in the autobiographical preface to the 1971 collection of his essays, *Éléments d'une critique de la bureaucratie*, the rupture "incited me to draw out the consequences of my political interpretation of totalitarianism, to rethink the idea of liberty, that of social creativity, within the framework of a theory of democracy that does not elude the division, conflict and unknown of history; to reject the revolutionary tradition in all its variants, a tradition in its own way just as oppressive, just as rigid as those which it combated."[33] Lefort's departure from Marxism had, in fact, been a longer good-bye, and leaving Socialisme ou Barbarie lifted a self-censorship that had restrained him from exploring his doubts. In subsequent years he radicalized his earlier efforts to develop a phenomenology of the social.[34] As he now saw it, the task of political philosophy was not to create a theoretical adjunct to revolutionary struggle, nor was it even to provide new or renewed normative foundations for democracy. Rather, the proper role of philosophy is to search for the formative principles of democratic pluralism or, put differently, to describe the conditions of modern democracy in its historical specificity. The process of reflection that led Lefort to this new sense of purpose has been described in detail several times, not least by Lefort himself.[35] Rather than retread that ground, let us identify some key elements of his mature political thought and relate them to his disagreement with Marx.

The impact of Maurice Merleau-Ponty is evident everywhere in Lefort's writing: in his rejection of a neutral standpoint outside phenomena and in his effort to develop a self-reflexive relationship to an object that is already dense with meaning, to understand phenomena from their inside, to describe rather than prescribe, and to let conclusions emerge out of description. The phenomenological orientation is also evident in his attempt to describe the *political* as a *mise en forme*, a shaping whereby a society institutes itself as *this* society, an action that further implies the engendering of meaning (*mise en sens*) and a staging (*mise en scène*). This formulation translates the phenomenological vocabulary of Merleau-Ponty into political terms. In *The Visible and the Invisible*, the enigmatic masterpiece left incomplete at his death in 1961, Merleau-Ponty presents the "invisible" as the "lining" and the "inexhaustible depth" of the visible, the necessary and constitutive relationship between figure and ground, surface and depth, presence and absence. These are not static ratios, but chiasmatic exchanges in which the visible and the invisible intertwine and reverse. Nor is the invisible the nonvisible or "absolute invisible, which would have nothing to do with the visible. Rather it is the invisible *of* this world, that which inhabits this world, sustains it, and renders it visible, its own and interior possibility, the Being of this being."[36] Together, the visible and the invisible form the "flesh of the world," Merleau-Ponty's key phrase designating the world as a horizon of general visibility in which the human is embedded as both seer and seen. Lefort, who edited and published *The Visible and the Invisible* after his teacher's death, took over the notion of flesh as a central category of his political philosophy. The "flesh of the social" signifies the political principle of general social visibility.

With this formulation, Lefort distinguished himself from both academic social science and Marxism. The social sciences have developed as discrete disciplinary fields by taking the social field as comprised of just so many distinct objects—politics, society, the private, the public, the economy, religion and values, and so on. By contrast, Lefort searched for the "originary *form*," the "political *form*," by which the social acquires its "original *dimensionality*."[37] By the same token, where the Marxist grants the class struggle or relations of production the status of foundational reality, Lefort urged us to see that social conflict can only be defined as representing an internal division, a division opening within and defined by a single milieu. To convey what he means, Lefort opened his *Essais sur le politique* by invoking the concept of *politeia* or *regime*. "The word is worth retaining," he wrote, "only if we give it all the resonance it has when used in the expression 'the Ancien Regime.'" Used in that sense, regime combines the idea of a "type of constitution," understood in the broad sense of "form of government" and "structure of power," and a "style of existence or mode of life." For Lefort, this definition of regime or "form of society" implies the "notion of a principle or an ensemble of generative principles of the relations that people maintain with each other and with the world."[38] In a fundamental distinction that he did much to propagate, Lefort distinguished "politics" (*la politique*) in the sense of partisan competition for power, quotidian governmental actions, and the normal functioning of institutions from the more primordial category of the "political" (*le politique*).[39] The political in this technical sense is not a historical development imposed on a preexisting social order, but rather the formative principle of social experience itself. Lefort called the political "a hidden part of social life, namely the processes which make people consent to a given regime—or, to put it more forcefully, which determine their manner of being in society—and which guarantee that this regime or mode of society has a permanence in time, regardless of the various events that may affect it."[40] In brief, the political is Lefort's translation of the visible and the invisible into political terms. Marcel Gauchet formulated this even more clearly when he wrote, "the political constitutes the most encompassing level of the organization [of society], not a subterranean level, but veiled in the visible."[41]

Lefort's approach to the political reveals a strong methodological holism.[42] The point is worth stressing, because the holism may easily be overshadowed by one of the most basic claims of Lefort's mature thought, namely that division is an ineradicable and, indeed, constitutive dimension of the social. In insisting on division against a background of holism, two influences flowed together. As always with Lefort, Merleau-Ponty was key. If, as Merleau-Ponty insisted, reflection arises out of and against a background of unreflective being, then consciousness is always in relation to "brute being" (*être brut*), with no possibility of a position outside being and no power to master or totalize it. In a major 1961 contribution to an issue of *Les Temps modernes* marking Merleau-Ponty's death, Lefort drew out the consequence that human subjectivity rests upon a constitutive division between reflection and the unreflective ground. Philosophical interrogation thus moves constantly in a circle between its own formulations and its encounter with a being that surpasses it. The philosophical *démarche* finds itself in an "ordeal of circularity that is one of constant and deliberate indetermination."[43] Brute being, the 1961 essay concludes, remains incommensurable with the "representations that science composes of it." A philosophical spirit that takes these lessons seriously will renounce the "'flat' being offered to the dreams of a sovereign consciousness" and in place of this old Cartesian dream embrace "the wild spirit (*l'Esprit sauvage*), the spirit that makes its own law, not because it has submitted everything to its will, but because submitted to Being, it awakens to the contact of the event to contest the legitimacy of established knowledge."[44] In later work Lefort would characterize this as a "heroism of mind" animated and "haunted" by the 'impossible' task of disclosing that which is—the being of history, of society, of man—and of creating, of bringing forth through the exercise of a vertiginous right to thought and to speech, the work in which meaning makes its appearance."[45]

If the ontological position inherited from Merleau-Ponty dictated to Lefort that human subjectivity rests upon constitutive division, this conviction was underscored in the early 1960s by Lefort's increasing interest in Jacques Lacan. As we saw in the previous chapter, this was precisely the moment when Lacan truly emerged as one of France's *maîtres à penser*. Lacan's insistence on a radical heteronomy within man's psyche dovetailed with Merleau-Ponty's ontology to convince Lefort that division is constitutive of human identity and immunize him against fantasies of overcoming this primordial alienation. In an interview Marcel Gauchet remarks on Lacan's direct influence on Lefort. As Gauchet recounts, in Lacan's seminar, newly shifted from Sainte-Anne Hospital to the Ecole Normale Supérieure, Lacan spoke of "'constitutive division,' and Lefort took up the formula in order to transpose it into the political domain." Gauchet pointedly separates this move from the more familiar examples of left-wing appropriations of psychoanalysis: "Here, it is not Freud with Marx, but Freud against Marx. In regard to Marx, Freud is the author who prompts one to conceive a certain irreducibility of human conflictuality." Conceding that Freud's own extrapolations from intrapsychic conflictuality to the collective level remained thin, Gauchet nonetheless notes that "the latent model of the irreducible character of psychical division, strongly accentuated by Lacan, supplied an effective lever by which to escape all philosophies of reconciliation. It permitted a number of authors to leave Marxism."[46] Lacan's influence on Lefort is so clear that, some twenty years later, Slavoj Žižek could quite simply call Lefort's theory of democracy a "Lacanian exposition."[47]

Undoubtedly, Lefort's engagement with Lacanian psychoanalysis was positive. There was never even a hint of the kind of critique, let alone

polemic, that Castoriadis directed at Lacan. Nonetheless, it seems clear
that Lacan became serviceable for Lefort because Lacan's idea of constitutive division could be integrated into Merleau-Ponty's ontological critique
of totalizing philosophies. In this sense Lefort had a model in Merleau-
Ponty himself, who toward the end of his life perceived points of contact
between his thought and psychoanalysis, particularly Lacan.[48] The relative superficiality of Lefort's engagement with Lacan may be detected in
his rather imprecise usage of key Lacanian terminology. Of Lacan's triadic
distinction between symbolic, imaginary, and real, Lefort uses the imaginary in a strongly Lacanian way. However, as we will see shortly, his use
of both the symbolic and the real did not remain faithful to Lacan. We
might also note that Lefort could not have been oblivious to the various
critical discourses that arose in the wake of Lacan's break with the Freudian orthodoxy. For example, he acknowledged the influence of Piera Aulagnier, the post-Lacanian analyst who became Castoriadis's wife in 1968.
As we saw in the previous chapter, Aulagnier led a group of apostate Lacanians into the Organisation psychanalytique de langue Française in 1969.
It was from Aulagnier that Lefort took the term *mise en sens*, which Aulagnier had developed in her work on psychosis and Lefort now applied to
the shaping power of the social institution.[49] Lefort maintained relations
with the circles engaged in debating the Lacanian legacy in the 1970s, not
only Aulagnier's Quartrième Groupe but also groups aimed at bridging
the schism, such as the seminar Confrontations, where Lefort presented
what would become one of his most important essays, "The Image of the
Body and Totalitarianism."[50]

When Lefort linked the terms *mise en forme* and *mise en sens* to a third
term, *mise en scène*, his self-conscious deployment of a theatrical image
tied the institution of the social to the order of representation. The process
whereby society shapes its shared existence through self-production and
reproduction is indissolubly united with the process whereby that life is
represented or interpreted. Indeed, as Hugues Poltier writes, "society sup-
poses the existence of a symbolic order and vice versa [*reciproquement*]."[51]
Yet it is one of the most important claims of Lefort's mature thought that
society and its symbolic representation cannot coincide. One of the earliest formulations of this principle comes in a pivotal text published shortly
after his exploration of "brute being." There he explicitly extended the
lesson of constitutive division from Merleau-Ponty's ontology to his new

thought of the political. "Society," he wrote, "cannot become an object of representation or a material that we can transform because we are rooted in it and discover in the particular form of our 'sociality' the sense of our undertakings and tasks."[52] True to his renunciation of all philosophies of reconciliation, including of course Marxism, Lefort viewed conflict as fundamental to social experience; indeed, conflict's appearance and operation belong constitutively to Lefort's notion of regime. This is the great theme of Lefort's opus on Machiavelli, which he began in the early 1950s and finally submitted to Raymond Aron as a *thèse d'état* in the early 1970s.[53] Yet what Lefort saw in Machiavelli was the insight that if power is to master social conflict, such power must rely on a representation lifting it above the contest of interests. That is, power involves a symbolic representation of society that is not anchored in the real, but absorbs the inner divisions of the social into a figure of unity.[54] The symbolic thus remains exterior or nonidentical to the social, even though the social world would be unimaginable without this symbolic institution.

One might say that this symbolic instance is imposed on the "real."[55] However, it would be even more accurate to say that the symbolic gives society *access* to the real—first, to its own reality insofar as the symbolic creates a figure of the unity of the social, as well as a sense of the lawful and the unlawful and of the difference between sense and nonsense, and then, second, to the world more broadly insofar as the symbolic establishes ontological categories of the existent and the nonexistent.[56] We can note that this sets Lefort at some distance from Lacan, who would distinguish between "reality," which is what society designates as real, and the "real," which is beyond symbolization, indeed even beyond the possibility of symbolization. Lefort's notion of the real is actually closer to the Lacanian definition of a symbolically instituted "reality" than to the Lacanian "real." A real beyond all symbolic orders is not a concern for him, nor does he thematize an unsymbolized and *unsymbolizable* real as a permanent source of disruption for the symbolic order in the way that is so fundamental to the political thought of Ernesto Laclau and Slavoj Žižek.

Lefort's emphasis on the symbolic institution of the social distanced him still further from Marxism. In a major essay in 1974 he criticized Marx for failing to recognize the symbolic institution. Collapsing the social institution into the real, Marx treated social division as a primary social datum. What is negated in such cases of epistemological realism, Lefort argued, is "the articulation of the division ... with the 'thought' of the division, a thought which cannot be deduced from the division since it is implicated in the definition of its terms. What is negated is the symbolic order, the idea of a system of oppositions by virtue of which social forms can be identified and articulated with one another; what is negated is the relation between the division of social agents and representation."[57] True to his roots in phenomenology, which had always tried to overcome dualisms between the subjective and the objective, Lefort insisted that he intended neither to "assert the primacy of representation" and thereby fall into the illusion of an "independent logic of ideas" nor to fall into a "naturalist fiction" by adhering to an analysis of social mechanisms. "We must appreciate," he continued, "that it is the social space which is instituted with the division, and it is instituted only in so far as it appears to itself. Its differentiation through relations of kinship or class, through the relation between state and civil society, is inseparable from the deployment of a discourse at a distance from the supposed real, a discourse which enunciates the order of the world."[58]

Lefort's claim that Marx had located social institution at the level of the real unmistakably echoes Merleau-Ponty's criticism of Marxist orthodoxy in *Adventures of the Dialectic*. Nonetheless, Lefort's appeal to a symbolic order created out of a system of oppositions would seem to align him with the structuralist position. There is without question a structuralist influence operating in Lefort. We have already seen that he was receptive to Lacan; even in the early 1950s he was very interested in Claude Lévi-Strauss, and he periodically taught seminars on structural anthropology. The authors of the two major book-length studies of Lefort rightly note that it is only in the early 1970s that Lefort introduced the concept of the symbolic in the "technical sense" that would henceforth be a key to his political interpretation of societies.[59] Yet it is necessary to proceed with caution. In his 1981 article on the theologico-political, in one of his most pregnant discussions of the symbolic, he indicates that he does not use the term in the way the social sciences understand it, but in the sense that the symbolic governs access to the world.[60] While it is not entirely clear *which* social sciences he means, it seems reasonable to assume that he is speaking of the structuralist model that was still powerful at that time. In a published discussion with colleagues at the Collège de psychanalystes in October 1982, Lefort underscored the complexity of the story: "is it not time to stop imputing to Lacan the invention of the notion of the symbolic? Some give the impression that one fine day Lacan came along and that notion of the symbolic was born. The notion of the symbolic is much older!"[61]

Certainly, Lefort's engagement with the notion of the symbolic was much older. Indeed, one of the first of his articles to draw wide attention was a critique of Lévi-Strauss's attempt to appropriate Marcel Mauss as the forerunner of his own symbolic anthropology. Even though Lefort chastises Mauss for ignoring Marx, his assessment of Mauss is mainly positive. He describes Mauss as "one of the most representative authors of our epoch," a figure dedicated to developing a "new rationalism" that does not "explicate a social phenomenon by relating it to another phenomenon judged to be its cause, but links all economic, juridical, religious, and artistic traits of a given society and [attempts] to comprehend how they conspire in the same meaning."[62] Taking aim at Lévi-Strauss, Lefort insisted that the ideal of mathematizing the symbolic relation was foreign to Mauss. Even more important, Lefort claimed that Mauss sought the *signification* of symbols, not the strictly internal relations of symbols between themselves. That is, Lefort read Mauss as a phenomenologist of the social world who tried to understand the immanent intentions of conduct without leaving the plane of the lived. Lévi-Strauss, by contrast, drained social life of its unmasterable complexity and reduced lived experience to a raw material for the construction of a symbolic logic.[63] Already in this criticism of Lévi-Strauss we see hints of the chiasmatic relation between the social and its symbolic representation that the later Lefort will describe, along with a rejection of reductionism, whether of a materialist or an idealist kind. Indeed, what we see is the same tension we observed in Merleau-Ponty, whose work in the 1950s rested on an expressivist theory of the symbolic even as he opened toward the constructivist view entailed in structuralism.

What is really striking in Lefort's early anthropological essays is that, despite his avowed Marxism, he already has a strongly formulated idea of symbolic institution. For example, in a 1952 essay addressing the question of historicity in societies "without history," he wrote: "an individual life is highly symbolic with regards to cultural becoming, in that [the symbolic] shows [this individual] what sorts of possibilities are given to humans, what relations link them to the group and what these relations tend toward, what perception of the past and of the future the institutions furnish them."[64] Lefort's final answer to the apparent absence of temporality in primitive societies is that stagnation is a specific mode of instituting historicity and temporality, a *mise en forme* that establishes a manner of coexistence, comportment, and collective practice.[65] One sees a similar sensibility at work in Lefort's 1952 attempt to outline a phenomenology of proletarian experience, which depicts the proletariat's productive activity extending to the production of social life in its entirety. These ideas emerge in close engagement with Merleau-Ponty, who was at that time working out the ideas on institution that would become the subject of his 1954–55 lectures.[66] Castoriadis was, as we saw in the preceding chapter, reluctant to acknowledge that Merleau-Ponty influenced his own thinking about the institution of society; but, with Lefort, Merleau-Ponty's impact is palpable. Or, perhaps more accurately, it is hard to tell how to assign priority— to the teacher or to the student— because their relationship might itself be taken as an intricate example of chiasma. At any rate, the continuity from this early thought to Lefort's mature ideas is patent.

Hugues Poltier notes that despite the heavy usage of the term *symbolic* in Lefort's later work, it is not easy to define its meaning exactly.[67] This seems true, but I would suggest that it is not because of a lack of rigor on Lefort's part. Rather, his concept does not remain restricted to the abstract and reduced notion advanced by structuralism but instead carries with it expressive and affective dimensions as well, not to mention a *spatial* dimension, at least in a negative sense insofar as symbolic *exteriority* creates the *interior* social space. Moreover, to expand a point already raised, Lefort's concept of the symbolic stands at some distance from Lacan's. For Lefort, the symbolic is a *dimension*, suggesting that it is not all there is to the social whole. It is not simply the system of signs *tout court*. Finally, to cite Lefort's most famous claim about modern democracy, if modern democratic society's quasi representation of itself remains an *empty place*, it is *empty* not because it is structured by lack or incompletion, which is the transcendental condition of the symbolic in Lacan's system, but because modern democracy institutes the symbolic dimension of power as empty.[68] This is a point made forcefully by the young Slavoj Žižek, when he insists that, "it is misleading to say that the 'democratic invention' *finds* the locus of Power empty—the point is rather that it *constitutes, constructs* it as empty; that it reinterprets the 'empirical' fact of interregnum into a 'transcendental' condition of the legitimate exercise of Power."[69]

The Religious and the Political

The *impurity* of Lefort's symbolic is well illustrated by his claim in "The Permanence of the Theologico-Political?" that "both the political and the religious bring philosophical thought face to face with the symbolic."[70] Both offer responses to the basic ontological experience of constitutive division, of humanity's noncoincidence with itself. Religion, however, interprets this as a division between the visible world and the invisible world of God or gods. As Bernard Flynn writes, "The doctrinal content of religion is a dramatization of this experience of noncoincidence."[71] Flynn proposes an appropriate formula for understanding "the religion of premodernity": it is "the symbolic dimension as interpreted by the imagination; the fundamental indeterminacy through which societies relate to themselves and the world is dramatized in terms of determinate figures existing in the visible world."[72] The symbolic is not, necessarily, contrasted to the imaginary as it would be by a Lacanian. For Lefort, the question is rather one of disentangling the imaginary from the symbolic through the course of history. If Lefort has an anthropological constant, it is that societies are symbolically instituted, which means that the domain of the political necessarily comes forth with the social institution. However, as Dick Howard has noted, the political may "be lived in a mode of non-recognition, through a concerted effort to avoid the decisions and divisions that it consecrates."[73] A discourse on the political as such, based on recognition of society's nonidentity with itself, emerged only in recent history. Such a discourse was not *repressed* in premodern society, it was simply impossible, because it was not symbolically enabled. Of premodern societies, Lefort asserts that "when reflection exercised itself on power, the organization of the City, the causes of its corruption, it remained rigorously subordinated to a theological representation of the world, which alone fixed the markers of the real and the imaginary, the true and the false, the good and the evil. There was not for thought a place of the political."[74]

Lefort's mature thought rests upon an argument for the emergence of the place of the political, the possibility of disentangling the symbolic, imaginary, and real, and living in the condition of indeterminacy that opens up once this disentanglement is underway. This entails a theory about the transition from premodern to modern society, from premodern forms of politics to modern democracy, and from the religious to the political. Yet the potential role played by both the religious and the political in the symbolic institution of society makes the story of their relationship particularly fraught. Indeed, to return to key terms in Lefort's vocabulary, the chiasmatic exchange between the near and the remote, between social visibility and its invisible lining, establishes points of contact between politics and religion. This is the case not only because both are constituted by specific forms of exchange between the visible and the invisible, but because throughout their long mutual history they have been intertwined as the visible and the invisible of each other.

The interrogative title of Lefort's major essay on religion and politics suggests this relationship. Indeed, one of the main arguments of "The Permanence of the Theologico-Political?" is that religion reveals something fundamental about the political. Or, more precisely, religion reveals an insight that philosophical thought should try to preserve, namely the

> experience of a difference which goes beyond differences of opinion . . . the experience of a difference which is not at the disposal of human beings, whose advent does not take place within human history, and which cannot be abolished therein; the experience of a difference which relates human beings to their humanity, and which means that their humanity cannot be self-contained, that it cannot set its limits, and that it cannot absorb its origins and ends into those limits. Every religion states in its own way that human society can only open on to itself by being held in an opening it did not create.[75]

Even if the political philosopher cannot accept the language in which religion expresses itself, he or she learns from the religious the "experience of alterity in language, and of a division between creation and unveiling, between activity and passivity, and between the expression and impression of meaning."[76]

Lefort aims this object lesson in exteriority at the political hubris and fantasies of social homogeneity that he considers the shadow side of modern democracy since the French Revolution. This recourse to otherness links him, in a way, to a broader strategy within the antitotalitarian discourse of French intellectuals in the late 1970s and 1980s. One sees this in the outright appeals to divine transcendence in the religiously inflected works of thinkers within the orbit of the new philosophers such as Maurice Clavel, Christian Jambet, and Guy Lardreau.[77] Among poststructuralist theorists such as Jean-Luc Nancy and Philippe Lacoue-Labarthe or the post-Marxists Chantal Mouffe and Ernesto Laclau, the deconstruction of stable identity—of persons, communities, and meaning—revealed an otherness that might provide a prophylaxis against a totalitarianism that seemed to lurk in all forms of politics. Among the various voices sounding this ground note, perhaps Jacques Derrida offers the most revealing contrast to Lefort.

Derrida entered this arena belatedly with *Specters of Marx* in the early 1990s. Numerous reviewers have accused Derrida of falsification or cynicism for claiming there that deconstruction had always "remained faithful to a certain spirit of Marxism."[78] He had in fact hinted in that direction for years; but, as he explained at a conference in 1981, he had remained silent so as to avoid contributing to the "anti-Marxist concert" of the post-1968 years. His strategy, he reported, was marked in his writings by a "sort of withdrawal or retreat (*retrait*), a silence with respect to Marxism—a blank signifying . . . that Marxism was not attacked like such and such other theoretical comfort. . . . This blank was not neutral. . . . It was a perceptible political gesture."[79] It was the triumphalism of the post–cold war era that finally provoked him to defend Marx or at least a "certain spirit" of Marx. That is, Derrida rejected Marx's determinist and foundational ontology, but affirmed Marxism's longing for justice.

There is much in this position that parallels the strategy followed by Nancy, Lacoue-Labarthe, Laclau, and Mouffe in the 1980s. What really distinguishes Derrida's intervention is his revival of Marxism's messianic impulse. After all, Nancy and Lacoue-Labarthe had sought to "retreat" God—in the sense of both revisit (re-treat) and drive back—in precisely the same way as politics, God and politics both being associated with a monological philosophy of the subject; Jean-François Lyotard had believed that a paralogical democracy must be godless; Laclau and Mouffe had criticized religion as hegemonic discourse. Even as late as 1989, Derrida himself was reluctant to link his idea of justice to messianism. By

1993, though still rejecting any determinate messianic content, Derrida insisted on the messianic form as a latent dimension in the structure of promises.[80] This too was not a sudden about-face for Derrida. Already, in his 1980 essay "Of an Apocalyptic Tone Recently Adopted in Philosophy," Derrida had lamented his contemporaries' hasty abandonment of Marxist eschatology.[81] Moreover, Derrida's periodic interest in deconstruction's relationship to negative theology foreshadowed his messianic yearning for the totally other.[82] Derrida's references to Walter Benjamin's notion of a "weak messianic force," as well as his opposition to any attempt to represent the messianic hope, suggest, finally, the possible influence of a more specifically Jewish tradition, a complex issue that exceeds the scope of this brief excursus.[83] Here it is enough to note that in *Specters of Marx* and subsequent work Derrida refused to tie the messianic impulse to a specific religion. Indeed, he vacillated between, on the one hand, treating the messianic as a general ontological form and, on the other, linking its universal form to the specific events of revelation in the three religions of the Book.[84] *Specters of Marx* leans heavily on the former hypothesis, resurrecting a messianism without content, what Derrida calls the "messianic and emancipatory promise . . . as *promise* and not as onto-theological or teleo-eschatological program or design."[85]

Separated from eschatology and teleology, messianism becomes a hope without hope, an impossible attachment to a democracy that is always *à venir*, always "to come." This formulation offers a precise political counterpart to the play on *à Dieu* and *adieu* that animates Derrida's *The Gift of Death* and other works of the 1990s. Hent De Vries presents the *adieu* as the core of Derrida's return to religion insofar as it summons up all "the ambiguity of a movement toward God, toward the word or the name of God, and a no less dramatic farewell to almost all the canonical, dogmatic, or onto-theological interpretations of this very same 'God.' "[86] As with the figure of the *adieu*, the messianic topos allows Derrida to affirm the yearning for democracy, while avoiding any hint of "Sameness" or closure that might raise the danger of totalitarian thinking. It must be said that Derrida's political position pays its dividends in paradoxes. While he reasserts Marx's desire for justice, he essentially neutralizes concrete democratic projects because, given his terms, the attempt to represent the democratic idea, let alone realize it, threatens to prematurely close down the messianic longing for an otherness that is forever to come.

In the more recent essay "Faith and Knowledge," this "messianicity without messianism" spills directly over into "religion without religion." Derrida the atheist attempts to separate religion from fundamentalism, identifying the religious instead with "reticence, distance, dissociation, disjunction," while naming futurity its temporal sensibility. This rather selective identification of religion with deferral and otherness serves his needs because they are precisely the qualities of the "democracy to come." Religion and democracy thus intertwine as mutually implicating origins and goals. Indeed, the religious and the political prove inseparable: "The fundamental concepts that often permit us to isolate or to *pretend* to isolate the *political* . . . remain religious or in any case theologico-political." Derrida presents this position as if it were opposed to Carl Schmitt, as if Schmitt had been forced grudgingly to acknowledge that his "ostensibly purely political categories" were in fact the "product of a secularization or of a theologico-political heritage." Yet it was Schmitt who articulated and embraced that theological genealogy and tried to mobilize it as the ultimate source of the power of political concepts. Ultimately, despite Derrida's effort to distance himself from Schmitt's political theology by linking politics to the deferrals of religion instead of to its potencies, he and Schmitt both end up at the conviction that the significant concepts of modern politics are secularized theological concepts.[87] Derrida's entanglement with Schmitt returns us by contrast to Lefort.

Lefort's claim that the philosopher should learn from religion would seem to identify him as another heir to Schmitt's political theology. After all, the lesson about alterity that religion teaches to political philosophy appears to unify religion and politics so long as politics manages to resist the illusion of pure self-immanence and clings to a primordial knowledge of otherness. However, Lefort resists this kind of conclusion, arguing that it threatens to negate the meaning of the historical separation of democracy from religion. A position such as Derrida's would lead us to the view that the appearance of a new representation of power that has no religious basis merely conceals the displacement and perpetuation of religious content. To be sure, looking at the practices of democracy since the French Revolution, Lefort finds ample evidence of democracy's entanglement in religion. For example, from the Jacobins onward, democracy has been haunted by the Christian logic of incarnation, by the impulse to represent the nation as an actual being or, in Jules Michelet's phrase, to imagine the sovereign "people" as the democratic Christ, and the desire to close the gap between the symbolic representation of power and the complexity of the real through the logic of embodiment lived on in twentieth-century fantasies of party, nation, class, race, and leader. Further, this desire to give a figure to social exteriority has been accompanied by the impulse to unite the existence of democracy in historical time with permanent duration. Hence the attempt to immortalize the institutions of democracy and, in the extreme instance, the "persistence of the theologico-political vision of the immortal body" expressed literally in mummification of the leader.[88]

Significantly, rather than take those entanglements as signs of democracy's intractable reliance on religion, Lefort read them as phenomena of a transitional epoch. In fact, he insisted on the radical novelty of democracy, which lies in the open, indeterminate, and unmasterable social experience that it generates. Lefort traced this experience to a "symbolic mutation" in the order of power, wherein power underwent a radical "disincorporation" in the period of transition from monarchy to democracy. As we saw, Lefort held that in premodern society the noncoincidence of society with itself was dramatized as the relationship between human society and an *other* place. Within this imaginary relationship to symbolic exteriority, power itself is draped in the mantle of the religious. Inspired by Ernst Kantorowicz's seminal work on the medieval image of the king's two bodies, mortal and immortal, individual and collective, Lefort argued that the doubled body of the king served as the coupling link between the visible and the invisible.[89] He saw this logic functioning right up to the collapse of the ancien régime, with the monarch representing the unity of the social in the unity of his own body. The radicalism of modern democracy thus lies in its novel disincorporation or disembodiment of power in the name of an egalitarian perception of social relations. Addressing this shift, Bernard Flynn writes, "In modern society, no figure of mediation can incarnate society's quasi representation of itself, its *mise-en-scène*. The *place* of the Other remains, but its determinate figuration is effaced. The place of the Other remains, but it remains as an *empty place*."[90]

Hence we arrive at Lefort's best-known claim, that democratic power is a *lieu vide,* an "empty place." Democratic power may be contested—indeed it depends on that contest—but no one can appropriate or incarnate it, nor can such power be "represented." With the disembodiment of power goes a

dispersal of power, knowledge, and law. They enter into contestatory relations, cannot be mastered by a single logic of representation, and are always in "excess" of each other. Modern democracy is thus marked by the
simultaneous loss of foundation and the interminable search for foundation, the loss of a notion of legitimate power and the opening of an interminable debate as to what is legitimate. Democracy institutes a society in
which division is not disruptive but constitutive of the social domain.
Modernity thus enables the possibility for an explicit discourse on the
political and recognition of the symbolic dimension as such, because, for
the first time, people are symbolically enabled to distinguish between the
symbolic and imaginary interpretations of the symbolic. As Lefort put it
in a particularly condensed formulation:

> of all the regimes of which we know, [modern democracy] is the
> only one to have represented power in such a way as to show that
> power is an *empty place* and to have thereby maintained a gap be-
> tween the symbolic and the real. It does so by virtue of a discourse
> which reveals that power belongs to no one; that those who exercise
> power do not possess it; that they do not, indeed, embody it; that
> the exercise of power requires a periodic and repeated contest; that
> the authority of those vested with power is created and re-created as
> a result of the manifestation of the will of the people.[91]

The advent of modern democracy is nothing less than a *metaphysical
event*, a tear in the tissue of human belief and symbolic order. Rather
than proceed as Carl Schmitt (and Derrida) would to identify this symbolic change as concealing an underlying continuity with religion, Lefort
emphasized the *efficacy* of the symbolic: namely that the appearance of a
new power that disavows the religious does have the power to constitute
a new practice. Accordingly, he endorsed Tocqueville's insight that democracy is important not for what it "does" but for what it "causes to be
done," its power to arouse constant agitation in people.[92] This means that
democracy continually moves forward into the open, indeterminate, un-
grounded space of political contestation. But, cautioned Lefort, the paradox of "any new adventure that begins with the formulation of a new idea
of the state, the people, the nation or humanity is that it has its roots in
the past."[93] Hence, in the unsettling early experience of democracy, people

grasped at religious forms in an attempt to avert any further dissolution of the social. Moreover, the collapse of theological representations of the world symbolically encouraged the emergence of a misleading representation of society as a sui generis creation of human will. Thus the theological image of a unified divine will replicated itself in the image of society as a unified subject, a fantasmatic identification that underwrites the democratic slogan "vox populi vox dei" as much as it does totalitarianism's dream of the "People-as-One."[94] Lefort detected a further impulse toward the restoration of the theologico-political in the psychical trauma that accompanied power's disembodiment. In thinly veiled references to Jacques Lacan, Lefort's essay "The Image of the Body and Totalitarianism" suggests that subjects constitute themselves through a specular relation to the figure of power. The experience of democracy is thus akin to the individual's transition from imaginary unity to symbolic division, and as with the "ordeal of the division of the subject," so too is the traumatic loss of the substance of the body politic never fully overcome.[95] It is hard not to think that, beyond the Lacanian inflection of this idea, Lefort's detection of a traumatic core in democracy taps into the quite specific meaning of regicide within the French political imagination, wherein political modernity is tied to the destruction of the king's body, political liberty primordially connected to crime.[96]

Although Lefort argues that in times of crisis, at weak points of the social, the theologico-political formation may reassert itself within democratic culture, nonetheless he asks, "Far from leading us to conclude that the fabric of history is continuous, does not a reconstruction of the genealogy of democratic representations reveal the extent of the break within it?" Rather than seeing democracy as a new episode in the transfer of the religious into the political, Lefort urges us to reflect on the process of democracy's liberation from religion, what he calls the "adventure of their disintrication." Like Castoriadis, Lefort insists on a division between religion and the new social experience of democracy. Lefort remains much more guarded toward the project of autonomy, however. To a much greater degree than Castoriadis, Lefort circumscribes autonomy by placing the self-determining power of democratic society into an agonistic relationship with the enigma of the opening of the social world onto itself. Clearly, Lefort means to tie the enigma of this opening to democratic practice and discourse; for the otherness of the social institution no longer comes from a figure of the Other, but inheres in the latency of all identities claimed within and for democratic society. Nonetheless, in the history of democracy the enigma of social institution has produced its share of civil religions, and, as Derrida's example shows, the theologico-political remains capable of reactivation. Modern democracy may not conceal a religious core, but, from within Lefort's terms, the persistence of the theologico-political signifies the "unavoidable—and no doubt ontological—difficulty democracy has in reading its own story."[97] The adventure of disintrication seems tortuous and possibly interminable.

Marcel Gauchet and the Birth of Autonomy from the Spirit of Religion

The distintrication of the political from the religious is a central concern of Marcel Gauchet's *The Disenchantment of the World*, published in 1985 to considerable acclaim and controversy. Yet Gauchet was optimistic that complete disintrication is possible. Indeed, he believed it was already achieved. If Gauchet's thought reveals many deep debts to Lefort, his conclusions about the theologico-political problem differ fundamentally on precisely this most important point. In fact, despite Lefort's impact on his student, the basic problem addressed in *The Disenchantment of the World* is framed in terms that sound more like those of Castoriadis. Gauchet followed Castoriadis in viewing religion as a "way of institutionalizing *humans against themselves*," that is, as a form of human self-creation acting against autonomy. The core task of Gauchet's book thus resonates with Castoriadis: to trace the gradual breakdown of religious otherness and the transfer of the instituting power from the extrasocial source to society itself.[98] Strikingly, however, Gauchet's conclusions took him in a political direction quite at odds with either Castoriadis or Lefort.[99]

Gauchet's account of the emergence of modern autonomy remains anchored to an account of constitutive heteronomy or exteriority that imposes strict limits on his view of modern democracy. Hence, he steered sharply away from Castoriadis's vision of direct democracy. However, Gauchet's treatment of constitutive heteronomy led him away from Lefort as well. Lefort's mature vision of democracy placed little emphasis on the actual institutions of government; rather, he focused on the sociopolitical dynamics opened by democratic contestation within a context of historical indeterminacy. Despite his renunciation of revolution, Lefort's vision retains an element of the *esprit sauvage* he celebrated in his 1961 essay on Merleau-Ponty. By contrast, Gauchet's account of a postreligious world anchors the symbolic dimension in the institutions of the state, which take on the character of a quasi transcendentality. Gauchet's concern was less with the way in which the symbolic opens up an indeterminate space of democratic contest than with the way in which the symbolic status of the state creates the conditions for what he terms *effective* democracy. This preoccupation led him to increasingly embrace the principles of representative democracy and existing institutions of the state. From a youthful commitment to anarchism, Gauchet had become a liberal democrat at the time he wrote *The Disenchantment of the World*; in the 1990s he turned increasingly to a defense of what he considered the imperiled French republican tradition. Yet, as we shall see, the analytic framework he first developed to account for the exit from religion has proven to be a constraint in his ability to engage contemporary politics. A melancholic tone has come to inflect Gauchet's writings, and its cause may be the limits of his political model as much as the actual state of politics.

Born in 1946 in Normandy, Gauchet already aligned himself with the left as a high school student. However, as he relates in an interview, early encounters with dogmatic communist school teachers immunized him against the pull of the Communist Party. His sympathies were with anti-Stalinist libertarian and anarchist tendencies like those he encountered in the pages of *Socialisme ou Barbarie*, which he had been reading since he was fifteen.[100] At the university in Caen in 1966–67, a course with Claude Lefort on the "dimensions of the social field" proved a transformative experience for the young student. From Lefort he learned unforgettable lessons about the "irreducibility of democracy, the centrality of the political, the necessity to think together, from this point of view, democracy and totalitarianism in their ties and in their opposition."[101] In the same interview Gauchet emphasizes that at the time he was becoming "perceptibly more anti-Marxist than Lefort and Castoriadis." Lefort still admired Marx and saw "between the lines of the explicit Marx a hidden Marx that remained to be recuperated." Gauchet, by contrast, introduced what he calls "a consequential theoretical anti-Marxism" in "Sur la démocratie: Le politique et l'institution du social," a long text that he and Lefort coauthored in 1971.[102] In the early 1970s, this anti-Marxism did not yet mean a disengagement from critical radical politics. Indeed, it seemed to fit well with his anarchist convictions. During the 1970s Gauchet continued to collaborate with Lefort, for example in the short-lived journals *Textures* and *Libre*, undertakings that also involved the likes of Castoriadis and Furet. He also worked intensively with Gladys Swain, a friend from his student days in Caen and later his partner, on the history of psychiatry. This collaboration led to the publication of *La pratique de l'esprit humain: L'institution asilaire et la revolution démocratique* in 1980, the first of a series of major works that Gauchet has dedicated to the intersection of the histories of democracy and modern subjectivity.[103]

By the end of the 1970s, Gauchet's ideological trajectory had carried him from anarchism to liberalism, a development that culminated in his cofounding of *Le débat* with Pierre Nora in 1980. Gauchet's itinerary shared something with many in his generation, affected as he was by the radicalism of 1968 and disappointment in its aftermath, and then the antitotalitarian moment, with its attendant anxieties about the power of the state. Yet where some—most notably the New Philosophers—chose to denounce the state in all its forms, Gauchet ended up endorsing one version of the state, the liberal democratic state, as the best possibility for safeguarding human autonomy. There was also a singular dimension to Gauchet's political evolution, one that can be traced in yet another of the intellectual affiliations that indelibly stamped his thought.

Gauchet describes his first encounter with the work of the anthropologist Pierre Clastres as "one of the great shocks of my intellectual life."[104] Clastres formed a part of the milieus of the journals *Textures* and *Libres* up to his death in a car accident in 1977; his 1974 book *La Société contre l'état* exercised considerable influence on the antitotalitarian currents of French thought in the 1970s.[105] The book articulated, as Claude Lefort put it, "the question of the political" at the heart of primitive society.[106] Its radical claim was that such societies had made a preemptive choice against a power that might detach itself from the community. In the name of a thoroughgoing equality, primitive society rejected any form of internal division that might make possible the emergence of the state. This vision of an egalitarian society instituted against the state spoke directly to the anarchist sentiments of Gauchet; but he rapidly grew skeptical. For one thing, he was troubled by the fragile and anachronistic notion of such a *choice.* As he would later ask bluntly, "How can one be against something that does not yet exist?" Accordingly, he came to redefine Clastres' thesis as "society against political division."[107] Even more fundamentally, however, he realized the insufficiency of Clastres' ideal. If primitive society succeeded in creating a certain kind of egalitarian democracy, it was within an otherwise severely restricted context. That is, the price for the absence of masters was the exclusion of any possibility that the institution of society itself might become a matter for democratic discussion. "If there is self-rule [*autogestion*] on the practical level, in sum," wrote Gauchet in 1975, "it is by a rejection of self-rule on the 'theoretical' level. It is thus radical democracy through the narrowest conservatism."[108] In other words, primitive society offered equality without autonomy.

In an effort to better conceptualize the nature of primitive society, Gauchet resorted to the basic insight that he shared with Claude Lefort, namely that division is constitutive of social existence as such. And he turned to religion as the most primordial form of division. As he recollected in 2003, he was reluctant to invoke religion in "Politique et société: La leçon des sauvages," the 1975 essay that opened the breach between Clastres and himself. He recalled that at that time he was repulsed by religion and essentially ignorant of its history.[109] Nonetheless, he detected in religion a way out of the impasses of Clastres' model.[110] Primitive society did not win its form of equality simply by neutralizing all types of division; rather, it expelled division from within the social body only to erect a more primordial division between humanity and the gods. Where Clastres had scarcely mentioned religion at all, it now became Gauchet's key for unlocking the paradoxical secret that society's self-creation lay in an originary act that placed the symbolic institution of society at an infinite remove from human agency.

Indeed, religion became absolutely central to Gauchet's understanding of history and remains so up to this day.[111] Following on the opening he had made in the essay "Politique et société," he began to formulate a more elaborate theory of the role of religion not just in primitive society, but in the subsequent evolution of societies and the emergence of states. The 1977 essay "La Dette du sens et les racines de l'état: Politique de la religion primitive" marks a further significant development beyond the 1975 essay and foreshadows *The Disenchantment of the World*'s sweeping account of the birth of politics in religion, the dynamics of the great monotheisms, the specific role of Christianity in loosening the grip of religion, and the emergence of modern democratic autonomy out of this process of exiting from religion. This undertaking bears more than a passing resemblance to Max Weber's theoretical account of the gradual formation of a self-sufficient secular sphere as the actualization of potentialities existing within the religious domain itself. However, the similarities are ultimately rather superficial. Where Weber had stressed the specific role of the Protestant Reformation in creating conditions that would eventually legitimate this-worldly pursuits and instrumental rationality, Gauchet situates Weber's thesis within a much broader argument about the transformative effects of monotheism. Gauchet differs from Weber in another and still more revealing way. Weber never claimed that a religious, spiritual dynamic alone could explain the emergence of modernity, but Gauchet places extraordinary weight on historical transformation operating at the symbolic level. Indeed, in a published *table ronde* on his work, it is amusing to read Catholic theologians chiding him for neglecting material factors.[112] It is as if, in the rush to shed all vestiges of the Marxian model, Gauchet ends up with an unapologetic idealist account of the unfolding logic of an idea. But it is not surprising. After all, as he recalled in a 2003 interview, his ambition was to create "a *theory of history* capable of effectively giving the lie to Marxism, not only by attempting to critique it on specific points . . . but by proposing an alternative vision."[113] But such an aim comes with an ironic price. For beneath Gauchet's frequent insistence on the contingency of history is a historical model with a deterministic thrust.[114] The rather unbending logic of Gauchet's effort to surpass Marxism with an equally grand alternative theory gains in irony if we recall Gauchet's additional debt to Weber's great contemporary, Émile Durkheim. Gauchet's depiction of religion centers on its social function, and, in doing so, it certainly reveals the strong traces of Durkheim, for whom religion serves as a system of communication and a means of specifying and regulating social relationships. Seemingly unaware of the deterministic element in his own theory, Gauchet mixed praise of Durkheim with the criticism that he had lapsed into a determinist account of the necessity of religion instead of viewing religion as a "free instituting operation arising from an act of creation expressing a decision of society."[115]

The provenance and intentions of Gauchet's concern with religion are signaled immediately in the subtitle of *The Disenchantment of the World*: "A

Political History of Religion." Indeed, consistent with his appropriation of Pierre Clastres, Gauchet viewed religion as political from its very beginning. Rejecting evolutionary models of religious development, he argued that religion received its fullest expression in primitive societies, when the instituting power was allegedly most fully removed from human society. For such a society, the founding power lies at an unfathomable distance in the past; the present is in a position of absolute dependence on this mythic past, and human activities adhere to their inaugural truth. Such radical dispossession enforces an "ultimate political equality, which, although it does not prevent differences in social status or prestige, does prohibit the secession of unified power."[116]

Two great upheavals shook this originary form of religion, the birth of the state and the emergence of monotheism. Of the two, Gauchet considered the emergence of the state around five thousand years ago to have been the more epochal development. Where total dispossession had essentially neutralized the dynamics of group relations, the advent of political domination brought new instabilities and potencies into the heart of the collective process. Political domination also inaugurated a different relation between the visible and the invisible, for the distance between society and its origin now became a distance operating within human society between the dominant and the dominated, those who have the gods on their side and those who do not. Kings and priests could claim power through their access to and ability to interpret the invisible. The emergence of monotheism during the Axial Age (800 to 200 BC) introduced still another dimension of instability into the homeostatic form of primitive religion.[117] Monotheism brought an infinite increase in the potency and otherness of the divine, now imagined as a god-subject whose will not only created the cosmos but also sustains it at every present moment. Gauchet based the central thesis of his book on what he called the "dynamic of transcendence" inaugurated by the formation of the subjectivized God. Far from dispossessing humans, transcendence makes God more accessible: foundation no longer belongs only in the remotest past but also in the present. This vision of the world as the object of a single will opens up possibilities for a human understanding of the creation and at least partial decipherment of that divine will. The representation of absolute otherness yields a de facto reduction of otherness. Hence Gauchet's paradoxical formulation: "the greater the gods, the freer the humans are."[118]

Christianity radicalized the effects of the monotheistic revolution. With the incarnation, the divine enters the world, introducing new and transformative tensions into the dynamic of transcendence: the enigma of the wholly other and the human form of the God-Man, inscrutability of the father's message and the need to interpret the human voice of the son, hope in the beyond versus adherence to a here-below that had been graced by Christ's humanity, world rejection and the imperative to act upon the world. So explosive were these new instabilities that Gauchet named Christianity the "religion for departing from religion." Gauchet shared Lefort's interest in the relationship between the incarnation and politics, but he gave a more detailed account of the instabilities that Christianity introduced into the institution of monarchy. Where pre-Christian monarchs could function as both priests and kings, occupying the meeting place between the visible and the invisible, Christ took that place once and for all. The Christian monarch could no longer aspire to be the perfect mediator. However, if the Christian king could not be what Christ was, he could at least be like Christ "to the extent that he made Christ's absence present and symbolized his truth."[119] This preserved the sacral dimension of kingship, reinstating its mediating function between the beyond and the here-below. At the same time, the unbridgeable gap between Christ and the monarch meant that the legitimacy of the Christian ruler contained a destabilizing and transformative element. For the monarch represented not the point of meeting but the depth of separation between the two orders of reality marked as forever separated by having been *uniquely* consubstantial in Christ. Hence the sacral dimension of kingship derived from the management of the lowly world, but behind the apparent continuity of the sacral function Gauchet detects a great transformation. The monarch's mediating activity shifted toward a domain removed from the Church's control, the domain of justice. A great metamorphosis in the sacral function of kingship meant that the king emerged as the "archetypal mediating figure in the collective sphere, as opposed to the individual mediation between souls and God, guaranteed by the sacraments' absolving power."[120]

Gauchet followed Ernst Kantorowicz closely in dating this change to the thirteenth and fourteenth centuries, when new symbols emerged of political incorporation, the state as a secular *corpus mysticum* and the notion of the body politic.[121] However, Gauchet's conclusion was much bolder than any found in Kantorowicz, for he identified this as nothing less than the birth of political modernity. As he wrote, the emergence of the king as the mediating figure of the human order was a "radical turnaround of the relation between power and society. The monarch gradually evolved from incarnating sacral dissimilarity into realizing the collective body's internal self-congruence."[122] Political modernity deployed this symbolic reversal in two directions: the growth of a state oriented toward monopolizing collective organization and a form of political legitimacy based on a logic of representation. Political modernity thus replayed the paradox of monotheism—the dynamic of transcendence whereby humans become freer, even as God becomes greater—in the form of a tendency toward the democratic inversion of sovereignty.

> The democratic inversion of sovereignty was from its very beginning
> inscribed in sovereignty understood as an idea of the modern State,
> as an expression of the new relation between power and society re-
> sulting from the completed revolution in transcendence. Once the
> split between this world and the beyond has caused political author-
> ity to take responsibility for representing and organizing collective-
> being, then individuals will soon exercise sovereignty, whatever royal
> trappings of authority remain. The State colossus is first strengthened,
> only to open itself up later to its subjects. By deepening the separation
> from its subjects, the State ends up being identified with them, in
> that those who submit to power will eventually claim the right to
> constitute it.

The dynamic of transcendence thus acted as the great agent returning the instituting power to human society, transforming a transcendent logic of legitimacy into an immanent-democratic one. The history of the transition from heteronomy to autonomy is "religious to the core," writes Gauchet. If we have moved from being within religion to being outside it, our world nevertheless remains shaped by it. Hence, "If we have surpassed the religious, it has not left us, and perhaps never will, even though its historical effectiveness is finished."[123]

It is not my purpose here to evaluate the merits of this argument or weigh it against the other great macrolevel attempts to explain the emergence of the secular world. Rather, I want to emphasize one important point, namely the significance of the book within the intellectual and political context of France in the 1980s. The history of the disenchantment of the world, I would suggest, served Gauchet as a vehicle for expressing a generation's disenchantment with its former political commitments. A 1986 conversation between Gauchet and Pierre Manent published in *Esprit* is revealing. Manent was at that time just completing his book *An Intellectual History of Liberalism*, which depicts the history of liberalism as the protracted struggle of the secular city against the theologico-political problem, that is, the intertwining authority of the "religious sacred" and the "civic sacred." Manent complained that Gauchet's account of religion's decline erased the role played by the great polemical struggle waged from Machiavelli onward against the political power of sacred monarchy. Gauchet's reply had less to do with the relative historical merits of their respective positions than with contemporary politics: "a sober view of democratic development," he instructed Manent, "conducted on the base of a religious genealogy, permits the simultaneous rebuttal of ultra-democratic optimism, blind to the obstacles that lie in its route, and of conservative pessimism, obsessed exclusively by the factors of dissolution and the inviability of an individualist order."[124] Far from being the "other" of democratic politics, Gauchet presents the theologico-political as the invisible container for the experience of democracy. A religious genealogy serves here in the normalization and stabilization of a liberal democratic order, cautioning equally against both direct democratic aspirations and the religious critics of secular society.

It is a sign of Gauchet's intentions that for all the influence of Castoriadis, he entirely ignored the ancient Greek origins of democracy. This neglect fully inverts the democratic vision of Castoriadis, for whom the ancient Greek model of direct democracy remained the vital germ, if not the model for the modern project of autonomy. Against what he called the "metaphysics of representation," Castoriadis championed an uncompromising Aristotelian definition of the citizen as "capable of governing and being governed," and he devoted considerable energy to analyzing the institutional innovations of the first democratic regime.[125] Gauchet, by contrast, entirely neutralized the value of the Greek experience. For one thing, he directed his general argument that humans are freer under monotheism against modernist or postmodernist celebrations of paganism, citing specifically Marc Augé's celebration of polytheism, although one must also think of Lyotard's identification of paganism with heterogeneity.[126] For another, rather than consider Athenian democracy as a relative breakthrough to a new political form, Gauchet stressed instead how the polis remained embedded in a vision of a rational cosmos that acted as a constraint upon political innovation. Hence the political novelty of fifth-century Athens gets lost within its general participation in the religious transformations of the Axial Age.[127] The point is not so much whether Castoriadis understated the limitations of Greek political innovation. Rather, the point is that, for Gauchet, the ancient experience of democracy apparently has no meaning for the advent of modern democracy or the future possibilities of democratic action.

In Gauchet's genealogy, or—to use an even more appropriate Nietzschean phrase—his account of the birth of democracy from the spirit of religion, liberal individualism and representative democracy emerge as the natural heirs to the logic of Christian transcendence. As for direct democracy, Gauchet viewed it with the same suspicion as Furet. Indeed, Gauchet's contribution to Mona Ozouf and Furet's 1988 *Critical Dictionary of the French Revolution* argues that a totalitarian logic emerged when the "Declaration of the Rights of Man and Citizen" fused the legal protection of individual rights with the exercise of popular sovereignty.[128] The ideological reorientation of French intellectual life, which began with the rejection of Marxism and the affirmation of democratic commitments, here melts into the claim for a left-liberal consensus of the sort triumphantly presented in the 1989 bicentenary of the French Revolution, a commemoration so dominated by François Furet that he was anointed "roi Furet."[129] On the broadest historical scale imaginable, Gauchet's ambitious book confirms that the "revolution is over."[130]

Democracy Against Itself?

In 1985 Gauchet seemed quite convinced that the exit from religion was complete. The instituting power had been successfully transferred from the extrasocial source to society itself. Religious belief, he conceded, may survive as a matter of private conviction, but it is no longer an active or relevant force in the political realm. As he claimed in 1984, "If God doesn't exist, nothing happens."[131] There is, he wrote in 1998, a general consensus, even among believers, that society and politics are human creations. "In a word, we have become metaphysical democrats."[132] Nonetheless, it is crucial to an understanding of Gauchet's concerns in the years after *Disenchantment of the World* to see that in his account, even if religion, understood as a positive structure of belief, has vanished, the structuring function of the religious continues to underlie modern democracy. The exteriority of the gods may have been overcome, but not exteriority itself. Rather, it has been transferred to the modern liberal democratic division between state and society, between society as the true source of the instituting power and the state that represents that power, both in the sense of governing in the name of the collective and in the sense of giving that collective a symbolic representation of itself. Transcendence in the age-old sense of an otherworldly power may have disappeared, but transcendence survives as a this-worldly structure. Far from diminishing our autonomy, so runs Gauchet's argument, the "terrestrial transcendence" of the secular liberal democratic state guarantees it. Dispossession, which throughout history had been the precondition of humanity's heteronomy, now becomes constitutive of our autonomy and the only true bulwark against totalitarian dreams of overcoming social division and fully mastering our history.

It is hard not to hear a certain kind of triumphalism in what Camille Tarot has justly described as Gauchet's vision of a "reconciled modernity."[133] Yet the confidence expressed in *The Disenchantment of the World* proved shortlived. By the late 1980s Gauchet worried that modern democracy was moving in a self-destructive direction. Whereas Gauchet's concern in the 1970s and early 1980s centered on an overweening state's threat to liberty, his worries shifted as he observed the evident triumph of neoliberalism in America and western Europe. Since around 1990, he has maintained that the collective dimension of the political threatens to be fully eclipsed by hyperindividualism and free market idolatry. In what Gauchet has come to regard as a new phase of democracy emerging after 1968, the individual citizen bases his political sensibility strictly on the protection of personal rights, and his political horizon extends no further than the fulfillment of private interests. In such a regime the individual no longer recognizes his dependency on the institution of a collective power, or, at most, he sees that power as an instrument for the pursuit of individual interests. Indeed, faith in the auto-organization of the market

makes the steering powers of the government seem unnecessary or coun-
terproductive. In Gauchet's pathos-laden formulation, it turns out that
democracy operates against itself. He insists that he does not view this
situation fatalistically, but maintains that the situation is open and holds
out hope that democracies can recover a more robust sense of their collective nature.[134] Yet this claim for openness and optimism seems at odds
with the burdens of Gauchet's historical model. At a certain level the
speed with which Gauchet passed from a moment of confident synthesis to
a sense that democracy is caught in a self-defeating impasse may be surprising, but at a deeper level this more recent pessimism seems to be the
unsurprising outcome of the rigid theory of history that Gauchet developed in the 1970s and 1980s.

After all, Gauchet continues to rely massively on his hypothesis that
our autonomy is to be explained through the process of leaving religion.
The exit from religion continues in the present, he tells us in 1998; the
political and anthropological forms that have emerged beyond religion
never cease to be simultaneously haunted and supported by the vestiges of
the religious form, he insists in 2002.[135] Yet he claims that we have reached
a new stage in this process or, more precisely, France has reached a new
stage. (It must be noted that Gauchet's work after *Disenchantment of the
World* has become increasingly narrow in its focus on France, although he
repeats a move made by a long succession of forward-looking French nationalists insofar as he transmutes this provincialism into universalism by
insisting that France has experienced certain general trends of the modern
world with particular intensity.) In this allegedly new historical stage, the
political struggle against religion seems complete. Not only has the Catholic Church been pushed out of the political domain by the lay republic,
but all reference to the divine has been fully excised. Yet this turns out to
be a source of worry for Gauchet because democracy thereby loses the
object—the ultimate other—against which it had defined itself. Again,
Gauchet speaks here specifically of France, and he measures France's current condition against a model of politics shaped mainly by the Third
Republic.[136] Militant secularism, he insists, galvanized the sensibility of
the Third Republic's champions and gave them a meaningful horizon of
action and aspiration. Insofar as politics could pose as an "alternative" to
religion, politics could undergo an elevation (*sublimation*) to a higher
plane.[137] Moreover, the republic could function as an alternative form of

the sacred, as it did in Durkheim's analysis, or as a supreme moral instance over all the religions, as it did for Charles Renouvier.[138] The victory of the republic, however, turns out to be phyrrhic. With the complete triumph over religion, in the absence of its ultimate other, democracy loses its substance. Gone is the old spiritual energy of the priesthood of the citizen, the "moral majesty of the state," and "sacrifices on the altar of public affairs."[139] Amplifying this sense of loss is the decline of secular substitutes for religion, particularly communism. With the definitive end of the "revolutionary faith," we have lived through the end of eschatological history, a sea change that Gauchet dates very recently, effectively since the 1970s and especially since the collapse of the Soviet Bloc.[140] Like Furet's *The Passing of an Illusion*, which appeared in 1995, Gauchet's *Religion in Democracy* maintains that liberal democracy has become the unsurpassable horizon of our era; yet whereas Furet predicts that the austere and disenchanted world of liberal democracy will spawn new utopian dreams, Gauchet worries that it will only bring apathy and the citizen's ever greater retreat from identification with the collective institution of society.

To repeat, Gauchet tries to present all this as a contingent development within the open horizons of "historical society," his preferred term for the world that has emerged from the closed symbolic universe of religion. Yet this analysis of contemporary (French) democracy seems driven less by empirical study than by the internal logic of his theoretical model. The age of hyperindividualism, which has evidently grown to such a point that the collective power of society is imperiled, seems less like a contingent historical outcome than the next logical step in the dynamic of transcendence. In his historical analysis of French politics, Gauchet sees the period from roughly 1880 to 1914 as a crucial turning point. According to him, throughout the nineteenth century the power of civil society steadily waxed, meaning that the vital political question of the age was how the state could cope with this. The republican solution lay in the parallel growth of both society *and* the state; as society's claims became more and more extensive, the state expanded to meet them. Democratic pressures strained the state, but they did not in the end topple the state's edifice. Instead of accommodating individuals and social groups by descending down into the competitive jostling of society, the state grafted its authority onto its capacity to represent society as a whole. "In effect," writes Gauchet of the state, "far from being weakened by the democratization of its principle (in the name of the general will) and by the liberalization of its exercise (in the name of particular beliefs), the latter found itself justified and reaffirmed. By its grace, political debate and action became the alchemical crucible of collective transcendence."[141] Later in the same discussion, Gauchet insists that although the order that holds people together is their own creation, "politics conceived as the deliberate arrangement of an artificial collective body in this way constitutes for humanity the sublime vector of a transcendent affirmation of its liberty."[142]

So, to adapt Gauchet's succinct formulation for humanity's exit from religion to the new conditions of postreligious liberal democracy, the greater the state, the freer the individual. If this description bears any resemblance to the real situation of French politics, can it be any wonder that individuals drifted away from their republican vocation by the end of the twentieth century? Let us operate for a moment strictly within Gauchet's terms. Just as the gods mattered less and less once their transcendence put them at an insurmountable distance from the space of human thought and action, so too, as the state's distance from society grows, must the quasi transcendence of the republican state cease to have much hold on people. And then, too, just as the early modern king ceased to be a mediating figure between society and its extrasocial foundation and became instead the representative of the human collective body's internal self-congruence, is it not a further logical step that the state as a quasi-transcendent symbol of the collective is eventually penetrated by the plurality of conflicts and desires that mark the actual reality of society?

In a 2003 exchange with Régis Debray, Gauchet worried that with the loss of the phantom form of religion France lost that "collective transcendence of which the nation and the state are the main incarnations."[143] The symbolic representation of the collective, he writes in 1998, permits the collectivity to "see and conceive itself": the function of representation is "simultaneously specular, scenographic, and cognitive."[144] This capacity to comprehend our societies as coherent entities is what we lost along with the decline of religion, he asserts. Those readers inclined to regard politics as more than just an optical phenomenon may be mildly placated by Gauchet's concession that the difficulty of gaining such a symbolic comprehension weakens the possibility of collective action.[145] However, there is no mistaking that Gauchet's emphasis lies on the legitimizing function of symbolic form and not on the transformative possibilities of collective activism. If a malaise has settled over modern liberal democracies, it may have less to do with the decline in the authority of a transcendent representation of the collective than with the extremely thin conception of democracy that prevails in those regimes. And here Gauchet occupies an ironic position, for, even as he tries to diagnose the symptoms of a decline in democratic energy, his entire theoretical account of the rise of modern democracy pushes toward exactly this impasse. There is an insidious self-confirming circularity in Gauchet's assertion that the chief paradox of contemporary democracy is that the greater its triumph, the greater the indifference of its citizens.[146] For Gauchet has identified the march of history with the realization of a strikingly restricted and minimal conception of democracy. Collectivity emerges in his work as an ideally homogeneous agent beyond which lies the chaos of unintegrated social conflict among self-interested individuals. He speaks frequently of collective action, but collective action seems more like a strictly symbolic performance transacted within the representational domain of transcendent democracy. He has almost nothing to say about actual social movements or agents, except when they seem to pose a threat to the alleged stability of the process whereby collective power is integrated into the symbolic realm of the political. He tells us in an interview that he never shared in "that faith in the creative effervescence of the margins. I never succeeded in seeing in that irresponsible radicality anything other than a corruption of democracy."[147] In Gauchet's account both history and normative criteria channel social energies into a rigidly formalistic, homogeneous, and reified conception of democracy. It can hardly be surprising that people are less than motivated by democratic politics if this is all that democracy is. If democracy is *against* itself, that formulation has truth only if one accepts the narrow terms in which Gauchet has confined his thinking about democratic politics.

In *La condition historique* Gauchet describes himself as "veering to the right," which he equates with rallying to "normal politics." This turn, he acknowledges, involved distancing himself from Claude Lefort and what he calls "political inconsequence."[148] Lefort remained quite silent about the direction his student had taken, but another former Lefort student and erstwhile comrade of Gauchet's showed no such reticence. In 2008 Miguel Abensour published an open letter condemning a man with whom he had once collaborated, for example in the journals *Textures* and *Libre* or in the production of an edition of Étienne de La Boétie's *Le discours de la servitude volontaire* and a series of accompanying essays. Abensour was provoked by *La condition historique*, where Gauchet identifies Abensour as a "revoltist" in an interview tracing his path leading toward the founding of *Le Débat*. The interview recalls that Abensour had drawn upon Lefort to theorize a conception of democracy stressing the utopian imperative and the "protests of the margins as the authentic vector of collective invention."[149] For his part, Abensour's open letter reaffirms what he had long drawn from Claude Lefort, namely that Lefort's concept of democracy means more than simply a situation of permanent contestation.[150] Rather, he argues, Lefort offered a robust theory of the uncertainty and indeterminacy of the democratic condition, an uncertainty that reaches down to the very foundations of the democratic order.

This is the essence of the *démocratie sauvage* with which Abensour had for years identified Lefort.[151] In his letter against Gauchet, Abensour relinquishes this phrase in favor of "insurgent democracy," but the political vision remains unchanged. In place of Gauchet's image of a framework of quasi-transcendental democratic institutions, Abensour insists on the interminability of the democratic revolution. Where Gauchet identifies democracy with a specific political regime, Abensour recognizes democracy as a specific political institution of the social.[152] In an insightful article from 2006, the political theorist James Ingram traces out the divergent paths of Abensour and Gauchet and rightly notes that both derive from Lefort's ideas.[153] Ingram attributes these derivations to the ambiguity of Lefort himself, whose political philosophy could lend itself to "radicalization or restoration, the deepening or limiting of democracy, awakening from an old ideological slumber or falling into a new one."[154] Yet I do not think Lefort is quite so equivocal. After all, Lefort's idea of regime has little to do with a specific institutional arrangement, but with a specific *mise en forme* of social life. His praise of democracy, as he repeatedly emphasized, lies not in what it *does*, but in what it *causes to be done*; that is, its power to arouse constant agitation in people.

At the bottom of this interpretation of democracy lies Lefort's understanding of the symbolic dimension. Lefort's symbolic dimension is not a quasi-transcendental realm of representation. It is partially a specific *space*, or, to follow his own terminology, it is a *place*. But precisely because in modern democracy it is an empty place, it is both a place and no place. It is this ambiguity that links Lefort's idea of the symbolic dimension of the political to an expansive conception of democracy as a social experience. It allows Lefort to describe the political in the dynamic terms of Merleau-Ponty's philosophy. Democracy contains potential for chiasmatic exchanges of the ruled and the rulers, the represented and the representation. The symbolic construct not only anchors the action of the democratic subject by relating it to an institutional symbol of the collectivity. Rather the symbolic creates transversal relations. The political *mise en forme* may well produce a certain kind of democratic subject, but democratic subjects potentially produce that political *mise en forme* in an open and reversible process. To be sure, Lefort backed away from Cornelius Castoriadis's radical vision of autonomy when he insisted that the institution of the social is *no one's act*. Yet, even if he thereby acknowledged a debt to the insights of political theology, Lefort nonetheless envisioned modernity to be most fully characterized by a *démocratie sauvage*, animated by an *esprit sauvage*, sitting tenuously atop brute being. Though he renounced the dream of revolution decades before his death in 2010, Lefort never rallied to "normal" politics, whatever that vague phrase might mean. Indeed, his description of the symbolic dimension of modern democracy could feed into radical democratic projects such as those we shall encounter in Ernesto Laclau, Chantal Mouffe, and Slavoj Žižek.

CHAPTER FIVE

The Post-Marx of the Letter

*Laclau and Mouffe Between Postmodern Melancholy
and Post-Marxist Mourning*

IN A LATE TEXT LOUIS ALTHUSSER urged his readers to give "the crisis of Marxism" a "completely different sense from collapse and death." Instead of writing the epitaph for Marxism, he insisted, it was necessary to show "how something vital and alive can be liberated by this crisis and in this crisis."[1] This missive went unanswered by Althusser's French readers, and in fundamental ways it remains unanswered to this day. Indeed, by the time Althusser dispatched his call in 1977, the French intelligentsia was in "the process of full de-Marxification."[2] With the left-wing parties and unions compromised by their response to the events of May 1968, the 1970s witnessed the fragmentation of the left followed by the near wholesale collapse of the miscellany of Maoists, Trotskyists, *autogestionnaires* and council socialists, anarchists, and so on. The leading edge of radicalism had passed to the philosophers of desire and the postmodern critics of normativity, metanarratives, and metaphysical "humanism." The podium of moral declamation had been seized, albeit briefly, by the ex-Marxist New Philosophers, while, more quietly and more profoundly, the ground was shifting toward liberal democratic pluralism, a sea change that would thrust into prominence older figures like Claude Lefort and François Furet and prepare the way for younger talents like Marcel Gauchet and Pierre Rosanvallon. In such a climate, not only was Althusser's call unheeded but also his once extraordinarily influential brand of structural Marxism, his so-called theoretical practice, was permanently eclipsed.

Yet this seems to be a case verifying Jacques Lacan's remark that "a letter always arrives at its destination."[3] For if the call went unanswered in France, it was heard in England; or at least the spirit of a call that was not Althusser's alone animated a great deal of English intellectual labor of the late 1970s and 1980s. The contrast between the two contexts during that period is striking. For even though the post-1968 British left entered a period of crisis that only escalated with the success of Thatcherism in the early 1980s, the desire to liberate something "vital and alive" from this crisis remained powerful. Perhaps the most original, intellectually engaging, and influential of all such efforts was *Hegemony and Socialist Strategy*, the 1985 book written by Ernesto Laclau and Chantal Mouffe, an Argentine and a Belgian who had made their careers in England. Yet it was undoubtedly one of the most controversial as well, for Laclau and Mouffe sought to restore the theoretical dignity of Marxism by articulating a "post-Marxism without apologies."[4] Their double gesture of going beyond Marxism while incorporating it as a legacy and moral compass—signaled concisely in their claim to be both "*post*-Marxist" and "post-*Marxist*"— thematized the ambiguity of their intervention in relation to the various discourses that claimed patrimony from Marx. Yet another ambiguity resided in the fact that Mouffe and Laclau sought to rethink leftist politics using precisely the poststructuralist conceptual tools that in France had operated simultaneously as cause and symptom of the collapse of Marxist politics in the 1970s.

Laclau and Mouffe's post-Marxism belongs to the intellectual history of France after 1968, and this for two reasons. First, because they continued a trajectory launched in France but all but fully arrested there and, second, because the deflection of that trajectory into England offers an outstanding example of both the persistent importance of local context *and* the ultimate insufficiencies of the national paradigm in the study of intellectual history.[5] When we are dealing with a project firmly grounded in French poststructuralism, addressed to the international crisis of the left, and articulated in England by a Belgian woman educated in France and her English-educated Argentine husband teaching at Essex University and drawing on his formative political experience in the Argentine left, the question arises, just where *is* "French" thought in the decades after 1968?

The International Career of Hegemony

When Jacques Derrida addressed Marxism's collapse in his 1993 book *Specters of Marx*, he spoke of a sense of déjà vu that made the question of Marxism's fate resonate like "an old repetition."[6] Similarly, Mouffe and Laclau placed themselves in relation to a genealogy of distress within Marxism. As Laclau emphasized in a 1988 interview, "post-Marxism" is not a deviation from a pure source, but a radicalization of "the ambiguity of Marxism—which runs through its whole history" and is present even in Marx himself. "The act of constitution of post-Marxism is not different from its genealogy: that is, from the complex discourses through which it has been gradually gestating, including the Marxist tradition."[7] A substantial part of *Hegemony and Socialist Strategy* is devoted to this genealogical reconstruction of the conflict in twentieth-century socialist thought between a deterministic social metaphysics grounded in the essentialist categories of class and economy and the contingencies and exigencies of historical existence.

Antonio Gramsci holds pride of place in this history because of his radical reworking of the idea of hegemony, which he inherited from Russian debates about the gap between the "necessary laws of history" and the actual political demands of the Russian situation. Gramsci's emphasis on the importance of consent in the formation of bourgeois domination shifted the proletarian struggle onto the ideological terrain of civil society; at the same time, his conception of the materiality of ideology identified ideology not merely with ideas or mental representations, but with "an organic and relational whole, embodied in institutions and apparatuses, which weld together a historical bloc around a number of basic articulatory practices. This precludes the possibility of a 'superstructuralist' reading of the ideological."[8] Finally, and most important for Mouffe and Laclau, Gramsci's recognition of the historical and contingent character of the working class' assertion of its claims and identity subverted the essentialist determinist logic of Marxist thinking about class. Gramsci thereby pointed toward a new recognition of "social complexity as the very condition of political struggle," and thus his conception of hegemony "sets the basis for a democratic practice of politics, compatible with a plurality of historical subjects."[9]

Laclau and Mouffe's appropriation of the Gramscian concept of hegemony came as they distanced themselves from their earlier attachment to

Althusser. In an online interview in 1998, Mouffe, who had been a student of Althusser's in Paris, explained that, "I became a Gramscian when I ceased to be an Althusserian." Gramsci offered her a way out of an "Althusserian kind of dogmatism" that Althusser's followers were then putting into practice.[10] Laclau's attachment was more tenuous than that of his wife. Although the theory of ideology offered in his 1977 book, *Politics and Ideology in Marxist Theory*, contains a strong Althusserian dimension, Laclau emphasized in a 1988 interview that it was only insofar as Althusser seemed to subvert the totalizing character of Marxist discourse that his work attracted him. This disruptive resource lay in Althusser's "overdetermined contradiction," a concept with a psychoanalytic provenance that opened the way for Laclau and Mouffe's break with the economistic reductionism of classic Marxism. Yet, as Laclau has often noted, the nonreductionist theory suggested in Althusser's *For Marx*, the 1965 collection of his articles from the early 1960s, was belied by the tendency toward a closed structuralist system already discernible in *Reading Capital*, published also in 1965.[11] Given Althusser's increasing rigidity, Laclau maintained in the 1988 interview, it was not surprising that the Althusserian school "had little time to mature intellectually in a post-Marxist direction—the '68 wave created a new historical climate that turned obsolete all that analytical-interpretative lucubration around Marx's holy texts; but in the second place . . . the Althusserian project was conceived as an attempt at an internal theoretical renewal of the French Communist Party—a project that gradually lost significance in the seventies."[12] Althusser's own development may have been arrested by both his own internal impasses and the course of post-1968 politics, but Laclau acknowledged that "a great deal of my later works can be seen as a radicalization of many themes already hinted at in *For Marx*."[13] The recovery of Gramsci played an indispensable role in this process of radicalization.

In thus turning to Gramsci, Laclau and Mouffe were in fact participants in an international surge of engagement with the Italian theorist. In England the influence of Gramsci can be found as early as the post-1956 thaw, when de-Stalinization and the formation of the New Left found a resource in the 1957 edition of *The Modern Prince and Other Writings*.[14] The cultural and historical analysis pioneered by scholars like Raymond Williams and Edward Thompson drew on Gramsci, as did Tom Nairn and Perry Anderson's theoretical analyses of the British state and the labor movement. In the mid-1970s Gramsci's influence strengthened, as Grams-cians gained considerable influence in the British Communist Party and played a crucial role in the emergence of a Eurocommunist majority at the party's Thirty-fifth Congress in 1977. On a different plane, the cultural Marxist appropriation of Gramsci begun by figures like Thompson and Williams gained new momentum in cultural and media studies, most im-portantly at the Centre for Contemporary Cultural Studies at Birming-ham University and the Popular Culture group at the Open University. Surveying the Continent in 1977, Chantal Mouffe and Anne Showstack Sassoon argued that the end of the 1960s marked an important turning point in French and Italian Gramscian studies because the parochial and dogmatic treatment of Gramsci as the theorist of the Italian Communist Party had broken down. Freed from the narrow reading of the Italian communists, Gramsci emerged as the "theoretician of the revolution in the West." Mouffe and Sassoon reserved special praise for the works of Leonardo Paggi and Christine Buci-Glucksmann, who offered compelling readings of Gramsci as the theorist of the superstructures.[15] Even more important, both Paggi and Buci-Glucksmann used Gramsci to criticize Althusser's insistence upon distinguishing "ideology" and "science" as well as his characterization of Marxist philosophy as the "theory of theoretical practice." Gramsci, by contrast, rejected the notion of philosophy as a "science with a specific object" and recognized philosophy as a vital politi-cal action in the ideological struggle.[16] In Mouffe and Sassoon's reading, Gramsci thus emerges as a kind of post-Althusserian. As Mouffe wrote, "If the history of Marxist theory during the 1960s can be characterized by the reign of 'althusserianism,' then we have now, without a doubt, entered a new phase: that of 'gramscism.'"[17] In Britain, too, the decline of Althus-serianism coincided with the rise of Gramsci, as structuralist analysis gave way to awareness of the need for historical modes of analysis to account for the "surging conservative revival coalescing around the person of Mar-garet Thatcher."[18]

Mouffe's own contribution to her 1977 edited volume on *Gramsci and Marxist Theory* points toward important dimensions of *Hegemony and Socialist Strategy*, but it remained within a Marxist framework as did most of the international engagement with Gramsci. In the intervening years leading up to the publication of *Hegemony*, Mouffe and Laclau became convinced that Marxism was not only inadequate but was rather an obstacle to the effort to understand the post-1968 proliferation of new social movements—"feminisms, ecology, peace, Third World solidarities, gay-lesbian rights, and antiracism, as well as squatting and the broader alternative scenes"—and the distinctive forms of democratic politics that had emerged after '68.[19] Gramsci offered a promising resource for this project, but only if his ideas were detached from his own ultimate reliance on the essentialist core of Marxism: its insistence on the foundational status of the material base. Hence Laclau and Mouffe grafted the notion of hegemony onto the stem of French poststructuralism, seeing hegemony as the process whereby the social world is constructed through discourse. Viewed in this light, the relationship between workers and socialism, for example, is not a necessary relationship, but rather the outcome of a process of articulation and political contestation. Social agents do not discover their common interests in an underlying shared essence, but forge them through "articulatory practices" that construct discourses operating within a political space that is itself not determined by the logic of anything exterior to it. "The relation of articulation is not a relation of necessity," wrote Laclau and Mouffe. "What the discourse of 'historical interests' does is to *hegemonize* certain demands. . . . Political practice constructs the interests it represents."[20]

This detachment of interests from some anterior social base might alone have been sufficiently blasphemous to draw the wrath of many Marxists, but the real novelty and radicalism of Laclau and Mouffe came from their appropriation of poststructuralism. Following Derrida's deconstructive strategy, they argued that there is no "transcendental signified," no "eidos, arché, telos, energia, ousia, alétheia, etc."[21] Lacking a point of anchor, meaning is purely relational, emerging out of a mobile play of differences, presences, and absences. Insofar as society is discursively constructed, this differential element ensures that society itself can never be a closed, fixed system of meaning. "Society" is *impossible*, in the strict sense that society can never be fully present as an objective field, "a sutured and self-defined totality."[22] But Mouffe and Laclau were also careful to insist that if society is not "totally possible, neither is it totally impossible."[23] This play of possibility and impossibility within an overdetermined field opens up the potentiality of hegemonic politics. Hegemony works by establishing equivalential links among entities within a field of difference. Hence, for example, the articulation of the Rights of Man and Citizen opens further arguments that those rights require an extension to people of color as well as to women, thereby displacing democratic discourse from the field of political equality among citizens to the field of equality between the sexes or between races. Hegemony is not "an irradiation of effects from a privileged point," but "basically metonymical: its effects always emerge from a surplus of meaning."[24] Hegemony combines elements around a core, what Mouffe and Laclau named a *point de capiton*, borrowing Lacan's term for the "privileged signifiers that fix the meaning of a signifying chain" and thereby establish the positions that make predication possible.[25] In a key statement, Mouffe and Laclau wrote: "The practice of articulation, therefore, consists in the construction of nodal points which partially fix meaning; and the partial character of this fixation proceeds from the openness of the social, a result, in its turn, of the constant overflowing of every discourse by the infinitude of the field of discursivity."[26]

In the 1990s Laclau's work became increasingly stamped by Lacan, inspired in part by Slavoj Žižek's efforts to fully integrate post-Marxism into the field of Lacanian psychoanalysis. This is a topic to which we will return in the concluding pages of this chapter, but, at present, it suffices to note that in *Hegemony and Socialist Strategy* Lacan was just one resource underlying Laclau and Mouffe's insistence that the "meaning-giving" human subject cannot be defended as the last redoubt of essentialism. Having abandoned the straitjacket of Marxism, Laclau and Mouffe refused to have their identities bounded by any specific theoretical frontier. Many theoretical legacies tattoo the body of their text. Hence they located themselves in a continuum with Nietzsche, Freud, Wittgenstein, Heidegger, and, of course, the French poststructuralists in contesting the view of the subject as an "agent both rational and transparent to itself" and the "conception of the subject as origin and basis of social relations."[27] In place of "subjects," they spoke of "subject positions" formed within a discursive structure. The subject is itself a *point de capiton*, a nodal point that is implicated *within* and created *by* the practices of articulation. As with every other element of the discursive field, the subjectivity of the agent is penetrated by the same precariousness and polysemy that overflow all attempts to conceal or "suture" the indeterminacy of meaning. Ultimately, then, hegemonic politics is about the struggle for the creation of new subjects or, more precisely, new subject positions, through the practices of articulation. The distance from Marxism is clear; as with any other social identity, class identity is a subject position created through articulation. The classic socialist struggle over the relations of production has no primacy, but is itself the outcome of a certain discursive practice. Indeed, even though Mouffe and Laclau went to great lengths to emphasize that the preoccupations of traditional socialist politics remain important dimensions of democratic struggle, they become just one dimension of "radical democracy," the concept offered by Laclau and Mouffe to describe the political project opened by the much more fractured, pluralistic, and mobile front of new social movements contesting social, sexual, racial, and gender hierarchies.

Laclau and Mouffe's concept of the construction of the subject through language "as a partial and metaphorical incorporation into a symbolic order" has led some critics to argue that they were insufficiently detached from Althusser's view of the subject as passively produced through the process of ideological interpellation.[28] Laclau went to some lengths to dispel this view in a 1988 interview. While acknowledging that his first works had drawn on Althusser's "Spinozan notion of a 'subject effect,' which merely stems from the logic of the structures," he emphasized that the production of subjects through interpellation works only if the individuals thus being hailed *identify* with ideology. Given this view, he and Mouffe conceived interpellation "as part of an open, contingent, hegemonic-articulatory process which can in no sense be confused with Spinozan 'eternity.' "[29] Laclau and Mouffe's resistance to Althusser found a striking expression in their intervention in the debate prompted by Edward Thompson's attack on the Althusserians in *The Poverty of Theory*.[30] In opposition to Thompson's essentialist humanism, Laclau and Mouffe emphasized the complexity of the discourses that have produced the modern subject and hence the fragility and incomplete project of "humanism," and, contrary to Althusser's relegation of humanism to the field of ideology, they insisted not only on the effective power of humanist discourse in emancipatory struggles since the eighteenth century but also on the forms of overdetermination that always put subjects in excess of any symbolic order.[31] Between the essentialism of the humanist "subject" and the excessive swing of poststructuralist thought toward the metaphor of dispersal, Laclau and Mouffe insisted that an analysis of subjectivity "cannot dispense with the forms of overdetermination of some positions by others," a conception of relation that resists both dispersal and suture.[32]

This intervention offers a striking instance of the contextual hybridity of Laclau and Mouffe's text. They act here as *mediators* in the conflict between "humanists" and "antihumanists," which in France reached something of an apex in Alain Renaut and Luc Ferry's *La pensée 68: Essai sur l'anti-humanisme contemporain*, published the same year as *Hegemony*. The fact that their mediation comes through a commentary on the climactic clash between British Marxist humanism and Althusser, or at least his British proxies, suggests the multiple levels at which Laclau and Mouffe acted as cultural *brokers*, standing at the point of exchange between two intellectual and political traditions.

Mourning or Melancholy?

Post-Marxism reinvents social struggle in terms of postmodernism's general critique of logocentrism and essentialism. Post-Marxism thereby taps directly into a main intellectual trend in French thought since the 1960s. After 1968, when orthodox Marxism and the Parti communiste français revealed their bankruptcy in the streets, French theorists turned to new forms of critical thought emphasizing the importance of contingency, microresistance, cultural rebellion, and a conception of the political no longer bounded by the state. Waves of theory ceased to refer to Marx and socialism and celebrated new forms of liberation instead. Hence Deleuze and Guattari's schizopolitics, Foucault's micropolitics, Lyotard's gaming, Derrida's aesthetic play, and Baudrillard's celebration of the hyperreal simulacrum.

In an essay entitled "The Apocalyptic Imagination and the Inability to Mourn" Martin Jay explores the double meaning of these febrile gestures of postmodernism. Jay takes his point of departure from Eric Santner's suggestion that much postmodernism represents itself as a healthy mourning for the lost hopes of the modernist project. However, drawing on Freud's distinction between mourning and melancholia, Jay underscores the apparent endlessness of postmodern mourning. The insistence on the inability of language to achieve a plenitude of meaning leads to "a valorization of repetition that is closer to melancholy than mourning *per se*."[33] As Jean Baudrillard wrote in 1981, "Melancholy is the quality inherent in the mode of disappearance of meaning, in the mode of volatilization of meaning in operational systems. And we are all melancholic."[34] In Freud's famous discussion, writes Jay, the work of mourning is "conscious of the love-object it has lost," and "it is able to learn from reality testing about the actual disappearance of the object and thus slowly and painfully withdraw its libido from it. The love-object remains in memory, it is not obliterated, but it is no longer the target of the same type of emotional investment as before."[35] Instead of gradually withdrawing his libidinal attachment from the lost object, the melancholic internalizes the object as a form of self-identification. According to Freud's model, the melancholic ego's regressive narcissistic identification with the lost object couples with guilt to produce alternating states of manic elation and self-punishing low-esteem. From this perspective it might be suggested that postmodernism's celebration of excess is the manic side of a melancholia that manifests itself in fantasies of obliteration and endless dispersal. Martin Jay argues that this vacillation helps to explain the peculiarity of the postmodern apocalyptic imagination, which works with only one side of the apocalyptic tradition: the threat of destruction, but not the promise of revelation.

Post-Marxism would seem to compound the sources of melancholy, as it not only inhabits the loss of meaning but also the specific loss of Marxism as a privileged object, intellectual investment, and emotional cathexis. Certainly, the language of mourning is not absent. Laclau and Mouffe viewed Marxism as a tradition, a culture, a collective memory, a personal past, and a personal identity. As Laclau said in 1988, "The loss of collective memory is not something to be overjoyed about. It is always an impoverishment and a traumatic fact. One only thinks *from* a tradition."[36] Jacques Derrida, who entered this discussion with *Specters of Marx*, oriented the discussion of Marxism toward bereavement. Derrida wrote of an uncanny situation in which Marx has vanished but continues to haunt us. Marx's specter becomes a way for Derrida to activate the *trace* of meaning as a political principle; the ghostly presence of Marx's demand for justice disrupts the seamlessness of contemporary time. It orients Derrida's call for justice toward the ghosts of those who were and those yet to be. The logic of spectrality, further, furnishes Derrida with a weak—a deliberately weak—hold on the Marxian tradition or at least a "certain spirit of Marxism." That is to say, a dimension of "radical critique" and a "certain emancipatory and messianic affirmation" of a democracy that is always a "promise that can only arise in . . . failure, inadequation, disjunction, disadjustment, being 'out of joint.' "[37]

Although *Specters of Marx* is elegiac in tone, it aims to further the work of mourning by preserving Marxism's radical spirit while rejecting the *strong* messianism, determinism, and ontological foundationalism that overburdened the Marxist tradition. In a lengthy 1999 response to his Marxist critics, Derrida sharply distanced his book from despair or nostalgia. He insisted that "one can discuss the work of mourning, analyze its necessity and political effects across the globe (after the alleged 'death of Marx' or of the communist idea)—one can be constrained to do so for all kinds of reasons, without therefore relinquishing a certain gaiety of affirmative thinking. Even without recalling the many texts and talks I have devoted to this possibility, I think it fair to say that *Specters of Marx* is anything but a sad book."[38]

Despite their admission of trauma, Laclau and Mouffe do not write in the elegiac mode. Indeed, their post-Marxism reverses many of the signs of postmodern melancholia. Whereas the indefinite deferral of meaning had fed a "tone of dread and hysteria" that Derrida described in the 1980 article "Of an Apocalyptic Tone Recently Adopted in Philosophy," the "impossibility of society" furnished a source of optimism for Laclau and Mouffe. Hence Laclau insisted in 1990 that the poststructuralist critique of the rationalism of the project of modernity does not undermine the emancipatory project linked to it. Instead, he argued that the renunciation of the Enlightenment's "rationalistic epistemological and ontological foundations" and a true acceptance of our historicity and contingency expand the democratic potentialities of the Enlightenment tradition, while "abandoning the totalitarian tendencies arising from the [Enlightenment] reoccupation of the ground of apocalyptic universalism."[39] The arrested apocalypse of the postmodern imagination thus furnishes an unexpected principle of hope. As Laclau wrote, "this final incompletion of the social is the main source of our political hope in the contemporary world: only it can assure the conditions for a radical democracy."[40] Recognition of ontological openness, as the condition for the articulation of multiple contestatory subject positions, performs the work of mourning. The post-Marxist can disengage from the lost object of Marxism and form a new cathexis to the self-constituting community of radical democracy. It allows the post-Marxist to "restore Marxism to its theoretical dignity" by creating a genealogy of post-Marxism "from the complex discourses through which it has been gradually gestating, including the Marxist tradition. In this sense, post-Marxism restores to Marxism the only thing that can keep it alive: its relation with the present and its historicity."[41]

At its most fundamental, this post-Marxist principle of hope rests on the recovery of "historicity," that is, the final liberation of the historical world from all vestiges of determinism. Derrida's *Specters of Marx* reminds the reader of deconstruction's basic critique of "the onto-theo- but also archeo-teleological concept of history—in Hegel, Marx, or even in the epochal thinking of Heidegger." This is to be a critique, Derrida wrote, undertaken for the sake of "thinking another historicity . . . another opening of event-ness as historicity that permit[s] one not to renounce, but on the contrary to open up access to an affirmative thinking of the messianic and emancipatory promise as promise: as *promise* and not as onto-theological or teleological program or design."[42] Laclau and Mouffe likewise urge a "radical historicism" based on an "acceptance of our contingency and historicity."[43] Ultimately, both Derrida and the post-Marxists invoke an ontological condition wherein the impossibility of closure defines our "historicity" as the condition of all "history," eventness the condition of the specificity of the event.

Yet if they all draw on a conception of *ek-stasis* that is ultimately of Heideggerean provenance, they move from there in quite different directions. In a very perceptive essay on *Specters of Marx*, Laclau agreed with much of what Derrida had to say, but he sharply parted company over the ethico-political consequence to be drawn from Derrida's "hauntology." Laclau wrote: "The illegitimate transition is to think that from the impossibility of a presence closed in itself, from an 'ontological' condition in which the openness to the event, to the heterogeneous, to the radically other is constitutive, some kind of ethical injunction to be responsible and to keep oneself open to the heterogeneity of the other necessarily follows." For one thing, if the "promise implicit in an originary opening to the 'other'" is an "'existential' constitutive of all experience," then it is always already there, and an injunction would be superfluous. More importantly, Laclau could discern no necessary link between the "impossibility of ultimate closure and presence" and "an ethical imperative to 'cultivate' that openness or even less to be necessarily committed to a democratic society."[44] For Laclau, deconstruction's consequences for politics and ethics could be developed only if deconstruction truly radicalizes undecidability as the "condition from which no necessary course of action follows." And this requires freeing deconstruction from the ethics of Levinas, "whose proclaimed aim," he wrote, "to present ethics as *first* philosophy, should from the start look suspicious to any deconstructionist."[45] In short, Derrida's ethico-political injunction must itself enter into a hegemonic logic if it is to become politically operative.

Similar concerns animate Žižek's more recent critique of Derrida's *Specters of Marx*, which he conducts in a text whose title—in Žižek's typically vaudevillian way—shines a light down one path leading from the French exit from Marxism: "MELANCHOLY AND THE ACT in which the reader will be surprised to learn that anyone who is not a melancholic, or does not agree that we are thrown into a contingent finite universe, can today be suspected of 'totalitarianism.' "[46] Žižek offers a drastic redefinition of the melancholic, whom he no longer sees as "primarily the subject fixated on the lost object, unable to perform the work of mourning it, but, rather, the subject who *possesses* the object, but has lost his desire for it, because the cause which made him desire this object has withdrawn, lost its efficacy." Melancholia "occurs when we finally get the desired object, but are disappointed with it."[47] Derrida's spectral turn to a "certain spirit of Marxism" may indeed be melancholic in this way, or, even better, it may be a melancholic prophylaxis insofar as the messianic promise of a democracy *à venir* remains ineluctably distant from all positive incarnations of democracy. Watching Derrida address his Marxist critics in "Marx & Sons," one shares his irritation at the proprietary and censorious tones of unreconstructed hardliners like Terry Eagleton, but it is hard not to be struck by his double prohibition—against bringing his vision into focus, let alone acting upon it. Derrida's affirmative gaiety seems a very different affair from the recognizably *political* contours of Laclau's hegemonic logic, not to mention from Žižek's call for specific "economico-political measures" to address poverty and other injustices.[48]

The National Contexts of Marxism's Crisis

Supporters and critics of poststructuralism alike have frequently imputed a specific politics to it. In response, Laclau has insisted that "there is nothing

that can be called a 'politics of poststructuralism.'" Rejecting the idea
that there are philosophical systems with "unbroken continuities" that go
from metaphysics to politics, Laclau held in an interview that "the correct
question . . . is not so much which is *the* politics of poststructuralism, but
rather what are the *possibilities* a poststructuralist theoretical perspective
opens for the deepening of those political practices that go in the direction of a 'radical democracy.'"[49] Likewise, in his review of *Specters of Marx*
Laclau maintained that, "with any deconstruction worthy of the name,
there is a plurality of directions in which one can move."[50] Certainly, if
one looks to the early 1980s, when Laclau and Mouffe were composing
their book, there can be no question of the lability of deconstructive politics. Derrida may have praised Laclau and Mouffe in 1993 for their "novel
elaboration, in a 'deconstructive' style, of the concept of *hegemony*,"[51] but
in the early 1980s the most prominent deconstructive variation on the
much-remarked "return of the political" in France was the work of Jean-
Luc Nancy and Philippe Lacoue-Labarthe and the Center for Philosophical Research on the Political that they founded in 1980. For Nancy and
Lacoue-Labarthe, politics is, *à la* Heidegger, implicated in the long history
of humanism's forgetting of Being. Tying political action to the human
subject's "exorbitant" drive toward unity, essence, and domination, Nancy
and Lacoue-Labarthe could at best offer the paradoxical ideal of the "inoperative community," a *being-in-common* that only works so long as it does
not work. Ruling out all exercise of will as a recuperation of the totalitarian
mania for fusion, communion, and substance, Nancy could only invoke
Gelassenheit, or resignation, as the means by which the inoperative community would be "exposed" as "this strange being-the-one-with-the-
other."[52] The contrast to Laclau and Mouffe grows sharper if one measures
their different perspectives on *autogestion*, the political goal of self-management first articulated by Cornelius Castoriadis and *Socialisme ou Barbarie*
in the 1950s and revived as an ideal by student activists in 1968 and then by
the Deuxième Gauche, the post-'68 leftist tendency that repudiated the
bureaucratized politics of the PCF in favor of direct democracy. Where
Laclau and Mouffe criticized self-management only because they believed
that shop-floor politics should not be limited to workers themselves but
should be articulated hegemonically with the interests of other political
agents, Lacoue-Labarthe acknowledged the politics of self-management as
the only viable "provisional politics" in the broken landscape of the left,

even as he fretted that councilist politics focus "unduly on what could indisputably lead to 'Marxist metaphysics,' on the motif of *self*-organization, and that is to say on the conception of the proletariat as Subject."[53]

We may readily accept Laclau's claim that undecidabilty and contingency accompany the moves that political thinkers make, but does that mean there are no other considerations – dare one say, determinations – that might contribute to an understanding of the specific moves that Laclau and Mouffe chose to make? Here it is necessary to expand the discussion of the contextual complexities of their intervention. *Hegemony and Socialist Strategy* is a hybrid product, drawing on various theoretical legacies and responding to various contexts. Differences between the French and English contexts, the remaining pages of this section will argue, help to explain the differences in tone and project that we have noted in the contrast between Laclau and Mouffe, on one side, and figures like Derrida, Lacoue-Labarthe, and Nancy, on the other.

The Soviet invasion of Hungary in 1956 had some similar effects among both English and French left-wing intellectuals. For many, profound disillusionment led them to break with the Communist Party and embark on the various political and intellectual projects that may be loosely grouped as the New Left. In the French context, as we saw in chapter 2, membership in Socialisme ou Barbarie spiked briefly after the Hungarian invasion, while anti-Stalinist groups like the Situationist International and the *Arguments* circle emerged in direct reaction against the Soviet aggression. Yet it was Althusserian Marxism that profited most in the 1960s from French leftist intellectuals' disenchantment with communism. The events of May 1968 shook Althusserianism, as it did structuralism as a whole. Nonetheless, as Dosse notes, the second wind of Marxism among intellectuals after 1968 actually raised Althusser's stocks to unprecedented highs. With Althusser enjoying a growing readership, new enthusiasts, academic consecration, and official PCF recognition, the Althusserians resumed their long march through the structures. Yet "the triumphal period" proved to be as "ephemeral as it was exciting."[54] Indeed, the intellectual left unraveled with stunning speed, and episodes like Althusser's self-criticism, an act of self-destruction that he considered more radical than suicide, or the scathing critique of the apostate Jacques Rancière were local events within a larger story that includes the effects of the "Common Program" that brought the PCF and the Socialist Party into an electoral alliance in

1972, the French publication of Alexander Solzhenitsyn's *Gulag Archipelago*, and the paradoxical effects of François Mitterrand's electoral victory in 1981 upon the leftist sympathies of intellectuals.[55] The rise of the *Nouveaux Philosophes*, the apotheosis of Raymond Aron, the impact of François Furet and Claude Lefort, the revival of political liberalism in the 1980s, the hyperallergic reaction of postmodernists to any manner of totalizing thought—all these mark a reversal that is stunning in its suddenness and depth.

The causes of this sea change are too complex to explore in detail here, but I do want to mention two possible factors. First, numerous commentators have remarked the loaded historical relationship between the state and the political intellectual in France. From at least Émile Zola through Jean-Paul Sartre, the politically engaged intellectual, the universal intellectual who speaks as the voice of reason or the people was an icon in French culture, intimately tied to French national identity and the horizons of possible political action. Historically, this defense of universal values had moved in close step with the Jacobin ideal of the republican state as the agency for the realization of the general will. Identification with this ideal of a power that fully manifests democratic unity combined with commitment to a revolution that would attain this goal at a stroke. This affective-intellectual constellation exercised a powerful hold on the political imagination of the French left even as its object shifted from the French to the Bolshevik Revolution, from republicanism to Marxism. It tended to produce an "ideological manichaeism" that became intense in moments of crisis from the Dreyfus affair, through the 1930s, defeat and resistance in the 1940s, the cold war, right up to 1968.[56] Indeed, we may recognize its continuation into the 1970s in the New Philosophers, in whom Dosse sees "equally violent thinking, the same propensity for exaggeration in other directions, as Althusser had counseled, in order to be heard."[57] The melancholic impasses so common to French poststructuralism seem yet another expression of this Manichaean form. It would assign far too much power to one writer to say that François Furet led the French beyond this impasse, but his 1978 declaration that the French Revolution is "over" may be taken as symptomatic of a shift in intellectual mood and French politics.[58] Furet's conviction that Jacobin-Bolshevism had given way to a liberal consensus and a "normalized" liberal democratic state seemed confirmed in 1986, when a socialist president and a conservative government proved capable of cohabitation in the name of centrist pragmatism. By the 1989 bicentenary of the Revolution, an editorial in *Le Point* could write that "the revolutionary dream of a change of society is abandoned" and celebrate the advent of a "pacified, banalized republic shorn of its passions."[59]

It has become customary to date the decline of the iconic figure of the French intellectual to the development of the liberal consensus and the centrist republic. However, a second factor that might help explain the abrupt reversal of intellectual leftism runs in a somewhat different direction. In a 1983 interview, Michel Foucault evoked wistfully the exciting currents of left-wing thought that had existed since at least 1960 but had disappeared by the early 1980s. Foucault ventured that the crisis of Marxism was the result not of the disappearance of the public intellectual but rather of the democratization of the intellectual function. New circumstances since the 1960s had given "university activity an echo which reverberated widely beyond academic institutions or even groups of specialists, professional intellectuals."[60] Although he acknowledged some gains in terms of public awareness, he essentially endorsed Régis Debray's influential argument that French intellectual life had entered a "media cycle" by the 1970s. As Debray wrote, "Marx called France the land of ideas. The Atlantic world lives in the era of the scoop. Atlantic France has manufactured the ideological scoop. It teaches newsmen nothing, still less men of thought. But it satisfies a certain 'national intellectual personality.' "[61] Under the pressure of the mass media, Foucault argued,

a fairly evolved discourse, instead of being relayed by additional work which perfects it (either with criticism or amplification), rendering it more difficult and even finer, nowadays undergoes a process of amplification from the bottom up. Little by little, from the book to the review, to the newspaper article, and from the newspaper article to television, we come to summarize a work, or a problem, in terms of slogans. This passage of the philosophical question into the realm of the slogan, this transformation of the Marxist question, which becomes "Marxism is dead," is not the responsibility of any one person in particular, but we can see the slide whereby philosophical thought, or a philosophical issue, becomes a consumer item.[62]

In France, a context unusual for the extent of the centralization of education, intellectual life, the media, and the public sphere, the media could perhaps play a particularly strong role in transforming an unsettled debate into the decided conviction of public opinion. That this amplification-effect could stifle debate is made clear if we recall Derrida's announcement at a conference in 1981 that he had maintained "a silence with respect to Marxism" at a time when critical reflection on Marx would simply get sucked into the "anti-Marxist concert."[63]

In his memoir, Eric Hobsbawm recalls with distaste the "militant and ill-tempered anti-communism of so many of the formerly left-wing 'intellocrats'" in the France of the 1980s and 1990s. He writes, "As a by now quite well-known Marxist historian, I found myself for a while a champion of the embattled and besieged French intellectual Left."[64] Although Hobsbawm, a self-described "heterodox communist" right up to his death in late 2012, was by no means typical of contemporary British leftists, his remarks suggest something of the relevant comparison between France and Britain in the post-1968 period. Without question, the British left entered an open-ended period of crisis, defined by the defeat of the Labour Party, the disastrous miners' strikes, eighteen years of Conservative rule, and the return to power in the late 1990s of a Labour Party transformed almost beyond recognition, led by a man whom Hobsbawm calls "Thatcher in trousers."[65] The 1980s saw much discussion around the question, "What's Left?" Despairing as that question was, however, it did not suggest a massive rejection of left-wing allegiances among the intellectuals who continued to pose and explore it. In fact, although the 1980s were politically disastrous for the British left, a left-wing intellectual culture continued in Britain. Lin Chun, a historian of the British New Left, details the growth of left-wing publications and activities during the 1970s. She writes, "All these developments had combined to transform the environment of the intellectual work of the Left. By the end of the decade, Marxist traditions had been much strengthened in some fields in this notoriously parochial country, in sharp contrast to the collapse of Marxist strongholds on the continent at exactly the same time."[66]

To overcome British parochialism had been one of the stated goals of the younger generation of new leftists. Perry Anderson's "Origins of the Present Crisis" was instrumental in opening this direction in the mid-1960s when he lamented the inability of the New Left to develop any "structuralist analysis of British society" and traced the older New Left's intellectual style to Britain's antitheoretical empiricist culture. The poverty of cultural and intellectual life in Britain became a recurrent theme for the contributors to *New Left Review*, and the effort to fill what Anderson called the "absent centre" of British society and culture increasingly took the form of a widening engagement with continental Western Marxism. After 1968 the turn toward Western Marxism deepened as the *New Left Review* group worked to acquaint English readers with the writings of European Marxist thinkers, terra incognita with the exception of Gramsci and, since the mid-1960s, Althusser. Through translations, anthologies of critical essays, and books like Anderson's measured *Considerations on Western Marxism* (1976), British leftist intellectuals became increasingly conversant with Karl Korsch, Georg Lukács, Theodor Adorno, Max Horkheimer, Sartre, and Althusser.[67] Looking back from 1990 to this sustained effort to overcome the British left's intellectual isolation, Anderson noted that 1968 was not merely a political break but a "geo-cultural" one as well.[68]

These circumstances bore directly on the British reception of French poststructuralism. According to Antony Easthope, author of the major survey of British poststructuralism, "Whereas the 'new ideas' and the 'new criticism' were assimilated in America to a liberal and libertarian tradition, in Britain they acquired a radical and political force because they were adopted into the British Marxist and left-culturalist inheritance."[69] In America the reception first began with Derrida and then moved on to Lacan, thus bypassing almost entirely the work of Althusser. In Britain, Easthope shows, the reception began with Althusser in the 1960s and then progressed, through the analysis of ideology, to Lacan.[70] To be sure, with the growth of analytical Marxism, much of the energy on the intellectual left had swung back from the French to the native English "linguistic turn" by the mid-1980s, and even at the height of the British enthusiasm for French theory there were many left-wing dissenters who attacked Althusserian sectarians and regarded structuralism and poststructuralism to be antithetical to the socialist project. One thinks immediately of Edward Thompson, but Perry Anderson can be added to the list of prominent opponents. Despite his willingness to defend Althusser against Thompson, Anderson's *In the Tracks of Historical Materialism* (1983) damns the French theorists; and that condemnation extends to his ill-informed, indeed outright wrong inclusion of Pierre Clastres, Claude Lefort, and Marcel Gauchet among the priests of "Desire," the latest "fashionable philosophy of Parisian irrationalism."[71]

Dogged by controversy as British Althusserianism and Lacanianism undoubtedly were, the important point is that French theory unfolded within, not against, the broad culture of the British left.

Left-wing British intellectuals had often envied the partisan vitality of French intellectual life, the prominence of the public intellectual in France, and the subtleties of French political discussion.[72] Perhaps, however, the more decentralized nature of intellectual life in Britain, the weaker hold of revolution on the political imagination of the left, the strong orientation of leftist intellectuals to questions of culture, the greater distance of intellectuals from the mass media, indeed, the greater marginality of intellectuals within a culture that remained suspicious of abstraction and never appointed its leading writers to a higher moral tribunal, had the effects of immunizing the British left against the more extreme swings that accompanied the collapse of Marxism in France. Post-Marxism may have been vigorously attacked by its staunchest British Marxist critics as quite simply "ex-Marxism,"[73] but we would miss a crucial dimension of the tone and substance of Mouffe and Laclau's appropriation of poststructuralism if we failed to see it as partly a product of the British context, where the crisis of Marxism was not accompanied by an "antitotalitarian moment," public rituals of self-abasement, and the manic-depressive tone of so much French thought of the period.

Hegemony and Socialist Strategy was a relay between two political and intellectual cultures that responded quite differently to the crisis of the left after 1968. Lest we fall into a simple image of a two-way trade between the British and French elements of this construction, it is important to at least mention yet another context haunting their discourse, namely the impact of their Latin American experiences. Mouffe, who had moved from Belgium to Paris in the mid-1960s, became involved in anti-imperialist movements and Latin American politics. This led her to go to Colombia, where she lectured in philosophy at the National University from 1967 to 1973. Mouffe credits the specific dynamics of Latin American politics with accelerating a critical revaluation of structural Marxism that had begun even before she left Paris.[74] To an even greater extent, Ernesto Laclau's formative experiences were Latin American, due to his involvement in the Argentine Socialist Party of the national left during the 1960s. Within that context, Laclau has emphasized, the classical issues and divisions of the European left were overshadowed by the political legacy of Juan Perón, who had been elected president in 1946 by "a heterogeneous coalition of the most diverse kind, ranging from the far-left to the far-right."[75] The challenges of left-wing politics in a situation dominated by Peronist populism gave Laclau the "experience of the ambiguity of democratic banners—what we would today call 'floating signifiers'—as well as the recognition of the centrality of the categories of 'articulation' and 'hegemony.'" It was unnecessary, Laclau has maintained, to read poststructuralist texts to learn the lessons of contingency and undecidability. "I'd already learnt this through my practical experience as a political activist in Buenos Aires. So when today I read *Of Grammatology*, *S/Z*, or the *Écrits* of Lacan, the examples which always spring to mind are not from philosophical or literary texts; they are from a discussion in an Argentinian trade union, a clash of opposing slogans at a demonstration, or a debate during a party congress."[76] After he came to Europe in 1969, earned a Ph.D. at the University of Essex, and began teaching there, these experiences continued as points of reference for a "nondogmatic" reflection on Marxist theory and politics.

Placing the Post-Marxist Intellectual

From the time when Marx declared that the proletariat finds its *intellectual* weapons in philosophy, through to the Leninist vanguard, Gramsci's war of position, Sartre's committed writer, and Althusser's "theoretical practice," the Marxist tradition reserved a privileged place for the radical intellectual. In the French context a Marxist belief in the unity of theory and practice amplified a long association of the French intellectual with the defense of universal values. Although the figure of the *philosophe engagé* has continued to haunt the French imaginary, the collapse of Marxism ushered in an ongoing discussion of the disappearance of the great intellectual as well as a widespread critique of universal values and the *maîtres à penser* (including structuralists like Lévi-Strauss and Althusser) who had spoken for them. The late 1970s and the 1980s witnessed numerous efforts to demystify that figure. One immediately thinks of Pierre Bourdieu's sociology of academia as well as attempts to reconceptualize the political role of intellectuals, such as Foucault's idea of the "specific intellectual" or Julia Kristeva's notion of the dissident, the latter privileging the Freudian and the avant-garde writer, but *not* the rebel who confronts political power directly.[77] What was the fate of the radical intellectual's political vocation for Mouffe and Laclau, thinkers who situated themselves within the discourses of suspicion directed against the universalism and essentialism that had sustained the traditional intellectual, who nonetheless still claimed, however ambiguously, a legacy in Marxism?

Post-Marxism would seem to imply a greatly diminished place for the political intellectual. After all, the identity of theory and practice seems to be the first casualty of the post-Marxist critique of historical determinism and foundationalist logics. With no logical historical process to discover and no foundation upon which to articulate normative arguments about justice and the good, the older privilege of the intellectual would seem irretrievably shattered. Laclau addressed this issue directly in a 1988 interview, when he described his and Mouffe's role as an extension of Gramsci's idea of the organic intellectual. Like Gramsci, Laclau rejected the definition of intellectuals as a segregated group and instead emphasized "the intellectual function," which establishes "the organic unity of a set of activities, which, left to their own resources, would remain fragmented and dispersed."[78] The intellectual function is thus the practice of articulation. Far from diminishing the intellectual function, the dissolution of rationalist social ontologies like Marxism actually amplifies it because "hegemonic articulations are not a secondary or marginal effect but the ontological level itself of the constitution of the social." Where the tradition of "great intellectuals" had rested on a claim that the intrinsic truth of things could be recognized by certain persons possessing the means of access, the organic intellectual participates in the construction of a truth that is "essentially pragmatic" and "democratic."[79] The intellectual function thus "consists in the invention of languages. If the unity of historical blocs is given by 'organic ideologies' that articulate into new projects fragmented and dispersed social elements, the production of those ideologies is the intellectual function *par excellence*." Laclau emphasizes that these ideologies are not "utopias" proposed to society, but "inseparable from the collective practices through which social articulation takes place."[80]

This radicalization of the Gramscian organic intellectual raises as many problems as it resolves, however. For one thing, it suffers the dilemma common to pragmatist arguments, for it dispenses with the effort to confirm truth claims in any manner beyond the validation that comes when an argument works politically. A glaring example of this problem comes when Mouffe and Laclau seek support in Georges Sorel's concept of "myth."[81] Even leaving aside the troubling political vacillations in Sorel's career and considering only strategic concerns, the Sorelian myth of the general strike seems to illustrate precisely the inadequacy of an articulation that no longer searches for verification beyond the discursive terms set by itself. After all, it can be plausibly argued that the myth of the general strike lulled socialists into complacency, blinded them to their real situation, and impeded their strategic thinking in the years leading up to the outbreak of war in 1914. Laclau and Mouffe's detachment of truth claims from a materialist foundation was, of course, what most upset Marxists. However, even among postfoundationalist political thinkers, one sees a striking contrast. Jürgen Habermas's attempt to develop a discourse theory of democratic legitimation springs immediately to mind; even closer to the discursive tradition within which Laclau and Mouffe operate, their position contrasts sharply with a figure like Claude Lefort. Lefort, whose discussion of the dynamics of the democratic revolution that has unfolded ever since 1789 figures prominently in the final pages of *Hegemony and Socialist Strategy*, approaches their position when he writes that "the quest for truth and the truth itself are one and the same," but his argument that both politics and truth depend on utterance, performance, and a "process of questioning" that is implicit in modern social practices opens a different prospect for the intellectual.[82] Lefort describes the intellectual pursuit as requiring a "heroism of mind" animated and haunted by "the 'impossible' task of disclosing that which is—the being of history, of society, of man—and of creating, of bringing forth through the exercise of a vertiginous right to thought and to speech, the work in which meaning makes its appearance."[83] In admittedly quite different ways, Habermas and Lefort each insists upon the intellectual's responsibility to the argument itself as well as the possibility of deliberative capacities within the public(s) construed in the broadest terms. Vexed though the question of validity has become, there remains a compelling need to understand the process whereby we test our claims as something that reaches beyond the pragmatic goal of constructing historical blocs, even if we also recognize the impossibility of foundational guarantees and the untenability of the traditional intellectual's privileged position vis-à-vis truth.

Even on Laclau and Mouffe's own terms, there seems to be a deep division between the organic intellectual's role in inventing languages that will unify fragmented social elements into new political projects and the deconstructive intellectual's understanding of the constitutive impossibility of identity. Social movements, even ones occupying the fragmented space of contemporary politics, do not thrive on a sense of their own impossibility, nor do movements coalesce around a sense of their own arbitrariness and contingency. Indeed, the new social movements have not been without their essentialisms. So, for example, the Women's Peace Camp founded at Greenham Common U.S. Air Force Base in 1981 by the Women for Life on Earth Peace March banned men throughout the thirteen years of its existence. Nature, not nurture, let alone choice, is most likely to figure in gay, lesbian, and transgendered claims for rights. Foucault's caution about queer politics is revealing here, for he saw in queer politics a tendency to repeat the essentializing politics of identity he spent his career battling. When English activists connected the closure of coal pits with the expansion of nuclear energy in England, then the women's protest movement at Greenham Common, the global context of nuclear fuels, and finally anti-apartheid and peace groups, organizing a conference called "Make the Links—Break the Chains," which brought all these groups together in 1986, were they *constructing* the connections or *discovering* them?[84] Viewed analytically, this is a perfect example of hegemonic articulation operating within an overdetermined field; however, the agents themselves would likely have been surprised and possibly skeptical to be told that the links were not accurate descriptions of a real state of affairs.

Laclau maintained that even after toppling the pillars of Marxist orthodoxies, the concept of ideology could be retained, "even in the sense of 'false consciousness,' if by the latter we understand that illusion of 'closure' which is the imaginary horizon that accompanies the constitution of all objectivity."[85] Yet the constitution of "objectivity" seems to be a condition of all social movements, thereby rendering all of them instances of false consciousness. To update a Leninist dictum according to post-Marxist logic, left to themselves political agents will never develop more than a predicative consciousness. But how many social movements could survive in the full light of Laclau and Mouffe's knowledge? There seems to be a clear divide between the organic intellectual of the social movement and the deconstructive analyst who exposes the ontology of the social. Possessed of this knowledge, the post-Marxist seems condemned to what Roland

Barthes called "theoretical sociality": "we constantly drift between the object and its demystification, powerless to render its wholeness. For if we penetrate the object, we liberate it but destroy it; and if we acknowledge its full weight, we respect it, but restore it to a state which is still mystified."[86]

Trauma and the Post-Marxist Subject: Žižek's "Beyond Discourse-Analysis"

This observation returns us to the question of trauma. This chapter has argued that Laclau and Mouffe redirected the sources of postmodern melancholia toward the work of mourning, of working through the loss of Marxism and, indeed, the redemptive project of revolution itself. I have tried to delineate their appropriation of poststructuralist theory and suggest reasons—both internal to their own trajectories and related to the contextual hybridity that stamps their work—why they embraced an affirmative stance vis-à-vis the collapse of Marxism, moving beyond a potential impasse into a fruitful theory of social antagonism and the role of discourse in the formation of political movements, in short, why their theory is so French and so very un-French. Yet if the "final incompletion of the social" offers the main source of hope for the project of radical democracy, have the post-Marxists worked through their own mourning at the risk of minimizing a deeper trauma connected to democracy itself? Claude Lefort, whose work represents the best that issued from the French reflection on totalitarianism, speaks of the traumatic core of democracy itself, which was born in the symbolic disincorporation of power. The loss of the visible unity of the body politic, the experience of social division and indetermination haunt the democratic experience. The death of embodied power was the enabling condition of modern democracy, but it also marks an originary scene of loss that still seems to exert power over the psychical life of democracy. "Is it not true," Lefort writes, "that in order to sustain the ordeal of the division of the subject, in order to dislodge the reference points of the *self* and the *other*, to depose the position of the possessor of power and knowledge, one must assume responsibility for an experience instituted by democracy, the indetermination that was born from the loss of the substance of the body politic?"[87]

Lefort's influence is explicit in *Hegemony and Socialist Strategy.* His description of the "empty place" at the center of power in modern democracy forms an essential component of the theory of radical democracy advanced there. Yet Mouffe and Laclau's account of the indetermination that accompanied the disincorporation of power focuses on the enabling effects of this symbolic mutation for a pragmatic politics of radical contestation, while disregarding the traumatic undertow that Lefort believed exerts a permanent drag on the adventure of democracy. Trauma returned to the foreground in one of the earliest and most penetrating discussions of *Hegemony and Socialist Strategy.* In 1985 the obscure Slovenian philosopher Slavoj Žižek published an enthusiastic review of the book in the Paris journal *L'Age.* Two years later, on the occasion of the publication of the Slovenian edition of *Hegemony and Socialist Strategy,* Žižek underscored the importance of the book in an essay that eventually appeared as an appendix in a collection of Laclau's essays in 1990.[88] By then Žižek had published *The Sublime Object of Ideology,* the first of a remarkable and ceaseless flood of works that has carried him to the highest shores of global intellectual celebrity.[89] In "Beyond Discourse-Analysis," Žižek claimed that the breakthrough of *Hegemony and Socialist Strategy* lay in Mouffe and Laclau's concept of social antagonism: "far from reducing all reality to a kind of language-game, the socio-symbolic field is conceived as structured around a certain traumatic impossibility, around a certain fissure which *cannot* be symbolized." In short," Žižek continued, "Laclau and Mouffe have, so to speak, reinvented the Lacanian notion of the Real as impossible, they have made it useful as a tool for social and ideological analysis."[90]

In many respects, this reading of *Hegemony and Socialist Strategy* looks like a textbook example of one of Slavoj Žižek's favorite moves, retroactive reinscription or resymbolization. Lacan, after all, was but one of a number of putatively "poststructuralist" theorists mobilized in Laclau and Mouffe's eclectic book, and their concept of antagonism arguably had more to do with the poststructuralist critique of the metaphysics of presence than with the traumatic encounter between the symbolic and the real.[91] Indeed, in an otherwise laudatory preface to *The Sublime Object of Ideology,* Laclau worried about Žižek's overly "drastic" separation between Lacanian theory and poststructuralism; likewise, having firmly identified Hegel with the kind of totalizing and deterministic thinking that he and Mouffe aimed to overcome, Laclau voiced skepticism about the Slovenian school's "special combination of Hegelianism and Lacanian theory."[92] As for Žižek, his firmer rooting in Lacanian theory manifests itself in a significant recasting of the notion of antagonism as an effect of the traumatic dynamics of the symbolic and the real.

Certainly, Laclau and Mouffe disclosed a debt to Lacan when they described the linguistic construction of the subject "as a partial and metaphorical incorporation into a symbolic order."[93] Yet in many ways their formulation had affinities with Louis Althusser. Of course, Althusser himself had drawn on Lacan, but only on a rigidly structuralist version of Lacanianism that depicted the subject as the interpellated product of the "big Other," that place where the authority of the symbolic order is assumed to lie, that ultimate "quilting point" that stabilizes the entire system of signification and loads individuals with a symbolic mandate and a place in the intersubjective network of symbolic relations.[94] We have already seen that Laclau attempted to distance himself and Mouffe from Althusser, insofar as he insisted that an adequate theory of interpellation would require three elements missing from Althusser: an accompanying theory of the process whereby subjects come to identify themselves with ideology, a view of interpellation as part of a contingent hegemonic-articulatory process, and full recognition that forms of overdetermination ensure that subjects will always be in excess of any symbolic order. Notwithstanding these objections to the Althusserian theory of subjectivation, *Hegemony and Socialist Strategy* remained predominantly within the framework of a linguistic conception of the subject. To be sure, Althusser's rigid structuralism has given way to a more dynamic decentered model animated by surplus and slippage, and interpellation is now imagined as the outcome of political contestation, not an automatic effect irradiating from the big Other. However, Laclau and Mouffe still understand subjectivity as a product of the symbolic order, with identities being relayed up and down the chain of signification, while they see the "overdetermination" that exceeds the symbolic as stemming from the indeterminacies of signifiers themselves. Laclau's recognition that interpellation must be supplemented by a theory of subjective identification does not find its way into the pages of *Hegemony and Socialist Strategy*. In short, Laclau and Mouffe did not provide a theory of the subject so much as a more supple theory of subjectivation, that is, of the creation of subject positions.[95]

Žižek's work in the late 1980s steps directly into the lacuna left open by Laclau and Mouffe. Indeed, *The Sublime Object of Ideology* opens by staging a confrontation between Althusser and Lacan. Althusser's work, writes Žižek,

> embodies a certain radical ethical attitude which we might call the heroism of alienation or of subjective destitution. . . . In contrast to this Althusserian ethics of *alienation* in the symbolic "process without subject," we may denote the ethics implied by Lacanian psychoanalysis as that of *separation*. The famous Lacanian motto not to give way on one's desire . . . is aimed at the fact that we must not obliterate the distance separating the Real from its symbolization: it is this surplus of the Real over every symbolization that functions as the object-cause of desire.[96]

Žižek's contrast between Althusser's reliance upon the symbolic and Lacan's emphasis upon the real rests on one of the central gambits of Žižek's work, namely his insistence on a deep contrast between Lacan's structuralist phase in the 1950s and his subsequent phase as the analyst of the real.[97] In the final stage of his career, Lacan became intensely concerned with that kernel or remainder that can never be integrated into the symbolic order, but produces effects that may be constructed retroactively in the ways it distorts the symbolic reality of subjects. Žižek illustrates this by contrasting the structuralist Lacan's concept of symptom to the later Lacan's notion of fantasy. In the early fifties Lacan conceived symptoms as

> white spots, non-symbolized imaginary elements of the history of the subject, and the process of analysis is that of their integration into the symbolic universe of the subject: the analysis gives meaning, retroactively, to what was in the beginning a meaningless trace. So the final moment of the analysis is reached when the subject is able to narrate to the Other [i.e., the Symbolic Order] his own history in its continuity; when his desire is integrated, recognized in "full speech."

In Lacan's final period, writes Žižek, "we have the big Other, the symbolic order, with a traumatic element at its very heart."[98] This big Other bears no resemblance to Althusser's description of the big Other as an "Absolute Subject" that "occupies the unique place of the Centre, and interpellates around it the infinity of individuals into subjects."[99] Instead, the big Other, the symbolic order, is flawed. It is not-all, carrying an unsymbolizable element at its very heart, an empty place.

Fantasy, in this late Lacanian view, is "conceived as a construction allowing the subject to come to terms with this traumatic kernel." So, writes Žižek, "the final moment of the [analytic process] is defined as 'going through the fantasy': not its symbolic interpretation but the experience of the fact that the fantasy-object, by its fascinating presence, is merely filling out a lack, a void in the Other. There is nothing 'behind' the fantasy; the fantasy is a construction whose function is to hide this void, this 'nothing'— that is, the lack in the Other."[100] Far from trying to exhaustively translate the symptom into the language of the other, the later Lacan focuses on the way the subject organizes itself around the lack or void of the real; a successful analysis would end with the patient *identifying* himself with his symptom, recognizing in the real of his symptom the only support of his being.[101] From the perspective of the later Lacan's understanding of the subject's fantasmatic projections onto the big Other, Žižek offers a corrective to Althusser's account of interpellation that answers to Laclau's call for a theory of identification—namely, before being caught in an ideological identification, in a process of symbolic recognition or misrecognition, the subject is "trapped by the Other through a paradoxical object-cause of desire in the midst of it."[102] That is to say, identification with ideology rests on the constitutive "lack" in the subject itself, which fuels fantasies that somewhere out there is the lost object that will plug the gap in its own makeup. The internalization of ideology never fully succeeds, Žižek argues, because of the residue of the real, but *"this leftover, far from hindering the full submission of the subject to the ideological command, is the very condition of it:* it is precisely this non-integrated surplus of senseless traumatism which confers on the Law its unconditional authority."[103]

Žižek's understanding of Lacan's final phase allowed him to assert the connection between psychoanalysis and social analysis by arguing that both the individual subject *and* the "big Other, the symbolic order itself," are *"barré*—crossed-out—by a fundamental impossibility, structured around an impossible/traumatic kernel, around a central lack."[104] Arguably, then, when he credited Laclau and Mouffe with reinventing the Lacanian real as a tool for social and ideological analysis, Žižek offered empty praise, not only because it is not clear that they were really doing *that* but also because this was in fact the defining core of Žižek's own enterprise, visible already in his first published book, *Hegel: Les plus sublimes des hysteriques*, and spectacularly elaborated in *The Sublime Object of Ideology*, which, incidentally, repackages much of his first French book for an English readership. In recasting Laclau and Mouffe's concept of antagonism he brings to bear the full weight of his *own* reading of Lacan.

"Beyond Discourse-Analysis" endorsed Laclau and Mouffe's basic claim that antagonism arises from the impossibility of society ever achieving fullness or self-identity, yet Žižek argues that they did not take this idea to its most radical conclusion, for they stopped with a vision of various competing subject positions encountering others as impediments to the attainment of full identity.[105] To track antagonism to its most radical dimension, Žižek emphasized the need to move beyond the idea of subject positions and recognize the "traumatic kernel the symbolization of which always fails; and—this is our hypothesis—it is precisely the Lacanian notion of the subject as 'the empty place of the structure' which describes the subject in its confrontation with the antagonism, the subject which isn't covering up the traumatic dimension of social antagonism."[106] Prior to social conflict, Žižek insisted, "every identity is already in itself blocked, marked by an impossibility, and the external enemy is simply the small piece, the rest of reality upon which we 'project' or 'externalize' this intrinsic, immanent impossibility."[107] The antagonistic fight between subject positions is merely a part of "social *reality*," already a part of the symbolic order; by contrast, "pure antagonism" is *real*, a "limit of the social . . . the impossibility around which the social field is structured," the "internal limit preventing the symbolic field from realizing its full identity."[108] Žižek ended the core section of the essay by returning to the Lacanian subject, "a paradoxical entity which is so to speak its own negative, i.e. which persists only insofar as its full realization is blocked—the fully realized subject would be no longer subject but substance." The subject is therefore "beyond or before subjectivation," for whereas subjectivation already implies integration into a "universe of meaning," the subject is precisely the failure of subjectivation, the "left-over which cannot be integrated into the symbolic universe."[109]

Žižek's analysis amounts in many respects to a dramatic reorientation of Laclau and Mouffe's theory of antagonism, from the social and pragmatic register to a seemingly anterior psychical domain. Nonetheless, Laclau, for his part, readily accepted Žižek's identification of antagonism with the Lacanian real, and his theoretical work in the early 1990s moved more decidedly onto Lacanian terrain.[110] By contrast, Lacan remains one among many theorists kept in circulation in Mouffe's work after *Hegemony and Socialist Strategy*. Indeed, his presence in her own work is quite minor. That is not the only difference marking Laclau and Mouffe's thought after their collaboration in *Hegemony and Socialist Strategy*. From the early 1990s to the present, Mouffe has focused on the conditions for a radically pluralistic conception of democracy. She explicitly rejects consensus models of liberal democracy like those of John Rawls or Jürgen Habermas, arguing instead that political orders are always hegemonic. That means that they involve frontiers and processes of inclusion and exclusion; it also means that the political is passionate, conflictual, and dissensual. This has led Mouffe to an engagement with Carl Schmitt, the thinker whose conception of the political concentrates most emphatically on conflict. While this has brought some to attack Mouffe as a left-wing Schmittian, such critiques miss the crucial point, namely that Mouffe is deeply intent on counteracting Schmitt's inflexible "friend-foe" distinction with an agonistic model of liberal democracy. Antagonism persists as a central term in Mouffe's work, but the goal is now to transform struggles between enemies into democratic contests between adversaries. Agon, after all, signifies a de-escalation of the existential struggle implied in the concept of antagonism, and, in this sense, the presiding figure in Mouffe's later work is not Schmitt, but Hannah Arendt. Mouffe remains committed to a project that challenges the hegemonic self-understanding of liberal democracy, but she does so from a position that explicitly embraces the legitimacy of liberal democratic values and institutions.[111]

In the 1990s, although there continued to be many overlaps between the erstwhile collaborators, Laclau pursued a quite different agenda. His commitment centered on the desire to revitalize the leftist political project, and here he became convinced that the viability of such a project depends on the possibility of recovering the concept of universalism. We have seen that redeeming universality was not part of the agenda of *Hegemony and Socialist Strategy*, where "the classic discourse of socialism" was identified as "a discourse of the universal, which transformed certain social categories into depositories of political and epistemological privileges."

Indeed, rejecting the idea of a global logic of the social, as well as the classic Marxist commitment to the proletariat as a universal revolutionary subject, Mouffe and Laclau issued an unequivocal statement in the last pages of the book, that "there is no radical and plural democracy without renouncing the discourse of the universal.[112] A crucial statement in 2000 stands in stark contrast:

> This, in my view, is the main political question confronting us at this end of the century: what is the destiny of the universal in our societies? Is a proliferation of particularisms—or their correlative side: authoritarian unification—the only alternative in a world in which dreams of a global human emancipation are rapidly fading away? Or can we think of the possibility of relaunching new emancipatory projects which are compatible with the complex multiplicity of differences shaping the fabric of present-day societies?[113]

In the course of the 1990s, Laclau's work came to be driven by his conviction that emancipatory politics would not survive the ceaseless fragmentation that underpins the postmodern vision of politics at its most extreme. Indeed, he came to believe that fragmentation threatens the very space of politics where antagonistic struggles take place, insofar as some common ground is necessary even for the sharpest of rivals.[114] Yet, if the idea of universality must accompany any viable concept of progressive politics and democratic renewal, it would not be enough simply to reassert the purity of the universal.

Laclau's growing preoccupation with the problem of universality signals another apparent convergence with Slavoj Žižek. Undoubtedly, in contrast to Laclau, Žižek was from the outset more interested in exploring the problem of universality, but in his first major works Žižek's aim was to expose the ideological functions of the concept of universality in its "intact purity" and to contrast the "utopian" idea of a universality untainted by particularity to a concrete universality always distorted by exceptions and deformations. To be sure, the early Žižek acknowledged a greater role for universal concepts than *Hegemony and Socialist Strategy* would have allowed, insofar as Žižek conceded that "although 'in reality' there are only 'exceptions' and 'deformations,' the universal notion of 'democracy' is none the less a 'necessary fiction,' a symbolic fact in the absence of which effective democracy, in all the plurality of its forms, could not reproduce itself."[115] Yet his emphasis on the pluralism of effective democracy brings this claim into line with the core of Laclau and Mouffe's view.

By the end of the 1990s, Žižek had abandoned the view of a necessary fictional universal disconnected from particular practice. Instead, he came to insist on a *committed* universality, a universal truth worth fighting for, but, paradoxically, a universalism that only emerges from the position of engaged particularity. Like Laclau, Žižek renounced received ideas about really existing universality and sought instead a new understanding of the inextricable and mutually tainting relationship between universality and particularity. Yet behind the shared Lacanian vocabulary and the apparent similarities of their attempts to reconnect leftist thought with universalism, Žižek and Laclau were in fact on sharply diverging paths. Indeed, in Žižek's trajectory, we see an increasing impatience with the constraints and restraints imposed on post-Marxism by its formative context in the antitotalitarian discourse of French thought. In the name of a renewed radicalism, Žižek has shrugged off many of the taboos that shaped post-Marxism. With this act, he has reopened the themes and tropes of precisely the revolutionary tradition that post-Marxism had pronounced exhausted. Consistent with Žižek's Kierkegaardian definition of *repetition*— indeed consistent with everything about Žižek—his return to revolution is anything but straightforward. To trace out and evaluate Žižek's development from post-Marxism to self-avowed revolutionary will be the task of the next and final chapter.

CHAPTER SIX

Of Empty Places

Žižek and Laclau; or, The End of the Affair

> Insofar as we play the democratic game of leaving the place
> of power empty, of accepting the gap between this place and
> our occupying it (which is the very gap of castration), are we—
> democrats—all not . . . faithful to castration?
> —SLAVOJ ŽIŽEK, *WELCOME TO THE DESERT OF THE REAL*

CLAUDE LEFORT'S DESCRIPTION of the "empty place" at the center of power in modern democracy resonates in the pages of Ernesto Laclau and Chantal Mouffe's *Hegemony and Socialist Strategy*. This is equally true of the young Slavoj Žižek, for whom Lefort seemed to offer a "complete theory of democracy."[1] Yet, at the same time, Žižek shifted the register of the "empty place" in his 1987 essay on Mouffe and Laclau. He praised them for conceptualizing antagonism in Lacanian terms as the traumatic confrontation between the real and the symbolic and thereby converting the Lacanian notion of the real into a useful tool for "social and ideological analysis," but Žižek nonetheless dramatically shifted the locus of their concept of antagonism from the social domain to a more originary antagonism in the individual subject. More precisely, Žižek returned the trope to its originary place in Lacanian theory when he described the human subject as the "empty place of the structure."[2] Of course, as we have seen, Lefort was fully aware that his account of democracy drew upon the Lacanian theme of the divided subject, but for Lefort this connection remained at the level of enabling metaphor, because he regarded the political as a sui generis domain, not as part of a series of repeated structural features. By contrast, Žižek early on offered an account of a certain structure or, more precisely, of *lack* in structure, which could then be seen repeating itself at the levels of both the individual human subject and the sociopolitical order. In this sense, Žižek's repositioning of the "empty place" can be seen as both a return to the Lacanian provenance of the topos and as its redeployment in a new discursive context and expanded framework.

Ernesto Laclau readily accepted Žižek's comparison of the theory of antagonism to the Lacanian idea of the real, and the Lacanian theory of the subject, already at play in *Hegemony and Socialist Strategy*, thereafter became a more prominent element in his work. Žižek was equally happy to form an alliance. He defended the idea of radical democracy and, in a feat of retroactive reinscription, he named Hegel—one of his major touchstones, along with Lacan—the "first post-Marxist," for having disclosed a field of "difference and contingency" that Marxism subsequently sutured.[3] This friendship and intellectual convergence proved short-lived, however. By 1997 Žižek insisted that "what is needed today" is a "strictly dogmatic Lacanian approach combined precisely with a not-post-Marxist approach."[4] *The Ticklish Subject*, clearly a turning point in Žižek's intellectual career, expressed disagreement with Laclau on a number of key issues. *Contingency, Hegemony, Universality*, a three-way conversation between Laclau, Žižek, and Judith Butler elaborated differences on all sides. Toward the end of that series of exchanges, Laclau acknowledged "serious disagreements," but also "important coincidences" and grounds for "some sort of permanent alliance."[5] But this looks like wishful thinking. After all, Žižek lumped both Butler and Laclau into a "'postmodern' Left" that accepts the fundamentals of the capitalist market economy and liberal democracy, abandons the possibility of "a completely *different* economico-political regime," and is content to play at the game of identity politics. Žižek, on his side, issued a call for a "revolutionary stance pursuing its goal with an inexorable firmness. . . . If this radical choice is decried by some bleeding-heart liberals as *Linksfaschismus*, so be it!"[6] Žižek's theoretical commitment to revolutionary resoluteness came with a sharpening anticapitalism and an idiosyncratic revival of the Marxian tradition, from Marx himself through to Lenin and Mao, with even a side trip back to Robespierre. For his part, Laclau responded by mocking the "naïve self-complacence" of Žižek's "r-r-revolutionary" talk of total change, dismissing Žižek's attempt to return to the centrality of class struggle and the "logic" of Capital, and concluding that, all along, Žižek had merely been using politics to illustrate psychoanalytic concepts instead of conducting a political inquiry proper.[7] A lengthy exchange in the pages of *Critical Inquiry* in 2006 drops the last pretense of politeness and mixes principled dispute with ad hominem attacks. The "fruitful intellectual exchange" that Laclau had hoped for in 1989 had come to a crashing end.[8] The collapse of Žižek and Laclau's friendship and sense of common project suggests the end of a stage in the history of post-Marxism.

There is, in this implosion, a strange and ironic repetition of history, a kind of replay of the revisionist controversy that rent the Second Socialist International in the first years of the twentieth century. If that struggle pitted revolutionary socialists against evolutionist parliamentary socialists, the controversy between Laclau and Žižek pits a poststructuralist Eduard Bernstein against a Hegelio-Lacanian Vladimir Lenin supplementing his arsenal with borrowings from Saint Paul, Schelling, and Jesus Christ. This is, it must be emphasized, a controversy propelled mainly by the transformation of Žižek's thought and by Žižek's mise-en-scène of his theoretical interventions. If the first revisionist crisis played out on the public stage of western European socialist politics on the eve of the First World War, this latest revisionist controversy unfolds mainly in an esoteric theoretical theater constructed by Žižek himself. If it takes only the slightest historical imagination to see the resemblance to the first revisionist crisis, it takes only the slightest skepticism to recall Marx's maxim that history happens twice, first as tragedy, then as farce.

How did this situation develop? Žižek's reworking of Laclau and Mouffe's conceptual framework in "Beyond Discourse-Analysis" has led some commentators to identify the nature and depth of their respective theories of antagonism as the source of the rupture.[9] Undoubtedly, Žižek's divergent perspective forecast trouble ahead. Yet, in what follows, I want to supplement this by arguing that the initial fissures in the concept of antagonism became an ever deepening rift once Laclau and Žižek started to foreground the need to rethink the concept of universalism. As we saw in the concluding pages of the previous chapter, both Žižek and Laclau came to believe that the left must move beyond the radical pluralism, dispersal and deferral of meaning, identity politics, and focus on particularism that had characterized the politics of postmodernism; if there was to be any possibility of revival of the leftist project, the category of universality had to be recaptured. Of course, accompanying this conclusion is an acute awareness that there is no such thing as a pure universal, one untainted by particularity and awaiting discovery in a metaphysical beyond. This conviction unites

Žižek and Laclau in a paradoxical and tortuous enterprise. The universal does not exist. We must have the universal. The universal is impossible. The universal is necessary.

The paradoxes of this search for a plausible notion of the universal dimension of politics assigned a new function to the notion of the "empty place." From a description of the historically specific nature of modern democracy, the empty place became for both Žižek and Laclau a structural feature of any viable notion of universality. The use of a common theoretical term and the apparent proximity of many of their concepts masks, however, sharply divergent ways of conceptualizing the universal. Tracking the shifting fortunes of the concept of the empty place may provide privileged access to the issues that led to the breach between Laclau and Žižek and, more broadly, Žižek's trajectory toward a self-styled (if you will) post-post-Marxist "revolutionary" stance. Indeed, the empty place seems not to be empty at all. Shaped in each case by strong theoretical assumptions, that place turns out to be an accident-ridden intersection, full of collisions between competing visions of left-wing politics, the radical intellectual, the possible and proper contribution of the Lacanian approach to politics, and the relation or nonrelation between Lacanian and poststructuralist thought.

Žižek the Radical Democrat

In light of Žižek's late-1980s essay on Laclau and Mouffe, with its displacement of antagonism from the social domain where Laclau and Mouffe had treated it to a seemingly anterior psychical register, it may be surprising that it took until 2000 for Laclau to conclude that Žižek's thought is not "organized around a truly *political* reflection but is, rather, a *psychoanalytic* discourse."[10] Yet Laclau's bitter remark seems only partly correct. Certainly, Laclau is right to note that Žižek's thought lacks "strategic reflection," but it is not true that Žižek reduces the political dimension to a set of illustrations for an ultimately individualistic psychoanalytic perspective. There is, first of all, the general point already made: Žižek develops an explanatory structure that he applies repetitively and homologically to individual and politico-social levels in their separation as well as in their intersection. Second, political imperatives have always been at work in

Žižek's work. In his first English-language books, *The Sublime Object of Ideology* and *For They Know Not What They Do,* the political imperative is decidedly the defense of a posttotalitarian, pluralistic vision of radical democracy.

Two contexts seemed to intertwine in shaping Žižek's politics at that early stage. Most immediate was the situation in Žižek's native Slovenia and the broader collapse of the Soviet Bloc in eastern Europe. *For They Know Not What They Do* was first delivered the winter semester of 1989–90 as lectures in Ljubljana during the turbulent period between the General Assembly of the Yugoslav Republic of Slovenia's September 1989 assertion of the right to secede from Yugoslavia and the December 1990 referendum that overwhelmingly supported Slovenian independence. Žižek remembered it as

> a time of intense political ferment, with "free elections" only weeks ahead, when all options still seemed open, the time of a "short circuit" blending together political activism, the "highest" theory (Hegel, Lacan) and unrestrained enjoyment in the "lowest" popular culture— a unique utopian moment which is now, after the electoral victory of the nationalist-populist coalition and the advent of a new "scoundrel time," not only over but even more and more *invisible*, erased from memory.[11]

Žižek's involvement in this moment even extended to a candidacy for the collective presidency in the 1990 election and a nearly successful run for election on the Liberal Party ticket.[12]

Pressing as the needs of this immediate context were, Žižek's response as a theorist was filtered through an intellectual frame profoundly shaped by France. By his own account, Slovenia's philosophical community in the 1960s and 1970s was provincial but eclectic. While very young, he read his way through standard Marxist works and began the forays into early German idealism that would become a defining feature of his mature work. Heidegger was the first to exercise a powerful hold on Žižek's philosophical imagination, but it was French theory that began to command his attention in the very early 1970s. He remembers that he and his friends read everything they could from Lévi-Strauss, Foucault, Kristeva, Lacan, and Althusser. These figures were prominent in the voluminous masters thesis he submitted in 1975 on "French theories of symbolic practice" under the title "The Theoretical and Practical Relevance of French Structuralism."[13] He credits Derrida with providing him the first push to move away from Heidegger; but, as he relates in a 2004 interview, he and his circle made a partisan choice for Lacan around 1975–76. This decision led a few years later to the formation of the Society for Theoretical Psychoanalysis, a loose grouping of Lacanian theorists including Žižek, Joan Copjec, Renata Salecl, Mladen Dolar, Miran Bozovic, and Alenka Zupančič.[14] Žižek's master's thesis had made him politically suspect to the Yugoslav authorities, but, despite the handicaps they placed on him, Žižek deepened his engagement with French thought, particularly, of course, Lacan. Between 1981 and 1985, he lived off and on in Paris, studying Lacanian theory with Jacques-Alain Miller and completing a second doctorate in psychoanalysis in 1985. Immersed in the Paris milieu, but a core member of the emerging Slovenian anticommunist opposition movement, Žižek, not surprisingly, absorbed something of the antitotalitarian spirit that was still an important feature of Paris's cultural landscape, even if by the early 1980s it had already passed its peak. Nor is it surprising that, of the antitotalitarian writers, Žižek should have been drawn to Claude Lefort, in whom he recognized a fellow Lacanian. A measure of the regard he held for the French political philosopher comes in a 1985 interview where Žižek refers to him by way of illustrating Lacanian engagements in a series of public struggles: "We have, along with others, a complete theory of democracy, thanks to Claude Lefort's Lacanian exposition."[15]

Lefort's influence on Žižek is present in the political direction of *The Sublime Object of Ideology* and *For They Know Not What They Do*. Or, more precisely, Lefort's theory of democracy gets metabolized into Žižek's philosophical preoccupations. In fact, consistent with his interest in the fantasmatic dimension of ideology, what really intrigued Žižek was not the empty place of power as such, but the way in which emptiness gets filled with specific content. Here Žižek insisted on his distance from deconstructionists like Derrida, thus foreshadowing the increasingly sharp critique of poststructuralism that became a marked feature of Žižek's work from the mid-1990s onward. The "fundamental gesture of poststructuralism," he wrote in *The Sublime Object of Ideology*, "is to deconstruct every substantial identity, to denounce behind its solid consistency an interplay of symbolic overdetermination."[16] That is, deconstruction presupposes a constituted field of identity in order to set to work on subverting it. Where the deconstructionist struggles to dissolve the inert solidity of identity, Žižek reversed the procedure to demonstrate the way the fluidity of being passes into a "point of inert, fixed identity-with-itself." Žižek continued the sentence by way of an example: "the way the State as the agency of rational 'mediation' of society acquires full actuality, realizes itself, only in the inert, 'irrational' immediacy of the monarch's body."[17] It is perhaps unsurprising that the image of the monarch should make its appearance in these early works, given the background influence of Lefort. After all, Lefort's work circulated around the issue of the symbolic power of the monarch's body and the radical effects ensuing when that body was divested of power. It is surprising, however, to realize just how frequently the issue of the monarch surfaces in *The Sublime Object of Ideology* and *For They Know Not What They Do*. Or, more to the point, *Hegel's* monarch, as theorized in the *Philosophy of Right*. The Hegelian monarch, brought into contact with Lefort's theory of democracy, performs considerable work in Žižek's early political thought. But, true to the image of metabolization invoked previously, the monarch does double duty, for it also provides Žižek with a privileged example of the interaction between universals and particulars.

To return again to the contrast with poststructuralism, the deconstructionist starts with the presupposition of a universal and then demonstrates its impossibility by showing that it is in fact only one term within a chain of terms. No element can dominate, because the meaning of each element is recorded by all the elements in a ceaseless movement of deferral and supplement. Žižek, by contrast, maintained that the universal is always a particular element within a series, elevated to fill the empty place of the series itself. An *empty* place, it must be emphasized, because the series as such, the genus, can never perfectly encompass the particular species it groups under it. Žižek offered both Hegelian and Lacanian formulations of this claim. In Lacanian terms, Žižek rejected the pluralist and relativist position of postmodernism and fully endorsed Lacan's insistence that "in every concrete constellation, *truth is bound to emerge* in some contingent detail."[18] In Hegelian terms, Žižek took this to be the essence of Hegel's idea of the "concrete universal," that is, a universal that is not distinct from and merely externally related to the particular, but, rather, a universal that finds embodiment in the particular. Žižek undoubtedly departed from conventional Hegel interpretation not only when he insisted that there is no "abstract" universal over and against the concrete but also when he maintained that all concrete universals are such only through a contingent and arbitrary process.[19] In Žižek's work of the late 1980s and early 1990s, Hegel's monarch serves as a key example of that contingent process whereby a particular element within a series creates the universal.

Critics have long attacked Hegel for placing a nonrational, biologically determined man at the head of the rational state. But, according to Žižek, the crucial point is precisely the abyss separating the state as an organic rational totality from the "'irrational' *factum brutum* of the person who embodies supreme power."[20] As the political actor who has only to "say 'yes' and dot the 'I,'" the monarch has often nothing more to do "than sign his name." "But this name is important," Hegel emphasizes: "it is the last word beyond which it is impossible to go."[21] The monarch's entire authority and actuality thus consists in his name, in a signifier. So, stated Žižek, "The monarch thus embodies the function of the Master-Signifier at its purest; it is the One of the Exception, the 'irrational' protuberance of the social edifice which transforms the amorphous mass of 'people' into a concrete totality of mores."[22] Žižek treated this as a specific instance of a more general process that finds its clearest formulation in *The Sublime Object of Ideology*: "it is the universal itself which is constituted by way of subtracting from a set some Particular designed to embody the Universal as such: the Universal arises . . . in the act of radical split between the wealth of particular diversity and the element which, in the midst of it, 'gives body' to the Universal."[23] For Žižek, it is precisely the fact that the Hegelian monarch exceeds the dialectic, or, even better, short-circuits the dialectical mediation between "individual" and "totality," that allows the dialectic to work. Hence, from the argument that "the State as a rational totality exists only insofar as it is embodied in the inert presence of the King's body," Žižek offered a more general statement about Hegel's dialectic: "the greatest speculative mystery of the dialectical movement is not how the richness and diversity of reality can be reduced to a dialectical conceptual mediation, but the fact that in order to take place this dialectical structuring must itself be embodied in some totally contingent element."[24]

This highly idiosyncratic reading of Hegel immediately takes on political significance in that, for Žižek, the value of dialectical procedure lies in its power to reveal moments of genesis whereby a necessity springs up as the "positivization" or "coagulation" of a "radically contingent decision."[25] In short, a radically contingent, scandalous act of violence stands at the origin of the new master signifier.[26] And this act "succeeds" the moment it conceals its own past, its own conditions, its scandalous character.[27] Hence, the new master signifier becomes naturalized, necessary, part of the order of things. As the original violence sinks into forgetfulness, people come to identify with the master signifier. It becomes an *objet petit a*, a fantasy object that seems to hold some key, some promise of completion. This creates the conditions for the strange transubstantiation of the monarch whereby the king becomes a Thing, a sublime body, or, more precisely, we the subjects act *as if* he is the Thing embodied. The contemporary relevance of this surfaced when Žižek noted that, "within the post-revolutionary 'totalitarian' order, we have witnessed a re-emergence of the sublime political body in the shape of Leader and/or Party." In "post-democratic" totalitarianism, revolutionaries fully assume the role of an instrument of an objective historical order or law, and, by doing so, the body of the revolutionary redoubles itself and assumes a sublime quality. Thus, the Stalinist vow of the Bolshevik Party: "We, the Communists, are people of a special mould. We are made of special stuff." Hence the uncanny affiliation between communism and the mausoleum, the compulsion to preserve intact the body of the dead leader. "How," Žižek asked, "can we explain this obsessive care if not by reference to the fact that in their symbolic universe, the body of the Leader is not just an ordinary transient body but a body redoubled in itself, an envelopment of the sublime Thing?"[28]

How does one kill such a body? Regicide is one of the recurring motifs of *For They Know Not What They Do*. It is, significantly, a book first delivered as lectures to a public that had just symbolically overturned an objective order, symbolically killed a master signifier. By the end of 1989, Slovenia's neighbors, the Romanians, had actually executed their leader after a hastily convened revolutionary court judged him guilty of crimes against the people. But because of the uncanny fusion of physical body and sublime thing, Žižek was, in fact, not optimistic that regicide can really achieve its goal. The Jacobins recognized this fusion and rightly refused to distinguish between the empirical person and the symbolic mandate of the king. Yet

Žižek judged the Jacobin regicide negatively. For it seems like an "impotent *acting out* which was simultaneously excessive and empty." The decapitation of the king was fundamentally superfluous *and* a terrifying sacrilege confirming the king's charisma by the very act of his physical destruction. Žižek claimed that the same effect is at work in all similar cases, including the execution of Nicolae Ceauşescu: "when confronted with the picture of his bloodstained body, even the greatest enemies of his regime shrank back, as if they were witness to excessive cruelty, but at the same time a strange fear flashed across their mind, mixed with incredulity: is this really *him*?"[29]

So how does one kill such a body? Karl Marx's answer was that we must destroy the symbolic system in which some men are kings; but Žižek was too much the psychoanalyst not to believe that an emperor without clothes might still be a fantasmatic object. Ultimately, Žižek's answer lay with Lacanian psychoanalysis, or more exactly with the process of going through the fantasy, of recognizing that the fantasy object is merely filling a lack, a void in the Other. The early Žižek gave this act of "subjective destitution," of stripping subjectivity of its fantasmatic props, a strongly emancipatory meaning. *Tarrying with the Negative* opens with the striking image of the Romanian rebels during the violent overthrow of Ceauşescu waving the "national flag with the red star, the Communist symbol, cut out, so that instead of the symbol standing for the organizing principle of the national life, there was nothing but a hole in its center." Žižek applied the moral of this episode directly to his own work: "the duty of the critical intellectual—if, in today's 'postmodern' universe, this syntagm has any meaning left—is precisely *to occupy all the time*, even when the new order (the 'new harmony') stabilizes itself and again renders invisible the hole as such, *the place of this hole*, i.e., to maintain a distance toward every Master-Signifier."[30] *The Plague of Fantasies* offers perhaps the strongest statement of the alleged political effects of this procedure: "the crucial precondition for breaking the chains of servitude is thus to 'traverse the fantasy' which structures our *jouissance* in a way which keeps us attached to the Master—makes us accept the framework of the social relationship of domination."[31]

This position would seem to be the point of intersection between Žižek and the project of radical democracy espoused by Mouffe and Laclau. Echoing Lefort, Mouffe and Laclau had argued that democracy's loss of foundation translates into the possibility of a contingent, open-ended struggle to extend the meaning and reach of democracy. Yet even in his early works, where Žižek ultimately shared their democratic orientation, he followed a different path, one that assigned the state a role not visible in *Hegemony and Socialist Strategy*. It was, perhaps, the situation in Slovenia that explains this detour. Ian Parker argues that during the 1980s, as Yugoslavia disintegrated, Žižek developed considerable suspicion of the forces of civil society. Where dissidents in communist Czechoslovakia and Poland put their hopes in the pluralistic web of social interests and nonstate associations, Žižek saw in civil society "a network of moral majority, conservatives and nationalist pressure groups, against abortion." With Croat and Serb nationalists rushing to fill the vacuum left by the collapse of the Yugoslavian state, Žižek declared, "in Slovenia I am for the state and against civil society!"; and he championed the "establishment of an 'alienated' state that would maintain its distance from civil society."[32] As Parker suggests, Žižek thus retained something of Hegel's misgivings about the autonomous powers of civil society. Yet, of course, Žižek's mode of articulating this was his own amalgam.

Consider his discussion of the Jacobins in the final chapter of *For They Know Not What They Do*. Žižek wrote that the "tragic grandeur" of the Jacobins lies in their refusal to occupy the empty place of power. Following Lefort's description of the Terror, Žižek noted that the Jacobins set themselves up as the guardians of that empty place, preventing anybody from occupying the empty center of power, protecting this place against false pretenders. But, asked Žižek, does not the guardian reserve for himself a privileged place, "does he not function as a kind of King-in-reverse?" That is to say, is not the position from which he acts and speaks the position of absolute power? "Is not safeguarding the empty locus of Power the most cunning and at the same time the most brutal, unconditional way of occupying it?"[33] At this point, Hegel's monarch makes another return, this time as the speculative resolution to the Jacobin impasse. Both the Hegelian monarch and the Jacobin terrorist protect the empty locus of power. However, Hegel limited the monarch's power to a formal act of endorsement of legislation, and he carefully divested the personal attributes of the monarch of any significance vis-à-vis his political role.[34] In contrast to the Jacobins, the monarch protects the empty place only as an empty, formal agent whose main task is to prevent the current performer of power from identifying himself immediately with the locus of power.

Wrote Žižek: "The 'monarch' is nothing but a positivization, a material-
ization of the *distance* separating the locus of Power from those who exert
it."[35] The monarch thus interrupts the vicious circle of "democrats cutting
off each other's heads indefinitely."

Žižek's concern with the process whereby emptiness gets filled with
content was thus, at this stage in his career, not really so sharply opposed
to the forces of civil society. Indeed, his defense of the embodiment of
power in the form of a symbolic figure was intended to safeguard a pluralistic space of political contestation.[36] That political intent was inseparable
from his general theoretical interest in the function and operation of universals. This concern, we have seen, contained a strongly demystifying
impulse to expose the tainted relations between universals and particulars, recollect the repressed memory of the contingent and even violent
acts by which a particular gets thrust into the place of the universal, and
establish a critical distance toward every master signifier that claims to
occupy the empty place of power. At the same time, his insistence on necessary fictions, whether that of the *alien* state, the monarch or his republican surrogates, or the "universal notion of 'democracy,'" introduced a
strange tension between the duty of the critical intellectual and the evident necessity for a "kind of 'active forgetfulness'" that allows us to accept
a symbolic fiction even though we know in reality that things are not like
that. The only solution the early Žižek could offer to this conundrum was
to make fetishism an integral component of really existing democracy. As
he wrote in a 1991 essay: "The democratic attitude is always based upon a
certain fetishistic split: *I know very well* (that the democratic form is just a
form spoiled by the stains of 'pathological' imbalance), *but just the same* (I
act as if democracy were possible)."[37]

Žižek's willingness to tolerate what he viewed as a fetishistic attachment
to the democratic attitude proved relatively short-lived. Given his clear-
sighted view into the necessary fictions of democracy, one might have suspected that the impulse of the critical intellectual would grow stronger and
stronger, directing itself against each and every attempt to establish a new
positive order or erect a new master signifier. Yet that is not the direction
he pursued. Writing a preface for the second edition of *For They Know Not
What They Do* in 2002, Žižek observed of his works from the late eighties
and early nineties that they oscillate "between Marxism proper and praise
of 'pure' democracy, including a critique of 'totalitarianism' along the lines

of Claude Lefort. It took me years of hard work to identify and liquidate these dangerous residues of bourgeois ideology clearly at three interconnected levels: the clarification of my Lacanian reading of Hegel; the elaboration of the concept of act; and a palpable critical distance towards the very notion of democracy."[38] Though he might have added his clarification of the relationship between universality and "militant" politics, this list accurately sums up the main trajectory of his thought since the early nineties: his insistence on partisan commitment, the affirmation of Marx and "class struggle," his turn to Lenin, his summons to anticapitalist revolution, his idea of the "act," his opening toward Christianity, his mobilization of antidemocratic rhetoric. Taken together, Žižek's work since the later 1990s, particularly from *The Ticklish Subject* onward, conveys a profound shift in tone and emphasis, the emergence of new themes, and a striking reorientation of his political commitments.

It is worth pausing here to consider the debate that has emerged over the question of how to understand Žižek's development over time. Geoffrey Harpham, author of a penetrating and sharply critical essay on Žižek, treats all of his work as if it were of a piece. This rather ahistorical position is already signaled in Harpham's opening observation that "even in what was apparently his first work, Žižek displayed no trace of apprenticeship."[39] Žižek's Hegel and Lacan seem to be there right from the start, even if Zizek himself has indicated a more complicated itinerary involving early attractions to Heidegger and Derrida.[40] While a reading of Zizek's oeuvre suggests substantial changes in theme and tone, one finds so many elements and traces of the allegedly "later" concerns in the earlier writings that it can seem as if those texts could—and did—contain everything. This is especially the case if one applies Žižek's own habit of retroactive reinscription to the wide span of Žižek's prodigious output. If Harpham's presentation sometimes edges toward parthenogenesis, Ian Parker goes to an opposite extreme in arguing that Žižek was born in chaos and has remained there ever since. One of Žižek's most astute critics, Parker captures well the vexing experience of reading Žižek when he speaks of oscillating between the conviction that "there is no theoretical system as such in Žižek's work" and the sense that behind the impression of "chaotic movement" lies the "lucid elaboration of a theoretical argument."[41] Parker hints at a calculated madness when he speaks of an "element of motivated inconsistency" in Žižek's writing, but ultimately he comes down firmly in support of the conviction that there is no system or lucid and sustained elaboration of an argument. Sarah Kay, author of *Žižek: A Critical Introduction*, comes in for criticism from Parker, for she treats Žižek as a more or less conventional type of theorist, elaborating a consistent project across his career.[42] Kay notes the shifts in Žižek's work, but handles them with studied neutrality. Enthusiastic supporters Rex Butler and Scott Stephens, by contrast, acknowledge the self-contradictions and sometime chaos of Žižek's utterances, but explain these as conscious strategies to prevent his readers from domesticating him and, ultimately, to force a separation between well-meaning leftists and the "Hegelio-Marxism" that he champions.[43] Not surprisingly, Rex Butler's book on Žižek is sensitive to the shift in his thought, as is Jodi Dean's.[44] Butler and Dean both regard the more recent work of Žižek to be a promising path for leftist renewal, though Dean draws limits on her acceptance of Žižek's particular brand of provocation. She thus becomes "Exhibit A" for Butler and Stephen, who claim that Žižek's "plea for Leninist intolerance" does indeed separate the weak from the strong.[45]

My own position, it should be clear, is that Žižek's thought is not at all devoid of theoretical coherence or system, which is not to say that there are not many instances of inconsistency, motivated or not. At the same time, although there are strong continuities across the entirety of his oeuvre, the breaks are significant enough to militate against an image of seamless theoretical elaboration. In thinking about Žižek's career, I find myself in agreement with Adam Kotsko, author of *Žižek and Theology*, although, as we will see later, I disagree with his presentation of the later Žižek.[46] Kotsko counters Žižek's objection that to periodize an author is to domesticate and classify him by pointing to the various instances when Žižek himself insists on such periodization, starting, of course, with Lacan. Thus emboldened, Kotsko divides Žižek's work into three periods. The early period runs roughly to the mid-1990s and is characterized by the development of a new form of ideology critique and support of liberal democracy. *Tarrying with the Negative* (1993) initiates a break based on a critique of liberal democracy. Kotsko describes the second period, running through to *The Ticklish Subject*, as a "retreat into theory." The third period, from around 2000 to the present, coincides with Žižek's return to Marx, deployment of revolutionary language, and deepening engagement with Christianity. My own discussion thus far has focused on the early Žižek, and in what follows I will more or less elide the distinction between the second and third periods or, more precisely, I will concentrate on Žižek's work from *The Ticklish Subject* on. Nonetheless, it is crucial to consider the possible reasons why this later work insists upon a "palpable critical distance towards the very notion of democracy."

One answer lies in Žižek's analysis of the putative relationship between liberal democracy and nationalism in *Tarrying with the Negative*.[47] This book appeared several years after the exuberant hopes for democratic reform in eastern Europe, which formed the context for the lectures that eventually became *For They Know Not What They Do*. In those intervening years, radical democratic movements like the Neues Forum in former East Germany had disappeared before the juggernaut of West German liberal-democratic capitalism, while the former Yugoslavia had descended into a cauldron of nationalist and ethnic conflict. In trying to explain this distressing development, Žižek returned again to a Lacanian reading of the empty place. The collapse of eastern European socialism broke the "spell" overnight, he argued, and wiped out the big Other, the ultimate guarantee of social order. "This experience," wrote Žižek, "of how the 'throne is empty' (of how the big Other does not exist) is bound to trigger panic."[48] With the sudden disappearance of the Leader or the Party, the empty place of power, the void, stands exposed. This is, of course, the condition of democracy according to the Lefortian description that Žižek embraced in his first books. Yet the dynamics of post-Soviet eastern Europe seemed to verify an insight expressed forcefully by Jacques-Alain Miller and eventually quoted by Žižek in his book on Iraq:

> Democracy as empty place means: the subject of democracy is a barred subject. Our limited algebra enables us to grasp immediately that this leaves out the small *a*. That is to say: everything that hinges on the particularity of enjoyment. . . . We are told: once the empty place is there, everybody, if he respects the law, can bring in his traditions and his values. . . . However, what we know is that, in actual fact, the more democracy is empty, the more it is a desert of enjoyment.[49]

In such conditions of destitution in eastern Europe, the "Nation, the national Thing, usurps, fills out, the empty place of the Thing."[50] Far from hindering this process, Žižek argued that liberal democracy helps produce it, precisely by its ideological insistence on emptying the center of power. Not only does liberal democracy thereby stimulate reactive formations like nationalism, but insofar as its history has been thoroughly implicated in national projects, it conceals its own impure particularisms behind a self-representation of univeralism. Liberal democracy's insistence on its own universalism in turn makes it complicit in the triumph of global capitalism; from the perspective of liberal universalism, resistance to globalization can only look like an obstinate and pathological attachment to the particular. In pushing to overcome such particularisms, liberal democracy smoothes the way for capitalist globalization.

This analysis of the misfiring of democracy in parts of eastern Europe is quite penetrating, though it must be said that numerous analysts in the early 1990s identified the rise of fundamentalisms and ethnic nationalisms as reactions to the homogenizing brand of globalization exported by the West, and did so without Žižek's laborious Lacanian machinery. Moreover, whatever the merits of Žižek's critique of liberal democracy, it seems a disproportionate response to announce his distance from the "very notion of democracy." For one thing, *Tarrying with the Negative*'s damning critique of democracy centers only on the former Soviet Bloc, and it was written before the dust of the Berlin Wall had even settled. Without wanting to diminish the traumatic events in the former Yugoslavia or the disappointment that came with the foreclosure of more expansive democratic possibilities in former East Bloc countries like East Germany, the Czech Republic, or Romania, one might be relieved that the collapse of really existing socialism did not unleash even more violence than it did. Žižek's rhetoric, adopted by his sympathetic commentators, forces a situation in which any claim for progress looks like complacency or deluded complicity, but such denunciations are trivial compared to the importance of pointing out that, some fifteen to twenty years later, the situation in the former East Bloc looks sufficiently checkered that it is too early for any final judgment. Žižek's analysis of the process whereby the empty place gets filled by the fantasy of the unitary "Nation Thing" is in its essentials not all that different from Lefort's account of the obverse of the democratic adventure. Yet, in sharp contrast to Žižek, Lefort does not draw down the shades on democracy, but instead argues for a historical process that creates the democratic subject.

Strikingly, this is exactly Žižek's position in his earlier work:

> What was at one moment a terrifying defect, a catastrophe for the
> social edifice—the fact that "the throne is empty"—turns into a
> crucial prerogative. The fundamental operation of the "democratic
> invention" is thus of a purely symbolic nature: it is misleading to say
> that the "democratic invention" *finds* the locus of Power empty—
> the point is rather that it *constitutes, constructs* it as empty; that it
> reinterprets the "empirical" fact of interregnum into a "transcenden-
> tal" condition of the legitimate exercise of Power.[51]

The point is not to deny either the imperfections of liberal democracy or
its compromising entanglements in capitalism; what is disturbing and puz-
zling about Žižek is that he insists on conflating liberalism and democracy, rather than trying to disentangle them and theorize their relationship. Instead of contesting the way in which capitalism has laid hegemonic
claims to the idea of democracy in the postcommunist world, Žižek declares his opposition to the very notion of democracy. It may be that Žižek
is ultimately playing a game of provocation, whereby his denunciation of
democracy is a strategy for obstructing the short circuit that fuses democracy and capitalism together. But that is difficult to judge because, for
reasons that we will explore, he stoutly refuses to suggest the positive contours of an alternative social order. So we cannot gauge what role, if any,
Žižek hopes democracy could play should the "impossible" happen, and
the liberal-democratic capitalist world collapse. The tendency of his thought,
however, is not encouraging for those who are both critical of the existing
order and committed to the expansion of democratic practices.

Politics Needs a Vacuum

In contrast to the dramatic shift in his own politics, Žižek is not just generous but also accurate in his description of Ernesto Laclau:

> We philosophers are madmen: we have a certain insight that we
> affirm again and again. That is why, although there are now some
> political and theoretical misunderstandings between Ernesto Laclau

and myself, I think that here you can see that he is a true theoretician philosopher. He has a certain, what Germans would call in
their nice way, *Grundeinsicht*, a fundamental insight, and he clari-
fies again and again the same points: antagonism, hegemony, empty
signifier. Doesn't he basically tell the same story again and again?
This is not a criticism.[52]

Žižek's turn to the idea of a committed, partisan universality is entirely
permeated by his changing preoccupations in the late 1990s. By contrast,
Laclau's concern with universality builds coherently on the theoretical
and political project of radical democracy articulated in *Hegemony and
Socialist Strategy* and, having articulated this view of universality in the
early 1990s, Laclau's approach has remained stable right up to the present.
A clear measure of this coherence is the fact that only three years after the
publication of *Hegemony and Socialist Strategy*, which lacked any attempt
to theorize a viable form of universalism, Laclau rearticulated hegemonic
struggle in a way that rejected both "relativist parochialism" and "foundationalist universalism" in favor of a conception of "relative universalism"
that is "pragmatically constructed through the 'equivalential' effects of
struggles carried out by actors that are always limited."[53] At a certain level,
this repeats Marx's insight that a particular class emancipates itself by
universalizing its own standard,[54] yet Marx insisted that this process belonged to *political* revolution, not to the social revolution of the proletariat, which he considered a truly universal class. Where Marx embedded
the hegemonic struggle in the determinant stratum of the social base,
Laclau remained committed to the original impulses of post-Marxism by
theorizing relative universalism as a contingent process of social construction with no reference to a base that determines, whether in the first or
last instance. This project finds expression in the long essay "New Reflections on the Revolution of Our Time" (1990) and receives a fuller elaboration in the essays collected in *Emancipation(s)* (1996).[55]

It has been noted that in the 1990s Laclau's work took on an increasingly Lacanian inflection; yet, in fact, another continuity from *Hegemony and Socialist Strategy* is the eclectic theoretical mix, particularly
Laclau's readiness to draw equally on Derrida and Lacan. This is clear in
the way Laclau constructed the central term of this new phase of his
thought, namely the universal as "an empty but ineradicable place."[56]

Why empty? Why ineradicable? Laclau mobilized both Derridean and Lacanian resources to answer these questions. The universal is the fullness of society itself; yet that fullness itself cannot be symbolized. Viewed through a Lacanian lens, this means that the social totality is itself the real, a void that Laclau, like Žižek, detected in both the individual subject and the social structure.[57] Like Žižek, Laclau argued that this void is revealed precisely by the "retroactive failure of the Symbolic" in its attempt to name it and, again like Žižek, Laclau emphasized that this emptiness itself, this negativity, "produces a series of crucial effects in the structuration/destructuration of social relations."[58] That is to say, social relations will be driven by the impossible desire to fill the empty place of the universal with positive content and the inevitable failure of every such attempt. Laclau even edged up toward the explanatory role of fantasy in supplementing the lack in the Other when he describes the content of subjective identification and social representations of totality.[59] Yet ultimately the Lacanian dimension remains at the level of a few repeated analogies between what Laclau was attempting and the dominant motifs of Lacanianism.[60]

The same results can evidently be arrived at through Derrida. Here Laclau worked in deconstructive fashion with the paradoxes of thinking about system on the basis of differential relations. If a system is to be a system and not just a random assemblage or simply the sum of all things, it must be bounded but if the system's limit is to be a real limit, it cannot be just another differential element within the system. The constitutive ground of the system must, therefore, be outside the system, excluded, a negativity vis-à-vis the system itself. Hence the limit of the system, or the system as such, cannot be represented within the system. So we get yet another formulation of the empty place, though this time it is as much shaped by Derrida's notion of a "constitutive outside" as by the Lacanian real: "any system of signification is structured around an empty place resulting from the impossibility of producing an object which, none the less, is required by the systematicity of the system."[61] Totality thus becomes a necessary but impossible object, which Laclau further illustrated with a passing reference to Kant's concept of the sublime.[62] There is a certain irony in Laclau's willingness to establish the empty place of the universal through both Lacanian and Derridean logics. What is this, if not a case of undecidability? And undecidability is precisely the point where Laclau maintained "deconstruction and hegemony cross each other," with deconstruction discovering "the role of the decision out of the undecidability of the structure" and "hegemony as a theory of decision taken in an undecidable terrain" requiring deconstruction's exposure of the "contingent character of the connections existing in that terrain."[63]

If the system, the totality, universality, cannot be represented as such, then particular signifiers must perform this function. Laclau again built on the paradox of differential systems, for if elements only gain identity within a system of differences, they nonetheless share a certain equivalence insofar as they all stand on this side of an exclusionary limit. Each element is split between difference and equivalence, but, far from hindering the operation of a system, this split is constitutive of any actually existing system. This description gave Laclau a means to reformulate the notion of equivalential links he and Mouffe had first articulated in a way that opens it to universality. *Hegemony and Socialist Strategy* presents equivalences in terms of metonymic links within a system of differences, where the openness of the social world is itself the result of that system, "the constant overflowing of every discourse by the infinitude of the field of discursivity."[64] In Laclau's reformulated theory, equivalence now also orients itself to the system itself or, more precisely, to the empty place of the system. If universality cannot itself be represented, then a particular signifier will have to assume the function of representing the universal, of becoming the "symbol of a missing fullness."[65]

Laclau insisted that this is a contingent process, with no rational or ontological ground granting priority to certain signifiers. Rather, the elevation of a particular into the position of universality is always the result of hegemonic struggle within an antagonistic political field, and hegemony always involves a synecdoche in which a particularism lays claim to a constitutively absent social fullness. This is an inherently unstable process. In order to symbolize universality, a signifier must lose its particular meaning. Laclau routinely called these signifiers "empty"; however, he was at his most precise when he spoke of *tendentially* empty signifiers. After all, he insisted that the formation of empty signifiers involves a reciprocity between universality and particularity. On one side, emptiness weakens the particularity of a concrete signifier, subordinating its differential identity to its equivalential potential. So, for example, a "right" in the modern world is understood not as the privileged property of a specific individual or group, but as the proper attribute of the human as such. On the other side, particularity responds by giving universality "a necessary incarnating body."[66] Thus, to continue the example, under the modern human rights regime, the universal human is neither a featherless biped nor the image of God nor the plaything of the Devil, but the subject as bearer of rights. The duality of *tendentially* empty signifiers exposes them to instability on both sides: as a specific representation extends its reach and embraces more, it risks dilution or fragmentation, while the validity of a representation of universality is at risk because its inescapable tie to particularity threatens to reduce the incarnate body to clay feet.

The inadequacy of any representation to fill the lack of the social is constitutive of the hegemonic relation, for hegemony requires that the particular goals of a sectorial group operate as a locus or even the name for a universality transcending them, a phenomenon that Laclau believed operates even in the most emphatic identity politics. This impossible hegemonic operation is possible, wrote Laclau, because certain signifiers—words like *freedom, right,* or *order*—have been emptied of their particular, differential meaning and, through a logic of equivalence, have come to represent the absent totality.[67] Equivalential links ultimately come to form a horizon—a *horizon*, he emphasized, and not a *ground*, because universality is the result of a process, not its enabling precondition, although one might add that pragmatic mobilizations of political languages introduce an undecidable relationship between horizon and ground.[68]

In Laclau's developing vocabulary of the late 1980s and early 1990s, *horizon* becomes closely linked to his particular use of the term *social imaginary*.[69] The concept of horizon entailed a move away from the concept of a master signifier, insofar as an equivalential chain may extend so widely over a variety of concrete demands that the ground of equivalence finds no specific anchor. At that point, claimed Laclau in 2000, "the resulting collective will will find its anchoring point on the level of the social imaginary."[70] Once horizons "become the generalized language of social change, any new demand will be constructed as one more link in the equivalential chain embraced by those horizons." Conversely, social imaginaries decline when social demands cease to recognize themselves in the political language provided by that horizon. Laclau tied this general assertion directly to his own political commitments when he traced the crisis of the contemporary left's social imaginary to the decline of the two horizons that structured its twentieth-century discourse, communism and the Western welfare state. Finding its own social imaginaries crippled, the left has retreated since the 1970s into either the defense of specific causes or into postmodern identity politics. "But," he asserted, "there is no hegemony which can be grounded in this purely defensive strategy. This should be the main battlefield in the years to come. Let us state it bluntly: there will be no renaissance of the Left without the construction of a new social imaginary."[71]

It is a characteristic of post-Marxism that it shies away from offering practical political directives derived from theory. True to this restraint, Laclau's theory may advance a forceful account of how social actors construct relative forms of universality on an uneven and complex terrain of power relations and representative symbolic practices, but it offers little by way of suggestion for what that new social imaginary might be like. The one injunction for the new radical democratic left—and here Laclau continued a trajectory from his collaborative work with Chantal Mouffe—is to openness. While Laclau regarded contingency as the fundamental condition of all politics, he considered it essential to radical democracy that this instability becomes visible and that it be affirmed. Here he saw an ally in history itself, for modern society is characterized by greater instability and a more explicit contest between different claims to represent the social whole. If conditions of sociopolitical modernity thus heighten the visibility of contingency in the political, Laclau also relied on his general account of signification to assert that the inevitable failure of any specific content to occupy the structural gap reveals the gap itself or, more precisely, the difference between "the general form of fullness and the concrete content that incarnates that form."[72] The capacity to identify and somehow symbolize that general form as well as its impossibility is crucial to Laclau's conception of a revived left committed to radical democracy. This is an issue we encountered in the previous chapter, where we saw Laclau attempting to correct Derrida's Levinasian ethics by insisting that the ethico-political commitment to openness to the other must enter into hegemonic logic if it is to become politically effective.[73] We may end this section by noting that Laclau suggested a similar corrective to Claude Lefort.

In their polemical exchange in 2006, Žižek accused Laclau of confusing the emptiness of certain signifiers with the emptiness of the place of power.[74] Žižek's charge seems to miss the point that should be clear from the preceding discussion that, while the two are not identical, the theory of empty signifiers would make no sense without theorizing an empty place in the social. In his reply Laclau insisted on distinguishing himself from Lefort, though he acknowledged an intersection: "Over several years I have resisted the tendency of people to assimilate my approach to that of Lefort, which largely results, I think, from the word *empty* being used in both analyses. But that the notion of emptiness is different in both approaches does not mean that no comparison between them is possible."[75] Still, it is clear that Laclau's intent was to put some distance between himself and Lefort. In *On Populist Reason* Laclau noted that Lefort's analysis of democracy focuses only on liberal-democratic regimes, whereas his own concern is with the "construction of popular-democratic *subjects*." He continued, "for Lefort, the *place* of power in democracies is empty. For me, the question poses itself differently: it is a question of *producing* emptiness out of the operation of hegemonic logics. For me, emptiness is a type of identity, not a structural location."[76] This attempt to give Lefort's description of the generative principle of liberal democratic regimes an activist inflection is even clearer in a text from 2001 where Laclau wrote, "Claude Lefort's argument should, I think, be supplemented by the following statement: democracy requires the constant and active production of that emptiness."[77] Ironically, Žižek made the same point repeatedly in his early works when he insisted that the "democratic invention" does not *find* the locus of Power empty, but rather "*constitutes, constructs* it as empty."[78] By the time Žižek accused Laclau of muddling different orders of emptiness, his own politics had ceased to circulate around the notion of the empty place.

Partisan Universality

In *The Ticklish Subject* Žižek described Laclau's notion of the universal as "a priori empty."[79] A year later, in his exchange with Laclau and Butler, Žižek sharpened the charge that Laclau was guilty of Kantian formalism. Responding to a passage where Laclau claims that although attempts to reach the impossible fullness of society will inevitably fail, they may still "solve a variety of partial problems," Žižek asked if this is not in fact a form of Kantianism in which the "infinite approach to the impossible Fullness" functions as a regulative idea.[80] Such a vision can only produce a gradualist politics, he argued, at best a radicalization of liberal pluralism that might bring more players onto the same field, but never imagines the possibility of transforming the field itself.[81] Of course, it was precisely the collapse of the latter possibility that precipitated the crisis of the left in the twentieth century, and, indeed, renunciation of the idea of total revolution can be taken as the founding gesture of post-Marxism itself. So the fact that Žižek's work since the late 1990s has demanded a thoroughgoing transformation of the existing order is the surest measure of his break with the political and intellectual temper of his first works. Not surprisingly, the combative language of "revolution" against "revisionism" has come to circulate freely in Žižek's text. In Žižek's mise-en-scène of a revisionist controversy between Hegelian-Lacanian revolutionism and postmodern revisionism, Žižek's Lenin assails Laclau's Eduard Bernstein, right down to the charge that revisionism transforms the socialist movement into a Kantian ethical project.

Žižek's demand appears on a number of different registers, but each returns to the crucial issue of universalism. First is his "unabashedly Marxist" insistence upon the repoliticization of the economic sphere.[82] Here Žižek noted that the recent politics of the left has tended to cluster around issues of identity that leave undisturbed basic questions of economic organization; the *"depoliticized economy is the disavowed 'fundamental fantasy' of postmodern politics."*[83] Žižek asserted that what he called "today's postpolitics cannot attain the properly political dimension of universality: because it silently precludes the sphere of the economy from politicization. The domain of global capitalist market relations is the Other Scene of the so-called repoliticization of civil society advocated by the partisans of 'identity politics' and other postmodern forms of politicization."[84] In *Contingency, Hegemony, Universality* Žižek directed this point against the basic political ideal of Laclau and Mouffe: " 'radical democracy' that was actually 'radical' in the sense of politicizing the economy *would, precisely, no longer be a '(political) democracy.' "*[85] Žižek's point unmistakably echoes the young Karl Marx's complaint that emancipation within the liberal democratic political state comes at the expense of alienating the "citizen" from his true universality as a social being.[86] Unlike Marx, who always insisted that any socialism worthy of the name *is* and *must* be democracy, Žižek frequently slipped from critique of liberal democracy to a general rejection of democracy: it is one thing to ask whether "liberal democracy" really must be the ultimate horizon of our political imagination, but it is another to assert that the master signifier of today's "global capitalist universe" *is* "democracy" without at all contesting this hegemonic identification.[87]

A second, closely related register is Žižek's ever sharpening rejection of what he typically calls, rather imprecisely, postmodernism. *The Sublime Object of Ideology* claims quite neutrally that the "fundamental gesture of poststructuralism is to deconstruct every substantial identity, to denounce behind its solid consistency an interplay of symbolic overdetermination."[88] By the mid-1990s this had hardened into a critique of poststructuralism's insistence on infinite deferral as a species of "bad infinity." Increasingly, he accused Jacques Derrida of a paranoid fear of any form of ontologization, that is, any anchoring of deconstruction's incessant movement.[89] Accordingly, Žižek attacked Derrida's notion of *démocratie à venir* as an impotent displacement of the need for concrete action.[90] Laclau got easily lumped into this "postmodern" or "poststructuralist" political camp.[91] In Žižek's reading, nothing ever *happens* within the postmodern vision of politics because there is no way to theorize radical rupture and the transition from one order to another.[92] Hence Žižek's own efforts, leaning on Alain Badiou, to mobilize concepts of the event, the act, and *creatio ex nihilo*.[93]

Badiou surfaces in a third register of Žižek's radical demand, namely in the contrast between *historicism* and *historicity*. In *On Belief* (2001) Žižek cited the "standard historicist criticism of Alain Badiou's work, according to which, the intervention *ex nihilo* of the Event into the historicity of Being is a laicized version of the religious Revelation through which Eternity directly intervenes in the temporal unfolding," only to mock it for kicking at an open door.[94] We will return shortly to the theological language of such passages, but for now it must be emphasized that this contrast forms a leitmotif in Žižek's entire oeuvre. So, for example, *For They Know Not What They Do* thematizes the opposition between "*historicism* in which all historical content is 'relativized,' made dependent on 'historical circumstances,'" and a *historicity* that involves a rupturing encounter with the real; later in the work the contrast sharpens between "absolute historicism" and "historicity [which] consists in the very fact that, at every given historical moment, we speak from within a finite horizon that we perceive as absolute."[95] In *Contingency, Hegemony, Universality* Žižek brought this directly to bear on Laclau, whose own intervention championed "radical historicism."[96] Having charged Laclau with Kantian formalism, Žižek wrote:

> *historicism* deals with the endless play of substitutions within the same fundamental field of (im)possibility, while *historicity* proper makes thematic different structural principles of this very (im)possibility. In other words, the historicist theme of the endless open play of substitutions is the very form of ahistorical ideological closure: by focusing on the simple dyad essentialism-contingency, on the passage from the one to the other, it obfuscates concrete historicity *qua* the change of the very global structuring principle of the Social.[97]

This defense of historicity returns full circle to Žižek's identification with the revisionist controversy of one century ago when he wrote elsewhere that the collapse of socialist solidarity in 1914 "cleared the ground for the Leninist event, for the breaking of the evolutionary historicism of the Second International."[98]

This adherence to the notion of historicity connects to a final register, that of *horizon*. We have seen that Laclau rejected the word *ground* and instead theorizes *horizon* as the outcome of hegemonic processes; accordingly, in *Contingency, Hegemony, Universality*, Laclau wrote that "while Žižek attempts to determine a systemic level which would 'totalize' social relations and would be universal in and for itself, both Butler and I tend to elaborate a notion of universality which would be the result of some form of interaction between particularities."[99] Žižek, for his part, insisted on the need to "distinguish more explicitly between contingency/substitutability *within* a certain historical horizon and the more fundamental exclusion/foreclosure that *grounds this very horizon*."[100] For Žižek, this is the proper and only level at which the question of radical change can be posed, that of the whole framework of the symbolic order. Hence, in his final remarks in *Contingency, Hegemony, Universality*, Žižek agreed with Laclau that the left needs a new imaginary, but he criticized Laclau and Mouffe's "radical democracy" for merely "radicalizing" the liberal democratic imaginary "while remaining within its horizon."[101] Žižek presented the left with a fundamental choice: it can fight limited battles on the ground defined by liberal democracy or it can risk *"the opposite gesture of refusing its very terms, of flatly rejecting today's liberal blackmail that courting any prospect of radical change paves the way for totalitarianism."*[102] Such a refusal involves a conception of universality fundamentally at odds with Laclau, for, in Žižek's view, struggle should be seen not "simply between the particular elements of the universality, not just about which particular content will hegemonize the empty form of universality, but between two exclusive *forms* of universality themselves."[103]

This claim applies a conviction that we have seen was a mainstay of Žižek's work since the late 1980s. For Žižek, universality emerges only concretely, always as a particular constellation formed by some type of exclusion. The Hegelian monarch functioned for the early Žižek as a privileged example of this process; yet the basic model is Lacan's description of the triumph of paternal law through renunciation of the incestuous object, the good mother.[104] Not surprisingly, he applied this directly to his debate with Laclau: "Lacan's 'primordial repression' of *das Ding* (of the pre-symbolic incestuous Real Thing) is precisely that which creates universality as an empty place" and, we can add, creates the desire for an object that can fill it. Typical of Žižek's fusion of Lacan with Hegel, he immediately recast this as a "Hegelian" insight—*contra* Kantian formalism—into the "violent operation of exclusion/repression" whereby a "universal frame" itself emerges.[105] Interestingly, Žižek also cast this as a "Schellingian" insight in *The Indivisible Remainder*, where he explored the question of grounding at a level of ontological depth not seen again in his work until *The Parallax View*, published in 2006.[106]

The Indivisible Remainder presents the Schelling of the various *Weltalter* drafts (circa 1810–12) as a philosopher who confronts directly the question, *"how does an Order emerge out of disorder in the first place?"*[107] In Schelling's mythopoeic depiction of God's emergence from a dark primordial ground into the light, Žižek saw another instance of violent expulsion, this time the act whereby God is first caught in a "vicious cycle of rotary motion" and emerges as a free Subject only by an "'act of primordial repression' by means of which God ejects the rotary motion of drives into the eternal past, and thereby 'creates time'—opens up the difference between past and present." Žižek insisted on a strict parallel with the way "man" *chooses* his character in a primordial act that separates "present-actual consciousness from the spectral, shadowy realm of the unconscious." Consistent with what we have seen in Žižek's earlier discussion of the emergence of master signifiers, *unconscious* does not mean in this context the "immediate opposite of consciousness . . . but the very founding gesture of consciousness, the act of decision by means of which I 'choose myself'— that is, combine this multitude of drives into the unity of my Self."[108] Žižek found remarkable parallels with his own position in Schelling's insistence that "the deed, once accomplished, sinks immediately into the unfathomable depth, thereby acquiring its lasting character. It is the same with the will which, once posited at the beginning and led into the outside, immediately has to sink into the unconscious."[109] What really interested Žižek was the way this primordial decision never obliterates what Schelling names the "indivisible remainder," that dark ground from which God and human subject alike liberate themselves; true to his understanding of the real, this stain is not only the external other of consciousness and symbolic order but is also repeatedly generated by the deadlocks of the symbolic itself.

This remainder, Žižek argued, assures Schelling a place in the history of materialism, which for Žižek was another way of saying that Schelling recognizes the unassimilable void that both obstructs and catalyses the symbolic order; Schelling repeatedly fails in his attempt to tackle the problem of the transition from "the pre-symbolic chaos of the Real to the universe of *logos*," but that fact situates his *Weltalter* among the great works of the materialist traditions, from Lucretius through Marx to Lacan, all of which remained *unfinished*.[110] The unfinished quality of the works of materialist thought in turn points to Žižek's conviction that materialism, far from being the source of a deterministic emphasis on the object, is actually the (groundless) ground of freedom and the enabling condition of creation. And here Žižek was able to graft his Lacanian account of the persistent stain of the real seamlessly onto Schelling's claim that "following the eternal act of self-revelation, all is rule, order, and form in the world as we now see it. But the ruleless still lies in the ground as if it could break through once again."[111] So the real, which is expelled in a primordial act of self-creation that lapses into oblivion, is always available to potentiate a repetition of that founding act.

We cannot move beyond this brief excursus on *The Indivisible Remainder* without remarking on a little irony of history. Throughout the book, Žižek insisted on the ultimate convergence of the later Schelling and

Hegel. This despite the animosity that historically divided Hegelians from Schelling because he sees in both philosophers a recognition that dialectic functions only through its relation to some other, nondialectical element. If the early Žižek archly insisted on naming Hegel the first "postmarxist," then *The Indivisible Remainder* suggests that the later Schelling must also share this rank. Yet in fact *The Indivisible Remainder* marks an important moment when Žižek turned away from the deconstructionist view of nature as a "discursive construct"—a position he recognized in his own earlier works—and embraced "materialism." So *The Indivisible Remainder* is a crucial text opening to the themes of the later Žižek, not only his self-described "dialectical materialism" but also his readiness to mix this materialist claim with theological motifs epitomized in the notion of "Pauline materialism." Surveying this trajectory, can we forget that when Marx arrived in Paris in 1844 he was aghast to discover that a leading French socialist like Pierre Leroux had taken Schelling for a materialist? *Mutatis mutandi* history happens twice. Žižek the avowed post-Marxist gradually returns to Marxism and dialectical materialism, but one of the mediators of this return is the post-Marxist *avant la lettre*, Schelling, with his sense of the contingent nature of being and account of the uncanny processes of creation. To invert Thomas Carlyle's famous phrase, Schelling presents a kind of supernatural naturalism that once attracted the romantic socialist Pierre Leroux and uncannily resurfaces in Žižek's materialism.

Whether cast in Lacanian, Hegelian, or Schellingian terms, the violent operation of exclusion/repression whereby a universal frame emerges shows us once again Žižek's conceptual strategy of repeating a homologous form that allegedly functions at both the individual and social levels. We can recall that, in the late 1980s, Žižek complained that Laclau and Mouffe's conception of antagonism operates only at the level of differences within social reality.[112] "Pure antagonism," by contrast, is based on division, *Spaltung*, which blocks every identity in itself, but is, paradoxically, the condition of possibility for the subject and for any structuration of the social field. Concrete universality is cast in the same terms, as the outcome of a *Spaltung* between the symbolic order and an excluded real. In Žižek's work from the mid-1990s onward, the privileged example is capitalism, which he describes as "more than ever . . . the concrete universal of today" that "overdetermines all alternative formations."[113]

Capitalism is structured by class antagonism, he writes; but, true to his understanding of concrete universality, he presents class antagonism as the real of capitalism, that element that cannot be fully symbolized or integrated as a "simple differential structural feature."[114] Though Derrida is a repeated target of Žižek's criticism, Žižek does not hesitate to borrow a Derridean image in speaking of a *spectral* logic in capitalism. Ernesto Laclau meets all this with derision. Dismissing the suggestion that capitalism is part of the real, Laclau argues that capitalism functions precisely because it is a symbolic system. As Sarah Kay summarizes Laclau's point, "Of course symbolic systems have holes in them, which is why capitalism is messy and contested; but it remains the system, not the hole."[115] Further, he argues, class struggle is a "species" of identity politics that is in fact becoming less and less important in advanced societies.[116] Above all, Laclau detects in Žižek's return to class struggle a schizophrenic split between a "highly sophisticated Lacanian analysis and an insufficiently deconstructed traditional Marxism."[117] Laclau's criticisms hit their mark.

Žižek, on his side, seems justified in insisting, within a given concrete constellation, that some element will overdetermine all others. Žižek's work is marked by various descriptions of this process: the dialectic demonstrated by Hegel's monarch; the "oppositional determination" whereby one term in a set of oppositions comes to embody the entire set, as in Marx's description of how finance capital comes to embody all forms of capital; the process by which the universal notion becomes fully implicated in the effort to exemplify it, a process that binds the universal to a *concrete* constellation of "particular figurations, precisely because [the universal] is forever prevented from acquiring a figure that would be adequate to its notion."[118] In *Contingency, Hegemony, Universality* he applies this understanding to his argument with Laclau: "my point of contention with Laclau here is that I do not accept that all elements which enter into hegemonic struggle are in principle equal: in the series of struggles . . . there is always *one* which, while it is part of the chain, secretly overdetermines its very horizon."[119] Ironically, *Hegemony and Socialist Strategy* explicitly accepts the role of overdetermination,[120] so the real difference is that, whereas Laclau and Mouffe saw overdetermination as the outcome of contingent struggle, Žižek increasingly takes on vestigial elements of the older Marxist emphasis on the necessary determining power of the economy.

Although this emphasis on capitalism as the concrete universal of the present day only clearly emerges in the Žižek of the mid-1990s, there is a remarkable level of consistency in his preoccupation with the question of how a contingent element comes to structure a field and his various attempts to describe this. Throughout his work, as we have seen, Žižek regards this as the great speculative mystery of dialectics; however, the repeated attempts to cast this process in Hegelian terms cannot conceal Žižek's heavy dependence on Lacanian logic. We see this if we consider the work performed by the term *short circuit*—now enshrined as the title of an MIT Press series edited by Žižek. Repeatedly, the image of the "short circuit" intervenes to account for the mechanism whereby universality is overdetermined by part of its content. So, for example, in *Revolution at the Gates*, Žižek notes that, for Laclau, "the short circuit between the Universal and the Particular is *always* illusory, temporary, a kind of 'transcendental paralogism.'" He then proceeds to contrast Laclau's skepticism to Badiou's (and Marx's) account of the proletariat not as just another specific class, but a "singularity of the social structure and, as such, the universal class, the non-class among the classes." Citing Marx's hope that the belated German nation could leap over the stage of bourgeois revolution and land directly in a revolution for the sake of universal human emancipation, Žižek generalizes this: "The dimension of universality thus emerges (only) where the 'normal' order that links the succession of particulars is disrupted. For this reason, there is no 'normal' revolution; each revolutionary explosion is grounded in an exception, in a short circuit of 'too late' and 'too early.'"[121] The short circuit is also a ruling motif in Žižek's account of Christ. So, he speaks of the "Christian insight" on the figure of Christ, that the only way to heal the wound of mortality is by "fully and directly identifying with it."[122] This phrasing occurs alongside reference to Wagner's Christ-like figure Parsifal, whose lesson Žižek again and again summarizes with the formula that "the wound is healed only by the spear which smote it." And this becomes a model for the "vicious cycle of subjectivity," wherein the subject is both "the gap, the opening, the Void which precedes the gesture of subjectivization" *and* "the gesture of subjectivization which, by means of a short circuit between the Universal and the Particular, heals the wound of this gap."[123]

True to Žižek's tendency to develop dynamic models that run up and down the chain from the individual psyche to the social order, these various instances of the short circuit are all bound to his heavy reliance on the later Lacan's idea of the symptom as *sinthome*. Where the early Lacan had seen symptoms as imaginary elements not yet integrated into the symbolic, the later Lacan regarded the symbolic itself as a symptomatic structure.[124] The *sinthome*, explains Žižek, is "a signifying formation penetrated with enjoyment." It supports our being by binding "our enjoyment to a certain signifying, symbolic formation which assures a minimum of consistency to our being-in-the-world."[125] This singular formulation is also the source of the subject's openness to and capacity for new symbolic meaning, because, as Hoens and Pluth put it, "one is always-already enjoying the structure within which meaning occurs."[126] Accordingly, Žižek presents the *sinthome* as a paradox, "a binding of enjoyment, an inert stain resisting communication and interpretation, a stain which cannot be included in the circuit of discourse, of social bond network, but is at the same time a positive condition of it."[127] One of the most astute students of this late stage in Lacan, Roberto Harari, notes that this is a logic of the symbolic based not on substitution but on attachment of signifiers, what Žižek would call "stuckness."[128] Jamie Murray's discussion of Lacan and legal theory—which makes no mention of Žižek—sheds direct light on the function of the *sinthome* in Žižek's thought. Murray writes that the *sinthome* is both a "point of attraction, and a process of dynamic ordering." It is, he continues, a "concrete universal," which he defines as a "topological invariant" that creates "effects at all scales of the system." The *sinthome* as a concrete universal produces new knots that tie together singularities across scales.[129] As Žižek says, the *sinthome* falls outside the "circuit of discourse," but it causes a whole series of short circuits, producing effects ranging from giving consistency to the psyche to bringing forth a concrete universal.

If we bring this discussion back to the explicitly political dimension of Žižek's work, we see another short circuit at work. The *sinthome* lies at the heart of the Lacanian notion of Cause. This is Cause understood as stubborn attachment, the kind of stuckness or fixity that gives the subject whatever consistency it has.[130] Yet Žižek applies the same terminology and conceptual framework to Cause meant in the sense of political commitment. We are now at the heart of the later Žižek's insistence on a *committed* universality, on a partisan universality. In a central passage in *The Ticklish Subject*, he writes: "The key component of the 'leftist' position is thus the equation of the assertion of *Universalism* with a militant, *divisive* position of one engaged in a struggle: true universalists are not those who preach global tolerance of differences and all-encompassing unity, but those who engage in a passionate fight for the assertion of the Truth that enthuses them."[131] At a certain level who would quarrel with the basic claim that passionate attachment is necessary for engaged struggle?

What is disturbing is that Žižek reduces political attachment entirely to a psychological process. Attachment to Truth is not the result of arguments but of a series of psychological short circuits. Numerous commentators have rightly worried about Žižek's "spontaneist" and "intuitivist" view of agency, the "gratuitousness" of political acts as he conceives them, and the impossibility on his terms of prefiguring alternative paths of action.[132] Indeed, Žižek produces a vision of political action that goes well beyond the decisionism of Carl Schmitt. Of Schmitt, one could say that, even if he saw no rational grounds for decision, it is nonetheless a *subject* who makes the decision through an act of will.[133] Žižek's subject is never really *present* in the moment of the act, but only discovers meaning retroactively. Consider more closely the model of retroactive causality that is one of the constants of Žižek's thought. Leaning on the Freudian notion of *Nachträglichkeit*, Žižek repeatedly employs a temporal structure in which performance or nomination constructs that which is retroactively discovered as the *Cause*. As Žižek puts this in *Metastases of Enjoyment*: "Subjects therefore posit the Cause, yet they posit it not as something subordinated to them but as their absolute Cause. What we encounter here is . . . the paradoxical temporal loop of the subject: the Cause is posited, but it is posited as what it 'always-already was.'"[134] It is emblematic that this formulation comes in a discussion of Christianity, for religious belief is in fact Žižek's privileged example. Whether one considers the discussion of Pascal in *The Sublime Object of Ideology* or the frequent invocation of Kierkegaard, we see this retroactive structure at work, whereby the believer performs rituals based on an "'empty' belief, the belief at work when we perform acts '*on faith*'—this belief, this trust that, *later*, sense will emerge."[135] Under the impression of Alain Badiou's work, Saint Paul emerges in *The Ticklish Subject* as the exemplar of the retroactive power of naming, transforming Christ into Cause. And, again, under Badiou's influence, Paul becomes a "proto-Leninist militant" passionately committed to a universal truth that allows no deviation.[136] The short circuit is complete: political engagement and religious belief both tighten into the dense knot of the *sinthome*. So, in *Revolution at the Gates*, Žižek asks:

> Why should we not . . . take the risk of shamelessly and coura-geously endorsing the boring classic criticism according to which Marxism is a "secularized religion," with Lenin as the Messiah, and so on? Yes, taking the proletarian standpoint is exactly like making a leap of faith and becoming fully engaged [in] its Cause; yes, the "truth" of Marxism is perceptible only to those who accomplish this leap, not to neutral observers.[137]

The victim here is not only a hackneyed cliché about Marxism but also the efforts of figures like Claude Lefort to describe the *disintrication* of emancipatory politics and religion.

Religion Without Religion

In *Contingency, Hegemony, Universality* both Judith Butler and Ernesto Laclau call Žižek *theological*. In Butler's case, she means the incantatory role that certain Lacanian formulae, such as sexual difference, play in his thought, while Laclau refers to Žižek's yearning for a "thoroughly differ-ent economico-political regime."[138] This is another case of kicking at an open door. Already in *The Ticklish Subject*, theological motifs become more central; since then Žižek has devoted three books to Christianity, and his 2006 opus, *The Parallax View*, continues this engagement.[139] If there is some truth to the claim that the earlier works look to theology mainly for illustrations of Hegelian and Lacanian concepts, whereas the later works treat theological questions more substantively, nonetheless these later works retroactively highlight just how much the early Žižek actually does address "the tradition which is ours," as he called Christian-ity in 1991.[140] The reopening of theological questions has, of course, been a dimension of post-Marxist discourse, as we have seen with Lefort, Gauchet, and in passing, Derrida. What they all have in common is their own stated distance from religious belief, of which Žižek's self-description as "fighting atheist" is the most emphatic.[141] Yet Žižek differs from these others.

Lefort interrogates the theologico-political in an effort to recover a dimension of alterity that had been lost in modern radical politics, but he strenuously adheres to the project of separating the theological from the political. Gauchet develops his own version of the grand narrative of secularization in order to account for the emergence of *liberal* politics from the empty form of religion. With Žižek there is no question of going back behind modernity to a world of naive faith. But the theological twines itself so tightly around the pillars of his thought that it becomes increasingly difficult to imagine a Žižek without a religious shroud. As for Derrida, the clearest measure of Žižek's distance comes, perhaps, in the foreword to the second edition of *For They Know Not What They Do*. There, Žižek adopts as his own John Caputo's formula of "religion without religion," which Caputo developed with specific reference to Derrida.[142] This is the "assertion of the *void* of the Real deprived of any positive content, prior to any content; the assertion that any content is a semblance which fills the void." Accordingly, Žižek offers Mallarmé's "rien n'aura eu lieu que le lieu" as the true formula of the atheist: "nothing will have taken place but the place itself." He cautions that although this may sound like the "Derridean/Levinasian 'Messianic Otherness,'" it is utterly different. Where Derrida orients himself toward a spectral Otherness—the place of the divine that is vacant yet continues to exercise effects or religion's "inner messianic Truth" sans external institutions—Žižek insists on the void within reality, the "fact that reality is not ultimate and closed." Consistent with the ontological position first clearly elaborated in his book on Schelling, Žižek describes this as the original *materialist* experience. Religion is unable to endure this void, so it "*fills it in* with religious content." Žižek immediately draws a parallel between his own distance from Derrida and the gulf between Kant's tension of "phenomena and Thing" and Hegel's "inconsistency/gap between phenomena themselves."[143]

This description of "religion without religion" would seem to connect Žižek's turn to theology with the vision of the critical intellectual that we encountered in *Tarrying with the Negative*, always occupying the "place" of the hole, maintaining a distance from every reigning master signifier.[144] And, indeed, it is an image that governs the most extensive study to date of Žižek and theology. Adam Kotsko's book connects Žižek's approach to Christianity to Lacan's formulae of sexuation, the distinction between the masculine logic of the master signifier and the feminine logic of the "nonall." The feminine is ostensibly *prior*, according to this scheme, because it is the logic of the real itself, that is, of the inherent incompletion and non-totalization of reality. The masculine logic of the constitutive exception, of the master signifier, follows as the attempt to establish harmonious order.[145] From this perspective, the crucifixion might be seen as the death of the master signifier. Interpreting the incarnation as a radical kenosis—the emptying out of divine attributes when God became human—Žižek argues that it was in fact God who died on the cross, or at least the "God of Beyond Himself."[146] What survives, even in death, is the miserable human. The Christian experience might thus align itself with Žižek's description of the psychoanalytic cure; that is, an experience of subjective destitution, the shattering encounter with the fundamental fantasy, and the realignment of subjectivity. Those who undergo analysis as "training" emerge into a community wherein the fantasmatic structure that erects the big Other is continually undermined. Both Christianity and the community of analysts would seem to offer models for a "non-ideological political practice," one that does not reinstate the master, but rather transforms the impossibility of the big Other into a positive and productive condition.[147] In yet another repetition of the "short circuit" and the Parsifalian image of the spear that wounds and heals, Žižek writes, in *Tarrying with the Negative,* that the "death of Christ is simultaneously a day of grief and a day of joy: God-Christ had to die in order to be able to come to life again in the shape of the community of believers (the 'Holy Spirit')."[148] The community of analysts, the community of the Holy Spirit: the chain of associations is completed in Žižek's work of the early 2000s when he suggests that this may also be a model for an authentic revolutionary collective.[149]

Kotsko links this to Hegel, who interpreted the resurrection as identical with the advent of the Holy Spirit.[150] Yet, how can we overlook in this Lacanian-Hegelian post-post-Marxist the surprising return of a structure of argument common to early nineteenth-century socialism, which Marx and Engels eventually consigned to the prehistory of revolutionary thought? I am referring, of course, to the revival of Joachimite theology to envision socialism as the age of the Holy Spirit in figures like Pierre Leroux, the Saint-Simonians, August Cieszkowski, and Moses Hess.[151] Žižek would be the first to emphasize that *repetition* occurs under changed conceptual circumstances, but nonetheless we encounter the crucial elements of Joachimism, right down to the organization of history into the ages of the Father,

the Son, and the Holy Ghost along with the lingering supersessionist logic
that has Christianity overcoming Judaism, the religion of humanity overcoming Christianity, love overcoming law. Perhaps the most significant
difference is that Žižek short-circuits the age of the Son, which effectively
means that he can regard the entire institutional history of Christianity as
incidental to its essential truth.

Kotsko's image of Žižek as an atheist recouping the spirit of Christianity
for a new model of community is sophisticated, but it overlooks the concerns that have been at the center of the present discussion, namely Žižek's
yearning for a total change of horizon and the formation of a new concrete
universal. These are, in fact, crucial elements of Žižek's engagement with
Christianity. They come to the fore if we consider the other side of Žižek's
critique of Derrida's religion without religion. We have already seen that
Žižek grew increasingly critical of the structure of infinite deferral that
underpins Derrida's thought. *Did Somebody Say Totalitarianism?* ties together a critique of two registers of this topos, Derrida's *démocratie à venir*
and the Derridean-Levinasian "Messianic longing for the Otherness that is
forever 'to come.'" This haunting specter, Žižek complains, "can never be
translated into a positive, fully present, existing entity." This messianic
yearning precludes the *act*, remaining forever suspended in a "melancholic
passive stupor."[152] What a contrast to the "'good news' of Christianity,"
presented by Žižek in the preceding section. Pre-Christian religions either
emphasized the inadequacy of all finite temporal objects, and hence the
need for moderation, or the retreat from temporal reality in favor of the "True
Divine Object." Christianity alone offers Christ as a "mortal-temporal
individual, and insists that belief in the *temporal* Event of Incarnation is
the only path to *eternal* truth and salvation."[153] Christianity is thus a "'religion of Love': in love one privileges, focuses on, a finite temporal object
which 'means more than anything else.'" We can supplement this point
with *The Fragile Absolute*'s citation from Saint Luke's Gospel: "If anyone
comes to me and does not hate his father and his mother, his wife and
children, his brothers and sisters—yes, even his own life—he cannot be my
disciple." This hatred is not, Žižek argues, the dialectical opposite of love,
but rather love's necessary demand for a fidelity that extends even to the
point of "unplugging" from all other attachments. Hence, in contrast to the
Greek philosophers, the champions of the "global Roman Empire," and

"those fully identified with the Jewish 'national substance,' " Christianity "asserts as the highest act precisely what pagan wisdom condemns as the source of Evil: the gesture of *separation*, of drawing the line, of clinging to an element that disturbs the balance of All."[154]

Returning to *Did Somebody Say Totalitarianism?* we see that Christianity's "good news" is the uniqueness of the incarnation, precisely the "positive, fully present, existing entity" that is precluded by the melancholic stupor of infinite messianic longing. And this transformative "love" is an act of divine grace that creates the conditions for a genuine rupture, a "Conversion" that can reorder reality and create a new symbolic order in which even our past (sin) can be retroactively resymbolized. How can we miss in the atheist Žižek's critique of the atheist Derrida a replay of the age-old tension between the Christian and the Jew? It is no wonder that the leader of the aggressively Christian "Radical Orthodoxy" movement, John Milbank, should contrast Žižek and Badiou to the Derridean/Levinasian concern with "irreducible plurality beyond totality." The reinstatement of totality in Žižek and Badiou, Milbank notes, comes not through a (pagan) reunification with the cosmos, but rather through "uniquely arising events, whose new logic, whose new rhythms, we all come to embrace." Their suspicion of "the politically correct discourse of pluralism causes them also unequivocally to favor the example of one religion over that of all the rest, and this religion is, of course, Christianity." Coming in an essay collection of which Žižek is an editor, we may reasonably assume Žižek agrees with this characterization.[155]

It would take us outside the scope of the present discussion to speculate about all the layers of motivation that have led the atheist Žižek to such an extensive engagement with Christianity. Yet within the terms of Žižek's politics Christianity performs two crucial functions. Despite Žižek's much-trumpeted return to Marx, very little of Marxism's analytical framework actually remains beyond an incantatory reference to the economy and class struggle and a bully pulpit call for total revolution. Missing is Marx's ontology and with it the dialectical logic of history that created grounds to hope for a total revolution. Derrida addressed this absence by transforming Marx into a specter, Marx's ontology into a hauntology, Marx's call for total revolution into an infinitely deferred demand for full justice. Žižek addresses it by resorting to a vision of history punctuated by

contingent acts that have the power to transform the horizon of the existing symbolic order. Having wagered on the impossible possibility that
total revolution can sweep away the compromised post-Marxist left, having embraced the advent of the New as an antidote to the *one-damned-
thing-after-another* stupor of postmodernism, Žižek is hard-pressed for
examples of sufficient magnitude to carry the weight of this gambit. His
frequent use of individuals like Antigone, Sethe from Toni Morrison's
Beloved, or the arch-criminal Keyser Soze from the film *The Usual Suspects*
to illustrate the "act" can only take us so far. Yes, one can concede that
these figures withdraw into a position not anticipated, preceded, or contained by the existing rules. Yes, these figures sacrifice what is most dear
to them, and in so doing they may disturb the fundamental fantasy of the
symbolic order. But these remain individual acts. The proper order of
magnitude is really only reached when Žižek presents "the ultimate example of such a gesture of 'shooting at oneself,' renouncing what is most
precious to oneself," namely "Christianity itself, the Crucifixion."[156] The
only other register that can equal Christianity's new dispensation in Žižek's
cosmology is the Bolshevik Revolution, and, as we have already seen,
Christianity and revolution become so thoroughly knotted together that
each threatens to become a metonymy for the other. The second service
that Christianity provides is an example of the transition to a new concrete
universality.

To understand this, it is necessary to consider what Žižek means by a
true act and to recall again his distinction between subject and subjectivation. Subject is the name for the negativity, the void, the leftover that cannot be integrated into the symbolic universe. A true act, Žižek emphasizes,
involves withdrawal beyond any support in the symbolic into the negativity of the real. This is for Žižek the ultimate definition of death drive and
the consummate expression of subjective destitution insofar as it affects the
fundamental fantasy. He contrasts this notion to both Badiou and Laclau,
whom he claims see the act as a positive gesture that fills in the void. Yet for
Žižek the "negative gesture of suspension-withdrawal-contraction" stands at
only a "minimal distance" from the "positive gesture" of filling the void.[157]
The negativity of the act is thus the necessary condition for creativity, although Žižek understands this creativity not as the action of bringing forth
the new, but of retroactively embracing what has emerged as a "Truth-
Event." Here Žižek leans heavily on Badiou's terminology, but again he in-

sists on the role of negativity. In an extended discussion that couples Saint Paul and Badiou at the same time as it collapses psychoanalysis and Christianity into one and the same discussion, Žižek emphasizes that subjective destitution does not directly create a "New Beginning": "it does not already *posit* a 'new harmony,' a new Truth-Event; it—as it were—merely wipes the slate clean for one." Yet negativity is not truly empty, it turns out; for Žižek immediately cautions that the word *merely* conceals the fact that in this negative gesture "something (a void) is confronted which is already 'sutured' with the arrival of a new Truth-Event. For Lacan, negativity, a negative gesture of withdrawal, precedes any positive gesture of enthusiastic identification with a Cause: negativity functions as the condition of (im)possibility of enthusiastic identification." The negative moment, death, is pregnant with resurrection: wiping the slate clean "opens up the domain of the symbolic New Beginning, of the emergence of the 'New Harmony' sustained by a newly emerged Master-Signifier."[158] Enter Saint Paul, who retroactively recreates Christ's death as a triumph. Or Lenin, who reconfigures the catastrophe of the Second International and the dire straits of Russia into grounds for revolutionary succcess.

To be fair, Žižek emphasizes that even if the negative gesture of withdrawal opens one to the New, it also persists as an element of instability, threatening to undermine the triumph of a new master signifier. Once again, we see Žižek, the critical intellectual, pointing to the void, to the empty place that bisects the big Other. Yet, as we proceed in *The Ticklish Subject*, Žižek's persona as critical intellectual becomes more and more imperiled by his commitment to the idea of revolution. Consider the role he assigns the "Master." The Master, whose "founding gesture" brings into being a "positive order," is, of course, an "impostor"—no one can escape the destabilizing effects of the real. Nonetheless,

the very fact that someone is ready to occupy this untenable place has a pacifying effect on his subjects—we can indulge in our petty narcissistic demands, well aware that the Master is here to guarantee that the whole structure will not collapse. The heroism of an authentic Master consists precisely in his willingness to assume this impossible position of ultimate responsibility, and to take upon himself the implementation of unpopular measures which prevent the system from disintegrating.[159]

Hence the "greatness of Lenin after the Bolsheviks took power: in contrast to hysterical revolutionary fervour caught in the vicious cycle, the fervour of those who prefer to stay in opposition and prefer (publicly or secretly) to avoid the burden of taking over, of accomplishing the shift from subversive activity to responsibility for the smooth running of the social edifice, he heroically embraced the onerous task of actually *running the State.*"[160]

How different this is from the Žižek of just a few years earlier. We still have the threat of revolutionaries cutting off each other's heads and we still have a leader bringing this vicious cycle to a close by occupying the empty place of power. But, for Žižek the radical democrat, Hegel's monarch was an enticing model precisely because the arbitrary selection of the leader guaranteed a distance between the place of power and those who exercised it. Instead of a dumb master, Žižek the revolutionary gives us the "authentic Master" whose willingness to occupy the impossible place of power guarantees the survival of a new order. Incidentally, this shift foreshadows yet another return of Hegel's monarch, this time in the final pages of Žižek's polemical exchange with Laclau in 2006. In this iteration, under the explicit rubric of Christology, the place of power seems to become fully identified with its occupant through the "mystery of incarnation." The fetishistic illusion that sustains our investment in a king now acquires a performative dimension whereby "the very unity of our state, that which the king embodies, actualizes itself only in the person of a king." What is striking, leaving aside the question of why Žižek speaks of an antiquated model of monarchy as if it were relevant to the reality of our political lives, is the rigidity with which Žižek now insists upon "the necessity for the universal to be incarnated in a contingent singularity."[161]

Returning to *The Ticklish Subject*, if the true master is willing to fill the place of power, then for the "true revolutionary" the acid test turns out to be "the heroic readiness to endure the conversion of the subversive undermining of the existing System into the principle of a new positive Order which gives body to this negativity."[162] Among the many interlocutors in the pages of *The Ticklish Subject*, Ernesto Laclau, Alain Badiou, Jacques Rancière, Judith Butler, Jacques Derrida, and so on, Žižek, it would seem, is the only one who might withstand this test. Žižek clearly recognizes that this logic will unnerve many of the readers who have followed him this far. So, he tries to dispatch the fear of "impending Ontologization" by emphasizing that every positive order already involves a preceding act. That is, no order of being is a "positive ontologically consistent Whole," so the commitment to a new order would seem to be shot through with awareness of the impossibility of a fully constituted social order. Yet the "void" that undermines the ontological consistency of any totality can itself never be represented; it only shows itself through the inevitable failure of whatever attempts to occupy this place. Žižek's politics, and indeed his thought generally, thus comes to oscillate between the image of radical subjective destitution and the plenitude of an order whose origin in a contingent act slips into oblivion.

Holding the Place or Filling It? Yes, Please!

Sarah Kay has suggested that Žižek's own writing may be viewed as an act, even a suicidal act in which Žižek strikes at himself.[163] Certainly, there are moments when that seems to be true, as when Žižek vows to hold to his position even if it means burning bridges and becoming one of the living dead.[164] However, it may be that the later Žižek's real gesture is not the nihilist's universal "no," but rather the positive gesture of filling the void. To name the revolution, to name the master, the savior, to avow passionate attachment to a cause, is bound to fail, but it may be worth it if failure reveals the negative place of political invention, of the emergence of the new, of the limits of the present horizon. This, at least, seems to be Žižek's wager; and it is the ultimate meaning of his return to Lenin. The Lenin Žižek wants to retrieve is not a source of dogmatic certainty, but the "Lenin whose fundamental experience was that of being thrown into a catastrophic new constellation in which the old co-ordinates proved useless, and who was thus compelled to reinvent Marxism." The *return* is actually meant as a *repetition* "in the Kierkegaardean sense: to retrieve the same impulse in today's constellation." Just as Lenin reinvented the revolutionary project in the conditions of the "politico-ideological collapse of a long era of progressivism," so should we in the context of the "emergence of the new form of global capitalism after the collapse of Really Existing Socialism."[165] The intimate link between Lenin's effort to create a positive order of being and its inevitable failure emerges later in *Revolution at the Gates* when Žižek emphasizes that "to repeat Lenin is to accept that 'Lenin is dead,' that his particular solution failed, even failed monstrously, but that there was a utopian spark in it worth saving. Repeating Lenin means that we have to distinguish between what Lenin actually did and the field of possibilities he opened up, the tension in Lenin between what he actually did and another dimension: what was 'in Lenin more than Lenin himself.' To repeat Lenin is to repeat not what Lenin *did* but what he *failed to do*, his missed opportunities."[166]

Ultimately, what "Lenin" means for Žižek is liberation from the *Denkverbot* that has made it almost impossible to imagine an alternative to the triumph of capitalism in the post–cold war world. The need to recover the radical imagination even at the cost of hyperbole is, after all, the driving force of all utopias. But Žižek's violation of the *Denkverbot* yields a welter of inconsistent and at times deeply disturbing pronouncements. Dominating everything, of course, is his call for an anticapitalist revolution. Anything short of a change in the horizon is just revisionism, at best a gradualist alteration within the general conditions of liberal capitalism: "Militant *politics*," he writes, "is a way of putting to use the terrific force of Negativity in order to restructure our social affairs."[167] At times this can lead Žižek to advocate the suicidal act; it can prompt him to endorse "in its basic intention," even if not as a "literal model to follow," the Sendero Luminoso's killing of UN and U.S. agricultural consultants and health workers or an incident where the Vietcong lopped off the left arms of village children who had been vaccinated by U.S. army doctors.[168] On other occasions Žižek's embrace of the purely negative is contradicted by his demand for specific action. So he complains that Derrida's messianic promise stifles "*any* determinate economico-political measures"; likewise, confronting Simon Critchley's Levinasian-Derridean notion of a politics of infinite demands, Žižek retorts that what we need is a politics that bombards "those in power with strategically well-selected, precise, finite demands," which cannot be dismissed because of their intrinsic impossibility.[169] (Apparently, to demand the impossible is OK so long as it is accompanied with the quasi-religious assurance that, like miracles, "THE IMPOSSIBLE DOES HAPPEN.")[170] At other moments he adopts a strange form of revolutionary *Attentismus*, exactly the opposite of the repetition of Lenin. Thus, in his book on Iraq, he claims that, "in a situation like today's, the only way really to remain open to a revolutionary opportunity is to renounce facile calls to direct action. . . . The only way to lay the foundations for a true,

radical change is to withdraw from the compulsion to act, to 'do nothing'—
thus opening up the space for a different kind of activity." A few pages later,
he complains about today's resistance to political action: "It is as if the
supreme Good today is that nothing should happen."[171] Then there is his
peevish and obtuse response to Laclau's critique of his fascination with
anticapitalist struggle, in which Žižek insists that of course he recognizes
the plurality of struggles. Class struggle may not be the actual content of
every struggle, he lectures, but it plays the *"structuring role"* in overdeter-
mining all emancipatory struggles. He offers this to Laclau and to us as if
it was not precisely the metaphysical bone on which Marxists have been
choking for the last hundred years. And that retort ends by claiming that,
in any case, "in today's constellation the primary focus should *not* be on
anticapitalism but on undermining the fetishist status of democracy as our
master-signifier."[172] This assertion is not only disturbing; it is hollow given
that the main justification Žižek offers for his indiscriminate rejection of
"democracy" is the allegation that democracy is the master-signifier of
liberal capitalism.

The hysterical cascade of positions and pronouncements slides into
bathos when Žižek places himself in line with the Jacobin Terror and the
Bolsheviks, each having brought the intellectual "game" to an end with an
idea that actually "seizes the masses." It is "up to us to repeat this same passage, and accomplish the fateful step from ludic 'postmodern' radicalism
to the domain in which the *games are over*."[173] Exactly which of Žižek's
ideas is going to seize the masses?

Let us return a final time to a telling moment in *Contingency, Hegemony, Universality*. Žižek addresses a series of rhetorical questions to
Laclau: "What if the Political itself (the radically contingent struggle for
hegemony) . . . *can be operative only in so far as it 'represses' its radically contingent nature, in so far as it undergoes a minumum of 'naturalization'?* What
if the essentialist lure is irreducible?"[174] Later in the text, Laclau returns to
these questions. Acknowledging that Žižek does not really believe that any
positive entity can truly fill the lack in the social, he proceeds to observe:
"in the endless play of substitutions that Žižek is describing, one possibility
is omitted: that, instead of the impossibility leading to a series of substitutions which attempt to supersede it, it leads to a symbolization of impossibility *as such* as a positive value. This point is important: although positivization is unavoidable, nothing prevents this positivization from symbolizing

impossibility as such, rather than concealing it through the illusion of taking us beyond it." The possibility of creating such a symbol, writes Laclau, "is important for democratic politics, which involves the institutionalization of its own openness and, in that sense, the injunction to identify with its ultimate impossibility."[175] This is the basic imperative of radical democracy, and, in one form or another, it is a value shared by each of the figures we have discussed including the younger Žižek.

The idea of symbolizing openness as such poses the challenge of naming an empty place without thereby taking possession of it. It presupposes a learning process whereby political actors formulate and pursue their specific political projects while simultaneously seeing the contingent and provisional nature of all political action. Indeed, Claude Lefort seems right in seeing this as the very condition of modern democracy, in which case Laclau and Mouffe's radical democracy is just what Žižek accuses it of being, namely the radicalization of liberal democracy's own fundamental impulses. Of course, it would be naive not to see that many political players do not perceive the game in this way and indeed are vehemently intent on keeping the field as closed as possible. Yet that recognition should not be met with an equally vehement demand for a new form of closure on the left, but rather with activism in the name of defending, extending, and radicalizing democratic openness. That is exactly opposite to the direction taken by Žižek. This chapter has tracked the trajectory of Žižek's career from his initial participation in the post-Marxist discourse that emerged from the crisis of Marxism and the development of the antitotalitarian left to his effort to retrieve and revitalize revolutionary fervor. Certain intellectual interlocutors, particularly Hegel and Lacan, have survived in the eye of the storm that is Žižek; others, like Marx, Schelling, Badiou, Saint Paul, and Lenin, have been swept up, knotted, and twisted in the whirlwind; still others, like Lefort and Laclau, have been spit out.

Žižek's most brilliant and exciting work came in his early years as he developed a unique account of ideology based on the fluid circulation of cultural and psychical energy around and through the hole that marks the meetings of the real and the symbolic. The only and proper place for the early Žižek, the place of the critical intellectual, was *"to occupy all the time, even when the new order (the 'new harmony') stabilizes itself and again renders invisible the hole as such, the place of this hole,* i.e., to maintain a distance toward every Master-Signifier." Just a few years later, disillusioned by the postcommunist world, the universal triumph of capitalism, and perhaps his own celebrity, Žižek's critical interest in undermining every fantasy of power had yielded to a militant call for the overcoming of the concrete universality of capitalism by a new and undreamt Order. It may be that he continues to honor his ideal of the critical intellectual, pointing tirelessly to the empty place at the center of society precisely by enacting the positive gesture of filling the void. By that reasoning, it may be that the only way to make that hole visible is to demonstrate the inevitable failure of any thing that might claim to fully occupy it. That would make his partisan advocacy of a strangely construed Christian-Bolshevik revolutionary tradition a topsy-turvy way of keeping the empty place open for the future.

This is a perilous game. It is hard not to see that Žižek is in danger of repeating the slippage of the Jacobins whom he analyzed in his early works, from a guardian of the empty locus of power to a brutal occupant of that place. There are numerous risks here, such as the exposure of Žižek's increasing detachment from the political needs of the present, or the self-destruction of what is genuinely interesting in his work, or the spread of a rather glib and vacuous vocabulary of militancy that merely adds to the *frisson* of "doing Theory," while masking theory's distance from any sort of actual political practice. Probably not among these perils is a new Committee of Public Safety with Žižek at its head, or a revived Lenin, beaten to drive out the moths, dressed in the new-old clothes of a first-century prophet, and ready to lead a revolution for the new millennium.

Epilogue

POST-MARXISM EMERGED in the 1970s and 1980s as Marxism lost its hold on the imagination of the western European intellectual left. The post-Marxism that we encounter in Ernesto Laclau, Chantal Mouffe, Jacques Derrida, and the young Slavoj Žižek attempts to hold onto the possibility of radical action and progressive transformation, while at the same time it renounces Marxism's idea of a privileged social actor, Leninism's insistence on a vanguard party possessing correct theory, and indeed, the basic Marxist-Leninist belief that a theory could ever adequately guide social movements operating within a complex historical reality. These theoretical projects intersected with many intellectual currents in twentieth-century thought, but, above all, they drew on the antifoundationalism that became especially potent in French intellectual life after, roughly, 1960. Contingency, indeterminacy, the complex relationship between sign and signifier, representation and represented, are all themes that bind post-Marxism to the French intellectual context, even if, as we have seen, that context cannot be spatially delimited to Paris or even to the Hexagon.

Post-Marxism owes still more to a French context, for it came to observe a certain number of prohibitions that emerged in the antitotalitarian discourse of French thought. It would be an error to see the antitotalitarian moment simply in terms of a renunciation of any lingering vestige of enthusiasm for the Soviet Union. It had much more to do with realignments in French left-wing politics and, at a deeper level, with an emotional and intellectual reorientation. The results were varied in the extreme: from the New Philosophers' denunciation of all power to Marcel Gauchet's long march from anarchism to liberalism to establishment republicanism. Generally, the antitotalitarian moment helped to detach the question of democracy from the question of revolution and launched a number of theoretical projects that together contemporaries heralded as the return of the political. Even more generally, antitotalitarianism may be taken as a factor in the widespread rejection of "totality" that became a hallmark of French thought. These were all developments in the 1970s and 1980s. Yet, as we have seen, Cornelius Castoriadis and Claude Lefort forged ideas in the 1950s and 1960s that opened up many of the questions and styles of thought that would gain greater traction in the wake of 1968.

In trying to arrive at generalizations, there is the ever present danger of effacing significant differences. Whereas Laclau, Mouffe, and the young Žižek named themselves post-Marxists, neither Castoriadis nor Lefort would have accepted the label other than, perhaps, as an incidental biographical detail. Marcel Gauchet, meanwhile, was never a Marxist. My argument has been that all of them pursued their projects within a horizon crucially defined by the collapse of Marxism. To adopt a formula from Hans Blumenberg, we might say that the old answer lost its power, but the questions persisted. Or at least some questions did, those centered on the critique of asymmetries of power and the transformative potential of democratic activism. Important commonalities run through the works of these theorists, first and foremost the turn to the symbolic, engagement with Lacan, emphasis on historical indeterminacy, the role of the imaginary, recognition of the fragmented landscape of modern society and whatever forms of emancipatory politics might emerge from it, and commitment to democracy. Yet the commonalities quickly fracture into the concrete articulations of these theorists. Instead of leading toward a unified picture, we end up with a kaleidoscope of positions on the prospects of democracy and the theory of modern culture and politics.

As we saw, Slavoj Žižek's career took him from an early allegiance to the idea of post-Marxist radical democracy to a militant call for the return of Marx, the critique of capitalism, and a fight against the one-sided universality of capitalism in the name of an equally one-sided and undreamt new order. Žižek's trajectory prompts a question akin to that asked of so-called postmodernism: insofar as most of us now use the term *postmodern* with skepticism, misgiving, or irony, are we in a post-postmodern condition or was postmodernity always merely part of modernity? In similar spirit, does Žižek's example suggest that we are entering (or have entered) a post-post-Marxist phase? Or might it be that post-Marxism is a dialectical moment in the history of Marxism? As Fredric Jameson has noted, "few intellectual movements have known quite so many internal schisms" as Marxism.[1] Is post-Marxism another internal schism? Where do things stand now? An impossible question admitting no definitive answer, but imperative nonetheless.

Alain Badiou insists that the "historical paradox" of the early twenty-first century "is that, in a certain way, we are closer to problems investigated in the first half of the nineteenth century than we are to those we have inherited from the twentieth century. Just as in around 1840, today we are faced with an utterly cynical capitalism, which is certain that it is the only possible option for a rational organization of society." Badiou goes on to note that now, as then, the poor are blamed for their own plight, widening gulfs separate rich nations from poor nations, while even in the wealthiest countries extreme poverty is contemplated with complacency, and political power does not even try to veil its function as an agent of capitalism. Now, as then, capitalism faces no other system that challenges its monopoly on the organization of really existing societies: as in the 1840s, "Revolutionaries are divided and only weakly organized, broad sectors of working-class youth have fallen prey to nihilistic despair, the vast majority of intellectuals are servile."[2] To Badiou's list I would add that elements of the intellectual habitus of the European left in the years just before Marxism began its ascent to dominance over the international socialist movement have resurfaced in the period after Marxism's collapse.

In my admittedly limited exploration of this theoretical landscape, we have seen unabashed appeals to the constructive power of imagination and the potential world-creating force of words, calls to untether utopianism from the leaden weight of an apparently self-evident reality, the deployment of the potencies of religion, the attempt to mobilize political energies around figures of impossibility. If, as Fredric Jameson has insisted, our age "demands a politics of ambivalence or ambiguity,"[3] its resources and the roots of its temperament will certainly not be found exclusively in the short twentieth century, Hobsbawm's "age of extremes." The figures I have discussed frequently turn back to the period prior to the rise of Marxism. Castoriadis finds inspiration for his concept of the radical imagination in Fichte's theory of productive imagination (*productive Einbildungskraft*). In his interrogation of modern democracy, Claude Lefort returns frequently to the years immediately after the fall of Napoleon, to writers who "still lived in the gap between a world that was disappearing and a world that was appearing" and whose "thought was still haunted by questions which knew no limits."[4] Miguel Abensour seeks resources for a revival of utopianism in Romantic socialism, including that of Pierre Leroux, to whom he dedicates numerous articles.[5] Jean Baudrillard, in the brief moment between his incarnations as Marxist radical and prophet of the postmodern simulacrum, turns for figures of revolt to the *poète maudit* and the revolutionary Romantic. Chantal Mouffe and Ernesto Laclau cite the Romantic mythologist Friedrich Creuzer's description of the symbol when they wish to illustrate the excess of the signified over the signifier, which for them conditions the operation of hegemony.[6] Slavoj Žižek returns again and again to Hegel, though not the Hegel of a rigid dialectic inexorably moving toward absolute reason, but the philosopher of a failed symbolic whose dialectic reveals the impossibility of resolution. And, to underscore this refashioning of Hegel, Žižek turns liberally to the work of Friedrich Schelling, whose later philosophy rested on an insight into the ontological incompleteness of being itself. To these examples from the figures treated in this book, we might add others. Jacques Rancière comes especially to mind: his recourse to Kant, Schiller, and Schlegel; his refusal, *contra* Habermas, of a "division between a rational order of argument and a poetic, if not irrational, order of commentary and metaphor"; his deflection of Walter Benjamin's classically *modernist* worries about the aestheticization of politics into an insistence that politics, properly understood, inevitably contains an aesthetic dimension insofar as "politics is always both argument and opening up the world where argument can be received and have an impact."[7]

Many of these resonances between the eras before and after Marxism's ascendancy may be tied to the prominent role of the symbolic, which has furnished us a red thread by which to track a number of thinkers wrestling with the challenge of reconceiving democratic theory in a context marked by the collapse of really existing socialism and the weakening hold of the Marxist model. We have seen that the notion of the symbolic construction of social reality was seized by figures like Merleau-Ponty or Althusser in various efforts to save Marxism from the economistic reductionism and epistemological realism of vulgar Marxism. Such attempts to rescue Marxism from its internal impasse moved rather seamlessly into attempts to rescue radical thought from Marxism itself. These strategies tie the various trajectories traced in this book to a great sea change in twentieth-century thought. Typically known as the linguistic turn, I have suggested in the introduction that the phenomenon might be better described as a symbolic turn. To invoke the term *symbolic* is inevitably to mobilize associations with the idea of the symbolic order articulated by structuralism and carried forward in poststructuralism. And, to be sure, Lévi-Strauss and, above all, Lacan exercised considerable influence over the theoretists explored here. Indeed, one way to sort out the positions we have explored is to weigh them in relation to Lacan's idea of the symbolic order. In this typology, Castoriadis emerges as an anti-Lacanian who views the symbolic order as the product and manifestation of the imagination working at both the individual and the anonymous social level; Lefort and Gauchet both draw on Lacan's idea of constitutive division to theorize the relationship of the symbolic and the real, yet their view of the symbolic is heavily influenced by phenomenological ideas about the background conditions of intelligibility; and, finally, Laclau, Mouffe, and Žižek all structure social theory around the basic Lacanian theory of desire, whereby the symbolic is driven by failed attempts to fill the lack in the heart of being. If the impact of structuralism upon these various post-Marxist styles is indisputable, nonetheless, a central assumption of this book has been that structuralism's relatively rigid semiotic conception of the symbolic order does not adequately accommodate the mode of the symbolic mobilized by post-Marxist theorists. The symbolic is, I have argued, an irreducibly polyvalent construct, one that oscillates between the theory of arbitrary signs and the ideal of motivated signs, between the power to "present" the thing and the demonstration of a gap between the thing and the sign, between the power to body forth an idea and the impossibility of fully adequate representation of it.

The critique of representation was, of course, the stock-in-trade of certain currents of what, for want of a better term, we can call postmodernism. At their worst, skepticism of representation could lead to the conclusion that all representations are equally inadequate or inadequate in the same way or that, as in the case of Baudrillard, the simulacrum has fully replaced social reality. Somewhat more soberly, and not surprisingly, postmodern critique gave a new relevance to the figure of the sublime. Most notable here is Jean-François Lyotard, who made the impossibility of representation the centerpiece of his critique of the modern projects of political emancipation. In truth, however, the extremes of postmodernist doubt have gained little purchase among the theorists discussed in this book. And even the idea of the sublime has been less important to post-Marxist thought than the idea that the representation of the ideas of political reason fails, but not in the absolute sense implied by Lyotard's deployment of Kant. We see a particularly clear version of this in Ernesto Laclau and Chantal Mouffe's theory of hegemony, in which the effort to represent becomes the driving engine of political contest. I would add that similar impulses are at the basis of Rancière's critique of Lyotard, whose turn to the sublime deflects politics into an ethics grounded in the insurmountable unrepresentability of the ideas of reason. For Rancière, the proper task of *politics*, which he defines as the demand for equality of that part of society that has no "part," as opposed to *police*, defined as the administration of social life, is to contest the very partition of the perceptible, whereby a social space opens onto those who have a part and those who do not, those who are visible in the common and those who remain invisible. And here Rancière sees an intersection between the egalitarian thrust of politics and the "fragile politics" of art, which "consists in bringing about a reframing of material and symbolic space."[8] From a different angle, Frank Ankersmit also develops a theory of politics that acknowledges both the imperative and the impossibility of representation. To be sure, Ankersmit himself evokes the sublime in his discussions of democratic politics and, especially, his treatment of historical knowledge.[9] But the real emphasis in his theory of politics falls upon the work of representation. In an unjustly neglected book, Ankersmit pursues a theory of democratic politics based on aestheticization; whereas Benjamin's famous anxieties circled around fascist yearnings for political spectacle and an organic state conceived as a *Gesamtkunstwerk*, Ankersmit bases his aesthetic politics not on the organic unity of the work of art, but on "the insurmountable *barrier* between the represented and its representation." Ankersmit calls this an aesthetic of "brokenness," and this particular aesthetic underpins his plea for a democratic politics that is aware of the irreducible nonidentity of the representation and the represented. "Political reality," he writes, "is not something we come across as if it has always existed; it is not found or discovered, but made, in and by the procedures of political representation."[10] In a pivotal chapter Ankersmit locates the emergence of this awareness of the complex work of political representation in the Romantic era.[11]

It has been a gambit of this book to open with two chapters on the Romantic theory of the symbolic. At the book's beginning, it may have struck readers as a curious choice for a study of post-Marxism and, at its end, it may remain so for some. I hope, though, that for many this initial focus has proven illuminating. My intention, in the first instance, was to create a certain narrative arc: Marxism inherited Left Hegelianism's hostility to Romanticism, including its politics, most obviously that of restorationist Romantics but also that of Romantic socialists such as Pierre Leroux. In the name of a this-worldly, disenchanting, desymbolizing logic, that hostility extended to a critique of the symbolic sensibility that governs so much of Romantic thought. Marx followed the Left Hegelians in associating human emancipation with the task of overcoming the otherness, heteronomy, and unmasterability implied by symbolic representation. Even if the subsequent history of Marxist theory contained many heterodox elements, the main current strongly embraced a desymbolizing impulse, epistemological realism, and economistic materialism. In the period of Marxism's most severe crisis, the intellectual left's suspicion of symbolic form eased. Recourse to the symbolic presented itself as an antidote to Marxism's perceived flaws and a more promising way to conceptualize a democratic politics that no longer orients itself toward a foundational logic of the historical world. With this move, the dialectic of desymbolization was in certain ways reversed. The symbolic offered a way to rethink the social space as contingent and open, irreducible to an anterior or prior instance or foundation beyond and outside representation; and the symbolic carried a certain lesson in moderation, fitting with the more ambivalent and ambiguous sensibility of leftist theorists chastened by the history of the twentieth-century socialist experience. Further, the symbolic furnished the lever switching left-wing theory from a preoccupation with the logic of the social to an exploration of the logic of the political. And, as I have argued, the return to the symbolic reopened the question of the immanent and the transcendent for political theory, a question that for the left had been foreclosed by Left Hegelian and Marxist thought. Attending that reopening of the problem of immanence and transcendence, we have seen, were revived concerns about the intersections of the theological and the political or, as in the case of Derrida, Žižek, and Badiou, outright borrowings from the archive of religion.

The mobilization of the symbolic brought with it much of the polyvalence, ambiguity, and paradoxical richness already evident when Romantic theorists struggled to articulate a new theory of the symbol around 1800. It is worth pausing for a moment to recall that, for a time, it was customary to describe postmodern culture as *allegorical*; in a canonical essay, Craig Owens equates postmodernism with the allegorical mode, which presents "the world [as] a vast network of signs . . . [which] continually elicits reading, interpretation."[12] In this framework, postmodernism's allegorical sensibility is explicitly contrasted to modernism's symbolist sensibility, that is, an aesthetic of fragmentation, displacement, and supplement is pitted against an aesthetic of presence, embodiment, and holism. Romanticism is habitually depicted as a culprit for introducing an aesthetic idealism that rests on an expressive theory of symbols, "the presentational union of the 'inner essence' and outward expression, which are in fact revealed to be identical."[13] Postmodernism, so this narrative runs, no longer proclaims the work's autonomy, self-sufficiency, transcendence, and fulfillment of desire, but rather it speaks of the work's contingency, insufficiency, lack of transcendence, and perpetual frustration.[14] Readers may well have been wondering if, when the post-Marxist theorists insist on the failure of representation, they are in fact expressing an allegorical, rather than symbolic sensibility. As I argued in chapter 1, however, the Romantics quickly blurred any rigorous distinction between the allegorical and the symbolic, with Friedrich Schlegel even using the terms interchangeably; in fact, the Romantic conception of the symbolic gained its fullest meaning precisely by reaching into the terrain of the allegorical, the impossibility of representation that theorists like Owens assign to postmodernism. I have chosen to stress the "symbolic" and its Romantic provenance because it is there that we see the characteristic tension between the power of symbols to present and their inevitable failure, which is precisely the tension that separates a properly postmodern theorist like Lyotard from the theorists of the political that I have discussed.

Thus my second motive in juxtaposing Romantic and post-Marxist thought: to counteract the all-too-frequent presentism that accompanies so much discussion of various currents of modern theory, including post-Marxism, by deepening the historical perspective. Here I need to repeat a disclaimer from the book's introduction. My aim has not been, in any way, to argue for direct lines of influence or causality stretching from Romanticism to post-Marxism, nor has it been to efface the significant differences between intellectual currents separated by wide gulfs of time and temper. Rather, in following the adventures of the symbolic, I have sought, in a manner that is, admittedly, itself somewhat Romantic, to create associations, resonances, and reverberations that may alter and inflect the way we read and hear contemporary theory. A comment from Georges Gusdorf, encountered as I approached the end of this task, more or less expresses my own sensibility and aim: "We are not masters of words; they come to us from the depths of ages charged with resonances and harmonies, with significations which continue to be enriched in usage by encounters, agreements, and disagreements with other words, whence arises unpredictable surges across mental space."[15]

In naming this book, I wanted to invoke a (modest) parallel between my assessment of an important current in recent left-wing theory and Maurice Merleau-Ponty's famous mid-twentieth-century evaluation of the state of Marxist thought and politics; further, I wished to suggest that something like a substitution might have occurred, with the symbolic coming to occupy in post-Marxism the place that the dialectic had occupied in Marxism. Certainly, one can find in the collapse of Marxism ample evidence to support Michel Foucault's insistence in 1966 that "a non-dialectical culture is in the process of taking shape."[16] Yet, if Foucault's assessment of postmodern culture seems confirmed, for example, in Jean Baudrillard's insistence that the symbolic is through and through undialectical because it permanently resists definition or masterability, Foucault would appear to be disproven by Slavoj Žižek, who insists that the symbolic is essentially dialectical precisely because of its unmasterability. Clearly, Žižek's dialectic, with its rejection of *Aufhebung* and its emphasis on contingency, incommensurabilities, and discontinuities, is won at the cost of relinquishing the main assumptions about dialectics that have dominated generations of thinkers. Nonetheless, it is not unprecedented within the history of the left; not only might Theodor Adorno's negative dialectics come to mind but also Ludwig Feuerbach's dialectic, with its disruptive positive remainder, discussed in chapter 1.

If, from certain vantage points in the 1970s or 1980s, it could look like dialectics was on its way out, the view from the present suggests a very different conclusion. One might be tempted to say that the relationship between the dialectical and the nondialectical is itself undecidable. In fact, however, I am inclined to see this relationship as precisely an instance of a dialectic that works through oppositions, conscious of their intertwining and reciprocal effects but also of the impossibility of their resolution. It is hard to disagree with Fredric Jameson that "this very opposition is itself dialectical: to resolve it one way or another is the non-dialectical temptation."[17]

The old dialectics, with its confidence or at least hope that thought and being, idea and history, are marching to the same drumbeat, the dialectics of the old communist movement against which thinkers like Cornelius Castoriadis set their teeth, is long dead. Indeed, that dialectics died several deaths, at the hands of post-Marxists and, before them, philosophically sophisticated Marxists at various moments in the twentieth century. With that death came anxieties that are familiar to anyone who has concerned herself with the possible pitfalls of embracing social constructivism, namely that critical theory falls into one-sidedness, losing its capacity or even its will to imagine processes beyond itself. Certainly, the idea that everything about the human world is a social construction has become a commonplace. Indeed, if at various points sophisticated Marxists, non-Marxists, and post-Marxists alike have found it useful to point to the symbolic constitution of the social as a corrective to the stale opposition between base and superstructure, this idea has become sufficiently uncontroversial that the billionaire George Soros has built his thinking on the notion that reflexivity shapes the economy right down to the fundamentals.[18] Yet undoubtedly the shift to the symbolic brings with it the danger that analysts come to think of the world as *just* representation and cease to believe that some representations may be more adequate than others and that, as David Harvey puts it, "the search for proper and powerful representations (theory) is always a matter of serious commitment for committed people"[19] or, at the very least, that they neglect the task of analyzing the economy outside the parameters of the symbolic dimension. Jameson expresses anxiety about this peril in a 2008 discussion of Pierre Bourdieu.[20] In his 2009 opus on dialectics he does an end run around this worry by arguing that contemporary Marxism must, appropriately, be a

Marxism of the superstructures because "late capitalism" has "profoundly and structurally modified" the relationship of base and superstructure.[21]

Ultimately, what was once taken as a heresy within the left, namely to overturn what a scathing attack on Laclau and Mouffe once called Marxism's "categorial priority,"[22] does not necessarily mean a lapse from materialism back into idealism. Indeed, the old idealist insistence that the human world is a construction of spirit is better understood through the theory of social institution, which emerged precisely as a means to get beyond the old spirit-matter dualism. The obstacle to the critique of political economy has stemmed not from the idea that the social world, including all facets of the economy, is instituted. That claim in itself does not at all deny that social processes function at various levels of agency and structure, all of which are open to analysis; and it has the entirely salutary effect of repeatedly unmasking capitalism's tendency to naturalize its operations, a tendency particularly pronounced in the era of neoliberalism's regnancy. The real problem has rested in the inclination, as the hold of a foundational logic of the social weakened, to accentuate contingency and indeterminacy while ignoring constraints. Undoubtedly, among poststructuralist and post-Marxist thinkers, the pendulum could swing too far in that direction, but nonetheless postfoundationalist theory presented a vital corrective within leftist thought. In turn, Moishe Postone offers a corrective to the corrective when he recognizes its value for thinking about action *but* calls for a crucial supplement: "Positions that ontologize historical indeterminacy emphasize that freedom and contingency are related. However, they overlook the constraints on contingency exerted by capital as a structuring form of social life and are, for this reason, ultimately inadequate as critical theories of the present."[23]

This summons back to the analysis of capitalism, and with it the return or reassertion of Marxism among many leading left-wing theorists in western Europe and America, is perhaps the best proof that, despite appearances, dialectics is alive and well. If the various strands of post-Marxist thought tended to minimize the sphere of the economy in favor of the shaping power of the political, the failure of what Rancière calls the "capitalist utopia" has reinvigorated the critique of political economy.[24] And here Marx's value turns out never to have been diminished. Indeed, as Dick Howard has put it, "Marxism in the postcommunist world could be thought of as a theory happily rescued from the weight of a failed experiment."[25] So, for example, David Harvey's brilliant analyses of global capitalism have, for several decades, drawn chiefly on Marx, while Chris Harman began writing his important book *Zombie Capitalism: Global Crisis and the Relevance of Marx* years before the crash in 2008.[26] At the opening of the twenty-first century, the list of important and creative work conducted within a Marxist analytic framework is not negligible.[27] Crucial to the reassertion of Marx's heuristic value is skepticism toward inflated claims of capitalism's historic transformation in recent decades. The stakes are clear. Just as Marxian political ideas might seem invalidated by the tragic course of communist totalitarianism, so too might Marxian economics be dismissed by the apparent fact that capitalism has changed beyond recognition in the many decades since Marx and Engels. Postindustrialism, postmodernism, the information society, the triumph of neoliberalism, globalization itself: all reinforced the sense that capitalism had moved beyond the Marxian framework.

In light of this, it is unsurprising to see recent champions of Marx warning that we must not overstate the extent of capitalism's alteration in recent times. Rather than overestimating the breaks and discontinuities of capitalism, we should develop a dialectical perspective on its continuities.[28] Likewise, even as we may recognize profound changes in the nature of labor, class, and the social bases of activism, we should not exaggerate the disappearance of the working class.[29] At the very least, North Americans who have become enamored of the idea of their postindustrial information society are well reminded by Žižek that the American working class is alive and well and living in China. Ultimately, Jameson seems right when he notes that "it seems paradoxical to celebrate the death of Marxism in the same breath with which you greet the ultimate triumph of capitalism. For Marxism is the very science of capitalism; its epistemological vocation lies in its unmatched capacity to describe capitalism's historical originality; its fundamental structural contradictions endow it with its political and its prophetic vocation, which can scarcely be distinguished from the analytic ones."[30]

The failure of the neoliberal capitalist utopia has put Marxist analysis back on the agenda. However, if this is true, we also see a dialectic at work whereby the sensibility expressed in post-Marxist theory finds its counterpart in a certain kind of Marxism. Hence, for example, in a perceptive essay from 1995, Douglas Kellner argues for the continuing relevance of "a reconstructed Marxism, a Marxism without guarantees, teleology, and foundations." Such a Marxism, he continues, "will be more open, tolerant, skeptical, and modest than previous versions. A Marxism for the twenty-first century could help promote democracy, freedom, justice, and equality, and counterattack conservative ideologies that merely promote the interests of the rich and powerful."[31] A similar spirit presides in the concluding remarks of Stuart Sim's intellectual history of post-Marxism. Sim foresees an important but diminished role for Marxism within a pluralistic political and theoretical landscape in which "one might be a Marxist on some issues, but not necessarily on all."[32] That seems like a position that almost all the figures discussed in this book might support. After all, even Castoriadis, the one most vociferously critical of Marx, concedes the "sociological" if not economic value of Marx's exploration of the mechanisms of capitalism.[33] Even Jameson's "postmodern Marxism" remains by and large consistent with a modest Marxism inhabiting a pluralist theoretical landscape.

Yet, although Marxian concepts might be appreciated as valuable tools in one's kit, it is not clear whether it makes any sense to call oneself a *Marxist* in certain regards but not in others. Throughout its history, Marxism's claims on its adherents have been much more demanding. It has not been a taxi that one can get out of at will, as Max Weber once said of the ethos promulgated by the Sermon on the Mount. Marxism has offered a comprehensive theory of historical process and society. Insofar as capitalism is an economic system that penetrates every corner of contemporary life, any theory of capitalism of necessity aspires to totality; and Marxism has been the aspirant par excellence.[34] Certainly in Slavoj Žižek's trajectory away from initial sympathy with post-Marxism to renewed fidelity to Marxism we see the return of a more encompassing claim on the theorist's identity and, with it, of the classic tropes of Marxist totalization: demand for a complete change of horizon, yearning for a new positive order to end the vicious cycle of revolt and its recuperation, centrality of class struggle and the agency of the working class, insistence on a *logic* of capital, spectral as that may be. Žižek's most recent writings have been much more explicit in tying this to the project of communism. "What is now required," he claimed in 2011, "is not a moralizing critique of capitalism, but the full re-affirmation of the Idea of communism."[35]

Among the dialectical twists that we have been tracing in these concluding pages, the return of communism as a kind of horizon of leftist thought is surely one of the more surprising. Žižek is by no means alone in shrugging off a prohibition that had descended upon the name of communism. Indeed, an anthology of essays on the "idea of communism" published in 2010 gathers a who's who of European and North American theorists.[36] Though not all the contributors are willing to accept the program, there is, nonetheless, an earnest engagement that is in itself striking. We saw in chapter 6 that Žižek's work had been moving in this direction for over a decade. But it is in fact Alain Badiou who has done the most to reactivate the question of communism. Badiou elaborated what he calls the "communist hypothesis" in his 2007 book *De quoi Sarkozy est-il le nom?* which subsequently appeared in English in 2010 as *The Meaning of Sarkozy*, accompanied by the volume *The Communist Hypothesis*.[37] "For about two centuries (from Babeuf's 'community of equals' to the 1980s)," Badiou notes, "the word 'communism' was the most important name of an Idea located in the field of emancipatory, or revolutionary, politics."[38] Insofar as that version of communism became linked to membership in a party that dreamed of capturing the state and establishing a regime grounded in radical egalitarianism, Badiou refuses nostalgia. "Marxism, the workers' movement, mass democracy, Leninism, the party of the proletariat, the socialist state— all the inventions of the 20th century—are not really useful to us any more."[39] Thus "the only real question is how to begin a second sequence of this Idea, in which it prevails over the clash of interests by means other than bureaucratic terrorism."[40] Badiou leaves this unanswered and seems mainly interested in holding open a dream for the future.[41] Yet if his communist idea has tendrils connecting it to the past and the future, the historicity of the communist horizon intersects with what he believes is an invariant, transtemporal core in the communist idea: "As a pure Idea of equality, the communist hypothesis has no doubt existed since the beginning of the state." This dehistoricizing, Platonizing move effectively means that communism appears "as soon as mass action opposes state coercion in the name of egalitarian justice."[42] In turn, he insists, in such confrontations the idea achieves materiality and symbolization, which produces a truth event that creates a new political subjectivity. Although emancipatory politics is essentially a politics of anonymous masses, Badiou warns his reader not to overlook the power of proper names in revolutionary politics, a pantheon of communist heroes: Spartacus, Thomas Münzer, Robespierre, Toussaint Louverture, Blanqui, Marx, Lenin, Rosa Luxemburg,

Mao, Che Guevara. "The anonymous action of millions of militants, rebels, fighters, unrepresentable as such, is combined and counted as one in the simple, powerful symbol of the proper name."[43] Badiou warns against fully accepting Kruschev's critique of the cult of personality; if the cult of the leader in really existing communism finds its consummation in the mausoleum, the pantheon should be an open shrine inspiring action and always ready to accommodate new heroes.

Badiou rejects compromises with parliamentary democracy, which he regards as inextricably complicit with capitalism, and he draws a hard line between socialism and communism; but, for all that, his communism is a tremulous creature. "Is it," he asks, "a question of a regulative Idea, in Kant's sense of the term, having no real efficacy but able to set reasonable goals for our understanding? Or is it an agenda that must be carried out over time through a new post-revolutionary State's action on the world? Is it a utopia, perhaps a plainly dangerous, and even criminal, one? Or is it the name of Reason in History?" Badiou surmises that this debate can never be concluded, because of the complex operation of the idea in history and subjective experience.[44] Yet it seems clear that Badiou's worries about the dangers of conceiving communism as a concrete political program are sufficiently strong that he inclines toward communism as a "very general set of intellectual representations" that fulfill a regulatory function in the Kantian sense.[45] The communist idea is eternal, its tasks infinite.

As with many aspects of his thinking, Žižek draws heavily from Badiou. Yet even if he affirms the "eternal idea of communism,"[46] he strongly rejects the notion that communism functions best as a regulative idea.[47] Here familiar themes from our earlier discussion of Žižek resurface. For one thing, he criticizes Badiou (and incidentally Rancière) for distinguishing between moments of authentic political contestation and the mere policing of men and goods. Ultimately, Žižek argues, Badiou (and Rancière) suffers from a fear that the purity of the idea will be sullied the moment communists truly struggle for power. Locating this anxiety in the longer history of the left, Žižek lumps Badiou (and Rancière) in with the "young Hegelian" rejection of the state, even as he himself takes the side of the "old Hegelians" in their quest for a "strong State grounded in a shared ethical substance."[48] Badiou's worries about power take him further into what Žižek regards as an almost "Gnostic" dualism between "the corrupted 'fallen world' of the economy and spiritual Truth." This leads Badiou to miss "the properly Marxist idea of *communism* whose core principle is precisely that this corrupt state of the economy is not an eternal fate, a universal onto-logical condition of man, but is a state that can be radically changed such that it will no longer be reducible to the interplay of private interests."[49] In sharp opposition to both Badiou and Rancière, Žižek insists that commu-nism should not consist only of a history of effervescent democratic mo-ments.[50] "Out of revolt," he writes in 2009, "we should shamelessly pass to enforcing a new order."[51] The task is not infinite, but finite: to translate and inscribe "the democratic explosion into the positive 'police' order, im-posing on social reality a *new* lasting order."[52] Strikingly, the impatience that drove a wedge between Žižek and Laclau reemerges in Žižek's treat-ment of his current allies in the new philosophical ultra-left.[53]

Badiou and Žižek represent two diverging tracks in the current revival of interest in communism, but both equally reveal the profound problems of this revival. There is, for instance, the question whether the communist idea can sufficiently free itself from the philosophical assumptions that prevailed in orthodox Marxist communism. As Simon Critchley puts it, "The idea of communism remains ontologically suspect because of the es-sentialist idealist metaphysics of species-being (*Gattungswesen*) that deter-mines the concept in Marx's work. Communism is a word that, in my view, remains captive to an essentially aestheticized and organicist notion of community."[54] In reply to Critchley, one might point to current discus-sions of "leftist ontology," which Bruno Bosteels emphasizes are aware of the need "to come to terms with the inherent gap or ghostly remainder in the discourse of being qua being." This imperative on "delinking" or "un-binding" the social, Bosteels reports, leads to the "stubborn, not to say hackneyed, insistence on motifs—here we can forgo the mention of proper names—such as the indivisible remainder or reserve, the constitutive out-side, the real that resists symbolization absolutely, the dialectic of lack and excess, or the necessary gap separating representation from presentation pure and simple."[55] Yet these motifs are exactly those that were, histori-cally, at the core of the post-Marxist turn away from communism to vari-ous conceptions of radical democracy. What is the imperative that drives the transfer of these motifs from their provenance in post-Marxism to their reappropriation as communist? Perhaps little more than impatience or the desire to occupy the ultra position within the spectrum of leftism. Precisely because in this brand of communism the social remains unbound by any underlying social logic, the theorist is at liberty to crank up the rhetorical volume.

Even more basic is the question whether communism can be detached sufficiently from the actual history of the twentieth century to serve as a productive register for the theory and practice of the left. The difficulty is compounded if that detachment can only be won by turning communism into the name of an eternal idea that periodically intersects with real history. If, as Žižek insists, communism is today not a *solution*, but the name of a *problem*, namely the "problem of the *commons* in all its dimensions,"[56] why burden this pressing concern with a name that is indissociable from such difficult recent history? Conversely, Žižek's insistent call for a communist politics that aims to create a new order sounds, simply put, so detached from the situation today that its usefulness wanes even as its compulsive rhetoric waxes. We are told at the opening of *Living in the End Times* that "the global capitalist system is approaching an apocalyptic zero-point."[57] It is hard not to agree that capitalism's four riders of the apocalypse do indeed bear tidings of catastrophe: the ecological crisis, effects of the biogenetic revolution, imbalances in the system itself, and the growth of ever deeper social divisions and exclusions. From this crisis scenario, Žižek spins out a dialectic in which communism is not merely the name of a generalized problem but also the portent of some not yet fully imagined solution. How, then, are we to react when we encounter Žižek telling a journalist, "The suggestion that capitalism is ready to collapse is perhaps, I admit it, wishful thinking"? Or, later in the same article, when he concedes, "I am utterly pessimistic about the future, about the possibility of an emancipated communist society. But that doesn't mean I don't want to imagine it"?[58] Moments of wishful thinking are allowed, but in light of Žižek's sober and, probably, self-ironizing concessions, would it not be more useful for Žižek to explore the possibility of the remotely possible, rather than constantly beating our breasts with the slogan that the impossible can happen? As for imagining, what could be a more basic exercise of the radical mind? Badiou has the virtue of honesty in urging his reader to "cling" to the hypothesis of a world freed from the reign of profit and private interest, writing that "I am telling you as a philosopher that we have to live with an idea."[59] By contrast, with Žižek, in view of his struggle between pessimism and imagination, why expend so much energy denouncing utopianism and regulative ideas when his own thought operates in those registers?

The summons to the idea of communism is meant to galvanize the left by restoring to it a positive vision. Yet in truth the divisive rhetoric of this revival—so thinly connected to likely prospects in the current world, so philosophically ethereal, so lacking in relation to any significant mass of political agents—is but a hollow echo of the schisms that tore apart the international left from 1900 to the 1930s. In the either/or, with-us-or-against us tone that is reemerging among some leftist theorists, an anachronistic cloud of suspicion settles back over electoral politics, democratic activism, reformism, and even socialism. And, ironically, suspicion also falls on the only truly visible political movements that contested neoliberal global capitalism during the past decade or so, organizations such as ATTAC, the World Social Forum, and the various groups within the *alter-globalization* movement. Through Žižek's eyes, radical as these groups may be, they are at best *ethical* anticapitalists who still treat the "democratic institutional framework of the (bourgeois) state" as a "sacred cow."[60]

In its retrospective for the year in which Žižek published that pronouncement, 2011, *Time* magazine declared the person of the year to be the Protester. Noting that, for at least two decades, large-scale protest had seemed "obsolete, quaint, the equivalent of cavalry to mid-20th-century war," the article proceeds: "'Massive and effective street protest' was a global oxymoron until—suddenly, shockingly—starting exactly a year ago, it became the defining trope of our times. And the protester once again became a maker of history."[61] Protest on this scale was indeed unpredicted and unforeseen as 2010 drew to a close. By mid-2011, massive and courageous demonstrations had toppled authoritarian regimes in Tunisia and Egypt, and protest had spilled over into armed conflict in Libya, eventually leading to the death of Muammar Gaddafi. Struggle continues in Arab countries like Bahrain and, above all, in Syria, where the regime of Bashar al-Assad has waged an ever more brutal campaign of repression that escalated into all-out civil war by mid-2012. Protest in Greece against austerity measures imposed by the European Union, the *Indignados* movement in Spain, unrest in the face of the corruption and ineptitude of Berlusconi regime's and the technocratic government of Mario Monti that succeeded him, mass demonstrations in Moscow against flawed electoral processes,

each of these protest movements exerted pressure on established powers
and political decision making; and, along with the Arab Spring, they entered into an international circuit of mutually reinforcing political activism. This dynamic helped spawn the Occupy Wall Street movement,
which began with protesters camping in Zuccotti Park in lower Manhat-
tan in late September 2011 and then spread rapidly to many American
cities. If the Occupy movement drew inspiration from protests in Europe
and the Middle East, it took its turn as a global inspiration on October 15,
when people marched in 951 cities in 82 countries around the world to
protest income inequality, political corruption, and economies skewed to
the benefit of a small wealthy minority.[62] By the end of November, police
had raided and cleared Zuccotti Park and other symbolically important
sites that protesters had physically occupied in other American cities. At
the end of 2012, when I write these words, Occupy's future is entirely uncertain. The anniversary of Occupy's birth came and went with little
fanfare. It has not yet launched any new prominent actions or recaptured
the media attention that it briefly enjoyed in the final months of 2011.
Nonetheless, it continues to build networks behind the scenes and its
ideas percolate, as evidenced in the aftermath of Hurricane Sandy, when
Occupy organized aid to the hardest hit areas of New York while linking
that action to a critique of income inequality and uneven access to government services. Still, whatever the movement's future, it undoubtedly
changed the "national conversation," as the bromide would put it, forcing
the theme of inequality into a political arena where it had been studiously
ignored for decades.[63]

Žižek was quick to emphasize the ostensibly anticapitalist orientation
of the uprisings that roiled the Arab world in 2011.[64] However, if we may
venture a brief comment on Egypt, generally seen as the bellwether for the
entire Middle East, reports in early 2011 indicated that, although they
were involved in demonstrations against Hosni Mubarak in Cairo's Tah-
rir Square, political communists were a small minority. And even if many
of the revolutionaries embraced solidaristic values and demands for social
and economic justice that were at odds with Western neoliberal capitalism, no one has dared claim that communism, however loosely defined,
was even remotely significant compared to the ideal of a democratic civil
society confronting a tyrannical regime. The Arab Spring's democratic
ideals have certainly come under tremendous strain in postrevolutionary

Egypt, first when a ruling military council meant to serve in the transition toward a new constitution and parliamentary government seemed reluctant to relinquish power and at times turned violently against peaceful protesters. The conflict between the generals and new civilian rulers was probably not resolved by the military's grudging recognition of Mohamed Morsi of the Muslim Brotherhood as the winner of Egypt's first competitive presidential election in late June 2012. In any case, the democratic values of Morsi and the Muslim Brotherhood, which was at the forefront of the struggle against Mubarak, have yet to be tested against their belief that "Islam is the solution" to the nation's woes or their ability to control even more fundamentalist Islamists to their right. Morsi's own motives became very murky in November 2012 when he attempted to elevate himself beyond any checks and balances, promising, like an ancient Greek tyrant, that these extraordinary powers would last only so long as necessary to steer the nation toward a new constitution. When protests against Morsi once again brought violent reprisals, this time not only from the police but from Muslim Brotherhood gangs, it was hard not to conclude that the Egyptian revolution was coming full circle back to dictatorship. Still, writing these sentences in mid-December 2012, with results of a referendum on a Muslim-backed draft constitution still pending, I am acutely aware that the situation in Egypt and the rest of the Arab world is far too fluid to venture any confident predictions. It seems safe to say, however, that the great struggle is first and foremost precisely for what Žižek so readily dismisses, the "democratic institutional framework of the (bourgeois) state."

Žižek seemed to forget his ambivalence toward *ethical* anticapitalism when he addressed the Occupy Wall Street movement at Zuccotti Park on October 9, 2011. Or, more to the point, he pressed the Occupy movement into the mold of his own preoccupations. "Don't be afraid to really want what you desire," he urged his listeners, and by this he meant nothing less than the overcoming of capitalism. Disavowing any attachment to the communism that collapsed in 1990, he nonetheless addressed his listeners—using the inclusive "we"—as "communists" insofar as "we care for the commons."[65] Occupy Wall Street is without question a very big tent, and there are undoubtedly participants who dream of a world beyond capitalism. Yet opposition to capitalism per se seems far less a driving force than does opposition to neoliberal capitalism, to the unbridled free market capitalism that over the last thirty years or so has allowed an unparalleled concentration of wealth in the hands of a few, great economic disparities, a retreat on environmental regulations, unevenly distributed tax burdens, and so forth.[66] The point of Occupy is certainly not to create an *ethical* capitalism, which may in any case be an oxymoron, but rather to subdue the most extravagant abuses of capitalism and contest the monopoly of capitalist form by imagining and possibly implementing other forms of economic interaction; the goal is not to overcome all inequality, but to contest a situation where inequality has reached such gross levels that social trust is collapsing.

In that effort the Occupy movement does not hesitate to address itself to the state. After all, among the protesters' demands are calls for a more equitable tax structure, elimination of corporate personhood, campaign finance reform, and, most generally, the liberation of society *and* government from corporate dominance. The movement does not make the state as such its target but rather took aim at a set of practices that have come to distort and gravely weaken the democratic foundation of American politics. Yet the democratic aspirations of Occupy Wall Street reached further than political reform, for, in the daily practices that emerged in Zuccotti Park and other sites of occupation, the movement tried to model a positive alternative form of sociality and politics in which equality was the core value and fundamental possibility of social and political relations. Occupy's general assemblies, with their time-consuming and patient processes of discussion and consensus, invited some ridicule from the mainstream media, but participants saw these as crucial and transformative exercises in the practice of deep democracy. Likewise, many onlookers attacked Occupy Wall Street for the absence of concrete demands. In rebuttal, one might simply ask why, after decades of more or less quiescence, anyone should expect a protest movement to instantly crystallize into a list of demands, especially when the immensity of the problems makes a specific agenda seem less important than contesting the basic values and organizing structures of present-day society. When members of the media tried to explain the aims of the Occupiers, they were frequently bemused by the apparent lack of leaders and designated spokespeople. Yet, here again, this was not a failure of organization, but a principle of organization—a movement without strong leaders, nonhierarchical and open, its decision making operating horizontally among participants rather than vertically between leaders and rank and file. Surveying what at times could seem like a carnivalesque inversion of how a movement might try to exert influence, the writer Jeff Sharlet aptly wrote, "In fact, the protesters *are* fools—but in the holy tradition, the tradition that speaks not truth to power but imagination to things as they are."[67] Or, expressed differently, Occupy Wall Street presented a form of prefigurative politics. As the anthropologist David Graeber put it in 2007, "Direct action is a form of resistance which, in its structure, is meant to prefigure the genuinely free society one wishes to create. Revolutionary action is not a form of self-sacrifice, a grim dedication to doing whatever it takes to achieve a future world of freedom. It is the defiant insistence on acting as if one is already free."[68]

Occupy Wall Street was very reluctant to identify leaders and intellectual figureheads, but, again and again, reports pointed to Graeber as an instrumental figure behind the movement's inception. An American teaching at the University of London's Goldsmiths College, Graeber was active in antiglobalization protests for over a decade and established himself as a prominent theorist of direct action.[69] In New York City in early August 2011 he helped steer protesters away from a rally near Wall Street that took on a conventional form with, as Andy Kroll reports, "speakers and microphones exhorting a mostly passive crowd."[70] More and more participants broke away from the rally and joined an informal discussion group with Graeber at its center. This became, more or less, the seed for the general assemblies that would come to define the movement's core consensual decision-making process.[71] Pointedly, three days after the demonstrations began, Graeber left New York. He wanted to prevent the formation of an intellectual vanguard. "We don't want to create a leadership structure," he told a reporter for the *Chronicle of Higher Education*. "The fact I was being promoted as a celebrity is a danger. It's the kids who made this happen."[72]

The *Chronicle* article suggested something of a genealogy of Graeber's ideas, emphasizing the impact of the long tradition of anarchist thought and politics as well as the lessons he had learned doing fieldwork between 1989 and 1991 on a community in central Madagascar that, more or less abandoned by the Malagasy state, had developed a form of self-governance based on direct participation and consensus decision making.[73] A fuller scrutiny of his writings suggests a specific influence much closer to the concerns of this book. In an extended essay on the antiglobalization movement published in 2007, Graeber calls for a form of political action based on what he describes as "a political ontology of imagination." Distancing himself from one of the most famous slogans of May '68, he continues, "It's not so much a matter of giving 'power to the imagination' as recognizing that the imagination is the source of power in the first place."[74] Earlier in the same volume, Graeber indicates what he calls "the key question" for revolutionary theory, namely "what precisely is the role of creativity, collective or individual, of the imagination, in radical social change? . . . The revolutionary theorist who grappled with the problem most explicitly was Cornelius Castoriadis."[75]

Elsewhere, in a passage that merits quotation at length, Graeber locates his own engagement with Castoriadis through specific reference to a "great intellectual rupture" he sees emerging out of 1968.

> If one goes to an anarchist bookstore or infoshop in almost any part of the world, this is what one is still likely to find: There will be works by and about the Situationists (particularly Guy Debord and Raoul Vaneigem), and the *Socialisme ou Barbarie* authors (certainly Cornelius Castoriadis, occasionally even Claude Lefort), alongside others continuing in the same tradition, and anarchist journals of every sort. Usually equally striking in their absence will be the work of the most famous poststructuralist authors like Michel Foucault, or Deleuze and Guattari. The absence of the latter can be partly attributed to the fact that they are so easily available elsewhere. University bookstores are crammed full of the stuff and rarely carry anything by the authors likely to be found in infoshops. It is very hard to avoid the conclusion that the readership for French theory has effectively split in two. Activists continue to read the works immediately preceding May '68: works that anticipated revolution. They also continue to develop them. Academics continue to read and develop the works from immediately afterwards. The result is two different streams of literature. Activists do draw from the academic stream to a certain degree, but the academics almost never read the other one.[76]

Castoriadis could not have said it better himself, or, in fact, he said exactly this, as we saw in chapter 3. My point here is not to end by suggesting the posthumous triumph of the frequently neglected Cornelius Castoriadis or to subordinate the complex and diverse phenomena of contemporary protest movements such as Occupy Wall Street to one or another theoretical progenitor. Rather, let us treat Graeber's emphatic remarks on Castoriadis as *pars pro toto* for a more general philosophical and political orientation that has been at the heart of this book. In that spirit, my aim is to underscore the pressing relevance of radical democratic theory to the prospects of protest movements for contesting and transforming the coordinates of the world as it is.

Back in 1999 Wendy Brown trenchantly analyzed the symptoms of "left melancholy" in a historical situation in which the left was awash in losses: "not only a lost movement but a lost historical moment; not only a lost theoretical and empirical coherence but a lost way of life and a lost course of pursuits."[77] The way out of melancholy, she insisted, lies not in clinging to old leftist truisms, but in "embracing the notion of a deep and indeed unsettling transformation of society rather than one that recoils at this prospect, even as we must be wise to the fact that neither total revolution nor the automatic progress of history will carry us toward whatever reformulated vision we might develop." The kinds of energies and ideas expressed in the Occupy Wall Street movement might buoy the spirits of leftists, at least those of a certain stripe; but it is still far too early to know what Occupy and related protest movements in Europe and elsewhere really mean. Are they the embryo of something bigger or have they already spent their most vital energies? Under these uncertain circumstances, it is impossible to say that the left has traveled very far toward realizing Wendy Brown's vision. The challenges are daunting, as the close of Brown's essay makes succinctly clear:

> What political hope can we nurture that does not falsely ground itself in the notion that "history is on our side" or that there is some inevitability of popular attachment to whatever values we might develop as those of a new left vision? What kind of political and economic order can we imagine that is neither state-run nor utopian, neither repressive nor libertarian, neither economically impoverished nor culturally gray? How might we draw sustenance from socialist ideals of dignity, equality, and freedom, while recognizing that these ideals were conjured from historical conditions and prospects that are not those of the present?[78]

To pursue whatever positive agenda the left might establish while also attending to prohibitions that reflection and historical experience alike have imposed points to the "politics of ambivalence or ambiguity" that Fredric Jameson believes is called for in our age.[79] Democracy is the regime of ambivalence and ambiguity par excellence—not the democracy of liberal capitalism, of elections, parliamentary representation, and plutocracy, but radical democracy. Žižek would tell us that *communism* is the name of a problem, not a solution, but a similar formula from Dick Howard seems more relevant to the prospects of the left: "democracy is not a solution; it is a problem, inseparably philosophical and political. After 1989, when its reified opposition to communism no longer made it into an unquestionable value, its problematic nature could and should again become manifest."[80] To the task of making democracy's problematic nature manifest, the thinkers examined in this book contributed vitally, and well before 1989. Above all, they have shown, in various ways, that, far from rendering it weak, democracy's problems are what enable it. Howard gives us one crucial formulation of that paradox: "Based on the protection of individual rights while seeking at the same time and for just that reason the common good, democracy is a problem, and democratic politics consists in maintaining that problem, not in solving it once and for all."[81]

The paradoxes that comprise the frame of radical democracy may be multiplied. The radical democrat recognizes the absence of any ultimate democratic legitimacy at the same time as she affirms the permanent search for legitimacy. She acknowledges the need for institutions, at the same time seeing that democracy survives by exceeding and contesting established forms. She knows that, *contra* Marx, democracy is neither a merely *formal* politics nor the real expression of man's social essence, but is rather a political activity aimed at redressing social injustice. She will know that democracy is not an accomplished form but a project, and, as such, it weaves together short-term struggles and long-term visions. The radical democrat stands between awareness of the impossibility of politics ever incarnating the social and the need for radical investment in a cause. He sees that even a democracy will entail forms of closure, even as he seeks to institutionalize democracy's dramatic openness. He will recognize the indispensability of symbols, even as he demystifies symbols as human creations, right up to and including the symbolization of democracy's openness. He will simultaneously acknowledge the importance of the old democratic dream of transparency and the play of absence and presence, disclosure and concealment, visibility and invisibility that marks the terrain between democracy as a mode of struggle and democracy as a form of regime. The radical democratic intellectual will believe in the value of theory but know that political action does not follow prescriptions.

Holding on to both sides of these formulations requires a measure of ambivalence and a goodly tolerance for ambiguity. Not without cause did Claude Lefort claim that the democrat requires a certain *heroism* of mind. Yet this particular form of heroism also demands a considerable degree of irony. Here it is worth recalling Friedrich Schlegel's comment, "it is equally fatal for the mind to have a system, and to have none." Of course, irony carries with it the risk of tempering enthusiasms and weakening commitment. One has only to think of the classic stereotype of the political Romantic made notorious by Carl Schmitt. Or, in our own time, Richard Rorty comes to mind, Rorty, whose ironic view on the impossibility of ever reconciling the multiplicity of personal beliefs and social inclusion led him, for a time, to advocate a sharp divide between a minimal liberal political regime and the self-cultivation of the private individual. Arguably, there have been times in the history of the left when a lesson in tempered passion might have been desirable. These days, two decades since the end of the cold war and with the agents of progressive politics in a desultory state, curbed enthusiasm may not be the most urgent thing that leftists need.

Still, I would plead for the place of irony, though of a very different kind from Rorty's, that is, one leading to engagement and sociability. What I have in mind is something akin to the lesson that Cornelius Castoriadis drew from ancient Greek tragedy, which he regarded as a preeminently political dramatic form. Reading Sophocles' *Antigone*, Castoriadis sees it not as a play about the supremacy of divine over human law or as the insurmountable conflict between these two principles, as Hegel had. Sophocles does not warn against the King of Thebes' insistence on the human law, but against Creon's unyielding will to apply the norms of the city without any cautionary sense of the uncertainty of the situation, the impurity of motives, or the inconclusive character of the reasoning upon which political decisions rest. Creon's son Aimon acknowledges that he cannot prove his father wrong, but begs him not to *"monos phronein,* 'not to be wise alone.'" With that, says Castoriadis, Sophocles formulates "the fundamental maxim of democratic politics."[82] Recognition of society's lack of foundation need not produce Rorty's withdrawal into the private or the postmodernist's celebration of endless dispersal or the conservative's reassertion of established practice. Rather, it may intensify the commitment to autonomy and emancipatory politics. An ironic perception of the situation of democracy may launch us into the spirit of mutuality, collective deliberation, and experimentation.

Notes

Introduction

1. Bertolt Brecht, *Die Dreigroschenoper* (Frankfurt: Suhrkamp, 1968), 94.

2. Reinhard Marx, *Das Kapital: Eine Streitschrift* (Munich: Pattloch, 2008).

3. Göran Therborn, *From Marxism to Post-Marxism?* (New York: Verso, 2008), 179–180.

4. Stuart Sim, *Post-Marxism: An Intellectual History* (London: Routledge, 2000), 70–91.

5. These themes have roots reaching deeper into the past, of course. For a significant tracing of an earlier critique of humanism, see Stefanos Geroulanos, *An Atheism That Is Not Humanist Emerges in French Thought* (Stanford: Stanford University Press, 2010).

6. Marcel Gauchet, *Le Débat* 50 (May-August 1988): 168.

7. Oliver Marchart, *Post-Foundational Political Thought: Political Difference in Nancy, Lefort, Badiou, and Laclau* (Edinburgh: Edinburgh University Press, 2007).

8. Yannis Stavrakakis, *The Lacanian Left: Psychoanalysis, Theory, Politics* (Albany: State University of New York Press, 2007).

9. This issue will be addressed in chapters 5 and 6. Anecdotally, a paper of mine, presented at a conference on Cornelius Castoriadis at Columbia University in December 2000, elicited from Ernesto Laclau the protest that he is not a Lacanian, but has drawn on Lacan only in thinking about the nature of the human subject.

10. Ian Parker, *Slavoj Žižek: A Critical Introduction* (London: Pluto, 2004), 117.

11. Alain Caillé, "Préface," in Camille Tarot, *De Durkheim à Mauss: L'invention du symbolique: Sociologie et science des religions* (Paris: Découverte, 1999), 12.

12. I paraphrase here the formulation of Adriano Rodrigues, "Quelques considérations à propos de la notion de symbole dans les sciences humaines," *Recherches Sociologiques* 7, no. 3 (Decembre 1976): 325.

13. Marcel Hénaff, *Claude Lévi-Strauss and the Making of Structural Anthropology*, trans. Mary Baker (Minneapolis: University of Minnesota Press, 1998), 6.

14. See, for example, Thomas Pavel, *The Feud of Language: A History of Structuralist Thought*, trans. Linda Jordan and Thomas Pavel (Oxford: Blackwell, 1989); Dan Sperber, *Rethinking Symbolism*, trans. Alice L. Morton (Cambridge: Cambridge University Press, 1975).

15. On this point in Ernst Cassirer, see Birgit Recki, "Cassirer and the Problem of Language," in Paul Bishop and R. H. Stephenson, eds., *Cultural Studies and the Symbolic: Occasional Papers in Cassirer and Cultural-Theory Studies, Presented at the University of Glasgow's Centre for Intercultural Studies* (Leeds: Northern Universities Press, 2003), 10.

16. In addition to structuralism, one sees a similarly conscious, though differently oriented reductionist impulse at play in logical positivism and analytic philosophy.

17. Slavoj Žižek, *Sehr innig und nicht zu rasch: Zwei Essays über sexuelle Differenz als philosophische Kategorie*, trans. Erik M. Vogt (Vienna: Turia and Kant, 1999), 34.

18. See Claude Lévi-Strauss, "Structure and Dialectics," in *Structural Anthropology*, trans. Claire Jacobson and Brooke Grundfest Schoepf (New York: Basic Books, 1963), 232–241, and "History and Dialectic," in *The Savage Mind* (Chicago: University of Chicago Press, 1966), 245–270.

19. Jacques Lacan, "The Function and Field of Speech and Language in Psychoanalysis," in *Écrits*, trans. Bruce Fink (New York: Norton, 2006), 209.

20. Ibid., 225.

21. See Dirk Hülst, *Symbole und soziologische Symboltheorie: Untersuchungen zum Symbolbegriff in Geschichte, Sprachphilosophie, Psychologie und Soziologie* (Opladen: Leske and Budrich, 1999), 77.

22. Ernesto Laclau, "Why Constructing a People is the Main Task of Radical Politics," *Critical Inquiry* 32 (Summer 2006): 665.

23. Slavoj Žižek, *Tarrying with the Negative: Kant, Hegel, and the Critique of Ideology* (Durham: Duke University Press, 1993), 92.

24. Jacques Lacan, "The Subversion of the Subject and the Dialectic of Desire in the Freudian Unconscious," in Lacan, *Écrits*, 675.

25. Lacan, "The Function and Field of Speech," 242.

26. Jacques Lacan, "Aggressiveness in Psychoanalysis," in Lacan, *Écrits*, 96.

27. Friedrich Schlegel quoted in Azade Seyhan, *Representation and Its Discontents: The Critical Legacy of German Romanticism* (Berkeley: University of California Press, 1992), 157. Rüdiger Görner has suggestively renamed the *Frühromantik* dialectic a *Pluralektik*. See Görner, *Das Zeitalter des Fraktalen: Ein kulturkritischer Versuch* (Vienna: Passagen, 2007), 71–89.

28. Maurice Merleau-Ponty, *Adventures of the Dialectic*, trans. Joseph Bien (London: Heinemann, 1974), 64–65.

29. Ibid., 200–201.

30. Maurice Merleau-Ponty, "On the Phenomenology of Language," in *Signs*, trans. Richard C. McCleary (Evanston: Northwestern University Press, 1964), 88.

31. Maurice Merleau-Ponty, "From Mauss to Claude Lévi-Strauss," ibid., 115.

32. Hyppolite and Lacan quoted in Peter Dews, "Imagination and the Symbolic," *Constellations* 9, no. 4 (2002): 517.

33. Marcel Mauss, "Real and Practical Relations Between Psychology and Sociology," in *Sociology and Psychology*, trans. R. Brain (London: Routledge and Kegan Paul, 1972), 10.

34. Claude Lévi-Strauss, *Introduction to the Work of Marcel Mauss*, trans. Felicity Baker (London: Routledge and Kegan Paul, 1987), 56–61.

35. Ibid., 37.

36. Ibid., 39–42.

37. Durkheim quoted in Tarot, *De Durkheim à Mauss*, 223.

38. Mauss quoted in Hénaff, *Claude Lévi-Strauss*, 96.

39. Tarot, *De Durkheim à Mauss*, 252.

40. Daniel Fabre, "Le Symbolique, brève histoire d'un objet," in Jacques Revel and Nathan Wachtel, eds., *Une école pour les sciences socials: De la VIᵉ Section à l'École des Hautes Études en Sciences Sociales* (Paris: CERF, 1996), 230. For an illuminating history of the discourse of the gift, culminating in the work of Mauss, see Harry Liebersohn, *The Return of the Gift: European History of a Global Idea* (Cambridge: Cambridge University Press, 2011).

41. Tarot, *De Durkheim à Mauss*, 350.

42. Ibid., 57–58.

43. Saussure cited in Boris Gasparov, *Beyond Pure Reason: Ferdinand de Saussure's Philosophy of Language and Its Early Romantic Antecedents* (New York: Columbia University Press, 2012). See, more generally, Tzvetan Todorov, *Theories of the Symbol*, trans. Catherine Porter (Ithaca: Cornell University Press), chapter 9.

44. The contrast between Mauss's "living" symbols and Lévi-Strauss's "dead" ones was at the heart of Lefort's influential critique of Lévi-Strauss. See Claude Lefort, "L'Échange et la lutte des hommes," *Les Temps Modernes* 6, no. 64 (February 1951): 1400–1417. We will return to Lefort's criticism of Lévi-Strauss in chapter 4.

45. Tarot, *De Durkheim à Mauss*, 60.

46. Fabre, "Le Symbolique, brève histoire d'un objet," 230. Hénaff argues that in early formulations Lévi-Strauss tied "symbolic effectiveness" to an "inductive process," whereby meanings became linked and enchained, but this dimension got sidelined as Lévi-Strauss put ever greater emphasis on the systematic and social nature of the symbolic (*Claude Lévi-Strauss*, 122).

47. Tarot, *De Durkheim à Mauss*, 629.

48. Judith Butler, "Critical Exchanges: The Symbolic and Questions of Gender," in Hugh Silverman, ed., *Questioning Foundations: Truth/Subjectivity/Culture* (New York: Routledge, 1993), 141.

49. Rudolf Schlögl, "Symbole in der Kommunikation: Zur Einführung," in Rudolf Schlögl, Bernhard Giesen, and Jürgen Osterhammel, eds., *Die Wirklichkeit der Symbole: Grundlagen der Kommunikation in historischen und gegenwärtigen Gesellschaften* (Konstanz: UVK, 2004), 18.

50. Karl-Siegbert Rehberg, "Weltrepräsentanz und Verkörperung: Institutionelle Analyse und Symboltheorien—Eine Einführung in systematischer Absicht," in Gert Melville, ed., *Institutionalität und Symbolisierung: Verstetigungen kultureller Ordnungsmuster in Vergangenheit und Gegenwart* (Cologne: Böhlau, 2001), 26.

51. See especially Rehberg, "Weltrepräsentanz und Verkörperung," 33.

52. Ibid., 24.

53. Schlögl, "Symbole in der Kommunikation," 13.

54. Daniel Fabre, "Symbolisme en questions," in Martine Segalen, ed., *L'Autre et le semblable: Regards sur l'ethnologie des sociétés contemporaines* (Paris: CNRS, 1989), 61. See also Fabre, "Le Symbolique, brève histoire d'un objet," 250.

55. Vincent Descombes, "L'équivoque du symbolique," *MLN* 94, no. 4, French Issue: Perspectives in Mimesis (May 1979): 655–656, 674.

56. Jean-Joseph Goux, *Symbolic Economies: After Marx and Freud*, trans. Jennifer Curtiss Gage (Ithaca: Cornell University Press, 1990), 130, 124.

57. Ibid., 128.

58. Sven Lütticken, "Attending to Abstract Things," *New Left Review* 54 (November-December 2008): 113.

59. Jürgen Habermas, "The Liberating Power of Symbols: Ernst Cassirer's Humanistic Legacy and the Warburg Library," *The Liberating Power of Symbols: Philosophical Essays*, trans. Peter Dews (Cambridge: MIT Press, 2001), 1–29.

60. Lévi-Strauss cited in Hénaff, *Claude Lévi-Strauss*, 134.

61. Lévi-Strauss cited ibid., 134.

62. Ibid.

63. Umberto Eco, *Semiotics and the Philosophy of Language* (Bloomington: Indiana University Press, 1984), 154–155. See also Hülst, *Symbol und soziologische Symboltheorie*, 115.

64. Karl Marx, *Capital*, in *Collected Works*, vol. 35 (London: Lawrence and Wishart, 1996), 1:85.

65. Ibid., 83.

1. The Symbolic Dimension and the Politics of Young Hegelianism

1. François Dosse, *History of Structuralism*, vol. 1: *The Rising Sign, 1945–1966*, trans. Deborah Glassman (Minneapolis: University of Minnesota Press, 1997), 46.

2. Pierre Bourdieu, *Language and Symbolic Power*, ed. John B. Thompson, trans. Gino Raymond and Matthew Adamson (Cambridge: Harvard University, 1991), 164.

3. Bent Algot Sørenson, *Symbol und Symbolismus in den ästhetischen Theorien des 18. Jahrhunderts und der deutschen Romantik* (Kopenhagen: Munksgaard, 1963), 16; and Götz Pochat, *Der Symbolbegriff in der Ästhetik und Kunstwissenschaft*, trans. Märta Pochat (Cologne: DuMont, 1983), 13.

4. Immanuel Kant, *Critique of the Power of Judgment*, ed. Paul Guyer, trans. Paul Guyer and Eric Matthews (Cambridge: Cambridge University Press, 2000), 226.

5. Ibid., 227.

6. See Sørenson, *Symbol und Symbolismus*, 92f. Halmi suggests usefully that whereas the Kantian symbol is *analogical* but without inherent relation between the object of intuition and the concept, the Romantic symbol is *synecdochical*. See Nicholas Halmi, *The Genealogy of the Romantic Symbol* (Oxford: Oxford University Press, 2007), 63–64.

7. Tzvetan Todorov, *Theories of the Symbol*, trans. Catherine Porter (Ithaca: Cornell University Press, 1982), chapter 6.

8. Jean-François Lyotard, *The Postmodern Condition: A Report on Knowledge*, trans. Geoff Bennington and Brian Massumi (Minneapolis: University of Minnesota Press, 1984), 81.

9. Edward Larrissy, "Introduction," and Paul Hamilton, "From Sublimity to Indeterminacy: New World Order or Aftermath of Romantic Ideology," in Edward Larrissy, ed., *Romanticism and Postmodernism* (Cambridge: Cambridge University Press, 1999), respectively 5 and 12.

10. Andrew Bowie, *From Romanticism to Critical Theory: The Philosophy of German Literary Theory* (London: Routledge, 1997), 204.

11. See Friedrich Schlegel, *Philosophical Fragments*, ed. P. Firchow (Minneapolis: University of Minnesota Press, 1991), 24.

12. Kathleen Dow Magnus, *Hegel and the Symbolic Mediation of Spirit* (Albany: State University of New York Press, 2001), 84.

13. Jacques Derrida, "The Pit and the Pyramid: Introduction to Hegel's Semiology," in *Margins of Philosophy*, trans. Alan Bass (Chicago: University of Chicago Press, 1982).

14. I borrow here a formulation from Hans Blumenberg, who described nominalism as the second overcoming of Gnosticism. See Hans Blumenberg, *The Legitimacy of the Modern Age*, trans. Robert M. Wallace (Cambridge: MIT Press, 1983).

15. F. W. J. Schelling, *The Philosophy of Art*, ed. and trans. Douglas W. Simpson (Minneapolis: University of Minnesota Press, 1989), 8.

16. G. W. F. Hegel, *Aesthetics: Lectures on Fine Arts*, trans. T. M. Knox (Oxford: Clarendon, 1975), 1:303.

17. G. W. F. Hegel, *Vorlesungen über die Geschichte der Philosophie*, ed. Eva Moldenhauer and Karl Markus Michel (Frankfurt: Suhrkamp, 1970), 1:109.

18. See, for example, Manfred Lurker, "Symbol," in Thomas A. Sebeok, ed., *Encyclopedic Dictionary of Semiotics*, 2d ed. (Berlin: Mouton de Gruyter, 1994), 2:1027.

19. Arnold Ruge and Theodor Echtermeyer, "Der Protestantismus und die Romantik: Zur Verständigung über die Zeit und ihre Gegensätze. Ein Manifest (1839–1840)," in Walter Jaeschke, ed., *Philosophie und Literatur im Vormärz: Der Streit um die Romantik (1820–1854). Quellenband* (Hamburg: Felix Meiner, 1995), 4.1:298.

20. Ibid., 308.

21. Ibid., 316.

22. Halmi, *The Genealogy of the Romantic Symbol*, 18–19.

23. Friedrich Schlegel, *Geschichte der Alten und Neuen Literatur*, vol. 6: *Kritische Friedrich Schlegel Ausgabe*, ed. Hans Eichner (Munich: Ferdinand Schöningh, 1961), 394.

24. Novalis, *Notes for a Romantic Encyclopedia: Das Allgemeine Brouillon*, ed. and trans. David Wood (Albany: State University of New York Press, 2007), 155, #857.

25. See the opening discussion in Azade Seyhan, *Representation and Its Discontents: The Critical Legacy of German Romanticism* (Berkeley: University of California Press, 1992), 3f. See also Halmi, *The Genealogy of the Romantic Symbol*, 60. I have addressed some of these issues at greater length in "Introduction: A Revolution in Culture," in Warren Breckman, ed., *European Romanticism: A Brief History with Documents* (Boston: Bedford, 2007), 1–41.

26. Halmi reminds us that participation here is closely related to "partialness," a relationship between part and whole, as in Samuel Taylor Coleridge's claim that "by a symbol, I mean, not a metaphor or allegory or any other figure of speech, but an actual and essential part of that, the whole of which it represents." See Halmi, *The Genealogy of the Romantic Symbol*, 16.

27. Benjamin cited in Bainard Cowan, "Walter Benjamin's Theory of Allegory," *New German Critique*, no. 22 (1981), 111. For considerations of various aspects of this theme, see the essays collected in Beatrice Hanssen and Andrew Benjamin, ed., *Walter Benjamin and Romanticism* (New York: Continuum, 2002).

28. Paul de Man, "The Rhetoric of Temporality," in *Blindness and Insight: Essays in the Rhetoric of Contemporary Criticism*, 2d ed. (Minneapolis: University of Minnesota, 1969), 207–208.

29. See Gail Day, "Allegory: Between Deconstruction and Dialectics," *Oxford Art Journal* 22, no. 1 (1999): 103–118.

30. F. W. J. Schelling, *Sämmtliche Werke* (Stuttgart: J. G. Cotta, 1856), 5:407.

31. Ibid., 555.

32. Moritz quoted in Todorov, *Theories of the Symbol*, 162.

33. Moritz quoted ibid., 156.

34. J. W. von Goethe, "Maximen und Reflexionen," in *Werke*, vol. 12: *Schriften zur Kunst. Schriften zur Literatur. Maximen und Reflexionen*, ed. Erich Trunz and Hans Joachim Schrimpf (Munich: Beck, 1994), 471.

35. Sørenson suggests that whereas Goethe's 1797 essay "Über die Gegenstände der bildenden Kunst" explicitly formulated this contrast, it remained only implicit in Moritz. See Sørenson, *Symbol und Symbolismus*, 108–111.

36. Ulrike Morgner, *"Das Wort aber ist Fleisch geworden": Allegorie und Allegoriekritik im 18. Jahrhundert am Beispiel von K.Ph. Moritz' "Andreas Hartknopf. Eine Allegorie"* (Würzburg: Königshausen and Neumann, 2002), 14–15.

37. Goethe, "Maximen und Reflexionen," 471, 470.

38. Pochat, *Der Symbolbegriff*, 28.

39. Goethe, "Nachträgliches zu Philostrats Gemälde," in *Goethes Werke, Weimarer Ausgabe*, vol. 1 (Weimar: H. Böhlau, 1898), 49:142.

40. R. H. Stephenson, "The Proper Object of Cultural Study: Ernst Cassirer and the Aesthetic Theory of Weimar Classicism," in Paul Bishop and R. H. Stephenson, eds., *Cultural Studies and the Symbolic: Occasional Papers in Cassirer and Cultural-Theory Studies, Presented at the University of Glasgow's Centre for Intercultural Studies* (Leeds: Northern Universities Press, 2003), 90.

41. See generally Susanne Lanwerd, *Religionsästhetik: Studien zum Verhältnis von Symbol und Sinnlichkeit* (Würzburg: Königshausen and Neumann, 2002).

42. Michael Titzmann, *Strukturwandel der philosophischen Aesthetik 1800–1880: Der Symbolbegriff als Paradigma* (Munich: Fink, 1978), 113.

43. F. W. J. Schelling, *Schellings Werke*, ed. Manfred Schröter (Munich: Beck, 1928), 3:576.

44. Sørenson, *Symbol und Symbolismus*, 248f.

45. Vonessen argues that "allegory, metaphor, cipher, hieroglyph, analogy, trope, representation" were all potentially used as synonyms for "symbol" by the Romantics. See Renate Vonessen, "Der Symbolbegriff in der Romantik," in Manfred Lurker, ed., *Beiträge zu Symbol, Symbolbegriff und Symbolforschung* (Baden-Baden: Valentin Koerner, 1982), 193.

46. Friedrich Schlegel, *Dialogue on Poetry and Literary Aphorisms*, ed. E. Behler (University Park: Pennsylvania State University Press, 1968), 89–90.

47. Sørenson, *Symbol und Symbolismus*, 236.

48. Novalis quoted in Halmi, "An Anthropological Approach to the Romantic Symbol," *European Romantic Review* 4, no. 1 (Summer 1993): 17.

49. Morgner, *"Das Wort aber ist Fleisch geworden,"* 36.

50. Manfred Zahn, "Zeichen, Idee und Erscheinung: Symbolkonzepte in der Philosophie des Deutschen Idealismus," in *Beiträge zu Symbol, Symbolbegriff und Symbolforschung*, 224.

51. Friedrich Schlegel, *Literary Notebooks 1797–1801*, ed. Hans Eichner (Toronto: University of Toronto Press, 1957), 46.

52. Cordula Grewe, *Painting the Sacred in the Age of Romanticism* (London: Ashgate, 2009), 33.

53. Umberto Eco, *Semiotics and the Philosophy of Language* (Bloomington: Indiana University Press, 1984), 143.

54. Hegel, *Aesthetics*, 1:245 (translation emended).

55. Magnus, *Hegel and the Symbolic Mediation of Spirit*, 39.

56. Hegel, *Aesthetics*, 1:397.

57. Hegel quoted in Paul de Man, "Sign and Symbol in Hegel's *Aesthetics*," *Critical Inquiry* 8 (Summer 1982): 763–764.

58. Magnus, *Hegel and the Symbolic Mediation of Spirit*, 180.

59. Ibid., 144.

60. Hegel, *Aesthetics*, 1:360. See also Pochat, *Der Symbolbegriff*, 67. In emphasizing the *inadequacy* of the symbolic, that is, the overabundance of meaning in proportion to the sign meant to carry that meaning, Hegel was influenced by Friedrich Creuzer, whose magnum opus *Symbolik und Mythologie der alten Völker*, published in four volumes between 1810 and 1812, we will discuss in the next chapter.

61. Hegel, *Aesthetics*, 1:79 (translation emended). See G. W. F. Hegel, *Vorlesungen über die Ästhetik:* vol. 1, *Werke*, ed. Eva Moldenhauer and Karl Markus Michel (Frankfurt: Suhrkamp, 1990), 111.

62. Hegel, *Aesthetics*, 1:301.

63. See the excellent account offered by Magnus, *Hegel and the Symbolic Mediation of Spirit*, especially 153–155.

64. Hegel, *Aesthetics*, 1:11.

65. Ibid., 89.

66. Ibid., 318.

67. Peter Szondi, *Poetik und Geschichtsphilosophie* (Frankfurt: Suhrkamp, 1976), 1:391.

68. Titzmann, *Strukturwandel der philosophischen Ästhetik*, 53. Vischer's later work develops a more positive approach to symbols, but by then he was strictly interested in the psychological function of symbols. See Pochat, *Der Symbolbegriff*, 64.

69. Ruge and Echtermeyer, "Der Protestantismus und die Romantik," 315.

70. G. W. F. Hegel, "The Lectures of 1827," in *Lectures on the Philosophy of Religion*, vol. 1: *Introduction and the Concept of Religion*, ed. Peter C. Hodgson, trans. R. F. Brown, P. C. Hodgson, and J. M. Stewart (Berkeley: University of California Press, 1984).

71. G. W. F. Hegel, *Phenomenology of Spirit*, trans. A. V. Miller (Oxford: Oxford University Press, 1977), 417.

72. See Magnus, *Hegel and the Symbolic Mediation of Spirit*, 198. I have discussed this in Warren Breckman, *Marx, the Young Hegelians, and the Origins of Radical Social Theory: Dethroning the Self* (Cambridge: Cambridge University Press, 1999), 32–41.

73. Magnus, *Hegel and the Symbolic Mediation of Spirit*, 23.

74. Hegel quoted ibid., 221.

75. Bruno Bauer, "Was ist jetzt der Gegenstand der Kritik?" in Hans-Martin Sass, ed., *Feldzüge der reinen Kritik* (Frankfurt: Suhrkamp, 1968), 201.

76. Karl Marx, "Contribution to the Critique of Hegel's Philosophy of Law: Introduction," in *Collected Works* (New York: International, 1975), 3:181.

77. See Hans Frei, *The Eclipse of Biblical Narrative: A Study in Eighteenth and Nineteenth Century Hermeneutics* (New Haven: Yale University Press, 1974), chapter 7. See also David Aram Kaiser, "The Incarnated Symbol: Coleridge, Hegel, Strauss, and the Higher Biblical Criticism," *European Romantic Review* 4, no. 2 (Winter 1994): 134–135.

78. David Friedrich Strauss, *The Life of Jesus Critically Examined*, 4th ed., trans. George Eliot (London: Thoemmes, 1998), 1:48.

79. David Friedrich Strauss to Friedrich Theodor Vischer, November 13 and December 5, 1841, *Briefwechsel zwischen Strauss und Vischer*, ed. Adolf Rapp (Stuttgart: Klett, 1952).

80. Quoted in Zwi Rosen, *Bruno Bauer and Karl Marx: The Influence of Bruno Bauer on Marx's Thought* (The Hague: Nijhoff, 1977), 39.

81. Bruno Bauer, *The Trumpet of the Last Judgement Against Hegel the Atheist and Antichrist*, trans. L. Stepelevich (Berkeley: University of California Press, 1989), 97.

82. Bauer, *Kritik der evangelischen Geschichte der Synoptiker* (Leipzig: O. Wigand, 1841), 1:xiv–xv.

83. Ibid., xv.

84. Ernst Barnikol, *Bruno Bauer: Studien und Materialien* (Assen: Van Gorcum, 1972), 437.

85. Bauer, *The Trumpet of the Last Judgement*, 115.

86. Bauer quoted in John E. Toews, *Hegelianism: The Path Toward Dialectical Humanism, 1805–1841* (Cambridge: Cambridge University Press, 1980), 322.

87. Bauer, *Kritik der evangelischen Geschichte der Synoptiker*, xvi.

88. Walter Benjamin quoted in Cowan, "Walter Benjamin's Theory of Allegory," 114.

89. Bauer, *The Trumpet of the Last Judgement*, 67.

90. Bruno Bauer, "Die gute Sache der Freiheit und meine eigene Angelegenheit," in Ingrid Pepperle and Heinz Pepperle, eds., *Die Hegelsche Linke* (Leipzig: Reclam, 1985), 496.

91. Bruno Bauer, "Charakteristik Ludwig Feuerbachs," *Wigands Vierteljahrsschrift* (Leipzig: O. Wigand, 1845), 91. Regarding the charge of "substance," see especially 105–111.

92. Bruno Bauer, "The Genus and the Crowd," *Philosophical Forum* 8, nos. 2–4 (1978): 129.

93. Ludwig Feuerbach, *The Essence of Christianity*, trans. George Eliot (New York: Harper, 1957), xlii.

94. Ludwig Feuerbach, "Towards a Critique of Hegel's Philosophy," in *The Fiery Brook: Selected Writings of Ludwig Feuerbach*, trans. Zawar Hanfi (New York: Anchor, 1972).

95. Feuerbach, *The Essence of Christianity*, xxxv.

96. Manfred Frank, *Der unendliche Mangel an Sein: Schellings Hegelkritik und die Anfänge der Marxschen Dialektik* (Frankfurt: Suhrkampf, 1975), 169–206.

97. Ruge and Echtermeyer, "Der Protestantisimus und die Romantik," 252.

98. Schelling, *Sämmtliche Werke*, 13:90f.

99. See Breckman, *Marx, the Young Hegelians*, 126–128.

100. Ludwig Feuerbach, *Principles of the Philosophy of the Future*, trans. Manfred Vogel (Indianapolis: Bobbs-Merrill, 1986), 54.

101. Van A. Harvey, *Feuerbach and the Interpretation of Religion* (Cambridge: Cambridge University Press, 1995), especially 68f.

102. Feuerbach, *The Essence of Christianity*, xxxix.

103. Marcel Gauchet, *The Disenchantment of the World: A Political History of Religion*, trans. Oscar Burge (Princeton: Princeton University Press, 1997), 90.

104. Graham Ward, "Theology and the Crisis of Representation," in Gregory Salyer and Robert Detweiler, eds., *Literature and Theology at Century's End* (Atlanta: Scholars, 1995), 136.

105. Ibid., 133.

106. Feuerbach, "Towards a Critique of Hegel's Philosophy," 68.

107. Richard Rorty, *Philosophy and the Mirror of Nature* (Princeton: Princeton University Press, 1979), 360.

108. Feuerbach, *The Essence of Christianity*, xl.

109. Karl Barth, "An Introductory Essay," in Feuerbach, *The Essence of Christianity*, xix.

110. Feuerbach, *The Essence of Christianity*, xli.

111. Ibid., 276–277.

112. Christopher Clark, *Iron Kingdom: The Rise and Downfall of Prussia, 1600–1947* (Cambridge: Harvard University Press, 2006), 416.

113. Bruno Bauer, *Die evangelische Landeskirche Preussens und die Wissenschaft* (Leipzig: O. Wigand, 1840), 59.

114. Bruno Bauer, *Hegel's Lehre von der Religion und Kunst von dem Standpuncte des Glaubens aus beurtheilt* (Leipzig: O. Wigand, 1842), 198.

115. Douglas Moggach, "Die Prinzipien des Schönen: Bruno Bauers Kritik an Kants Aesthetik," in Bruno Bauer, *Über die Prinzipien des Schönen: De pulchri principiis. Eine Preisschrift*, ed. Douglas Moggach and Winfried Schultze (Berlin: Akademie, 1996), 99.

116. It should be noted that here Bauer does not mean "symbol" to designate an artistic image, but rather a coherent doctrine of faith. This was an accepted German usage of the term, as exemplified in titles like Friedrich Creuzer's *Symbolik und Mythologie der alten Völker* (1810–12) or Johann Adam Möller's *Symbolik: oder Darstellung der dogmatischen Gegensätze der Katholiken und Protestanten nach ihren öffentlichen Bekenntnissen* (1832). I take this point from George Williamson, *The Longing for Myth in Germany: Culture, Religion, and Politics from Romanticism to Nietzsche* (Chicago: University of Chicago Press, 2004).

117. Bauer, *Über die Prinzipien des Schönen*, 69.

118. Bauer quoted in Moggach, "Die Prinzipien des Schönen," 100. This passage may serve to illustrate Bauer's tendency toward the *Pragmatisierung* of speculative theory, as Ingrid Pepperle writes in *Junghegelianische Geschichtsphilosophie und Kunsttheorie* (Berlin: Akademie, 1978), 141.

119. Bauer, *Über die Prinzipien des Schönen*, 67.

120. Pepperle, *Junghegelianische Geschichtsphilosophie und Kunsttheorie*, 148.

121. Peter Uwe Hohendahl, "Literary Criticism in the Epoch of Liberalism, 1820–70," in Peter Uwe Hohendahl, ed., *A History of German Literary Criticism, 1730–1980* (Lincoln: University of Nebraska Press, 1988), 245. A similar judgment is found in Norbert Oellers, "Die 'Hallischen Jahrbücher' und die deutsche Literatur," in Walter Jaeschke, ed., *Philosophie und Literatur im Vormärz: Der Streit um die Romantik* (Hamburg: Felix Meiner, 1995), 4:141–152.

122. John Milbank, *Theology and Social Theory: Beyond Secular Reason* (Oxford: Blackwell, 1990), 18.

123. Ibid., 20.

124. Gauchet, *Disenchantment of the World*, 90.

2. The Fate of the Symbolic from Socialism to a Marxism

1. Karl Marx to Ludwig Feuerbach, October 3, 1843, *Ludwig Feuerbach. Briefwechsel*, ed. W. Schuffenhauer, vol. 2 (Berlin: Akademie, 1985).

2. Karl Marx and Friedrich Engels, "Manifesto of the Communist Party," *Collected Works* (New York: International, 1976), 6:516.

3. The conflict between the later Schelling and his followers and the Left Hegelians is a major theme of my book *Marx, the Young Hegelians, and the Origins of Radical Social Theory*

(Cambridge: Cambridge University Press, 1999). For a detailed discussion of Leroux's support of Schelling, see Warren Breckman, "Politics in a Symbolic Key: Pierre Leroux, Romantic Socialism, and the 'Schelling Affair,'" *Modern Intellectual History* 2, no. 1 (April 2005): 61–86.

4. One of Leroux's staunchest twentieth-century champions, Jacques Viard, complains of a conspiracy of silence against Leroux among Marxist socialists. See Jacques Viard, *Pierre Leroux, Charles Péguy, Charles de Gaulle et l'Europe* (Paris: L'Harmattan, 2004). For a good critique of Viard's eccentric book, see David Griffiths's review in *French History* 20, no. 3 (September 2006): 362–363. I am indebted to his review for my reference to Marx's desire to include Leroux and his supporters in the First International.

5. The German Hegelian Eduard Gans wrote of *Le Globe* that "everything that belongs to the young and intellectually striving young generation in France was gathered here." See Norbert Waszek, "Eduard Gans, die *Jahrbücher für wissenschaftliche Kritik* und die französische Publizistik der Zeit," in Christoph Jamme, ed., *Die "Jahrbücher für wissenschaftliche Kritik": Hegels Berliner Gegenakademie* (Stuttgart: Frommann-Holzboog, 1994), 111.

6. Pierre Leroux quoted in Horst Stuke, *Philosophie der Tat: Studien zur "Verwirklichung der Philosophie" bei den Junghegelianern und wahren Sozialisten* (Stuttgart: Klett, 1963), 87.

7. Pierre Leroux, "De l'individualisme et du socialisme," in Bruno Viard, ed., *A la source perdue du socialisme français* (Paris: Desclée de Brouwer, 1997), 163, 157.

8. Jonathan Beecher, *Victor Considerant and the Rise and Fall of Romantic Socialism* (Berkeley: University of California Press, 2001), 5.

9. For a positive assessment, see George Sand quoted in Jean-Pierre Lacassagne, introduction to *Histoire d'une amitié: Pierre Leroux et George Sand. D'Après une correspondance inédite 1836–1866*, ed. J.-P. Lacassagne (Paris: Klincksieck, 1973), 82. For an assessment that mixes praise for Leroux's democratic passion and criticism of his mysticism and eclecticism, see Considerant quoted in Beecher, *Victor Considerant*, 150.

10. I take the word *hazy* from George Armstrong Kelly, *The Humane Comedy: Constant, Tocqueville and French Liberalism* (Cambridge: Cambridge University Press, 1992), 137.

11. Philippe Régnier, "Les Saint-Simoniens, le Prêtre et l'Artiste," *Romantisme*, no. 67 (1990–1991): 38–39. Régnier argues that Leroux's ideas did go some distance toward changing the aesthetic ideas of the Saint-Simonian leaders before he and other dissidents broke from the group, and he is surely correct in insisting that some similarities continued to exist between the Saint-Simonians and dissidents like Leroux.

12. Leroux, "De la poésie de style," in *Oeuvres de Pierre Leroux (1825–1850)* (Geneva: Slatkine, 1978), 1:328.

13. Leroux, "Deuxième Discours. Aux Artistes," ibid., 1:65.

14. Leroux, "De la poésie de style," 330.

15. Ibid., 333.

16. Paul Bénichou, *Le sacre de l'écrivain 1750–1830: Essai sur l'avènement d'un pouvoir spirituel laïque dans la France moderne* (Paris: Corti, 1973), 243f.

17. Leroux, "Aux Artistes," 67.

18. Ibid., 67. Contrast this interpretation to that of the art historian Neil McWilliam, who argues that Leroux's theory of the symbol is not mystical, but rests on a natural process of psychological association. See McWilliam, *Dreams of Happiness: Social Art and the French Left, 1830–1850* (Princeton: Princeton University Press, 1993), 179.

19. Leroux, "De la poésie de style," 334.

20. Leroux, "Considérations sur Werther et en general sur la poésie de notre époque," in Leroux, *Oeuvres*, 1:450.

21. Leroux, *Réfutation de l'éclectisme* (Geneva: Slatkine, 1979), 245.

22. Bénichou discounts the importance of Creuzer's influence in *Le temps des prophètes: Doctrines de l'âge romantique* (Paris: Gallimard, 1977), 340. For the opposite argument, see D. O. Evans, *Le socialisme romantique: Pierre Leroux et ses contemporains* (Paris: M. Rivière, 1948), 147f.; Brian Juden, *Traditions orphiques et tendances mystiques dans le romantisme français (1800–1855)* (Paris: Klincksieck, 1971), 320f.; and Michel Espagne, "Le Nouveau Langage. Introduction de la Philosophie Allemande en France de 1815 à 1830," in Jean Moes and Jean-Marie Valentin, eds., *De Lessing à Heine: Un siècle de relations littéraires et intellectuelles entre la France et l'Allemagne* (Paris: Didier-Erudition, 1985), 269–270.

23. See Jean-Jacques Goblot, *La jeune France liberale: Le Globe et son groupe littéraire 1824–1830* (Paris: Plon, 1995), 238f., and *Aux origines du socialisme français: Pierre Leroux et ses premiers écrits (1824–1830)* (Lyon: Presses universitaires de Lyon, 1977), 47. On the German controversies, see George Williamson, *The Longing for Myth in Germany, 1790–1890: Culture, Religion, Politics* (Chicago: University of Chicago Press, 2004), chapter 3.

24. [Dubois], "Religions de l'antiquité," *Le Globe*, August 27, 1825, 775.

25. Leroux quoted in Jérôme Peignot, *Pierre Leroux. Inventeur du socialisme* (Paris: Klincksieck, 1988), 34.

26. On Creuzer's theory of the symbol, see Tzvetan Todorov, *Theories of the Symbol*, trans. Catherine Porter (Ithaca: Cornell University Press, 1982), 216–221.

27. Creuzer cited in Pochat, *Der Symbolbegriff in der Ästhetik und Kunstwissenschaft*, trans. Märta Pochat (Cologne: DuMont, 1983), 43.

28. Leroux, "De la poésie de style," 337–338.

29. Ibid., 330.

30. Leroux, "De l'individualisme et du socialisme," 163.

31. Pierre Leroux, *De l'Humanité: De son principe, et de son avenir* (Paris: Fayard, 1985), 129.

32. Constant quoted in Naomi J. Andrews, "'La Mère Humanité': Femininity in the Romantic Socialism of Pierre Leroux and the Abbé A.-L. Constant," *Journal of the History of Ideas* 63, no. 4 (October 2002): 706.

33. See Beecher, *Victor Considerant*, 152–153; Armelle Le Bras-Chopard, *De l'égalité dans la différence: Le Socialisme de Pierre Leroux* (Paris: Presses de la Fondation nationale des sciences politiques, 1986), 49–50.

34. Leroux, *De l'humanité*, 100.

35. Leroux, "Culte," *A la source perdue*, 225.

36. In the course of writing this chapter, I discovered a somewhat similar emphasis on the symbolic dimension in two studies of Leroux's thought. See Miguel Abensour, "Postface: Comment une philosophie de l'humanité peut-elle être une philosophie politique moderne?" in Pierre Leroux, *Aux philosophes, aux artistes, aux politiques: Trois discours et autres textes*, ed. Jean-Pierre Lacassagne (Paris: Payot, 1994), 295–320; and Georges Navet, *Pierre Leroux, Politique, socialisme et philosophie* (Paris: Payot, 1994). We will return to Abensour in chapter 4.

37. Leroux, "Culte," 225.

38. Leroux, "De l'individualisme et du socialisme," 158.

39. On the physiological metaphor in Saint-Simonianism, see Robert Wokler, "Saint-Simon and the Passage from Political to Social Science," in *The Languages of Political Theory in Early Modern Europe*, ed. Anthony Pagden (Cambridge: Cambridge University Press, 1987), 334.

40. Leroux, "De l'individualisme et du socialisme," 164.

41. On the centuries-long debates about the nature of Christ's body mystically uniting the two orders of the immanent and the transcendent, the specific nature of the "body" brought into presence in the consecrated host of the Eucharist, and the identity of the Church as the mystical body of Christ, the classic work is Henri du Lubac, *Corpus Mysticum: L'Eucharistie et L'Église au Moyen Age. Étude Historique,* 2d ed. (Paris: Aubier, 1949). On the use of this symbolic form within medieval theories of kingship, see Ernst Kantorowicz, *The King's Two Bodies: A Study in Mediaeval Political Theology* (Princeton: Princeton University Press, 1997). On the persistent association of *corpus mysticum* with the nation in early modern France, see Paul Friedland, *Political Actors. Representative Bodies and Theatricality in the Age of the French Revolution* (Ithaca: Cornell University Press, 2002).

42. Leroux to Sand, September 16, 1841, in *Histoire d'une amitié,* 127.

43. Leroux's followers Luc Desages and Auguste Desmoulins took up that task in their *Aphorismes* (1848), which describes a new religion of humanity centered on "prayer and on communion or the act of fraternization." See Frank Paul Bowman, "Religion, Politics, and Utopia in French Romanticism," *Australian Journal of French Studies* II, no. 3 (1974): 307–324.

44. Warwick Gould and Marjorie Reeves, *Joachim of Fiore and the Myth of the Eternal Evangel in the Nineteenth and Twentieth Centuries,* 2d ed. (Oxford: Clarendon, 2001), 107.

45. Leroux quoted in Bras-Chopard, *De l'égalité dans la différence,* 316.

46. Leroux, *De l'humanité,* 191.

47. Leroux, "De l'individualisme et du socialisme," 164.

48. Leroux, Pierre, "Aux Artistes," 73, 80–82.

49. Claude Lefort, "The Permanence of the Theologico-Political?" in *Democracy and Political Theory,* trans. David Macey (Minneapolis: University of Minnesota Press, 1988), 249.

50. See Reeves and Gould, *Joachim of Fiore,* chapter 4.

51. On this point, see Michael Behrent, "Society Incarnate: Association, Society, and Religion in French Political Thought, 1825–1912" (Ph.D. diss., New York University,

2006), chapter 3: "The Mirror Stage of Society: Religion and the Dilemmas of Republicanism in the Thought of Pierre Leroux."

52. For a discussion of this socialist tendency, see Edward Berenson, "A New Religion of the Left: Christianity and Social Radicalism in France, 1815–1848," in François Furet and Mona Ozouf, eds., *The French Revolution and the Creation of Modern Political Culture*, vol. 3: *The Transformation of Political Culture, 1789–1848* (Oxford: Pergamon, 1989), 3:543–560. On this tendency in Considerant, see Beecher, *Victor Considerant*, 164–165.

53. Leroux, *De l'humanité*, 303.

54. Ibid., 191.

55. Leroux, "Du cours de philosophie de Schelling: Aperçu de la situation de la philosophie en Allemagne," in *Discours de Schelling à Berlin. Du cours de philosophie de Schelling. Du christianisme*, ed. Jean-François Courtine (Paris: Vrin, 1982), 44, 53.

56. Leroux, "Du Cours de Philosophie de Schelling," 42.

57. Ludwig Feuerbach, "Zur Kritik der positiven Philosophie," in *Gesammelte Werke*, ed. Werner Schuffenhauer (Berlin: Akademie, 1981), 8:207.

58. Leroux, "Du Cours de Philosophie de Schelling," 68.

59. Marcel Gauchet, *The Disenchantment of the World: A Political History of Religion*, trans. Oscar Burge (Princeton: Princeton University Press, 1997).

60. Miguel Abensour also explores the importance of alterity in Leroux's thought in "L'affaire Schelling: Une controverse entre Pierre Leroux et les jeunes hégéliens," in Patrice Vermeren, ed., "Victor Cousin suivi de la correspondance Schelling-Cousin," special issue, *Corpus*, nos. 18/19 (1991): 117–131.

61. For this point, I am indebted to the discussion of Leroux's *Du Christianisme et de son origine démocratique* (1848) in Behrent, *Society Incarnate*, chapter 3.

62. Leroux, "Du Cours de Philosophie de Schelling," 56.

63. Limayrac, "La poésie symbolique et socialiste," *Revue des deux mondes* (February 15, 1844): 672.

64. Frank Paul Bowman, "Symbol and Desymbolizing," in *French Romanticism: Intertextual and Interdisciplinary Readings* (Baltimore: Johns Hopkins Press, 1990), 155–164.

65. See Leonard P. Wessell Jr., *Karl Marx, Romantic Irony, and the Proletariat: The Mythopoetic Origins of Marxism* (Baton Rouge: Louisiana State University Press, 1979), 71f.

66. Stefan Morawski concludes more generally that both Engels and Marx had quite an extensive conversancy with the aesthetic thinking of German idealism. See Stefan Morawski, "Introduction," in Lee Baxandall and Stefan Morawski, eds., *Karl Marx and Frederick Engels on Literature and Art: Documents on Marxist Aesthetics 1* (Nottingham: Critical, Cultural and Communications, 2006), 34f.

67. For a detailed discussion of the background of Marx's essay, particularly in relation to Romantic painting, see Margaret A. Rose, *Marx's Lost Aesthetic: Karl Marx and the Visual Arts* (Cambridge: Cambridge University Press, 1984).

68. See ibid., 63.

69. See the nuanced assessment in Mcdonald Daly, "A Short History of Marxist Aesthetics," in *Karl Marx and Frederick Engels on Literature and Art*, vii–viii.

70. See Morawski, "Introduction," 14.

71. Alvin W. Gouldner, *The Two Marxisms: Contradictions and Anomalies in the Development of Theory* (New York: Continuum, 1980), 201.

72. Maurice Merleau-Ponty, *Adventures of the Dialectic*, trans. Joseph Bien (London: Heinemann, 1973), 59–60.

73. See Martin Jay, *Marxism and Totality: The Adventures of a Concept from Lukács to Habermas* (Berkeley: University of California Press, 1984), 475.

74. J.-J. Goux, *Symbolic Economies: After Marx and Freud*, trans. Jennifer Curtiss Gage (Ithaca: Cornell University Press, 1990), 132.

75. Bernard Flynn, *Political Philosophy at the Closure of Metaphysics* (Atlantic Heights, NJ: Humanities, 1992), 26–29.

76. Karl Marx, "Economic Manuscripts of 1857–1858," in *Collected Works*, 28:47.

77. Karl Marx, *Capital*, vol. 1, *Collected Works*, 35:93, note 1. Kain cites this passage to argue that Marx believed that the symbolic predominated in ancient and medieval society. See Philip J. Kain, *Marx and Modern Political Theory: From Hobbes to Contemporary Feminism* (Lanham, MD: Rowman and Littlefield, 1993), 290. Yet Kain's argument seems beside the point. Marx clearly maintained that the different modes and functions of the symbolic within various societies are all products of the organization of production.

78. Marx, "Economic Manuscripts of 1857–1858," 47.

79. Claude Lévi-Strauss, *Structural Anthropology*, trans. Claire Jacobson and Brooke Grundfest Schoepf (New York: Basic Books, 1963), 95.

80. Marx, *Capital*, 188.

81. I take this point from Peter Worsley, *Marx and Marxism*, rev. ed. (London: Routledge, 2002), 22–23.

82. Rastko Mocnik, "After the Fall: Through the Fogs of the 18th Brumaire of the Eastern Springs," in Michael Sprinker, ed., *Ghostly Demarcations: A Symposium on Jacques Derrida's Specters of Marx* (New York: Verso, 2008), 111.

83. Mocnik, "After the Fall," 115. The *locus classicus* for the discussion of symbolic efficacy is Lévi-Strauss, "The Effectiveness of Symbols," *Structural Anthropology*, 186–205.

84. Mocnik, "After the Fall," 117.

85. Marx, *Capital*, 85

86. Ibid., 83.

87. Anitra Nelson, *Marx's Concept of Money: The God of Commodities* (New York: Routledge, 1999).

88. Thomas Hobbes quoted in Valenze, *The Social Life of Money in the English Past* (New York: Cambridge University Press, 2006), 63.

89. See Carl Wennerlind, "Money Talks, but What Is It Saying? Semiotics of Money and Social Control," *Journal of Economic Issues* 35, no. 3 (September 2001): 562.

90. Nelson, *Marx's Concept of Money*, 8.

91. Hess quoted in Nelson, *Marx's Concept of Money*, 6.

92. Ibid., 8.

93. Ibid., 50.

94. Immanuel Kant, *Critique of the Power of Judgment*, ed. Paul Guyer, trans. Paul Guyer and Eric Matthews (Cambridge: Cambridge University Press, 2000), 226.

95. Marx, "Economic Manuscripts of 1857–1858," *Collected Works*, 28:91.

96. See Nicholas Halmi, *The Genealogy of the Romantic Symbol* (Oxford: Oxford University Press, 2007), 63–64.

97. Marx, "Economic Manuscripts of 1857–1858," 82.

98. Ibid., 103–104.

99. Ibid., 82.

100. Ibid., 146. It is hard not to hear in Marx's formulation an echo of Hegel's description of the Sphinx as the "symbol of the symbolic itself." See G. W. F. Hegel, *Aesthetics: Lectures on Fine Arts*, trans. T. M. Knox (Oxford: Clarendon, 1975), 1:360.

101. This point is made in Peter Hitchcock, *Oscillate Wildly: Space, Body, and Spirit of Millennial Materialism* (Minneapolis: University of Minnesota Press, 1999), 159–160.

102. Merleau-Ponty, *Adventures of the Dialectic*, 59–60. For a detailed discussion of orthodox Marxist thought in twentieth-century France, see William S. Lewis, *Louis Althusser and the Traditions of French Marxism* (New York: Lexington, 2005), especially chapters 3 and 5.

103. Merleau-Ponty, *Adventures of the Dialectic*, 62.

104. Ibid., 29.

105. Gouldner, *The Two Marxisms*, 201–202.

106. Gouldner places Louis Althusser on the side of "scientific Marxism." Martin Jay recognizes significant differences between Althusser and the Hegelian inflections that typify Western Marxism, but he argues that Althusser should ultimately be viewed as part of Western Marxism. See Jay, *Marxism and Totality*, 387f.

107. Jay, *Marxism and Totality*, 371–372.

108. Maurice Merleau-Ponty, *Signs*, trans. Richard C. McCleary (Evanston: Northwestern University Press, 1964), 9.

109. Merleau-Ponty, *Adventures of the Dialectic*, 65 (translation corrected).

110. Maurice Merleau-Ponty, "On the Phenomenology of Language," in *Signs*, 88.

111. Maurice Merleau-Ponty, *In Praise of Philosophy*, trans. John Wild and James M. Edie (Evanston: Northwestern University Press, 1963), 55–56.

112. Maurice Merleau-Ponty, "From Mauss to Claude Lévi-Strauss," in *Signs*, 115.

113. See François Dosse, *History of Structuralism*, vol. 1: *The Rising Sign, 1945–1966*, trans. Deborah Glassman (Minneapolis: University of Minnesota Press, 1997), 38.

114. Merleau-Ponty, "From Mauss to Claude Lévi-Strauss," 123.

115. See Maurice Merleau-Ponty, "The Philosopher and Sociology," in *Signs*, especially 110–112.

116. Ibid., 113.

117. See Taylor Carman and Mark B. N. Hansen, "Introduction," in Taylor Carman and Mark B. N. Hansen, eds., *The Cambridge Companion to Merleau-Ponty* (Cambridge: Cambridge University Press, 2005), 17.

118. See Nick Crossley, "Phenomenology, Structuralism and History: Merleau-Ponty's Social Theory," *Theoria: A Journal of Social and Political Theory* 51, no. 103 (April 2004), 98.

119. Philippe Gottraux, *"Socialisme ou Barbarie": Un engagement politique et intellec-tuel dans la France de l'après-guerre* (Lausanne: Payot Lausanne, 1997), 77–129.

120. François Furet, "French Intellectuals: From Marxism to Structuralism," *In the Workshop of History*, trans. Jonathan Mandelbaum (Chicago: University of Chicago Press, 1984), 30.

121. Dosse, *History of Structuralism*, 1:294.

122. Furet, "French Intellectuals," 38.

123. Louis Althusser, *Reading Capital*, trans. Ben Brewster (London: New Left, 1977), 97.

124. Althusser cited in Lewis, *Louis Althusser and the Traditions of French Marxism*, 174.

125. Louis Althusser, "Freud and Lacan," in *Lenin and Philosophy and Other Essays*, trans. Ben Brewster (New York: Monthly Review Press, 1971), 210–211.

126. Louis Althusser, "Ideology and Ideological State Apparatuses," in *Lenin and Philosophy*, 162. In *Lacan in Contexts* (New York: Verso, 1988), David Macey argues rightly that this use of the term *real* to signify something like *actual social conditions* violates Lacan's definition of the real as beyond and resistant to symbolization (19). On the general circumstances of Althusser's interest in Lacan, see Elizabeth Roudinesco, *Jacques Lacan: Outline of a Life, History of a System of Thought*, trans. Barbara Bray (New York: Columbia University Press, 1997), chapter 23.

127. The view that the symbolic is excluded is represented by Macey, *Lacan in Contexts*, 19. I find myself strongly in agreement with Valente's claim that at the same time that Althusser shifts from agency to ideology, he also shifts interpretive focus from the imaginary to the symbolic. See Joe Valente, "Lacan's Marxism, Marxism's Lacan (from Žižek to Althusser)," in Jean-Michel Rabaté, ed., *Cambridge Companion to Jacques Lacan* (New York: Cambridge University Press, 2003), 158.

128. Valente, "Lacan's Marxism, Marxism's Lacan," 168.

129. Daniel Fabre, "Symbolisme en questions," in Martine Segalen, ed., *L'Autre et le semblable: Regards sur l'ethnologie des sociétés contemporaines* (Paris: CNRS, 1989), 61.

130. Vincent Descombes, "L'équivoque du symbolique," *MLN* 94, no. 4, French Issue: Perspectives in Mimesis (May 1979): 655–656, 674.

131. Goux, *Symbolic Economies*, 130, 124.

132. Camille Tarot, *De Durkheim à Mauss: L'invention du symbolique. Sociologie et science des religions* (Paris: La Découverte, 1999), 629. On the impure sacred, see, for example, Alexander T. Riley, "'Renegade Durkheimianism' and the Transgressive Left Sacred," in Jeffrey C. Alexander and Philip Smith, eds., *The Cambridge Companion to Durkheim* (New York: Cambridge University Press, 2005), 274–304. See, more generally, Michèle Richman, *Sacred Revolutions: Durkheim and the Collège de Sociologie* (Minneapolis: University of Minnesota Press, 2002).

133. Guy Debord, *The Society of the Spectacle*, trans. Donald Nicholson-Smith (New York: Zone, 1994), 24.

134. Steven Best, "The Commodification of Reality and the Reality of Commodification: Baudrillard, Debord, and Postmodern Theory," in Mike Gane, ed., *Jean Baudrillard* (London: Sage, 2000), 1:241.

135. Jean Baudrillard, *For a Critique of the Political Economy of the Sign*, trans. Charles Levin (St. Louis: Telos, 1981), 149.

136. Ibid., 149, note 5.

137. Ibid., 150.

138. Ibid., 161.

139. Ibid., 163.

140. Jean Baudrillard, *The Mirror of Production*, trans. Mark Poster (St. Louis: Telos, 1975), 120.

141. Martin Jay, "The Apocalyptic Imagination and the Inability to Mourn," in Gillian Robertson and John Rundell, eds., *Rethinking Imagination: Culture and Creativity* (New York: Routledge, 1994). We will return to this theme in chapter 5.

3. From the Symbolic Turn to the Social Imaginary

1. François Furet, "French Intellectuals: From Marxism to Structuralism," in *In the Workshop of History*, trans. Jonathan Mandelbaum (Chicago: University of Chicago Press, 1984), 30.

2. Cornelius Castoriadis, "The Movements of the Sixties," in *World in Fragments: Writings on Politics, Society, Psychoanalysis, and the Imagination*, ed. and trans. David Ames Curtis (Stanford: Stanford University Press, 1997), 52.

3. Cornelius Castoriadis, "Psychoanalysis, Project and Elucidation: The 'Destiny' of Analysis and the Responsibility of Analysts," in *Crossroads in the Labyrinth*, trans. Kate Soper and Martin H. Ryle (Cambridge: MIT Press, 1984), 88 (translation emended).

4. See, for example, the two articles by Brian Singer, which offer pioneering overviews of Castoriadis's thought, but do little to bridge the years between the "early" and the "late" years: "The Early Castoriadis: Socialism, Barbarism, and the Bureaucratic Thread," *Canadian Journal of Political and Social Theory* 3, no. 3 (Fall 1979): 35–56, and "The Later Castoriadis: Institution Under Interrogation," *Canadian Journal of Political and Social Theory* 4, no. 1 (Winter 1980): 75–101. A similar tendency characterizes the two recent French books on Castoriadis: Gérard David, *Cornelius Castoriadis: Le projet d'autonomie* (Paris: Michalon, 2000); and Nicolas Poirier, *Castoriadis: L'imaginaire radical* (Paris: Presses Universitaires de France, 2004). Dick Howard shows more sensitivity to the historical complexity of Castoriadis's development in what remains one of the most valuable discussions of Castoriadis. See Howard, *The Marxian Legacy*, 2d ed. (Minneapolis: University of Minnesota Press, 1988). The first book-length study of Castoriadis in English, Jeff Klooger's *Castoriadis: Psyche, Society, Autonomy* (Leiden: Brill, 2009), offers a rich systematic presentation and nuanced evaluation, but it shows little interest in historicizing or contextualizing Castoriadis's thought. More recently, Suzi Adams's work *Castoriadis's Ontology: Being and Creation* (New York: Fordham University Press, 2011) argues that in the years after publication of *The Imaginary Institution of Society* Castoriadis extended his theory of self-creation to all regions of being, not just human regions, in effect articulating a second ontology. I believe that Adams overstates the break between these

two phases, but nonetheless her book is a deep and signal contribution to the philosophical literature on Castoriadis.

5. Paul Cardan [Cornelius Castoriadis], "Marxisme et théorie révolutionnaire," *Socialisme ou Barbarie*, no. 36 (April-June 1964): 1–25; no. 37 (July-September 1964): 18–53; no. 38 (October-December 1964): 44–86; no. 39 (March-April 1965): 16–66; no. 40 (June-August 1965): 37–71.

6. Cornelius Castoriadis, *The Imaginary Institution of Society*, trans. Kathleen Blamey (Cambridge: MIT Press, 1987), 2.

7. On the general situation after the German withdrawal, see Mark Mazower, *Inside Hitler's Greece: The Experience of Occupation, 1941–44* (New Haven: Yale University Press, 1993), 355–377.

8. Cornelius Castoriadis, "Institution and Autonomy," in Peter Osborne, ed., *A Critical Sense: Interviews with Intellectuals* (London: Routledge, 1996), 9. See also Philippe Gottraux, *"Socialisme ou Barbarie": Un engagement politique et intellectuel dans la France de l'après-guerre* (Lausanne: Payot Lausanne, 1998), 364.

9. Cornelius Castoriadis, "Socialism or Barbarism," in *Political and Social Writings*, vol. 1: *1946–1955: From the Critique of Bureaucracy to the Positive Content of Socialism*, ed. and trans. David Ames Curtis (Minneapolis: University of Minnesota Press, 1988), 79.

10. Cornelius Castoriadis, "Modern Capitalism and Revolution," in *Political and Social Writings*, vol. 2: *1955–1960: From the Workers' Struggle Against Bureaucracy to Revolution in the Age of Modern Capitalism*, ed. and trans. David Ames Curtis (Minneapolis: University of Minnesota Press, 1988), 296–297.

11. Cornelius Castoriadis, "The Content of Socialism, II," in *Political and Social Writings*, 2:91.

12. Cornelius Castoriadis, "Recommencing the Revolution," in *Political and Social Writings*, vol. 3: *1961–1979: Recommencing the Revolution: From Socialism to the Autonomous Society*, ed. and trans. David Ames Curtis (Minneapolis: University of Minnesota Press, 1993), 33.

13. Ibid., 29.

14. Letter to readers and supporters of *Socialisme ou Barbarie*, October 28, 1963, reprinted in Cornelius Castoriadis, "Postface to 'Recommencing the Revolution,'" in Castoriadis *Political and Social Writings*, 3:81.

15. See Howard, *The Marxian Legacy*, 225; for Castoriadis, the group's efforts at a dynamic and dialectical integration of workers and intellectuals in a collective practice of elaboration and action was meant to prefigure future socialist society. See Gottraux, *"Socialisme ou Barbarie,"* 98f.

16. Gottraux, *"Socialisme ou Barbarie,"* 142–155.

17. Ibid., 162.

18. Castoriadis, "Institution and Autonomy," 7.

19. Castoriadis Archive: (Bbis B) Phi 30/40–5.

20. Castoriadis Archive: Letter to *Les Temps Modernes*, July 28, 1948 (BbisB) Corr 40/60.

21. Castoriadis Archive: Lefort to Castoriadis, August 12, 1949 (BbisB) Corr 40/60.

22. Castoriadis, *The Imaginary Institution of Society*, 44–45.

23. Ibid., 54.

24. Ibid., 108. Castoriadis used the term *social-historical world* to unify the synchronic and diachronic elements that structuralism separated.

25. Ibid., 111.

26. Ibid., 247.

27. Ibid., 313.

28. Cornelius Castoriadis, "The Discovery of the Imagination," in *World in Fragments*, 245.

29. Castoriadis, "Institution and Autonomy," 11.

30. Ibid., 10–11.

31. On Bachelard and Jung, see Richard Kearney, *The Poetics of Imagining: Modern to Post-modern* (New York: Fordham University Press, 1998), 105–107; further, see passing references to Jung in Gilbert Durand, *Champs de l'imaginaire*, ed. Danièle Chauvin (Grenoble: ELLUG, 1996).

32. Later in his career, Castoriadis described Durand's idea of the imagination as "traditional" insofar as Durand saw in imagination a "dynamic power that deforms copies furnished by perception," as if, Castoriadis added, "perception could ever furnish 'copies.'" See Cornelius Castoriadis, "Complexité, magmas, histoire: L'exemple de la ville médiévale," in *Fait et à faire: Les carrefours du labyrinthe V* (Paris: Seuil, 1997), 225.

33. Jean-Paul Sartre, *The Imaginary: A Phenomenological Psychology of the Imagination*, trans. Jonathan Webber (New York: Routledge, 2004), 10–11.

34. Ibid., 182.

35. Castoriadis, "Institution and Autonomy," 10.

36. Castoriadis, *The Imaginary Institution of Society*, 127 (translation emended).

37. Castoriadis, "Institution and Autonomy," 10.

38. See, for example, Castoriadis, *The Imaginary Institution of Society*, 104.

39. Sartre, *The Imaginary*, 184.

40. Robert D. Cumming, "Role-Playing: Sartre's Transformation of Husserl's Phenomenology," in Christina Howells, ed., *The Cambridge Companion to Sartre* (Cambridge: Cambridge University Press, 1992), 48.

41. Castoriadis, "Institution and Autonomy," 10.

42. Castoriadis, *The Imaginary Institution of Society*, 124.

43. Ibid., 262–263.

44. Husserl quoted in Kearney, *The Poetics of Imagining*, 16.

45. Ibid., 16–17. Casey argues even further that, because he makes sensory perception the foundational act of consciousness, when Husserl then treats images as modifications of such sensory impressions, he essentially reduces the presentational features of images to "second-order extensions of sensations." See Edward S. Casey, "Imagination: Imagining and the Image," *Philosophy and Phenomenological Research* 31, no. 4 (June 1971): 483–485.

46. Castoriadis, "The Discovery of the Imagination," 245.

47. An excellent recent discussion of Fichte's theory of imagination is found in Frederick Beiser, *German Idealism: The Struggle Against Subjectivism, 1781–1801* (Cambridge: Harvard University Press, 2002), esp. 253f.

48. See, for example, Richard Kroner, *Von Kant bis Hegel*, 2d ed. (Tübingen: Mohr, 1961), 450. Castoriadis cites Kroner and elaborates on Kant, Fichte and *produktive Einbildungskraft* in *The Imaginary Institution of Society*, 391n.53.

49. Cornelius Castoriadis, "Epilegomena to a Theory of the Soul Which Has Been Presented as a Science," in *Crossroads in the Labyrinth*, 22 (translation emended).

50. Jerrold Seigel, *The Idea of the Self: Thought and Experience in Western Europe Since the Seventeenth Century* (Cambridge: Cambridge University Press, 2005), 27 and 366.

51. I draw this formulation from Thomas Pfau, "From Autonomous Subjects to Self-Regulating Structures: Rationality and Development in German Idealism," in Michael Ferber, ed., *A Companion to European Romanticism* (Oxford: Blackwell, 2005), 109.

52. Interpreters sometimes overlook this duality, too quickly seeing Castoriadis as an extreme subjectivist. See for example, Glen Newey, "Albino Sea-Cucumber," *London Review of Books*, February 5, 1998, 6–7; Lucian Boia, *Pour une histoire de l'imaginaire* (Paris: Belles Lettres, 1998), 208; and Slavoj Žižek, *The Ticklish Subject: The Absent Center of Political Ontology* (New York: Verso, 1999), 24. For a more nuanced approach to this question, see Joel Whitebook, *Perversion and Utopia. A Study in Psychoanalysis and Critical Theory* (Cambridge: MIT Press, 1996), 170f.

53. Castoriadis, *The Imaginary Institution of Society*, 108.

54. I have discussed this in "Democracy Between Disenchantment and Political Theology: French Post-Marxism and the Return of Religion," *New German Critique*, no. 94 (Winter 2005): 72–105, especially 80–86.

55. Castoriadis, "Institution and Autonomy," 8.

56. See Cornelius Castoriadis, "The Sayable and the Unsayable: Homage to Maurice Merleau-Ponty," in *Crossroads in the Labyrinth*, 119–144, and "Merleau-Ponty and the Weight of the Ontological Tradition," in *World in Fragments*, 273–310.

57. For information on this course, scholars drew until recently on the brief description in Maurice Merleau-Ponty, *Résumés de cours: Collège de France, 1952–1960* (Paris: Gallimard, 1968); now see Maurice Merleau-Ponty, *L'Institution dans l'histoire personnelle et publique: Le problème de la passivité. Le sommeil, l'inconscient, la mémoire. Notes de cours au Collège de France (1954–1955)* (Paris: Belin, 2003).

58. Merleau-Ponty, *L'Institution*, 34f.

59. Ibid., 35 and again 38.

60. Ibid., 47.

61. Castoriadis, "Institution and Autonomy," 8.

62. Merleau-Ponty, *L'Institution*, 41–42.

63. On the point about Merleau-Ponty and perception, see Bernhard Waldenfels, "Der Primat der Einbildungskraft: Zur Rolle des gesellschaftlichen Imaginären bei Cornelius Castoriadis," in Giovanni Busino, ed., *Autonomie et autotransformation de la société: La philosophie militante de Cornelius Castoriadis* (Genève: Droz, 1989), 157, note 22. See also the discussion of Merleau-Ponty's critique of Sartre's *L'Imaginaire* in Fabrice

Colonna, "Merleau-Ponty Penseur de l'Imaginaire," *Chiasmi International: Merleau-Ponty. Le Réel et l'Imaginaire* (Milan: Mimesis, 2003), 111–147.

64. For an overly hasty conflation of Castoriadis and Lévi-Strauss based on their allegedly shared view of the symbolic constitution of society, see Richard Kearney, *Poetics of Modernity. Toward a Hermeneutic Imagination* (Atlantic Highlands, NJ: Humanities, 1995), 74.

65. Claude Lévi-Strauss, *Introduction to the Work of Marcel Mauss*, trans. Felicity Baker (London: Routledge and Kegan Paul, 1987), 59.

66. Castoriadis, *The Imaginary Institution of Society*, 164.

67. Ibid., 117.

68. Ibid., 127.

69. Ibid., 127 (translation emended).

70. Lévi-Strauss, quoted ibid., 390, note 39.

71. Ibid., 136.

72. Castoriadis, "The Sayable and the Unsayable," 122.

73. Hans Joas, "On Articulation," *Constellations* 9, no. 4 (December 2002): 510.

74. Castoriadis, *The Imaginary Institution of Society*, 136.

75. Ibid., 138.

76. Pierre Bourdieu, *Language and Symbolic Power*, trans. Gino Raymond and Matthew Adamson (Cambridge: Harvard University Press, 1991), 164–166.

77. Karl-Siegbert Rehberg, "Weltrepräsentanz und Verkörperung: Institutionelle Analyse und Symboltheorien—Eine Einführung in systematischer Absicht," in Gert Melville, ed., *Institutionalität und Symbolisierung: Verstetigungen kultureller Ordnungsmuster in Vergangenheit und Gegenwart* (Cologne: Böhlau, 2001), 26.

78. Castoriadis, *The Imaginary Institution of Society*, 141.

79. Ibid., 355.

80. Ibid.

81. Ibid., 243.

82. The English and French titles of Schopenhauer's main work (*Le monde comme volonté et représentation*) point to the different translation conventions for phenomenology and classic German idealism, for, in the latter, *Vorstellung* (representation) contrasts with *Darstellung* (presentation). Another relevant word in the Husserlian tradition, *Vergegenwärtigung*, is translated as "presentification" in both English and French. Presentification bears directly on the phenomenology of imagination, most famously in Eugen Fink's "Vergengenwärtigung und Bild. Beiträge zur Phänomenologie der Unwirklichkeit," *Jahrbuch für Philosophie und phänomenologische Forschung* 11 (1930): 239–309. Undoubtedly with Husserl and Fink in mind, Sartre introduced *présentifier* as an "indispensable neologism" in *The Imaginary*, 105.

83. Castoriadis, *The Imaginary Institution of Society*, 329 (the second set of ellipses is Castoriadis's). Jeff Klooger recognizes the importance of the concept of presentation in Castoriadis's thought, but also his failure to develop systematically the distinction between presentation and representation. See Klooger, *Castoriadis*, especially 120.

84. Castoriadis, *The Imaginary Institution of Society.*, 329.

85. Ibid., 355–356.

86. Cornelius Castoriadis, "Modern Science and Philosophical Interrogation," in *Crossroads in the Labyrinth*, 172, see also "The Ontological Import of the History of Science," in *World in Fragments*, 342–373. I have discussed this aspect of Castoriadis's theory in "Cornelius Castoriadis *Contra* Postmodernism: Beyond the 'French Ideology,'" *French Politics and Society* 16, no. 2 (Spring 1998): 30–42.

87. Cornelius Castoriadis, "The Logic of Magmas and the Question of Autonomy," in *The Castoriadis Reader*, ed. and trans. David Ames Curtis (Oxford: Blackwell, 1997), 307. See also Castoriadis, "Modern Science and Philosophical Interrogation," 145–226.

88. Cornelius Castoriadis, "Technique," in *Crossroads in the Labyrinth*, 240.

89. For a discussion and relevant literature, see Seigel, *The Idea of the Self*, 363.

90. Castoriadis, *The Imaginary Institution of Society*, 371.

91. Castoriadis, "The State of the Subject Today," in *World in Fragments*, 148. Elsewhere, Castoriadis claims a more radical view than Fichte insofar as he believes that the imagination is the capacity to pose an image prompted by a shock or prompted by *nothing at all*. See Cornelius Castoriadis, "Imagination, imaginaire, réflexion," in *Fait et à faire*, 248–249.

92. Castoriadis Archive: Castoriadis to Jean Finkelstein, May 16, 1974, (Mar)A6.

93. Castoriadis, *The Imaginary Institution of Society*, 102–103.

94. Lacan, "The Instance of the Letter in the Unconscious, or Reason Since Freud," *Écrits*, trans. Bruce Fink (New York: Norton, 2006), 436.

95. Sherry Turkle, *Psychoanalytic Politics: Jacques Lacan and Freud's French Revolution*, 2d ed. (New York: Guildford, 1992), 116.

96. Elisabeth Roudinesco, *Jacques Lacan*, trans. Barbara Bray (New York: Columbia University Press, 1997), 102.

97. Hélène Troisier, *Piera Aulagnier* (Paris: Presses universitaires de France, 1998), 6; see also Elizabeth Roudinesco, *Jacques Lacan & Co.*, trans. Jeffrey Mehlman (Chicago: University of Chicago Press, 1990), 338.

98. Castoriadis Archive: Box (Mar) A6. "La psychanalyse, projet et elucidation" first appeared in the journal of the *Quatrième Groupe*, *Topique*, no. 19 (April 1977) and was reprinted in *Crossroads in the Labyrinth*.

99. See especially Cornelius Castoriadis, "The Construction of the World in Psychosis," *World in Fragments*, 196–210.

100. On the pre-Lacanian history of the "mirror stage," see Roudinesco, *Jacques Lacan & Co.*, 129–134. In *Jacques Lacan* (111), Roudinesco argues that whereas Wallon viewed mirroring as a stage in the development of the ego, Lacan transformed the mirror stage into the mechanism whereby the human consciousness comes to exist *as such*.

101. Jacques Lacan, "The Mirror Stage as Formative of the *I* Function as Revealed in Psychoanalytic Experience," in *Écrits*, 76.

102. Lacan quoted in Richard Boothby, *Death and Desire: Psychoanalytic Theory in Lacan's Return to Freud* (New York: Routledge, 1991), 21–22.

103. Ibid., 32.

104. Lacan, "The Mirror Stage," 76.

105. Castoriadis, *The Imaginary Institution of Society*, 3.

106. Castoriadis, "The State of the Subject Today," 150–151.

107. Seigel, *The Idea of the Self*, 366. For a detailed discussion of Reinhold's post-Kantian theory of reflection, see Frederick Beiser, *The Fate of Reason: German Philosophy from Kant to Fichte* (Cambridge: Harvard University Press, 1987), chapter 8.

108. Castoriadis, *The Imaginary Institution of Society*, 283.

109. Castoriadis periodically expressed dissatisfaction with the notion of primary narcissism. See, for example, his preference for the term *autism* (*The Imaginary Institution of Society*, 294). See also Castoriadis, "The Psychical and Social Roots of Hate," *Free Associations* 7, no. 3 (1999): 402.

110. Castoriadis, *The Imaginary Institution of Society*, 301.

111. Castoriadis borrowed a metaphor of metabolization developed by Aulagnier to describe the psyche's powerful attempt to allow only what it can "metabolize" to *enter* it. Aulagnier, in turn, drew on Freud's analogies between a cell and a psyche. Given Castoriadis's strong links to Fichte, it is difficult not to see resonances with Fichte's argument that imagination internalizes the matter of sensation to the extent that it can *determine* it, and, to the extent that it cannot, it repels that matter, externalizes it. See Beiser, *German Idealism*, 253.

112. Castoriadis, *The Imaginary Institution of Society*, 296.

113. Whitebook, *Perversion and Utopia*, 172.

114. Castoriadis, *The Imaginary Institution of Society*, 163.

115. Ibid., 299. The links to Aulagnier are clear in "The Construction of the World in Psychosis," 196–210. Among these manifestions of the *same* is the "self." Whitebook perceptively likens this to the Kantian transcendental unity of apperception, though here it is the psyche as such and not the synthetic function of the ego that is the source of the "I think" accompanying all representations and making them *my* representations (Whitebook, *Perversion and Utopia*, 172).

116. Castoriadis, *The Imaginary Institution of Society*, 288–289.

117. Castoriadis, "Psychoanalysis, Project and Elucidation," 91.

118. Malcolm Bowie, *Structuralism and Since: From Lévi-Strauss to Derrida*, ed. John Sturrock (Oxford: Oxford University Press, 1979), 131.

119. Ibid., 133.

120. Jürgen Habermas, *The Philosophical Discourse of Modernity: Twelve Lectures*, trans. Frederick G. Lawrence (Cambridge: MIT Press, 1987), 334.

121. Cornelius Castoriadis, "Done and to Be Done," in *The Castoriadis Reader*, 376.

122. Cornelius Castoriadis, "From the Monad to Autonomy," in *World in Fragments*, 190.

123. Castoriadis quoted in Fernando Urribarri, "The Psyche, Imagination and History: A General View of Cornelius Castoriadis's Psychoanalytic Ideas," *Free Associations* 7, no. 3 (1999): 385.

124. Joel Whitebook, "Requiem for a *Selbstdenker*: Cornelius Castoriadis (1922–1997)," *Constellations* 5, no. 2 (1998): 143.

125. Peter Dews, "Imagination and the Symbolic: Castoriadis and Lacan," *Constellations* 9, no. 4 (2002): 517.

126. Castoriadis, *The Imaginary Institution of Society*, 312.

127. See Peter Dews, *Logics of Disintegration: Poststructuralist Thought and the Claims of Critical Theory* (New York: Verso, 1987), 234ff. and Whitebook, *Perversion and Utopia*, especially 179–196.

128. Lacan, "The Instance of the Letter in the Unconscious," 424.

129. Castoriadis, *The Imaginary Institution of Society*, 293. Around a year before his death, in typewritten notes on Whitebook's *Perversion and Utopia*, Castoriadis articulated this position with particular clarity: "That Lacan takes «dream-images . . . as signifiers», that is as inserted in the same «literal or phonematic structures» as the signifiers in language» . . . is the result, inter alia, of his forgetting that the dream as we «know» it is but the end-result of various stages of transformation, up to and including the «secondary elaboration» which is responsible for its final presentation in the awaken [*sic*] memory." A further note reads: "emph that 'translation' of unconscious contents is a 'transposition into words of entities ultimately *untranslatable*, entities just *labeled* with words during the analytic process. And this is true whenever we speak, even in common parlance, about something psychical.'" Cornelius Castoriadis, "Notes on Whitebook, Perversion and Utopia (typing begun on Friday, January 24, 1997)," Castoriadis Archive: E bis 5.

130. Turkle, *Psychoanalytic Politics*, 73.

131. Ibid., 76–77.

132. Peter Starr, *Logics of Failed Revolt: French Theory After May '68* (Stanford: Stanford University Press, 1995), 38.

133. Ibid., 48.

134. Ibid., 73.

135. Castoriadis, "The Diversionists," in *Political and Social Writings* 3:274.

136. Castoriadis, "The Movements of the Sixties," in *World in Fragments*, 50–51.

137. See ibid., 53.

138. Castoriadis, "La Révolution anticipée," in Cornelius Castoriadis, Claude Lefort, and Edgar Morin, *Mai 1968: La Brèche* (Paris: Fayard, 1968).

139. This paragraph picks up on Starr's discussion of Castoriadis in *Logics of Failed Revolt*, 21. It is perhaps indicative of Castoriadis's fate that, even though Starr believes that May 1968 vindicated the sociopolitical analyses of *Socialisme ou Barbarie* (24–29) and that Castoriadis's tempered corrective to the paralyzing anxieties of some of his contemporaries was essentially right, Castoriadis in fact gets what amounts to a nod in the opening pages of a book that then devotes lengthy analysis to theorists caught in the impasse structure.

140. Castoriadis, "Epilegomena to a Theory of the Soul," 36.

141. Castoriadis, "The State of the Subject Today," 155.

142. Ibid., 156.

143. Castoriadis, "Epilegomena to a Theory of the Soul," 26 (translation emended).

144. Cornelius Castoriadis, "General Introduction," in *Political and Social Writings* 1:31.

145. Cornelius Castoriadis, "Power, Politics, Autonomy," in *Philosophy, Politics, Autonomy: Essays in Political Philosophy*, ed. and trans. David Ames Curtis (New York: Oxford University Press, 1991), 172.

146. Castoriadis, "The State of the Subject Today," 169.

147. Castoriadis, "Complexité, magmas, histoire," 212.

148. Here, one can note some discrepancy between the copious and careful reading notes in Castoriadis's archive and the often blunt and sometimes unnuanced criticisms that he leveled against many thinkers in his published work.

149. Claude Lefort, "An Interview with Claude Lefort," *Telos* 30 (1976–77): 192.

150. Slavoj Žižek, *On Belief* (London: Routledge, 2001), 23.

4. Democracy Between Disenchantment and Political Theology

1. Paul Bénichou, *Le sacre de l'écrivain 1750–1830: Essai sur l'avènement d'un pouvoir spirituel laïque dans la France moderne* (Paris: Corti, 1973), 243f.

2. Claude Lefort, "The Permanence of the Theologico-Political?" in *Democracy and Political Theory*, trans. David Macey (Minneapolis: University of Minnesota Press, 1988), 222.

3. Cornelius Castoriadis, "Institution of Society and Religion," in *World in Fragments: Writings on Politics, Society, Psychoanalysis, and the Imagination*, ed. and trans. David Ames Curtis (Stanford: Stanford University Press, 1997), 329.

4. See also Cornelius Castoriadis, "The Revolution Before the Theologians: For a Critical/Political Reflection on Our History," in *World in Fragments*, 72.

5. Pierre Rosanvallon, "Inaugural Lecture, Collège de France," in Pierre Rosanvallon, *Democracy Past and Present*, ed. Samuel Moyn (New York: Columbia University Press, 2006), 36.

6. See the account in Marcel Gauchet, "De *Textures* au *Débat* ou la revue comme creuset de la vie intellectuelle," in Marcel Gauchet, *La condition historique: Entretiens avec François Azouvi et Sylvain Piron* (Paris: Stock, 2003), 158.

7. Michael Scott Christofferson, *French Intellectuals Against the Left: The Antitotalitarian Moment of the 1970s* (New York: Berghahn, 2004).

8. Pierre Rosanvallon, "Le politique," in J. Revel and N. Wachtel, eds., *Une école pour les sciences sociales: De la VIe section à l'École des Hautes Études en Sciences Sociales* (Paris: CERF, 1996), 300.

9. Pierre Rosanvallon cited in Andrew Jainchill and Samuel Moyn, "French Democracy Between Totalitarianism and Solidarity: Pierre Rosanvallon and Revisionist Historiography," *Journal of Modern History* 76, no. 1 (March 2004): 107–154.

10. Jeremy Jennings, "The Return of the Political? New French Journals in the History of Political Thought," *History of Political Thought* 18 (Spring 1997): 148–156, and, more broadly, "'Le retour des émigrés'? The Study of the History of Political Ideas in Contemporary France," in Dario Castiglione and Iain Hampsher-Monk, eds., *The History of Political Thought in National Context* (Cambridge: Cambridge University Press, 2001), 204–227.

11. On the general role that Furet played in the intellectual reorientation of those years, see Sunil Khilnani, *Arguing Revolution: The Intellectual Left in Postwar France* (New Haven: Yale University Press, 1993), especially chapter 6.

12. See especially Claude Lefort, "Interpreting Revolution with the French Revolution," in *Democracy and Political Theory*, 89–114. Moyn has correctly pointed out that Furet in fact drew some of his chief political concepts from Claude Lefort. See Samuel Moyn, "On the Intellectual Origins of François Furet's Masterpiece," *Tocqueville Review* 29, no. 2 (2008): 1–20.

13. Gauchet, "De *Textures* au *Débat*," 167.

14. Jacques Derrida, *Specters of Marx: The State of the Debt, the Work of Mourning, and the New International*, trans. Peggy Kamuf (New York: Routledge, 1994), 122.

15. Karl Marx, "On the Jewish Question," in *Collected Works of Karl Marx and Friedrich Engels, 1843–1844* (Moscow: Progress, 1973), 3:156.

16. I discuss this in some detail in *Marx, the Young Hegelians, and the Origins of Radical Social Theory: Dethroning the Self* (New York: Cambridge University Press, 1999), chapter 7.

17. François Furet, *The Passing of an Illusion: The Idea of Communism in the Twentieth Century*, trans. Deborah Furet (Chicago: University of Chicago Press, 1999), 502.

18. See especially the lead essay in François Furet, *Interpreting the Revolution*, trans. Elborg Forster (Cambridge: Cambridge University Press, 1981).

19. Marcel Gauchet, *Le Débat* 50 (May-August 1988): 168.

20. Olivier Mongin, *Face au scepticisme (1976–1993): Les mutations du paysage intellectuel ou l'invention de l'intellectuel democratique* (Paris: Découverte, 1994), 17.

21. Gianni Vattimo, "The Trace of the Trace," in Jacques Derrida and Gianni Vattimo, eds., *Religion* (Stanford: Stanford University Press, 1998), 79–94.

22. Marcel Gauchet and Pierre Nora, "Aujourd'hui," *Le Débat* 50 (May-August 1988): 157.

23. Jean-Claude Monod, "Le 'problème théologico-politique' au XXe siècle," *Esprit*, no. 250 (February 1999): 179–192.

24. Gauchet and Nora, "Aujourd'hui," 147.

25. Claude Lefort, "An Interview with Claude Lefort," *Telos* 30 (1976–77), 185.

26. Ibid., 173.

27. Ibid., 175–176.

28. See, especially, Claude Lefort, "L'expérience prolétarienne," *Socialisme ou Barbarie* 11 (November-December 1952): 1–19, reprinted in *Éléments d'une critique de la bureaucratie* (Genève: Droz, 1971), 71–97.

29. See Claude Lefort, "Préface," in *Éléments d'une critique de la bureaucratie*, 14.

30. Claude Lefort [Montal], "Le proletariat et le problème de la direction révolutionnaire," *Socialisme ou Barbarie* 10 (July-August 1952): 18–27.

31. See Philippe Gottraux, *"Socialisme ou Barbarie": Un engagement politique et intellectuel dans la France de l'après-guerre* (Lausanne: Payot, 1998), 50–52.

32. Ibid., 87f.

33. Lefort, "Préface," 14.

34. Hugues Poltier, *Passion du politique: La pensée de Claude Lefort* (Genève: Labor et Fides, 1998), 19.

35. See Lefort, "An Interview," especially 179–185. For excellent recent accounts, see Poltier, *Passion du Politique*; Dick Howard, *The Specter of Democracy* (New York: Columbia

University Press, 2002); and Bernard Flynn, *The Philosophy of Claude Lefort: Interpreting the Political* (Evanston: Northwestern University Press, 2005). Samuel Moyn's forthcoming book *A New Theory of Politics: Claude Lefort and Company in Contemporary France* will offer the most detailed historical reconstruction of the development of Lefort's thinking. For the time being, see especially Samuel Moyn, "Marxism and Alterity: Claude Lefort and the Critique of Totality," in Warren Breckman, Peter E. Gordon, A. Dirk Moses, Samuel Moyn, and Elliot Neaman, eds., *The Modernist Imagination: Intellectual History and Critical Theory* (New York: Berghahn, 2009), 99–116.

36. Maurice Merleau-Ponty, *The Visible and the Invisible*, trans. Alphonso Lingis, ed. Claude Lefort (Evanston: Northwestern University Press, 1968), 151.

37. I cite the translation of this passage from Lefort as emended by Bernard Flynn, *Political Philosophy at the Closure of Metaphysics* (Atlantic Highlands, NJ: Humanities, 1992), 178. See Lefort, "Permanence of the Theologico-Political?" 218.

38. Lefort, "Introduction," in *Democracy and Political Theory*, 2–3.

39. I paraphrase terms used by Pierre Rosanvallon in an excellent discussion of these categories. See Rosanvallon, "Inaugural Lecture, Collège de France," 36.

40. Lefort, "Permanence of the Theologico-Political?" 215–216.

41. Marcel Gauchet, "Changement de paradigme en sciences sociales?" *Le Débat* 50 (May-August 1988): 168–169.

42. Within the scholarly literature, Poltier's *Passion du politique* in particular emphasizes this holistic orientation.

43. Claude Lefort, "L'idée d'être brut et d'esprit sauvage," *Les Temps Modernes* 17, nos. 184–185 (October 1961): 275.

44. Ibid., 286.

45. Claude Lefort, "How Did You Become a Philosopher?" in Alan Montefiore, ed., *Philosophy in France Today* (Cambridge: Cambridge University Press, 1983), 90.

46. Marcel Gauchet, "Freud et après," in *La condition historique*, 174.

47. Slavoj Žižek, "The Society for Theoretical Psychoanalysis in Yugoslavia: An Interview with Éric Laurent," in Rex Butler and Scott Stephens, eds., *Interrogating the Real* (New York: Continuum, 2008), 21.

48. Numerous commentators have remarked upon Merleau-Ponty's interest in psychoanalysis, including Gauchet in "Freud et après," 175. As Gauchet notes, it was within Merleau-Ponty's circle that Lacan and Lefort came to know each other personally. Samuel Moyn explores these relations in greater detail in his forthcoming *A New Theory of Politics*. I am grateful to him for sharing a draft of chapter 1.

49. See Lefort, "Permanence of the Theologico-Political?" 219. In this context, the most relevant works by Piera Aulagnier are *La Violence de l'Interprétation* (Paris: Presses Universitaires de France, 1975) and *Un interprète en quête de sens* (Paris: Payot, 1986). Aulagnier has not yet attracted much scholarly attention, despite her importance in the recent history of French psychoanalysis. For useful discussions, see Hélène Troisier, *Piera Aulagnier* (Paris: Presses Universitaires de France, 1998); and *Topique: Revue Freudienne* 39, no. 74 (2001), an issue dedicated to her in the journal she founded.

50. See Howard, *The Specter of Democracy*, 303, note 14.

51. Poltiers, *Passion du politique*, 187.

52. Claude Lefort, "La politique et la pensée de la politique," *Les Lettres Nouvelles*, no. 32 (1963): 19–70

53. Claude Lefort, *Le Travail de l'oeuvre: Machiavel* (Paris: Gallimard, 1972).

54. Oliver Marchart formulates this view well in *Post-Foundational Political Thought: Political Difference in Nancy, Lefort, Badiou, and Laclau* (Edinburgh: Edinburgh University Press, 2007), 93: "The role of power is precisely to institute society by *signifying* social identity—and only by relating to this representation/signification of identity can people relate to the space in which they live as a coherent ensemble."

55. Hent de Vries, "'Miracle of Love' and the Turn to Democracy," *New Centennial Review* 8, no. 3 (2009): 244.

56. See Lefort quoted in Dick Howard, *The Marxian Legacy*, 2d edition (Minneapolis: University of Minnesota Press, 1988), 221.

57. Claude Lefort, "Outline of the Genesis of Ideology in Modern Societies," in John B. Thompson, ed., *Political Forms of Modernity: Bureaucracy, Democracy, Totalitarianism* (Cambridge: MIT Press, 1986), 194.

58. Ibid., 194.

59. The quote comes from Poltier, *Passion du politique*, 184; see also Flynn, *The Philosophy of Claude Lefort*, 84–86.

60. Lefort, "Permanence of the Theologico-Political?" 222.

61. Lefort, "Le Mythe de l'Un dans le Fantasme et dans la Réalité Politique," *Psychanalystes: Revue du College de Psychanalystes* 9 (October 1983): 41.

62. Claude Lefort, "L'Échange et la lutte des hommes," *Les Temps Modernes* 6, no. 64 (February 1951): 1400.

63. Ibid., 1402. Dosse claims that "both the proclamation of a program [in Lévi-Strauss's *Introduction to the Work of Marcel Mauss*] and Claude Lefort's critiques provided the rational kernel for all the debates and polemics that developed in the fifties and sixties around the structuralist banquet." François Dosse, *History of Structuralism*, vol. 1: *The Rising Sign, 1945–1966*, trans. Deborah Glassman (Minneapolis: University of Minnesota Press, 1997), 31.

64. Claude Lefort, "Société 'sans historie' et historicité," *Cahiers internationaux de sociologie* 12 (July 1952): 97.

65. Ibid., 110–111. The term *mise en forme* appears on pages 95 and 108.

66. Maurice Merleau-Ponty, *L'Institution dans l'histoire personnelle et publique: Le problème de la passivité. Le sommeil, l'inconscient, la mémoire. Notes de cours au Collège de France (1954–1955)* (Paris: Belin, 2003).

67. Poltiers, *Passion du politique*, 184.

68. For an account that too readily equates Lefort's and Lacan's concepts of the symbolic, see Saul Newman, "The Place of Power in Political Discourse," *International Political Science Review* 25, no. 2 (2004), especially 150.

69. Slavoj Žižek, *For They Know Not What They Do: Enjoyment as a Political Factor*, 2d ed. (London: Verso, 2002), 276, note 52.

70. Lefort, "Permanence of the Theologico-Political?" 222.

71. Flynn, *The Philosophy of Claude Lefort*, 124.

72. Ibid., 125.

73. Howard, *The Marxian Legacy*, 212.

74. Lefort cited in Flynn, *Political Philosophy at the Closure of Metaphysics*, 188–189.

75. Lefort, "Permanence of the Theologico-Political?" 222.

76. Ibid., 224.

77. See Julian Bourg, *From Revolution to Ethics: May 1968 and Contemporary French Thought* (Montreal: McGill-Queen's University Press, 2007), chapters 21–23.

78. Derrida, *Specters of Marx*, 75.

79. Report from Séminaire "politique," July 23–August 2 1980, *Les fins de l'homme: À partir du travail de Jacques Derrida* (Paris: Galilée, 1981), 527.

80. John Caputo, *The Prayers and Tears of Jacques Derrida: Religion Without Religion* (Bloomington: Indiana University Press, 1997), 117.

81. Jacques Derrida, "Of an Apocalyptic Tone Recently Adopted in Philosophy," *Semeia* 23 (1982): 80.

82. In addition to Caputo, see Harold Coward and Toby Foshay, ed., *Derrida and Negative Theology* (Albany: State University of New York Press, 1992); and Kevin Hart, "Jacques Derrida: The God Effect," in *Post-Secular Philosophy: Between Philosophy and Theology*, ed. Phillip Blond (New York: Routledge, 1998), 259–280.

83. On Derrida's relationship to Benjamin, see the subtle discussion in Hent de Vries, *Religion and Violence: Philosophical Perspectives from Kant to Derrida* (Baltimore: Johns Hopkins University Press, 2002), esp. 266–87.

84. Caputo, *Prayers and Tears*, 136.

85. Derrida, *Specters of Marx*, 75.

86. Hent De Vries, *Philosophy and the Turn to Religion* (Baltimore: Johns Hopkins University Press, 1999), 24.

87. Derrida, "Faith and Knowledge: The Two Sources of 'Religion' at the Limits of Reason Alone," *Religion*, 25–26. See Schmitt, *Political Theology. Four Chapters on the Concept of Sovereignty*, trans. George Schwab (Cambridge: MIT Press, 1988) 36. For a subtle, albeit strongly Derridean discussion of the differences between Derrida and Schmitt, see De Vries, *Religion and Violence*, esp. 353–70.

88. Lefort, "The Death of Immortality?" in *Democracy and Political Theory*, 274. Ironically, Lenin railed against Christianity's "corpse-worship" in a 1913 letter to Maxim Gorki reprinted in *Lapham's Quarterly* 3, no. 1 (Winter 2010): 38.

89. Ernst Kantorowicz, *The King's Two Bodies: A Study in Medieval Political Theology* (Princeton: Princeton University Press, 1957). Both Lefort and Gauchet played an important role in Kantorowicz's reception in France, where people have tended to read him not only as historian but also as a political theorist. For example, Gauchet acknowledged that even though Kantorowicz only cursorily recognized the relevance of the theologico-political doubling of the king's body for the modern myth of the state, nonetheless his book offers a "veritable red thread of the history of political representations in Europe." See Marcel Gauchet, "Des deux corps du roi au pouvoir sans corps: Christianisme et politique," *Le Débat*, no. 14 (July-August 1981): 136. On Kantorowicz's reception among

French medievalists, see Alain Bourreau, *Kantorowicz: Stories of a Historian*, trans. Stephen G. Nichols and Gabrielle M. Spiegel (Baltimore: Johns Hopkins University Press, 2001).

90. Flynn, *The Political Philosophy of Claude Lefort*, 126.

91. Lefort, "Permanence of the Theologico-Political?" 225.

92. Claude Lefort, "Reversibility: Political Freedom and the Freedom of the Individual," in *Democracy and Political Theory*, 169.

93. Lefort, "Permanence of the Theologico-Political?" 255.

94. Claude Lefort, "The Image of the Body and Totalitarianism," in John Thompson, ed., *The Political Forms of Modern Society: Bureaucracy, Democracy, Totalitarianism* (Cambridge: MIT Press, 1986), 304.

95. Ibid., 306.

96. See Susan Dunn, *The Deaths of Louis XVI: Regicide and the French Political Imagination* (Princeton: Princeton University Press, 1994). Dunn ends her study with Albert Camus, but the polyvalent meaning of regicide seems to continue in Lefort, not to mention figures like Jean-Luc Nancy and Michel Foucault.

97. Lefort, "Permanence of the Theologico-Political?" 255.

98. I advanced this argument in "Democracy Between Disenchantment and Political Theology: French Post-Marxism and the Return of Religion," *New German Critique*, no. 94 (Winter 2005): 94–95. More recently, a similar observation may be found in Camille Tarot, *Le Symbolique et le sacré: Théories de la religion* (Paris: Découverte, 2008), 608–609.

99. My emphasis on the tensions between these three figures contrasts with the depiction of a harmoniously unfolding refinement of a single theory from Castoriadis to Lefort to Gauchet in Natalie Doyle, "Democracy as Sociocultural Project of Individual and Collective Sovereignty: Claude Lefort, Marcel Gauchet, and the French Debate on Modern Autonomy," *Thesis Eleven* 75 (November 2003): 69–95.

100. Marcel Gauchet, "Un parcours, une generation," *La condition historique*, 22–27.

101. Ibid., 23.

102. Ibid., 24. The interviews in *La condition historique* describe a growing distance between Gauchet and Lefort, beginning with tensions over this 1971 article, which Gauchet claims was mostly his creation and furnished Lefort with some of his key ideas about the political institution of society (see especially 160).

103. Gladys Swain and Marcel Gauchet's 1980 magnum opus is partially available in English as *Madness and Democracy: The Modern Psychiatric Universe*, trans. Catherine Porter (Princeton: Princeton University Press, 1999). Gauchet has consistently maintained that the histories of psychiatry, psychoanalysis, and neurophysiology are particularly sensitive registers of the modern upheaval in forms of subjectivity. This is a theme that will not be pursued here. For Gauchet's own description of these intersecting histories, see "The Democratic Malaise: An Interview with Marcel Gauchet," *Thesis Eleven* 38 (1994), especially 138–146. For a comprehensive assessment of this side of Gauchet's work, see Samuel Moyn, "The Assumption by Man of His Original Fracturing: Marcel Gauchet, Gladys Swain, and the History of the Self," *Modern Intellectual History* 6, no. 2 (2009): 315–341.

104. Marcel Gauchet, "La leçon de l'ethnologie," in *La condition historique*, 64.

105. On Clastres, see the special tribute issue of *Libre* 4 (1978); and Samuel Moyn, "Of Savagery and Civil Society: Pierre Clastres and the Transformation of French Political Thought," *Modern Intellectual History* 1, no. 1 (2004): 55–80.

106. Claude Lefort, "Dialogue with Pierre Clastres," in *Writing: The Political Test*, ed. and trans. David Ames Curtis (Durham: Duke University Press, 2000), 214.

107. Marcel Gauchet in Pierre Colin and Olivier Mongin, eds., *Un monde désenchanté: Débat avec Marcel Gauchet sur le désenchantement du monde* (Paris: CERF, 1988), 72.

108. Gauchet quoted in Samuel Moyn, "Savage and Modern Liberty: Marcel Gauchet and the Origins of New French Thought," *European Journal of Political Theory* 4, no. 2 (2005): 169. This paragraph draws quite heavily on Moyn's detailed account.

109. Gauchet, "La leçon de l'ethnologie," 70. As Behrent has noted, Gauchet's first published discussion of religion, in a 1971 article on monarchic sovereignty, treats it merely as an ideological tool for power. See Michael Behrent, "Religion, Republicanism, and Depoliticization: Two Intellectual Itineraries—Régis Debray and Marcel Gauchet," in Julian Bourg, ed., *After the Deluge* (Lanham, MD: Lexington, 2004), 331.

110. Gauchet, "La leçon de l'ethnologie," 75.

111. See Gauchet, *La Condition Politique* (Paris: Gallimard, 2005), 13.

112. Colin and Mongin, *Un monde désenchanté*.

113. Gauchet quoted in Behrent, "Religion, Republicanism, and Depoliticization," 329.

114. I am not alone in detecting this. See, for example, Geneviève Souillac, *Human Rights in Crisis: The Sacred and the Secular in Contemporary French Thought* (Lanham, MD: Lexington, 2005), chapter 1. In the interview that concludes Antoon Braeckman, ed., *La démocratie à bout de souffle? Une introduction critique à la philosophie politique de Marcel Gauchet* (Louvain: Peeters, 2007), Gauchet is asked whether his work is marked by a "certain Hegelianism" (153). Among the essays in the volume, see also André Cloots, "Marcel Gauchet et le désenchantement du monde: La place significative de la religion dans les transformations de la culture occidentale," 34.

115. See Marcel Gauchet, "La dette du sens et les racines de l'état: Politique et religion primitive," *Libre* 2 (1977): 10–11.

116. Marcel Gauchet, *The Disenchantment of the World: A Political History of Religion*, trans. Oscar Burge (Princeton: Princeton University Press, 1997), 25.

117. Gauchet here used the term introduced by Karl Jaspers to describe the transformations of the first millenium BC. See Jaspers, *Vom Ursprung und Ziel der Geschichte* (Zurich: Artemis, 1949). See also S. N. Eisenstadt, "The Axial Age: The Emergence of Transcendental Visions and the Rise of the Clerics," *Archives européennes de sociologie* 23 (1982): 294–314, and S. N. Eisenstadt, ed., *The Origins and Diversity of Axial Age Civilizations* (Albany: State University of New York, 1986).

118. Gauchet, *The Disenchantment of the World*, 51.

119. Ibid., 140.

120. Ibid., 142.

121. See Kantorowicz, *The King's Two Bodies*, 192f. on the secular *corpus mysticum* and 210f. on the "body politic."

122. Gauchet, *The Disenchantment of the World*, 143.

123. Ibid., 58–59.

124. Marcel Gauchet, "Le christianisme et la cité moderne: Discussion entre Marcel Gauchet et Pierre Manent," *Esprit* (April-May 1986): 99.

125. Cornelius Castoriadis, "Fait et à Faire," in *Fait et à Faire* (Paris: Seuil, 1997), 65, and "La démocratie comme procédure et comme régime," *La montée de l'insignifiance* (Paris: Seuil, 1996), 240. More generally, see "The Greek *Polis* and the Creation of Democracy," in *The Castoriadis Reader*, ed. and trans. David Ames Curtis (Oxford: Blackwell, 1997), 267–289, and "The Greek and the Modern Political Imaginary," in *World in Fragments: Writings on Politics, Society, Psychoanalysis, and the Imagination*, ed. and trans. David Ames Curtis (Stanford: Stanford University Press, 1997), 84–107.

126. Marc Augé, *Génie du paganisme* (Paris: Gallimard, 1982); Jean-François Lyotard, *Instructions paiennes* (Paris: Galilée, 1977). See, more generally, Martin Jay, "Modern and Postmodern Paganism: Peter Gay and Jean-Françoise Lyotard," in Mark S. Micale and Robert L. Diele, eds., *Enlightenment, Passion, Modernity: Historical Essays in European Thought and Culture* (Stanford: Stanford University Press, 2000), 249–262.

127. Johann Arnason weighs the merits of Castoriadis's autonomy model and Eisenstadt's Axiality (without mention of Gauchet) against the state of historical research in "Autonomy and Axiality: Comparative Perspectives on the Greek Breakthrough," in J. Arnason and P. Murphy, eds., *Agon, Logos, Polis: The Greek Achievement and Its Aftermath* (Stuttgart: Steiner, 2001), 155–206.

128. Marcel Gauchet, "Droits de l'homme," in F. Furet and M. Ozouf, eds., *Dictionnaire critique de la Révolution française (1780–1880)* (Paris: Flammarion, 1988), 685–695.

129. See Steve Kaplan, *Farewell, Revolution: The Historians' Feud* (Ithaca: Cornell University Press, 1995), 86.

130. I take the title of the lead essay in Furet's *Penser la Révolution française* (Paris: Gallimard, 1975).

131. Gauchet quoted in Behrent, "Religion, Republicanism, and Depoliticization," 337.

132. Marcel Gauchet, *La Religion dans la démocratie: Parcours de la laïcité* (Paris: Gallimard, 1998), 8.

133. Tarot, *Le Symbolique et le sacré*, 605–606.

134. See the exchanges between Marcel Gauchet and his interlocutors in "La sortie de la religion: Des totalitarismes aux droits de l'homme," in *La condition historique*, 317–335.

135. Gauchet, *La Religion dans la démocratie*, 16, and *La Démocratie contre elle-même* (Paris: Gallimard, 2002), xvii.

136. Marcel Gauchet works out his interpretation of the Third Republic in *L'avènement de la démocratie*, tome 2: *La crise du libéralisme, 1880–1914* (Paris: Gallimard, 2007). Volume 1 of *L'avènement de la démocratie* provides a general overview of the rise of democratic autonomy from roughly 1500 to 1900. Volume 3 focuses on the "short twentieth century." The

"real revolution" in that century of extremes, according to Gauchet, occurred not in communism or fascism, but rather in the democracies, which completed "the work of five centuries" by finally instituting a new form of "human organization." Consistent with Gauchet's anxious reading of this process, he cautions against celebrating this new form, which he warns is itself "fraught with problems." See Gauchet, *L'Avènement de la démocratie*, tome 3: *À l'épreuve des totalitarismes, 1914–1974* (Paris: Gallimard, 2010), 14. A concise recent formulation of Gauchet's interpretation of the decades since the 1970s may be found in the small book *La Démocratie d'une crise à l'autre* (Nantes: Defaut, 2007).

137. Gauchet, *La Religion dans la démocratie*, 65.

138. For Gauchet's discussion of Renouvier, see ibid., 47f.

139. Ibid., 65.

140. Ibid., 18–22.

141. Ibid., 45.

142. Ibid., 58.

143. See "Du religieux, de sa permanence et de la possibilité d'en sortir. Régis Debray, Marcel Gauchet: Un échange," *Le Débat* 127 (November–December 2003): 3–19.

144. Gauchet, *La Religion dans la démocratie*, 114.

145. Gauchet, "Ce que nous avons perdu avec la religion," *Diogène* 195 (July–September 2001): 314.

146. I pick up here on a formulation in Behrent, "Religion, Republicanism, and Depoliticization," 342.

147. Gauchet, "De *Textures* au *Débat*," 160.

148. Ibid., 161.

149. Ibid., 160.

150. Miguel Abensour, *Lettre d'un "révoltiste" à Marcel Gauchet converti à la "politique normale"* (Paris: Sens and Tonka, 2008), 10.

151. Abensour's major essay "'Démocratie sauvage' et 'principe d'anarchie'" is now available as an appendix in Miguel Abensour, *Democracy Against the State: Marx and the Machiavellian Moment*, trans. Max Blechman (Cambridge: Polity, 2011), 102–124.

152. Abensour, *Lettre d'un "révoltiste,"* 12–13.

153. James Ingram, "The Politics of Claude Lefort's Political: Between Liberalism and Radical Democracy," *Thesis Eleven* 87 (November 2006): 33–50.

154. Ibid., 34.

5. The Post-Marx of the Letter

1. Louis Althusser, "The Crisis of Marxism," in *Power and Opposition in Post-Revolutionary Societies*, trans. P. Camiller (London: Ink Links, 1979), 225.

2. Fredric Jameson, *Late Marxism: Adorno, or, The Persistence of the Dialectic* (New York: Verso, 1990), 5.

3. Jacques Lacan, "Seminar on 'The Purloined Letter,'" in *Écrits*, trans. Bruce Fink (New York: Norton, 2006), 30.

4. See Ernesto Laclau and Chantal Mouffe, "Post-Marxism Without Apologies," in Ernesto Laclau, ed., *New Reflections on the Revolutions of Our Time* (London: Verso, 1990), 97–132.

5. See Malachi Hacohen, "The Limits of the National Paradigm in the Study of Political Thought: The Case of Karl Popper and Central European Cosmopolitanism," in Dario Castiglione and Iain Hampsher-Monk, eds., *The History of Political Thought in National Context* (Cambridge: Cambridge University Press, 2001), 247–279.

6. Jacques Derrida, *Specters of Marx: The State of the Debt, the Work of Mourning, and the New International*, trans. Peggy Kamuf (New York: Routledge, 1994), 14.

7. Ernesto Laclau, "Theory, Democracy, and Socialism," in Laclau, *New Reflections*, 236.

8. Ernesto Laclau and Chantal Mouffe, *Hegemony and Socialist Strategy: Towards a Radical Democratic Politics* (New York: Verso, 1985), 67.

9. Ibid., 71.

10. Ian Angus, "An Interview with Chantal Mouffe and Ernesto Laclau," in *Conflicting Publics* (1999), http://www.english.ilstu.edu/Strickland/495/laclau2.html (last accessed August 6, 2012).

11. Ibid.

12. Ernesto Laclau, "Building a New Left," in Laclau, *New Reflections*, 178–179.

13. Ibid., 178.

14. For discussions, see Don Forgacs, "Gramsci and Marxism in Britain," *New Left Review* 176 (1989): 70–88; Dennis Dworkin, *Cultural Marxism in Postwar Britain: History, the New Left, and the Origins of Cultural Studies* (Durham: Duke University Press, 1997); Lin Chun, *The British New Left* (Edinburgh: Edinburgh University Press, 1993).

15. See Leonardo Paggi, *Le strategie del potere in Gramsci: Tra fascismo e socialism in un solo paese, 1923–1926* (Rome: Riuniti, 1984); Christine Buci-Glucksmann, *Gramsci and the State*, trans. David Fernbach (London: Lawrence and Wishart, 1980).

16. Chantal Mouffe and Anne Showstack Sassoon, "Gramsci in France and Italy—A Review of the Literature," *Economy and Society* 6 (1977): 53.

17. Chantal Mouffe, ed., *Gramsci and Marxist Theory* (London: Routledge, 1977), 1.

18. Dworkin, *Cultural Marxism*, 232–233.

19. Geoff Eley, *Forging Democracy: The History of the Left in Europe, 1850–2000* (New York: Oxford University Press, 2002), 461.

20. Laclau and Mouffe, *Hegemony and Socialist Strategy*, 120.

21. Ibid., 112.

22. Ibid., 111.

23. Ibid., 129.

24. Ibid., 141.

25. Laclau and Mouffe translate *point de capiton* as "nodal point," but Žižek's term *quilting point* better conveys Lacan's image of upholstery gathered and anchored by a button.

26. Ibid., 112–113.

27. Ibid., 115 and 121.

28. Ibid., 126.

29. Laclau, "Theory, Democracy, and Socialism," 210.

30. Edward P. Thompson, *The Poverty of Theory and Other Essays* (London: Merlin, 1978). On the heated debate provoked by *The Poverty of Theory*, see Dworkin, *Cultural Marxism*, 219–245, and, of course, Perry Anderson, *Arguments Within English Marxism* (New York: Verso, 1980).

31. Laclau and Mouffe, *Hegemony and Socialist Strategy*, 117.

32. Ibid., 116.

33. Martin Jay, "The Apocalyptic Imagination and the Inability to Mourn," in Gillian Robertson and John Rundell, eds., *Rethinking Imagination: Culture and Creativity* (New York: Routledge, 1994), 47, note 36.

34. Baudrillard quoted ibid., 35.

35. Ibid., 39.

36. Laclau, "Building a New Left," 179.

37. Derrida, *Specters of Marx*, 64

38. Derrida, "Marx & Sons," in Michael Sprinker, ed., *Ghostly Demarcations: A Symposium on Jacques Derrida's Specters of Marx* (New York: Verso, 1999), 259. Galilée published Derrida's text in French in 2002 with the same title.

39. Laclau, "New Reflections on the Revolution of Our Time," in Laclau, *New Reflections*, 83.

40. Ibid., 82.

41. Laclau, "Theory, Democracy, and Socialism," 236.

42. Derrida, *Specters of Marx*, 75.

43. Laclau, "New Reflections on the Revolution of Our Time," 83.

44. Laclau, "'The Time Is Out of Joint,'" in *Emancipation(s)* (New York: Verso, 1996), 77.

45. Ibid., 78.

46. Slavoj Žižek , *Did Somebody Say Totalitarianism? Five Interventions in the (Mis)use of a Notion* (New York: Verso, 2001), 141.

47. Ibid., 148.

48. Ibid., 154.

49. Laclau, "Building a New Left," 191.

50. Laclau, "'The Time Is Out of Joint,'" 70.

51. Derrida, *Specters of Marx*, 180, note 31.

52. Jean-Luc Nancy, *The Inoperative Community*, ed. Peter Connor (Minneapolis: University of Minnesota Press, 1991), 121. See also Philippe Lacoue-Labarthe and Jean-Luc Nancy, *Retreating the Political*, ed. Simon Sparks (New York: Routledge, 1997).

53. Lacoue-Labarthe, "'Political' Seminar," in Lacoue-Labarthe and Nancy, *Retreating the Political*, 98.

54. François Dosse, *History of Structuralism*, vol. 2: *The Sign Sets, 1967-Present*, trans. Deborah Glassman (Minneapolis: University of Minnesota Press, 1997), 164–178.

55. See Diana Pinto, "The Left, the Intellectuals, and Culture," in George Ross, Stanley Hoffmann, and Sylvia Malzacher, eds., *The Mitterrand Experiment: Continuity and Change in Modern France* (New York: Oxford University Press, 1987), 217–228.

56. See Natalie Doyle, "The End of a Political Identity: French Intellectuals and the State," *Thesis Eleven* 48, no. 1 (February 1997): 46.

57. Dosse, *History of Structuralism*, 2:274.

58. François Furet, *Interpreting the French Revolution*, trans. Elborg Forster (Cambridge: Cambridge University Press, 1981).

59. Steven Kaplan, *Farewell Revolution: The Historians' Feud* (Ithaca: Cornell University Press, 1995), 86.

60. Michel Foucault, *Politics Philosophy Culture: Interviews and Other Writings, 1977–1984*, ed. Lawrence Kritzman (New York: Routledge, 1988), 44.

61. Régis Debray, *Teachers, Writers, Celebrities: The Intellectuals of Modern France*, trans. David Macey (London: New Left, 1981), 87. For an interesting approach to the media cycle, see Tamara Chaplin, *Turning on the Mind: French Philosophers on Television* (Chicago: University of Chicago Press, 2007).

62. Foucault, *Politics Philosophy Culture*, 44–45.

63. Report from Séminaire "politique," July 23–August 2 1980, *Les fins de l'homme: À partir du travail de Jacques Derrida* (Paris: Galilée, 1981), 527.

64. Eric Hobsbawm, *Interesting Times: A Twentieth-Century Life* (New York: Pantheon, 2002), 335–336.

65. Ibid., 276.

66. Chun, *British New Left*, 109.

67. Dworkin, *Cultural Marxism*, 110–136. See also Chun, *British New Left*, 110–127.

68. Anderson quoted in Chun, *British New Left*, 124.

69. Antony Easthope, *British Post-Structuralism: Since 1968* (London: Routledge, 1991), xiii. A similar point about the American reception is made by Jean-Philippe Mathy, "The Resistance to French Theory in the United States: A Cross-Cultural Inquiry," *French Historical Studies* 2, no. 19 (Fall 1995): 331–347.

70. Easthope, *British Post-Structuralism*, xiii. The pioneering film studies journal *Screen* played a major role in this mediation. For a superb example of this British leftist appropriation of Lacan, see Rosalind Coward and John Ellis, *Language and Materialism: Developments in Semiology and the Theory of the Subject* (London: Routledge, 1977).

71. Anderson, *Arguments Within English Marxism*, 161.

72. See the remarks of Raymond Aron, *The Opium of the Intellectuals*, trans. Terence Kilmartin (New York: Doubleday, 1957), 219. This envy is a recurrent theme in Stefan Collini, *Absent Minds. Intellectuals in Britain* (Oxford: Oxford University, 2006), especially chapter 11.

73. See Norman Geras, "Ex-Marxism Without Substance: A Rejoinder," in *Discourses of Extremity: Radical Ethics and Post-Marxist Extravagances* (New York: Verso, 1990); and Ellen Meiksins Wood, *The Retreat from Class: A New 'True' Socialism* (New York: Verso, 1986).

74. See Jacob Torfing, *New Theories of Discourse. Laclau, Mouffe and Žižek* (Oxford: Blackwell, 1999), 15.

75. Laclau, "Theory, Democracy, and Socialism," 198.

76. Ibid., 200.

77. Pierre Bourdieu, *Homo Academicus* (Paris: Minuit, 1984); Michel Foucault, "Truth and Power," in *Power/Knowledge: Selected Interviews and Other Writings, 1972–1977*, ed. and trans. Colin Gordon (New York: Pantheon 1980); Julia Kristeva, "A New Type of Intellectual: The Dissident," in *The Kristeva Reader*, ed. Toril Moi (New York: Columbia University Press, 1986).

78. Laclau, "Building a New Left," 195.

79. Ibid., 196. The links to pragmatism are explicitly thematized in Simon Critchley, Jacques Derrida, Ernesto Laclau, and Richard Rorty, *Deconstruction and Pragmatism*, ed. Chantal Mouffe (New York: Routledge, 1996).

80. Laclau, "Building a New Left," 196.

81. See Laclau, "Theory, Democracy, and Socialism," 232.

82. Claude Lefort, "The Question of Democracy," in *Democracy and Political Theory*, trans. David Macey (Minneapolis: University of Minnesota Press, 1988), 19.

83. Claude Lefort, "How Did You Become a Philosopher?" in Alan Montefiore, ed., *Philosophy in France Today* (New York: Cambridge University Press, 1983), 91.

84. I take these examples from Eley, *Forging Democracy*, 463–467.

85. Laclau, "Building a New Left," 186.

86. Barthes quoted in Dick Hebdige, *Subculture: The Meaning of Style* (London: Metheun, 1979), 140.

87. Claude Lefort, "The Image of the Body and Totalitarianism," in John Thompson, ed., *The Political Forms of Modern Society: Bureaucracy, Democracy, Totalitarianism* (Cambridge: MIT Press, 1986), 305–306.

88. Slavoj Žižek, "Beyond Discourse-Analysis," in Laclau, *New Reflections*, 249–260.

89. Strikingly, despite Žižek's intense engagement with recent French thought and the fact that his first book, *Le Plus Sublime des hysteriques: Hegel Passe* (Paris: Point hors ligne, 1988), first appeared in French, his impact in France has been very limited. See Jagna Oltarzewska, " 'So much depends on circumstances'. Žižek in France," *Études Anglaises: Revue du Monde Anglophone* 58, no. 1 (January-March 2005): 53–67.

90. Žižek, "Beyond Discourse-Analysis," 249.

91. See, for example, Laclau, "Building a New Left," 180.

92. Ernesto Laclau, "Preface," in Slavoj Žižek, *The Sublime Object of Ideology* (New York: Verso, 1989), xii.

93. Laclau and Mouffe, *Hegemony and Socialist Strategy*, 126.

94. See especially Louis Althusser, "Ideology and Ideological State Apparatuses," in *Lenin and Philosophy and Other Essays*, trans. Ben Brewster (New York: Monthly Review Press, 1971). For an excellent critique of Althusser's use of Lacan, see Joseph Valente, "Lacan's Marxism, Marxism's Lacan (from Žižek to Althusser)," in Jean-Michel Rabaté, ed., *Cambridge Companion to Lacan* (New York: Cambridge University Press, 2003), 153–172. See also Elizabeth J. Bellamy, "Discourses of Impossibility: Can Psychoanalysis Be Political?" *Diacritics* 1, no. 23 (Spring 1993): 28–29.

95. Laclau describes the concept of "subject positions" as "our immediate prehistory," a "subtle temptation [that] haunted the intellectual imaginary of the Left for a while," in "Universalism, Particularism, and the Question of Identity," in *Emancipation(s)*, 20.

96. Žižek, *The Sublime Object of Ideology*, 2–3

97. For particularly clear versions of this account, see Slavoj Žižek, *The Metastases of Enjoyment: Six Essays on Woman and Causality* (New York: Verso, 1994), 29; and *The Indivisible Remainder: An Essay on Schelling and Related Matters* (New York: Verso, 1996), 94f. In thus periodizing Lacan's career, Žižek draws heavily on Jacques-Alain Miller. See Geoffrey Galt Harpham, "Doing the Impossible: Slavoj Žižek and the End of Knowledge," *Critical Inquiry* 29 (Spring 2003): 457, note 3. Žižek discusses the impact of Miller on his thought in "Opening the Space of Philosophy," in Slavoj Žižek and Glyn Daly, *Conversations with Žižek* (Cambridge: Polity, 2004), 33–34.

98. Žižek, *The Sublime Object of Ideology*, 133.

99. Althusser, "Ideology and Ideological State Apparatuses," 180.

100. Žižek, *The Sublime Object of Ideology*, 133.

101. Ibid., 75.

102. Ibid., 44.

103. Ibid., 43.

104. Ibid., 122.

105. See, for example, Laclau and Mouffe, *Hegemony and Socialist Strategy*, 125.

106. Žižek, "Beyond Discourse-Analysis," 251.

107. Žižek, *The Sublime Object of Ideology*, 252.

108. Ibid., 253. This criticism persists in Žižek's later work. See, for example, Slavoj Žižek, *The Ticklish Subject: The Absent Centre of Political Ontology* (New York: Verso, 1999), 171–172; and the dialogue between Žižek, Judith Butler, and Ernesto Laclau, in Judith Butler, Ernesto Laclau, and Slavoj Žižek, *Contingency, Hegemony, Universality: Contemporary Dialogues on the Left* (New York: Verso, 2000), 171–172.

109. Žižek, "Beyond Discourse-Analysis," 254.

110. See Laclau, "Theory, Democracy, and Socialism," 235, and *Contingency, Hegemony, Universality*, 77. See, further, Yannis Stavrakakis, *The Lacanian Left: Psychoanalysis, Theory, Politics* (Albany: State University of New York Press, 2007), 67.

111. For an illuminating overview of Mouffe's ideas, see Nico Carpentier and Bart Cammaerts, "Hegemony, Democracy, Agonism, and Journalism: An Interview with Chantal Mouffe," *Journalism Studies* 7, no. 6 (2006): 964–975.

112. Laclau and Mouffe, *Hegemony and Socialist Strategy*, 57, 191–192.

113. Laclau, in Butler, Laclau, and Žižek, *Contingency, Hegemony, Universality*, 86.

114. A sharp contrast between the projects of Mouffe and Laclau is drawn in Mark Anthony Wenman, "Laclau or Mouffe? Splitting the Difference," *Philosophy and Social Criticism* 29, no. 5 (2003): 581–606. While Wenman's careful differentiation of Laclau and Mouffe's positions, even within the pages of *Hegemony and Socialist Strategy*, is illuminating, he overstates the differences. Wenman argues that, although Mouffe pursues a laudable pluralism, Laclau succumbs to the fantasy of totality, which leads to a theory that violates

personal freedom (601). We will examine Laclau in detail in the next chapter, but, with regard to Mouffe, it can be said that the logic of equivalences remains central to Mouffe, as does her partisan preference for certain kinds of social struggles. Indeed, Wenman's emphasis on value pluralism downplays the conflictual and agonistic nature of Mouffe's democratic theory.

115. Žižek, *The Sublime Object of Ideology*, 148–149.

6. Of Empty Places

1. Slavoj Žižek, "The Society for Theoretical Psychoanalysis in Yugoslavia: An Interview with Éric Laurent [1985]," in Rex Butler and Scott Stephens, eds., *Interrogating the Real* (New York: Continuum, 2005), 21.

2. Slavoj Žižek, "Beyond Discourse-Analysis," in Ernesto Laclau, *New Reflections on the Revolution of Our Time* (New York: Verso, 1990), 251.

3. Slavoj Žižek, *The Sublime Object of Ideology* (New York: Verso, 1989), 6–7.

4. Slavoj Žižek, "Slavoj Žižek Interview," in A. Long and T. McGunn, *Journal for the Psychoanalysis of Culture and Society* 2, no. 2 (1997): 133.

5. Ernesto Laclau, in Judith Butler, Ernesto Laclau, and Slavoj Žižek, *Contingency, Hegemony, Universality: Contemporary Dialogues on the Left* (New York: Verso, 2000), 281.

6. Žižek, ibid., 223, 326.

7. Laclau, ibid., 289; see also Ernesto Laclau, *On Populist Reason* (New York: Verso, 2005), 232–239, and "Glimpsing the Future," in Simon Critchley and Oliver Marchart, eds., *Laclau: A Critical Reader* (New York: Routledge, 2004), 314–315.

8. Ernesto Laclau, "Preface," in Žižek, *The Sublime Object of Ideology*, xii.

9. See especially Ian Parker, *Slavoj Žižek: A Critical Introduction* (London: Pluto, 2004), 83; Thomas Brockelman, "The Failure of the Radical Democratic Imaginary: Žižek Versus Laclau and Mouffe on Vestigial Utopia," *Philosophy and Social Criticism* 29, no. 2 (2003): 183–208; Linda Zerelli, "This Universalism Which Is Not One," in Critchley and Marchart, *Laclau: A Critical Reader*, 98.

10. Laclau, in Butler, Laclau, and Žižek, *Contingency, Hegemony, Universality*, 289.

11. Slavoj Žižek, *For They Know Not What They Do: Enjoyment as a Political Factor*, 2d ed. (London: Verso, 2002), 3; see more generally, M. Kovac, "The Slovene Spring," *New Left Review* 1, no. 171 (1988): 115–128.

12. Parker, *Slavoj Žižek*, 34.

13. See Slavoj Žižek, "Opening the Space of Philosophy," in Glyn Daly and Slavoj Žižek, *Conversations with Žižek* (Cambridge: Polity, 2004), 28.

14. An interview that Žižek gave to the journal *Ornicar?* in 1986–87 suggests an active and even hieratically organized society. See Žižek, "The Society for Theoretical Psychoanalysis in Yugoslavia," 21–25. By contrast, in conversation with Glyn Daly, Žižek paints a picture of a chaotic, improvised grouping that was little more than a front for Žižek and some of his friends. See Žižek, "Opening the Space for Philosophy," 36–37.

15. Žižek, in Butler and Stephens, *Interrogating the Real*, 21. The comment includes a reference to Claude Lefort's *L'Invention démocratique: Les limites de la domination totalitaire* (Paris: Fayard, 1981).

16. Žižek, *The Sublime Object of Ideology*, 72.

17. Žižek, *For They Know Not*, 88. The following discussion compresses my treatment of this subject in Warren Breckman, "The Return of the King: Hegelianism and Postmarxism in Zizek and Nancy," in Warren Breckman, Peter E. Gordon, Dirk Moses, Samuel Moyn, and Elliot Neaman, eds., *The Modernist Imagination: Essays in Intellectual and Cultural History* (New York: Berghahn, 2009). A shorter version appears as "Die Rückkehr des Königs: Radikaldemokratische Adaptionen eines hegelianischen Motivs bei Jean-Luc Nancy und Slavoj Zizek," in Ulrich Johannes Schneider, ed., *Der französische Hegel* (Berlin: Akademie, 2007), 205–218.

18. Žižek, *For They Know Not*, 196.

19. A more orthodox interpretation would likely suggest, as Taylor does, that the concrete universal is the "manifestation of the necessity contained in the idea concerned, and it is moreover a necessary manifestation, that is, [it] can be seen as posited by [the idea]." See Charles Taylor, *Hegel* (Cambridge: Cambridge University Press, 1975), 113.

20. Žižek, *For They Know Not*, 82.

21. Hegel quoted ibid., 82

22. Ibid., 83.

23. Žižek, *The Sublime Object of Ideology*, 44.

24. Ibid., 183.

25. Žižek, *For They Know Not*, 189.

26. Given this perspective, it is not surprising that Žižek would eventually argue that the "true politico-philosophical heirs of Hegel are authors who fully endorse the political logic of the excess constitutive of every established Order," chief among them Carl Schmitt. See Slavoj Žižek, *The Ticklish Subject: The Absent Centre of Political Ontology* (New York: Verso, 1999), 113.

27. Žižek, *For They Know Not*, 189.

28. Ibid., 260.

29. Ibid., 256.

30. Slavoj Žižek, *Tarrying with the Negative: Kant, Hegel, and the Critique of Ideology* (Durham: Duke University Press, 1993), 1–2.

31. Slavoj Žižek, *The Plague of Fantasies* (New York: Verso, 1997), 48.

32. Slavoj Žižek, "Eastern Europe's Republics of Gilead," *New Left Review*, 1, no. 183 (September-October 1990): 62. Žižek's insistence on an alienated state diverged not only from the civil society dissidents but also from the classical Marxist idea that communism overcomes the separation of state and society. On the latter, see Paul Thomas, *Alien Politics: Marxist State Theory Retrieved* (New York: Routledge, 1994).

33. Žižek, *For They Know Not*, 268–269.

34. There has been substantial controversy over the extent to which Hegel's monarch really is rendered powerless. For the debate among Hegel's contemporaries, see Warren Breckman, *Marx, the Young Hegelians and the Origins of Radical Social Theory: Dethroning*

the Self (Cambridge: Cambridge University Press, 1999). For one instance of the debate in the twentieth century, contrast Eric Weil, *Hegel et l'État* (Paris: Vrin, 1950) to Bernard Bourgeois, *Études hégéliennes: Raison et décision* (Paris: Presses universitaires de France, 1992), especially chapter 4.

35. Žižek, *For They Know Not*, 269.

36. See, for example, Žižek, *Tarrying with the Negative*, 211–212. Žižek here repeats phrasing from the conclusion of his essay "Eastern Europe's Republics of Gilead," 62.

37. Slavoj Žižek, "Formal Democracy and Its Discontents," in *Looking Awry: An Introduction to Jacques Lacan Through Popular Culture* (Cambridge: MIT Press, 1991), 168.

38. Žižek, *For They Know Not*, xviii.

39. Geoffrey Galt Harpham, "Doing the Impossible: Slavoj Žižek and the End of Knowledge," *Critical Inquiry* 29, no. 3 (Spring 2003): 453.

40. See Žižek, "Opening the Space of Philosophy," 28–30.

41. Parker, *Slavoj Žižek*, 115.

42. Sarah Kay, *Žižek: A Critical Introduction* (Cambridge: Polity, 2003).

43. Rex Butler and Scott Stephens, "Play Fuckin' Loud: Žižek Versus the Left," *Symptom: Online Journal for Lacan.com*, 2007, http://www.lacan.com/symptom7articles/ butler .html (last accessed June 20, 2012).

44. Rex Butler, *Slavoj Žižek: Live Theory* (New York: Continuum, 2006); Jodi Dean, *Žižek's Politics* (New York: Routledge, 2006).

45. The phrase is from Slavoj Žižek, "A Plea for Leninist Intolerance," *Critical Inquiry* 28, no. 2 (Winter 2002): 542–566.

46. Adam Kotsko, *Žižek and Theology* (New York: Clark, 2008), 5–8.

47. Here I have benefited from Adam Kotsko, ibid., 38–42; and Jodi Dean, "Žižek Against Democracy," *Law, Culture and the Humanities*, 1, no. 2 (June 2005): 154–177.

48. Žižek, *Tarrying with the Negative*, 232–236.

49. Jacques-Alain Miller quoted in Slavoj Žižek, *Iraq: The Borrowed Kettle* (London: Verso, 2004), 111.

50. Žižek, *Tarrying with the Negative*, 221. Žižek links the formalism of liberal democracy to the formalism of Kantian ethics, but this is a dimension I cannot explore.

51. Žižek, *For They Know Not*, 276, note 52; see also *Tarrying with the Negative*, 221.

52. "Opening the Space of Philosophy," 41.

53. Ernesto Laclau, "Theory, Democracy and Socialism," in Laclau, *New Reflections*, 219 and 229.

54. Karl Marx, "Contribution to the Critique of Hegel's Philosophy of Law: Introduction," in *Collected Works, 1843–1844* (New York: International, 1975), 3:175–187.

55. Laclau, *New Reflections*, and *Emancipation(s)* (New York: Verso, 1996).

56. Laclau, *Emancipation(s)*, 58.

57. This argument is scattered throughout Laclau's *New Reflections* and *Emancipation(s)*.

58. See Laclau, in Butler, Laclau, and Žižek, *Contingency, Hegemony, Universality*, 68, 58; see also Laclau, "Glimpsing the Future," 288.

59. See Laclau, "New Reflections on the Revolution of Our Time," in *New Reflections*, 63, and "Subject of Politics, Politics of the Subject," in *Emancipation(s)*, 53.

60. The centrality of Lacanian categories is taken for granted in Anna Marie Smith, *Laclau and Mouffe: The Radical Democratic Imaginary* (New York: Routledge, 1998); for a position arguing that certain key Lacanian concepts, particularly *jouissance*, are underdeveloped in Laclau's work, see Jason Glynos and Yannis Stavrakakis, "Encounters of the Real Kind: Sussing Out the Limits of Laclau's Embrace of Lacan," in Critchley and Marchart, *Laclau: A Critical Reader*, 201–216; and, more recently, Yannis Stavrakakis, *The Lacanian Left: Psychoanalysis, Theory, Politics* (Albany: SUNY Press, 2007), 66–108. Laclau challenges Glynos and Stavrakakis in "Glimpsing the Future," 298–304.

61. Ernesto Laclau, "Why Do Empty Signifiers Matter to Politics?" in *Emancipation(s)*, 40, see also "New Reflections on the Revolution of Our Time," 84, note 5.

62. Laclau, "Why Do Empty Signifiers Matter to Politics?" 40.

63. Ernesto Laclau, "Power and Representation," in *Emancipation(s)*, 90.

64. Ernesto Laclau and Chantal Mouffe, *Hegemony and Socialist Strategy: Towards a Radical Democratic Politics* (New York: Verso, 1985), 113.

65. Ernesto Laclau, "Universalism, Particularism and the Question of Identity," in *Emancipation(s)*, 28.

66. Ernesto Laclau, "Why Constructing a People Is the Main Task of Radical Politics," *Critical Inquiry*, 32, no. 4 (Summer, 2006): 647.

67. Laclau, "Why Do Empty Signifiers Matter to Politics?" 42.

68. Laclau, "Power and Representation," 103; he repeats this formulation in Butler, Laclau, and Žižek, *Contingency, Hegemony, Universality*, 211.

69. See, for example, Laclau, "New Reflections on the Revolution of Our Time," 64f.

70. Laclau, in Butler, Laclau, and Žižek, *Contingency, Hegemony, Universality*, 210.

71. Ibid., 211.

72. Laclau, "Power and Representation," 93, see also Laclau, in Butler, Laclau, and Žižek, *Contingency, Hegemony, Universality*, 85.

73. See also Laclau, "Glimpsing the Future," 291.

74. Slavoj Žižek, "Against the Populist Temptation," *Critical Inquiry*, 32, no. 3 (Spring 2006): 559.

75. Laclau, "Why Constructing a People," 675.

76. Laclau, *On Populist Reason*, 166.

77. Ernesto Laclau, "Democracy and the Question of Power," *Constellations* 8, no. 1 (March 2001): 12.

78. Žižek, *For They Know Not*, 276, note 52, see also *Tarrying with the Negative*, 221.

79. Žižek, *The Ticklish Subject*, 184.

80. Žižek, in Butler, Laclau, and Žižek, *Contingency, Hegemony, Universality*, 93, see also 258.

81. Ibid., 325.

82. See, for example, Slavoj Žižek, "Preface," in *The Žižek Reader*, ed. Elizabeth Wright and Edmond Wright (Oxford: Wiley-Blackwell, 1999), x.

83. Žižek, *The Ticklish Subject*, 355.

84. Ibid., 353–354.

85. Žižek, in Butler, Laclau, and Žižek, *Contingency, Hegemony, Universality*, 100.

86. Karl Marx, "On the Jewish Question," in *Collected Works*, 3:146–174.

87. The question of liberal democracy appears early in Žižek's work. See Žižek, *Tarrying with the Negative*, 221; see the more decisive formulation in Žižek, "Preface," x. The second quote comes from Slavoj Žižek, "The Rhetorics of Power," *diacritics* 31, no. 1 (Spring 2001): 96.

88. Žižek, *The Sublime Object of Ideology*, 72.

89. Žižek, *The Ticklish Subject*, 238.

90. Slavoj Žižek, *Did Somebody Say Totalitarianism? Five Interventions in the (Mis)use of a Notion* (London: Verso, 2001), 154.

91. Certainly, despite Laclau's own criticisms of Derrida, it must be said that Laclau's recent efforts to rebut the charge of Kantian formalism by insisting that politics is not the struggle to fill "a transcendentally established place, but the constant production and displacement of the place itself" within the immanent order of the "discursive structure" reinforce his ultimate proximity to poststructuralism. See Laclau, "Glimpsing the Future," 282–283. In that piece Laclau addresses not Žižek but Rodolphe Gasché, whose essay, "How Empty Can Empty Be? On the Place of the Universal," opens Critchley and Marchart, *Laclau: A Critical Reader*.

92. See *The Ticklish Subject*, 135

93. I have discussed this theme in "The Uses of '*Creatio ex nihilo*': On the Postmodern Revival of a Theological Trope," *Ideas in History* 4, no. 2 (2009): 39–61.

94. Slavoj Žižek, *On Belief* (New York: Routledge, 2001), 112.

95. Žižek, *For They Know Not*, 101, 217, see also *The Indivisible Remainder: An Essay on Schelling and Related Matters* (New York: Verso, 1996), which contains a section titled "Against Historicism."

96. Laclau, in Butler, Laclau, and Žižek, *Contingency, Hegemony, Universality*, 71. In contrast to Žižek, Laclau has not held these two terms firmly apart. See, for example, his discussion of "radical historicity" in "Building a New Left," 192.

97. Žižek, in Butler, Laclau, and Žižek, *Contingency, Hegemony, Universality*, 112.

98. Slavoj Žižek, "Introduction," in Slavoj Žižek, ed., *Revolution at the Gates: Žižek on Lenin, a Selection of Writings from February to October 1917* (New York: Verso, 2002), 4.

99. Laclau, in Butler, Laclau, and Žižek, *Contingency, Hegemony, Universality*, 207.

100. Žižek, ibid., 108.

101. Ibid., 325.

102. Ibid., 326.

103. Žižek, "Against the Populist Temptation," 564.

104. I borrow this formulation from Dean, "Žižek Against Democracy."

105. Žižek, in Butler, Laclau, and Žižek, *Contingency, Hegemony, Universality*, 257–258.

106. Slavoj Žižek, *The Parallax View* (Cambridge: MIT Press, 2006). The most penetrating study of this aspect of his thought is Adrian Johnston, *Žižek's Ontology: A Transcendental Materialist Theory of Subjectivity* (Evanston: Northwestern University Press, 2008).

107. Žižek, *The Indivisible Remainder*, 3.

108. Ibid., 32–33.

109. Schelling quoted in Žižek, *The Indivisible Remainder*, 21.

110. Ibid., 6; see also Žižek, "A Symptom—of What?" *Critical Inquiry*, 29, no. 3 (Spring 2003): 489.

111. Schelling quoted in Žižek, *The Indivisible Remainder*, 75.

112. Žižek repeats this point in *The Ticklish Subject*, 172, and in Butler, Laclau, and Žižek, *Contingency, Hegemony, Universality*, 92.

113. Slavoj Žižek, *Organs Without Bodies: Deleuze and Consequences* (New York: Routledge, 2004), 184; for an earlier formulation, see *Tarrying with the Negative*, especially 220.

114. Žižek, *The Ticklish Subject*, 187.

115. Kay, *Žižek*, 146.

116. Laclau, in Butler, Laclau, and Žižek, *Contingency, Hegemony, Universality*, 203.

117. Ibid., 205.

118. On oppositional determination, see Žižek, *Tarrying with the Negative*, 120; on the impossibility of directly embodying the universal, see especially *The Ticklish Subject*, 100–103; also in Butler, Laclau, and Žižek, *Contingency, Hegemony, Universality*, 316.

119. Žižek, in Butler, Laclau, and Žižek, *Contingency, Hegemony, Universality*, 320.

120. Laclau and Mouffe, *Hegemony and Socialist Strategy*, 116.

121. Žižek, *Revolution at the Gates*, 297–298.

122. Žižek, *On Belief*, 104.

123. Žižek, *The Ticklish Subject*, 159. See also *Tarrying with the Negative*, 171.

124. Dominiek Hoens and Ed Pluth, "The *sinthome*: A New Way of Writing an Old Problem?" in Luke Thurston, ed., *Re-Inventing the Symptom: Essays on the Final Lacan* (New York: Other Press, 2002), 13.

125. Žižek, *The Sublime Object of Ideology*, 75.

126. Hoens and Pluth, "The *sinthome*," 12.

127. Žižek, *The Sublime Object of Ideology*, 75.

128. R. Harari, "The *sinthome*: Turbulence and Dissipation," in Thurston, *Re-Inventing the Symptom*, 48. The Žižek reference comes from Stavrakakis, *The Lacanian Left*, 81.

129. Jamie Murray, "Sinthome Law: Theoretical Constructions Upon Lacan's Concept of the Sinthome," *Law and Critique*, 16, no. 2 (2005): 219–220.

130. The most extended discussion of this is found in Slavoj Žižek, "Does the Subject Have a Cause?" in *The Metastases of Enjoyment: Six Essays on Woman and Causality* (New York: Verso, 1994).

131. Žižek, *The Ticklish Subject*, 226.

132. See respectively, Parker, *Slavoj Žižek*, 78; Russell Grigg, "Absolute Freedom and Major Structural Change," *Paragraph* 24, no. 2 (2001): 118; Andrew Robinson and Simon Tormey, "A Ticklish Subject? Žižek and the Future of Left Radicalism," *Thesis Eleven*, 80, no. 1 (February 2005), 94–107. For an effort to rebut these worries, see Jodi Dean, *Žižek's Politics*, especially 184f.

133. This is implied by Žižek in a piece that criticizes Schmitt in terms reminiscent of his critique of Laclau and Mouffe's theory of antagonism. See Slavoj Žižek, "Carl Schmitt

in the Age of Post-Politics," in Chantal Mouffe, ed., *The Challenge of Carl Schmitt* (New York: Verso, 1999), especially 27f.

134. Žižek, *The Metastases of Enjoyment*, 39.

135. Žižek, in Butler, Laclau, and Žižek, *Contingency, Hegemony, Universality*, 119.

136. Žižek, *The Ticklish Subject*, 226. See Alain Badiou, *Saint Paul: The Foundation of Universalism*, trans. Ray Brassier (Stanford: Stanford University Press, 2003).

137. Žižek, *Revolution at the Gates*, 187.

138. Butler and Laclau, in Butler, Laclau, and Žižek, *Contingency, Hegemony, Universality*, 145, 289.

139. Slavoj Žižek, *The Fragile Absolute; or, Why Is the Christian Legacy Worth Fighting For?* (New York: Verso, 2000), *On Belief; The Puppet and the Dwarf: The Perverse Core of Christianity* (Cambridge: MIT Press, 2003).

140. On the periodization claim, see Kotsko, *Žižek and Theology*, 21; Žižek, *For They Know Not*, 29.

141. See Slavoj Žižek and Doug Henwood, "I Am a Fighting Atheist: Interview with Slavoj Žižek," *Bad Subjects* 59, http://eserver.org/bs/59/zizek.html (last accessed August 6, 2012).

142. Žižek, *For They Know Not*, xxix. See John Caputo, *The Prayers and Tears of Jacques Derrida: Religion Without Religion* (Bloomington: Indiana University Press, 1997).

143. Žižek, *For They Know Not*, xxix.

144. Žižek, *Tarrying with the Negative*, 2.

145. Žižek discusses this formula in many places. In my description I am drawing on Kotsko, *Žižek and Theology*, 49.

146. Kotsko focuses his discussion on the works of the early 2000s, but the "death of God" theme is present much earlier in Žižek's work, as in this quote from *Metastases of Enjoyment*, 46. See also *Tarrying with the Negative*, 170: "When God becomes man, he identifies with man qua suffering, sinful mortal. In this sense, the 'death of God' means that the subject verily finds himself alone, without any guarantee in substantial Reason, in the big Other."

147. Kotsko, *Žižek and Theology*, 83.

148. Žižek, *Tarrying with the Negative*, 170–71. Again, Kotsko's examples are all from the works of the early 2000s, but Žižek's invocation of the "Holy Spirit" also reaches back to his earlier works.

149. Kotsko, *Žižek and Theology*, 98.

150. Ibid., 95.

151. See chapter 2. See, generally, Warwick Gould and Marjorie Reeves, *Joachim of Fiore and the Myth of the Eternal Evangel in the Nineteenth and Twentieth Centuries*, 2d ed. (Oxford: Clarendon, 2001), 107.

152. Žižek, *Did Somebody Say Totalitarianism?* 152.

153. Ibid., 151.

154. Žižek, *The Fragile Absolute*, 121.

155. John Milbank, "Materialism and Transcendence," in Creston Davis, John Milbank and Slavoj Žižek, eds., *Theology and the Political: The New Debate* (Durham: Duke University Press, 2005), 399–400.

156. Žižek, *The Fragile Absolute*, 157.

157. Žižek, *The Ticklish Subject*, 160.

158. Ibid., 153–154.

159. Ibid., 237. This comes in a chapter that ends with yet another double contrast that pits Derrida's "hauntology" against Žižek's "ontology," Kant's regulative ideal against Hegel's concrete rational order. Yet, ironically, Žižek's formulation of the leader's relationship to his subject's squabbles resembles nothing so closely as Kant's paean to Frederick the Great in "What Is Enlightenment?"

160. Ibid., 237.

161. Slavoj Žižek, "Schlagend, aber nicht Treffend!" *Critical Inquiry*, 33, no. 1 (Autumn 2006): 210–211.

162. Žižek, *The Ticklish Subject*, 238.

163. Kay, *Žižek*, 126.

164. Žižek, "Preface," x.

165. Žižek, *Revolution at the Gates*, 11.

166. Ibid., 310.

167. Žižek, *The Ticklish Subject*, 162.

168. Žižek, *Iraq*, 83–84.

169. Žižek, *Did Somebody Say Totalitarianism?* 154; Žižek, "Resistance Is Surrender," *London Review of Books*, November 15, 2007.

170. Žižek, *On Belief*, 84. See also Žižek, in Butler, Laclau, and Žižek, *Contingency, Hegemony, Universality*, 326.

171. I draw these two examples from Stavrakakis, *The Lacanian Left*, 133.

172. Žižek, "Schlagend, aber nicht Treffend!" 193.

173. Žižek, *Revolution at the Gates*, 311.

174. Žižek, in Butler, Laclau, and Žižek, *Contingency, Hegemony, Universality*, 100.

175. Laclau, ibid., 199.

Epilogue

1. Fredric Jameson, *Valences of the Dialectic* (New York: Verso, 2009), 404.

2. Alain Badiou, *The Communist Hypothesis*, trans. David Macey and Steve Corcoran (New York: Verso, 2010), 258–259.

3. Jameson, *Valences of the Dialectic*, 408.

4. Claude Lefort, "The Permanence of the Theologico-Political?" *Democracy and Political Theory*, trans. David Macey (Minneapolis: University of Minnesota Press, 1988), 215.

5. See Miguel Abensour, "L'affaire Schelling: Une controverse entre Pierre Leroux et les jeunes hégéliens," in Patrice Vemeren, ed., "Victor Cousin suivi de la correspondance Schelling-Cousin," special issue, *Corpus*, nos. 18/19 (1991): 117–131, "Postface. Comment une philosophie de l'humanité peut-elle être une philosophie politique moderne?" in Pierre Leroux, *Aux philosophes, aux artistes, aux politiques: Trois discours et autres texts*, ed. Jean-Pierre Lacassagne (Paris: Payot, 1994), and *Le procès des maîtres rêveurs* (Arles: Sulliver, 2000).

6. Ernesto Laclau and Chantal Mouffe, *Hegemony and Socialist Strategy: Towards a Radical Democratic Politics* (New York: Verso, 1985), 42, note 5.

7. Jacques Rancière, *Disagreement: Politics and Philosophy*, trans. Julie Rose (Minneapolis: University of Minnesota Press, 1999), 55–60 (translation corrected).

8. Jacques Rancière, *Aesthetics and Its Discontents*, trans. Steven Corcoran (Cambridge: Polity, 2009), 24. See also the very useful article by Joseph J. Tanke, "Why Rancière Now?" *Journal of Aesthetic Education* 44, no. 2 (Summer 2010): 1–17.

9. See especially F. R. Ankersmit, *Sublime Historical Experience* (Stanford: Stanford University Press, 2005).

10. F. R. Ankersmit, *Aesthetic Politics: Political Philosophy Beyond Fact and Value* (Stanford: Stanford University Press, 1996), 48.

11. See the chapter "Romanticism, Postmodernism, and Democracy" ibid.

12. Craig Owens, "The Allegorical Impulse: Towards a Theory of Postmodernism," part 2, *October*, no. 13 (Summer 1980): 62.

13. Ibid., 82.

14. Ibid., 80.

15. Geoges Gusdorf quoted in Donald A. Kelley, *The Descent of Ideas: The History of Intellectual History* (Aldershot: Ashgate, 2002), 295.

16. Michel Foucault, "L'homme est-il mort?" *Dits et écrits*, vol. 1: *1954–1969*, ed. Daniel Defert and François Ewald (Paris: Gallimard, 1994), 542.

17. Jameson, *Valences of the Dialectic*, 4.

18. George Soros, *The Alchemy of Finance: Reading the Mind of the Market* (New York: Wiley, 1987).

19. David Harvey, "Postmodern Morality Plays," *Antipode* 24, no. 4 (1992): 316.

20. Jameson, "How Not to Historicize Theory," *Critical Inquiry* 34, no. 3 (Spring 2008): 577.

21. Jameson, *Valences of the Dialectic*, 405.

22. Norman Geras, "Post-Marxism?" *New Left Review* 1, no. 163 (May-June 1987): 56.

23. Moishe Postone, "History and Helplessness: Mass Mobilization and Contemporary Forms of Anticapitalism," *Public Culture* 18, no. 1 (2006): 95.

24. Jacques Rancière, "Communists Without Communism?" in Costas Douzinas and Slavoj Žižek, eds., *The Idea of Communism* (New York: Verso, 2010), 174.

25. Dick Howard, *The Specter of Democracy* (New York: Columbia University Press, 2002), 5.

26. Among David Harvey's many works, see, most recently, *The Enigma of Capital and the Crises of Capitalism* (Oxford: Oxford University Press, 2010). Chris Harman, *Zombie Capitalism: Global Crisis and the Relevance of Marx* (Chicago: Haymarket, 2010).

27. See the survey of such work in the final chapter of Göran Therborn, *From Marxism to Post-Marxism?* (New York: Verso, 2008).

28. Jameson, *Valences of the Dialectic*, 380.

29. See the spirited text by Terry Eagleton, *Why Marx Was Right* (New Haven: Yale University Press, 2011), especially 177.

30. Jameson, *Valences of the Dialectic*, 409.

31. Douglas Kellner, "The Obsolescence of Marxism?" in Bernd Magnus and Stephen Cullenberg, eds., *Whither Marxism? Global Crises in International Perpspective* (New York: Routledge, 1995), 26.

32. Stuart Sim, *Post-Marxism: An Intellectual History* (New York: Routledge, 2000), 164.

33. Cornelius Castoriadis, "The Crisis of Marxism, The Crisis of Politics," *Dissent* (Spring 1992): 221.

34. Of course, within the history of twentieth-century Marxism, there was a lively debate over the question of totalizing theory. The classic analysis is Martin Jay, *Marxism and Totality: The Adventures of a Concept from Lukács to Habermas* (Berkeley: University of California Press, 1984).

35. Slavoj Žižek, "Afterword to the Paperback Edition," in *Living in the End Times* (New York: Verso, 2011), 473.

36. Douzinas and Žižek, *The Idea of Communism*. See also Bruno Bosteels, *The Actuality of Communism* (New York: Verso, 2011).

37. Pierre Badiou, *De quoi Sarkozy est-il le nom?* (Paris: Nouvelles Éditions Lignes, 2007), *The Meaning of Sarkozy* (New York: Verso, 2010), and *The Communist Hypothesis*.

38. Badiou, *The Communist Hypothesis*, 235–236.

39. Badiou, "The Communist Hypothesis," *New Left Review*, no. 49 (January-February 2008): 37.

40. Badiou quoted in Daniel Bensaïd, "Permanent Scandal," in *Democracy in What State?* trans. William McCuaig (New York: Columbia University Press, 2011), 23.

41. Badiou writes of the communist hypothesis that "it is in fact mainly negative, as it is safer and more important to say that the existing world is not *necessary* than it is to say, when we have nothing to go on, that a different world is possible." See Badiou, *The Communist Hypotheis*, 64.

42. Ibid., 35.

43. Ibid., 250.

44. Ibid., 246.

45. Ibid., 35.

46. See, for example, Žižek, "Afterword to the Paperback Edition," in *Living in the End Times*, 475.

47. See ibid., 473; and Žižek, "How to Begin from the Beginning," in Douzinas and Žižek, *The Idea of Communism*, 211.

48. Bosteels reports that at a 2009 conference in London on the idea of communism, Žižek was almost entirely alone in his statism (Bosteels, *The Actuality of Communism*, 223). To be fair, Žižek insists that "the true task is to make the state itself work in a non-statal mode." That remark, however, prompts me to recall an anecdote from Castoriadis. When he heard a conference participant call for the debureaucratization of the state, Castoriadis retorted we might as well try to demilitarize the army.

49. Žižek, *Living in the End Times*, 200.

50. Žižek, "How to Begin from the Beginning," 198.

51. Slavoj Žižek, *First as Tragedy, Then as Farce* (New York: Verso, 2009), 130.

52. Slavoj Žižek, *In Defense of Lost Causes* (New York: Verso, 2008), 418–419.

53. One could track this out in various directions, including Žižek's vociferous critique of Simon Critchley's *Infinitely Demanding: Ethics of Commitment, Politics of Resistance* (New York: Verso, 2007), which argues for an anarchist politics that remains at a distance from state power. See Slavoj Žižek, "Resistance Is Surrender," *London Review of Books*, November 15, 2007.

54. Critchley, *Infinitely Demanding*, 118.

55. Bosteels, *The Actuality of Communism*, 51–52.

56. Žižek, "Afterword to the Paperback Edition," in *Living in the End Times*, 481.

57. Žižek, *Living in the End Times*, x.

58. Žižek quoted in Stuart Jeffries, "A Life in Writing: Slavoj Žižek," *Guardian.co.uk*, July 15, 2011, http://www.guardian.co.uk/culture/2011/jul/15/slavoj-zizek-interview-life-writing (last accessed July 28, 2011).

59. Badiou, *The Communist Hypothesis*, 63, 67.

60. Žižek, *Living in the End Times*, 446.

61. Kurt Andersen, "The Protester," *Time,* December 26, 2011/January 2, 2012, 58.

62. Occupy Wall Street's international connections are neatly summarized in Ishaan Tharoor, "Hands Across the World," in *What Is Occupy? Inside the Global Movement* (New York: Time, 2011), 25–33. The numbers for the global protest on October 15, 2011, come from Andy Kroll, "How Occupy Wall Street Really Got Started," in Sarah van Gelder and the staff of *Yes! Magazine*, eds., *This Changes Everything: Occupy Wall Street and the 99% Movement* (San Francisco: Berrett-Koehler, 2011) 21.

63. For a thoughtful and sympathetic consideration of the movement's prospects as of early 2012, see Michael Greenberg, "What Future for Occupy Wall Street?" *New York Review of Books* 59, no. 2 (February 9, 2012): 46–48.

64. Žižek's response to the Arab upheavals was positive and supportive, but also skewed toward his concerns. See, for example, "Why Fear the Arab Revolutionary Spirit?" *Guardian.co.uk*, July 15, 2011, http://www.guardian.co.uk/commentisfree/2011/feb/01/egypt-tunisia-revolt (last accessed August 8, 2011). For an interesting panel discussion that debates, among other things, the anticapitalist dimension of the Egyptian Revolution, see "Round Table 'Meaning of Maghreb'—Žižek, Habashi, Amin, Harvey, Bauman, 18th May 2011," Zagreb, Croatia, *Kasama*, http://kasamaproject.org/2011/07/12/zizek-habashi-amin-harvey-bauman-on-the-arab-spring/ (last accessed July 28, 2011).

65. Slavoj Žižek, "Don't Fall in Love with Yourselves," in Carla Blumenkranz, Keith Gessen, Mark Greif, Sarah Leonard, Sarah Resnick, Nikil Saval, Eli Schmitt, and Astra Taylor, eds., *Occupy: Scenes from Occupied America* (New York: Verso, 2011), 69. In the same volume, Jodi Dean likewise forces Occupy into the recently emerged language of the "communist hypothesis," describing the movement as the "expression of communist desire . . . a politics that asserts the people as a divisive force in the interest of over-turning present society and making a new one anchored in collectivity and the common" (88).

66. See the results of 453 interviews at seven Occupy locations reported in Ali Hayat, "Capitalism, Democracy and the Occupy Wall Street Movement," *Huffington Post*, November 29, 2011, http://www.huffingtonpost.com/ali-hayat/occupy-wall-street-capitalism_b_1119247.html (last accessed January 28, 2012).

67. Jeff Sharlet, "By the Mob's Early Light: The Ritual Significance of Occupy Wall Street," *BookForum* 18, no. 4 (December/January 2012), 7.

68. David Graeber, "On the Phenomenology of Giant Puppets: Broken Windows, Imaginary Jars of Urine, and the Cosmological Role of the Police in American Culture," in *Possibilities: Essays on Hierarchy, Rebellion, and Desire* (Oakland: AK, 2007), 378.

69. See, for example, David Graeber, *Direct Action: An Ethnography* (Oakland: AK, 2009).

70. Kroll, "How Occupy Wall Street Really Got Started," 18.

71. For a recounting, see Stephen Gandel, "The Leaders of a Leaderless Movement," *What Is Occupy?* 34–39.

72. Graeber quoted in Dan Berrett, "Intellectual Roots of Wall St. Protest Lie in Academe," *Chronicle of Higher Education* 58, no. 9 (October 21, 2011), A6. For Graeber's reflections on vanguardism, see "The Twilight of Vanguardism," in *Possibilities*, 301–311.

73. See David Graeber, *Lost People: Magic and the Legacy of Slavery in Madagascar* (Bloomington: Indiana University Press, 2007).

74. Graeber, "On the Phenomenology of Giant Puppets," 406.

75. David Graeber, "Fetishism as Social Creativity: Or, Fetishes Are Gods in the Process of Construction," in *Possibilities*, 113.

76. Stevphen Shukaitis and David Graeber, "Introduction," in Stevphen Shukaitis, David Graeber, and Erika Biddle, eds., *Constituent Imagination: Militant Investigations// Collective Theorization* (Oakland: AK, 2007), 20.

77. Wendy Brown, "Resisting Left Melancholy," *Boundary 2*, 26, no. 3 (1999): 22.

78. Ibid., 26–27.

79. Jameson, *Valences of the Dialectic* (New York: Verso, 2009), 408.

80. Howard, *The Specter of Democracy*, 17.

81. Ibid., 22.

82. Cornelius Castoriadis, "The Greek *Polis* and the Creation of Democracy," in *Philosophy, Politics, Autonomy*, trans. David Ames Curtis (New York: Oxford University Press, 1991), 119–120.

Index

112–13, 134, 140; on Kant, 108; on Lacan, 121, 127, 137; on language, 114; Lefort and, 147–49; Lefort on, 137; on Lévi-Strauss, 112–18; Lyotard on, 103; on madness, 126; on Marxism, 96–98, 102, 103; on May 1968, 131–32; on Merleau-Ponty, 110–11; on metabolization, 312n111; on metaphysics, 128; middle ground of, 132–33; in Paris, 101; political and, xiii, 6; on presence, 116, 117; on presentation, 310n83; on psychical monad, 125–26; psychoanalysis and, 120–21, 122; on reason, 126; on religion, 140; resistance to fads, 136; on science, 119–20; on self-management, 102; Singer on, 306n4; on social, xiii, 128, 133; on social-historical world, 97, 105; on socialism, 102; on society, 108; on Soviet Union, 101, 148; Starr on, 313n139; starting points, 118–38; on structuralism, 97–98, 112, 131, 137; on sublime, 129; on symbolic, 112–13, 114, 116; symbolic turn and, 112; on tragedy, 287–88; Trotskyism and, 148; on unconscious, 121, 123, 127, 130; on Whitebook, 313n129
Catholic humanism, 2
Cause, 248
Ceaușescu, Nicolae, 225
Center for Philosophical Research on the Political, 196
Centre for Contemporary Cultural Studies, 187
Chaulieu-Montal tendency, 101
Chevalier, Michel, 59
Christ: Gauchet on, 172; Leroux on, 71–72; Žižek on, 246, 251
Christianity: as absolute religion, 40; Gauchet on, 172; Hegel on, 39–40; Marx, on, 144; monotheism and, 172; revolution and, 254; Romantics and, 38; Žižek on, 249, 252–54
Chun, Lin, 200
Cieszkowski, August, 71
Clark, Christopher, 52
Class struggle, 259
Clastres, Pierre, 168–69

Clavel, Maurice, 160
Cold war, 160, 198, 258, 287
Coleridge, Samuel Taylor, 294n26
Collective action, 180
Collective mythic consciousness, 44
Collège de Sociologie, 89
Commodity: fetishism, 21, 78–79, 81, 116; as hieroglyph, 79; Marx on, 78–79; money as, 80–81
Common Programme, 142, 197
Communism, 21; Badiou on, 275–76, 337n41; Critchley on, 277; end of, 4; failure of, 2–3; heroes of, 275–76; Marx on, 144; as religion, 145; revival of interest in, 277; socialism differentiated from, 276; Žižek on, 274–78
The Communist Manifesto (Marx & Engels), 58
Considerations on Western Marxism (Anderson), 201
Constant, Abbé Alphonse-Louis, 67
Consumption, 90
Corpus mysticum, 301n41; body politic as, 68; society as, 68, 69
Cousin, Victor, 75
"Creation" (Marx), 75
Creativity, 7, 12, 22, 76, 95, 97, 102, 105, 136–37, 149
Creuzer, Friedrich, 295n60; Dubois on, 64–65; on symbol, 65
Critchley, Simon, 277
Cult of personality, 276

Dean, Jodi: on Occupy Wall Street, 338n65; on Žižek, 229
Le débat, 7, 142, 168
Debord, Guy, 90
Debray, Régis, 199
Deconstruction, 221–22
De l'Allemagne (de Staël), 64
Delécluze, Étienne, 61; on symbolism, 63
Deleuze, Gilles, 130
"De l'individualisme et du socialisme" (Leroux), 68
de Man, Paul: on allegory, 30; on Romanticism, 34; on symbol, 30

48; on religion, 46–49, 55; on Schelling, 48; on symbol, 51

Fichte, Johann Gottlieb: Castoriadis on, 108–9; on ego, 120; on imagination, 312n111; Seigel on, 109; on self-consciousness, 125

Financial crisis, 1–2

Floating signifier, 20

Flynn, Bernard, 163; on Marx, 77; on religion, 158

For a Critique of the Political Economy of the Sign (Baudrillard), 12, 89–91

For They Know Not What They Do (Žižek), 220

Foucault, Michel: on intellectual function, 199; on Marxism, 199; on mass media, 199; on postmodernism, 270; on queer politics, 206

Fouque, Antoinette, 130

Frank, Manfred, 47, 48

French Psychoanalytic Society, 122

French Revolution: Furet on, 142, 143, 145–46, 175, 198–99; Lefort on, 70–71; totalitarianism and, 143

Freud, Sigmund, 11, 16, 103, 116, 123, 125, 129, 152, 189; on autonomy, 121; Castoriadis on, 127; Gauchet on, 152; on mourning, 191–92; on religion, 145

"Freud and Lacan" (Althusser), 88

Furet, François, 96, 145, 178; on democracy, 145; on French Revolution, 142, 143, 145–46, 175, 198–99; on structuralism, 86–87

The Future of an Illusion (Freud), 145

Gans, Eduard, 299n5

"Die Gattung und die Masse" (Bauer), 46

Gauche Prolétarienne, 142

Gauchet, Marcel, 6, 49, 141, 142; on Abensour, 181; Abensour on, 180–81; on ancient Greece, 174–75; on autonomy, 177; background of, 167–70; on Christ, 172; on Christianity, 172; on Clastres, 168–69; on collective action, 180; on democracy, 167, 168, 174–76, 180, 321n136; on dynamic of transcendence, 73, 171–73, 178; on

emergence of state, 171; on Freud, 152; on historical society, 178; on history, 170; on institution, 166, 168–69, 178; on Kantorowicz, 318n89; on Lacan, 152; Manent conversation with, 174; on modernity, 146; on monarch, 172, 173; on monotheism, 171, 174–75; on political, 151; on political inconsequence, 180; on primitive society, 169; on psychoanalysis, 152; on religion, 146–47, 166, 169–75, 179, 320n109; Tarot on, 176; on transcendental, 56

"Gegen die spekulative Aesthetik" (Hettner), 53

Genius, 111

The Gift (Mauss), 17

Gift economies, 92

The Gift of Death (Derrida), 161

Le Globe, 58, 299n5

God, 73, 158, 160, 161, 175, 242–43, 251; Leroux on, 69, 71–72; Žižek on, 251, 334n146

Goethe, Johann Wolfgang von: on allegory, 31; on beautiful, 31; on genius, 111; Leroux on, 63, 64; on poetry, 31; on symbol, 25, 32; on symbolism, 31

Gottraux, Philippe, 86; on "Marxism and Revolutionary Theory," 103

Gouldner, Alvin, 83; on Marx, 76

Goux, Jean-Joseph: on Marx, 77; on symbolism, 19–20

Graeber, David, on revolution, 283–84

Gramsci, Antonio: on consent, 185; on hegemony, 185–91; influence on England, 186–87; Mouffe on, 186, 187; Showstak on, 187

Gramsci and Marxist Theory (Mouffe), 187

Green, André, 123

Grewe, Cordula, 34

Grundsätze der Philosophie der Zukunft (Feuerbach), 48

Guattari, Fèlix, 130

Guigniaut, Joseph, 64

Gulag Archipelago (Solzhenitsyn), 142, 198

Gusdorf, Georges, 270

Romantics and, 75; on Schelling, 57; on society, 76; on symbol, 21, 303*n*77; *Time* magazine on, 2

Marx, Reinhard, 2

Marxism: alternatives to, 6; Althusser on, 12, 87, 183; Castoriadis on, 96–98, 102, 103; collapse of, 4–5, 8, 203; critical, 83; Derrida on, 160, 185, 192–93, 200, 253–54; Dosse on, 87; Foucault on, 199; French intellectuals and, 4–6; Howard on, 272–73; intellectual underpinnings of, 3; Jameson on, 264, 273; Jay on, 304*n*106; Kellner on, 273–74; Laclau on, 187–88, 192, 193–94; Lefort on, 147, 149; Merleau-Ponty on, 76–77, 82–83; Mouffe on, 187–88; rescuing, 266; scientific, 83; Western, 82–83, 201, 304*n*106; Žižek on, 249, 253–54

"Marxism and Revolutionary Theory" (Castoriadis), 103

Materialism: historical, 93; Žižek on, 244

Mauss, Marcel, 15; education of, 18; Lefort on, 156; Lévi-Strauss on, 16; Merleau-Ponty and, 84–85; on symbolic, 16, 17–18; on symbols, 18; Tarot on, 89

May 1968, 142; Castoriadis on, 131–32; failure of, 131; fragmentation after, 183, 191; Starr on, 313*n*139; structuralism and, 130

"Mazeppa" (Hugo), 65–66

McWilliam, Neil, 300*n*18

The Meaning of Sarkozy (Badiou), 275

Melancholy, 191–95; Baudrillard on, 191–92; Brown on, 285; Žižek on, 195

Mélanges de littérature et de philosophie (Ancillon), 64

Merleau-Ponty, Maurice, xii, 13; Castoriadis on, 110–11; on history, 83; on institution, 110–11; on invisible, 150; on language, 84; on Lévi-Strauss, 84–85; on Marx, 82; on Marxism, 76–77, 82–83; Mauss and, 84–85; on perception, 111; on philosophy, 85–86; on revolution, 111; on Sartre, xi, 83, 85; on Stalinism, 83; on symbolic, 14–15; on theory related to practice, 15; on Western Marxism, 82–83

Messianism, 160–61, 162

Metaphysics, 128

Michelet, Jules, 162–63

Milbank, John: on allegory, 54; on Badiou, 253; on Spinoza, 54; on Žižek, 253

Miller, Jacques-Alain, 130, 221, 230; Žižek on, 327*n*97

Miller, Judith, 130

The Mirror of Production (Baudrillard), 89–93

Mise en sens, 153

Mitterrand, François, 198

Mocnik, Rastko, 78

Modernity: Barth on, 49–50; Gauchet on, 146

Moggach, Douglas, 53

Monarch: Gauchet on, 172, 173; Hegel on, 223; Lefort on, 222; Žižek on, 222–27, 256

Money: as commodity, 80–81; Hegel on, 79; Hess on, 79; Hume on, 79; Marx on, 79, 80–81, 90; as symbol, 79; Valenze on, 79

Mongin, Olivier, 146

Monotheism: Christianity and, 172; Gauchet on, 171, 174–75

Montrelay, Michèle, 130

Moritz, Karl Phillip: Bauer's relationship with, 44–45; on beautiful, 30

Morsi, Mohamed, 281

Mouffe, Chantal, xiv, 7, 9, 160, 265; on Althusser, 190; on antagonism, 212, 213; background of, 202; as cultural broker, 191; on Gramsci, 186, 187; on hegemony, 188, 189, 267; on language, 190; on Marxism, 187–88; on post-Marxism, 184; on poststructuralism, 188; on religion, 160; on self-management, 196; on society, 188; on universality, 214; Wenman on, 327*n*114

Mourning, 191–95; Derrida on, 193; Freud on, 192; Jay on, 192; post-Marxism and, 192

Mundt, Theodor, on art, 39

Murray, Jamie, on sinthome, 247

Muslim Brotherhood, 281

Mythology: Marx on, 77–78; Sorel on, 205

Nairn, Tom, 186

Nancy, Jean-Luc, 160, 196

Symbol: aesthetic, 32, 60–66; ambiguity in,
19–20; ancient meaning of, 13; art and, 27;
Bénichou on, 63, 64; Benjamin on, 29–30;
Castoriadis on, 112–13; Coleridge on,
294n26; Creuzer on, 65; cryptophoric,
19–20; de Man on, 30; Descombes on, 19;
Feuerbach on, 51; Goethe on, 25, 32;
Grewe on, 34; Halmi on, 29, 293n6;
imaginary and, 116; irreducible duplicity
of, 19; Kant on, 24–25, 80, 293n6; Left
Hegelians on, 41; Leroux and, 60–66;
Lütticken on, 20; Marx on, 21, 303n77;
Mauss on, 18; money as, 79;
naturalization of, 49–54; Novalis on,
51–52; resubstantialization of, 25;
Romantic, 29, 34, 51; Saussure on signs
and, 18, 25; Schelling on, 27, 30, 32, 70;
Todorov on, 25
Symbolic: as algebraic order, 19, 89; Althusser
on, 88, 89, 305n127; Baudrillard on, 13,
90–91, 270; Bowie, M., on, 128; Butler, J.,
on, 18–19; Cassirer on, 20; Castoriadis on,
112–13, 114, 116; conception, 64; defining,
13; de Staël on, 62–63; dialectic related to,
13, 14–15, 270–71; Fabre on, 18–19; Hegel
on, 26–27, 35–36, 295n60; Hénaff on, 20;
Lacan on, 266; Lefort on, 155–56, 157,
181–82; Left Hegelian rejection of, 21–22;
Lévi-Strauss on, 10, 11, 15–17, 113, 291n46;
Mauss on, 16, 17–18; Merleau-Ponty on,
14–15; return to, 268–69; Romantic,
18–19, 21–22, 269, 293n6; structuralism,
18–19; Tarot on, 17; Žižek on, 14, 270
Symbolic turn, 11; Castoriadis and, 112
Symbolik und Mythologie der alten Völker
(Creuzer), 65; controversy over, 64
Symbolism: Caillé on, 10; Castoriadis on,
112–13; conscious, 35, 39, 40; Delécluze on,
63; Durkheim on, 17; expressive, 115; as
foreign import, 63; Goethe on, 31; Goux
on, 19–20; Limayrac on socialism and, 74;
Magnus on, 36; presence-creating, 19;
Rehberg on, 19, 115–16; religious, 32, 36;
Romantic, 74–75; semiotic, 115;
structuralism and, 11–12
Szondi, Peter, 39

Tarot, Camille: on Durkheim, 18; on
Gauchet, 176; on Mauss, 89; on symbolic,
17
Tarrying with the Negative (Žižek), 225, 230
Tessera, 13
Textures, 142, 168
Thatcher, Margaret, 187
Therborn, Göran, 3–4
Thompson, Edward, 186, 187, 190, 201
The Ticklish Subject (Žižek), 217, 256–57
Time magazine: on Marx, 2; person of the
year, 279–80
Todorov, Tzvetan, 25; on beautiful,
30–31; on resubstantialization of
symbol, 25
Total social fact, 15
Trauma, 207–15; Lefort on, 165, 207
Trotskyism, 148
True act, 254–55
Turkle, Sherry, 130
Twardowski, Kasimir, 117
Two Marxisms (Gouldner), 83

Unconscious: Boothby on, 130; Castoriadis
on, 121, 123, 127, 130; Lacan on, 124,
129–30, 138; as language, 129–30;
Lévi-Strauss on, 16; Žižek on, 243
Universality, 219; committed, 215, 247–48;
Laclau on, xiv, 214, 233–36; Mouffe on,
214; partisan, 238–49; Žižek on, xiv,
214–15, 222–23, 233, 242, 246–48

Valenze, Deborah, 79
Vattimo, Gianni, 146
Viard, Jacques, 299n4
Vischer, Friedrich Theodor, 39
The Visible and the Invisible (Merleau-Ponty),
150
Vonessen, Renate, 295n45
Voyage en Icarie (Cabet), 67

Wallon, Henri, 124
Weber, Max, xii, 82; on Protestant
Reformation, 170
Wenman, Mark Anthony, 327n114
Wennerlind, Carl, 303n89

CPSIA information can be obtained at www.ICGtesting.com
Printed in the USA
LVOW10s2038291015

460264LV00004B/13/P